Uncovering Digital Evidence

Daniel B. Garrie • Leo M. Gordon
Bradford Newman

# Uncovering Digital Evidence

## A Comprehensive Guide for Legal Professionals in the Digital Era

Springer

Daniel B. Garrie
Arbitrator, Mediator, Discovery Referee,
Court Appointed Judge
JAMS
Bellevue, WA, USA

Leo M. Gordon
U.S. Court of International Trade
New York, NY, USA

Bradford Newman
Leader, AI and Blockchain Practice
Baker McKenzie
Palo Alto, CA, USA

ISBN 978-3-031-68117-2 ISBN 978-3-031-68118-9 (eBook)
https://doi.org/10.1007/978-3-031-68118-9



This Springer imprint is published by the registered company Springer Nature Switzerland AG
The registered company address is: Gewerbestrasse 11, 6330 Cham, Switzerland

*We dedicate this book to our families, colleagues, and the many others who have inspired and supported us throughout this journey. Your encouragement and belief in our work have been vital to our success.*
*To my wife Marci, and my children, Sarah and Derek, and Jen and Ben, and grandsons Wyatt and Emmett, for their support, encouragement, and love, which makes all things possible.*
*I also want to thank my amazing wife, Sarah, and kids, Ella and Leon, whose continued support afforded me this opportunity. As my children frequently remind me all the time that they and mom help me make everything go Boomshackalaka. Additionally, I extend a special dedication to Julie Cass, in her memory. Julie's patience and understanding as she supported both me and David Cass over the decades, and our constant need to work on projects like this one, have left an indelible mark on our lives. I also want to thank Sofia Mahairas, who without her diligent and tireless efforts, this book would never have come to be.*
*Gratitude to my wife Alexis, and my children Frankie, Marco, Lilly, Angelina, and Penelope. Family first; all else follows.*
*Together, we extend our heartfelt gratitude to everyone who has been a part of this project.*

# Preface

Advances in the power and efficiency of computers have intruded upon professional practices in ways that most knowledge professionals may not fully appreciate. Safeguarding confidential information is paramount to any such practice. With this in mind, our book is intended for lawyers, accountants, financial advisors, and anyone seeking a deeper appreciation of the technologies shaping the digital landscape.

Ten comprehensive chapters provide significant depth for understanding the digital world of computing and data collection. Each topic in a chapter and among the chapters constitutes a building block to help one's understanding of the complexities of how the digital world works and interacts. We begin with the basics of hardware and software operation. From there, we provide an overview of how computing systems interact with the internet and cloud computing. We then proceed to the growth of mobile communication and on to the inexorable and historical growth of artificial intelligence, with special emphasis on the high-tech pitfalls that knowledge professionals may not have contemplated, including examination of digital forensic investigation and eDiscovery in litigation. Also addressed is the importance of law firm cybersecurity and the growing use of blockchain technology.

More precisely, Chap. 1 covers fundamental information on the computer's historical development and the hardware on which it operates, while Chap. 2 details the evolution of software and how it is currently developed, tested, and debugged. Chapter 3's exploration of how the Internet operates as a global network connection of computers naturally segues to Chap. 4's focus on the various models of cloud computing and the risks associated with them. Risk is also explored in Chap. 5's examination of mobile phone technology, while in Chap. 6 we provide an overview of a digital forensic investigation and the eDiscovery process, before focusing on data encryption and its importance in cybersecurity in Chap. 7. Perhaps the biggest of the "elephants" in this space—law firm cybersecurity—is covered in Chap. 8. We thought it is important to cover in Chap. 9 the rising interest in blockchain technology, with a focus on its impact on the world of commerce and increasing efforts to regulate it. Last, but not least, Chap. 10 examines artificial intelligence, with its growing impact on so many aspects of daily life.

In sum, this volume provides knowledge professionals with valuable insights for considering how best to safeguard the confidentiality, property, and integrity of their own and their clients' data in a digital world that continues to be fraught with risk.

Bellevue, WA, USA Daniel B. Garrie
New York, NY, USA Leo M. Gordon
Palo Alto, CA, USA Bradford Newman

# Contents

# Chapter 1
# Hardware

## 1.1 Computer Hardware, in General

> Part of the inhumanity of the computer is that, once it is competently programmed and working smoothly, it is completely honest.—Isaac Asimov[1]

Computer hardware is any processing machine that accepts and translates input symbols and executes an action.[2] The inputs are processed according to a sequence of instructions called software.[3] In a computer, hardware includes all of the equipment that comprises the physical body of the computer, its electronic circuitry, and peripheral items such as keyboards, mice, readers, scanners, and printers.[4] Such hardware is of limited value without software. It is the software that produces a given result, such as outputting symbols or performing an action.[5] The input symbols as well as the output symbols can represent, among other things, numbers, characters in a word editing software, pictures in an email, images stored in your

---

[1] Asimov, Change! (1983).

[2] See Patterson & Hennessy, Computer Organization and Design: The Hardware/Software Interface 24 (4th ed. 2009); Davis, The Nature of Software and Its Consequences for Establishing and Evaluating Similarity, 5 Software L.J. 299, 302 (1992); Franklin, Computer Architecture and Organization: From Software to Hardware 2 (University of Maryland, College Park 2007), available at http://www.ece.umd.edu/~manoj/350/notes/book.pdf (last visited Mar. 14, 2013).

[3] Ricoh Co., Ltd. v. Quanta Computer Inc., 550 F.3d 1325, 1335 (Fed. Cir. 2008) (citing Microsoft Corp. v. AT & T Corp., 550 U.S. 437, 127 S. Ct. 1746, 1754, 167 L. Ed. 2d 737, 33 A.L.R. Fed. 2d 745 (2007)).

[4] Eitel, Microcode Copyright and the Protection of Microprocessors Under Current Intellectual Property Law, 21 Colum. JL & Soc. Probs. 53 (1987); *see also* U.S. v. Carson, 2012 WL 5866211 (C.D. Ill. 2012), report and recommendation adopted, 2012 WL 5866506 (C.D. Ill. 2012); Advent Systems Ltd. v. Unisys Corp., 925 F.2d 670, 674, 13 U.C.C. Rep. Serv. 2d 669 (3d Cir. 1991).

[5] Microsoft Corp. v. AT & T Corp., 550 U.S. 437, 127 S. Ct. 1746, 1754, 167 L. Ed. 2d 737, 33 A.L.R. Fed. 2d 745 (2007) (defining software); Fantasy Sports Properties, Inc. v. Sportsline.com, Inc., 287 F.3d 1108, 1118 (Fed. Cir. 2002) (same).

 
D. B. Garrie et al., *Uncovering Digital Evidence*,
https://doi.org/10.1007/978-3-031-68118-9_1

laptop as desktop backgrounds, or video and audio stored in your computer's video editing software.

Hardware coupled with software pervade every aspect of modern life.[6] More prominent examples include the following:

- The Large Hadron Collider collects and processes data through the GRID, an international network of computers.[7]
- The Parkes radio telescope was used during the Apollo 11 moon landing to relay communications between NASA and the command module.[8]
- Computer chips which designers make faster and denser through the extensive use of software and hardware.[9]
- Medical devices with complex hardware which physicians use to perform cutting-edge medical procedures.[10] Computer-assisted surgery is used in a range of operations from hip replacement to brain surgery.
- Automobiles incorporate computers to interact with their drivers: from voice commands to automatic parallel parking and navigation systems.[11]

These are only a few examples of a population that is, of course, essentially innumerable.[12] Computer hardware can seem endlessly complex to the

[6] "Whether the applications of physics and chemistry that are manifested in advances in computer hardware and software were more or less foreseeable than the advances in biology and biotechnology is debatable, but it is not debatable that these fields of endeavor have become primary contributors to today's economy and culture, as well as offering an untold potential for future advances." In re Bilski, 545 F.3d 943, 981 (Fed. Cir. 2008), aff'd but criticized, 130 S. Ct. 3218, 177 L. Ed. 2d 792 (2010).

[7] Geddes, "The Large Hadron Collider and Grid computing," in Philosophical Transactions of the Royal Society a Mathematical, Physical and Engineering Sciences, Volume 37 Issue 1961 (2012), https://royalsocietypublishing.org/doi/10.1098/rsta.2011.0465.

[8] Sarkissian, "On Eagle's Wings: The Parkes Observatory's Support of the Apollo 11 Mission," in 18(3) Publications of the Astronomical Society of Australia 287–310 (2001).

[9] Software used to design electronic circuits and systems is called electronic design automation. See ClearOne Communications, Inc. v. Bowers, 651 F.3d 1200, 1211 (10th Cir. 2011).

[10] See Kunkler, The Role of Medical Simulation: An Overview, 2 Int. J. Med. Robotics & Comput. Assist. Surg. 203–210 (Sept. 2006); Singh, New Medical Office Embraces Technology (Sept. 25, 2010), http://www.newstimes.com/news/article/New-medical-office-embraces-technology-674626.php (last visited Mar. 14, 2013).

[11] Nagle, Arnold, Wilson, et al., "Automotive Concepts for Use of the Modernized Global Positioning System (GPS)," SAE Technical Paper 2003-01-0538, 302–313 (Mar. 3, 2003).

[12] See, e.g., ScienceDaily.com, Biologists Use Computers To Study Bacterial Cell Division (Virginia Tech, Jan. 30, 2008), http://www.sciencedaily.com/releases/2008/01/080124233635.htm (last visited July 16, 2012); ScienceDaily.com, Engineers Use Computer Simulation To Design Synthetic Blood Vessels (North Carolina State Univ., Apr. 12, 2001), http://www.sciencedaily.com/releases/2001/04/010412080121.htm (last visited July 16, 2012).

uninitiated.[13] This chapter provides a foundational understanding of computer hardware, with a primary focus on those areas of computer technology most likely to impact litigation, such as product liability, electronic discovery, or digital forensic investigations.[14] With this specialized focus, a number of hardware components are intentionally excluded and are left for specialized textbooks that specifically address computer hardware.

To that end, this chapter provides the reader with a history of computer hardware and an overview of the basic foundation of computer hardware. Next, we examine the primary components of a computer, including the central processing unit, microprocessors, and the motherboard. Following that, we review the types of memory on computers. We then look at the types of hard drives available,[15] how those drives use allocated and unallocated space, and how disk arrays can be used to partition data among hard drives. We will then review external data storage devices. Finally, we discuss input and output devices.

## 1.2 History of Computer Hardware

Early computers were analog machines.[16] Such computers use continuously changeable aspects of physical objects to model the problem being solved.[17] Analog machines "employ distinct computing elements for each mathematical operation

[13] U.S. v. O'Keefe, 537 F. Supp. 2d 14, 24, 69 Fed. R. Serv. 3d 1598 (D.D.C. 2008). The complexity of the technologic/scientific evidence will of course vary with the issue. See, e.g., Brooktree Corp. v. Advanced Micro Devices, Inc., 977 F.2d 1555 (Fed. Cir. 1992) (color video display semiconductor chips); Scripps Clinic & Research Foundation v. Genentech, Inc., 927 F.2d 1565 (Fed. Cir. 1991), clarified on denial of reconsideration, 18 U.S.P.Q.2d 1896, 1991 WL 523489 (Fed. Cir. 1991) and (overruled on other grounds by, Abbott Laboratories v. Sandoz, Inc., 566 F.3d 1282 (Fed. Cir. 2009)) (blood clotting factor VIII); Halliburton Co. v. Schlumberger Technology Corp., 925 F.2d 1435 (Fed. Cir. 1991) (neutron logging of oil wells); Bey v. Kollonitsch, 806 F.2d 1024 (Fed. Cir. 1986) (irreversible enzyme inhibitors); Fromson v. Advance Offset Plate, Inc., 755 F.2d 1549 (Fed. Cir. 1985) (silicated lithography plates).

[14] See Chap. 6 for more information on eDiscovery and digital forensic investigation.

[15] See, e.g., Data Storage System, U.S. Patent No. 2,540,654, at 1–2 (issued Feb. 6, 1951) ("[T]he magnets 27 will be used to determine or create patterns of electrical values corresponding to digits or other code signals.").

[16] "When electronic data processing began, each electronic circuit was made up of a vacuum tube, such as is used in radio or television, plus wires and resistors. The development of transistors in the 1950s allowed the vacuum tubes to be replaced by transistors." *Telex Corp. v. International Business Machines Corp.*, 367 F. Supp. 258, 275 n.33 (N.D. Okla. 1973).

[17] "A digital computer, as distinguished from an analog computer, operates on data expressed in digits, solving problems by doing arithmetic as a person would do it by head and hand." *Gottschalk v. Benson*, 409 U.S. 63, 65, 93 S. Ct. 253, 34 L. Ed. 2d 273 (1972) (*citing* Benrey, Understanding Digital Computers 4 (1964). "[I]n the digital computer, the electrical signals are discrete in character, but in the analog apparatus they are continuous." Application of Prater, 415 F.2d 1378, 1380 (C.C.P.A. 1968), opinion superseded on other grounds, 415 F.2d 1393, 6 A.L.R. Fed. 134 (C.C.P.A. 1969) (quoting appellant's brief).

required to reach the solution of a given problem."[18] Consider the difference between an analog watch and a digital watch: The analog watch is able to model the time continuously, as the hands of the clock can represent every point in time during the day.[19] Technically, the accuracy is limited by the visible physical markings on the clock.[20] Conversely, a digital watch is limited by the number of decimal places visible, as digital computers show values in iterations. This means that usually a digital watch shows only hours and minutes and can tell time only in 1-minute iterations.

Another common analog/digital comparison is between a slide rule and a calculator. The slide rule, which at one time was essential equipment for scientists and engineers,[21] is limited only by the physical markings on the device, whereas the digital calculator is limited by the number of decimal points viewed on the screen. Succinctly put, analog computers represent information by physical quantities, whereas digital computers use numbers or bit patterns to represent quantities. As this comparison was described by another commentator: "In a digital machine, the data, whether numbers, letters, or other symbols, is represented in digital form."[22]

An analog computer, on the other hand, uses combinations of voltage amplitude, currents, frequencies, or phases from the inputs to determine the required output sequence.[23] The *Merriam-Webster Dictionary* defines analog computers as "a computer that operates with numbers represented by directly measurable quantities (as

[18] Rel-Reeves, Inc. v. U. S., 209 Ct. Cl. 595, 534 F.2d 274, 276 (1976).

[19] See generally A. Briggle, Representation in digital systems, 175 Current Issues in Computing and Philosophy116 (2008).

[20] An analog clock uses a static, unchanging display called a "dial" against which "hands" move to indicate time. Accuracy is limited by the precision of the alignment of the dial to the hands and also by observers' ability to note that alignment. Digital clocks, on the other hand, do not use a dial. Digital clocks display time in digits, which observers read as numbers, and accuracy is limited only by observers' ability to observe the numbers on the display.

[21] "Slide rules are instruments, used by engineers and others, to make computations involving multiplication and division, to determine square and cube roots, squares and cubes, to find the values of trigonometric functions, and to make computations involving them." Keuffel & Esser Co. v. Pickett & Eckel, 182 F.2d 581, 582 (7th Cir. 1950).

[22] Morris & Reilly, Encyclopedia of Computer Science 4th 539–45 (John Wiley and Sons Ltd 2003).

[23] Wagner, Patenting Computer Science: Are Computer Instruction Writings Patentable?, 17 J. Marshall J. Computer & Info. L. 5, 15 (1998). "Analog computers pertain to representation by means of continuously variable physical quantities; for example, to describe a physical quantity, such as voltage or shaft position, that normally varies in a continuous manner, or devices such as potentiometers and synchros that operate with such quantities." Declaration of Dr. Andrea Goldsmith in Support of Qualcomm Incorporated's Claim Construction Brief, in Qualcomm Incorporated v. Conextant Systems, Nos. 02CV2002 B (JFS), 02CV2429 B (JFS), 2004 WL 3607654, at ¶142 n. 44 (S.D. Cal. Aug. 19, 2014) (citing Institute of Electrical and Electronics Engineers, Inc., The New IEEE Standard Dictionary of Electrical and Electronics Terms 35 (Christopher J. Booth ed., 5th ed. 1993)); see also Power Integrations' Opening Claim Construction Brief, in Power Integrations, Inc. v. Fairchild Semiconductor International, Inc., No. 08-309 JJF-LPS, 2009 WL 2897986 (D.Del. Aug. 5, 2009). Further discussion of analog computers can be found in the IEEE Annals of the History of Computing, http://www.computer.org/portal/web/computingnow/annals

voltages or rotations)."[24] In the late 1950s, when digital computers became fast, accurate, reliable, and reasonable, analog machines began to phase out.[25] Some other key milestones in the evolution of computer hardware over the past 70 or so years are described briefly below:

Vacuum tubes were created in the 1940s and served as the initial hardware for modern day computers. Of course, at the time, these computers would take up whole rooms and were costly to operate energy hogs that often broke.[26] Vacuum based computing relied on machine languages to execute operations and was limited to solving a single problem that was input using punch cards and paper tape. Results were output on printouts.[27]

Transistors were created in 1947, but did not replace vacuum tubes until the late 1950s.[28] Transistors allowed computers to become inexpensive, more energy-efficient, dependable, and smaller than vacuum tubes—the first-generation predecessors. Though the transistor still generated a great deal of heat that subjected the computer to damage, it was a vast improvement over the vacuum tube.[29] Second-generation computers still relied on punched cards for input and printouts for output.[30]

In 1964, the integrated circuit emerged, begetting the third generation of computers. Integrated circuits are miniaturized transistors placed on silicon chips, referred to as semiconductors.[31] Integrated circuits enabled computers to operate much more efficiently and at several magnitudes faster than second-generation transistor computers.[32] It was in this generation of computing that computers began to enter the mass market.[33] More importantly, these computers utilized keyboards and monitors via an operating system. The operating system enables the computer to operate many different applications at any one point.[34]The next big step came about with the

[24] Merriam-Webster Dictionary. Revised Edition (July 2004).

[25] See generally Freed & Ishida, History of Computers (Ziff-Davis Publishing Co. 1995); Bashe, Johnson, et al., IBM's Early Computers: A Technical History (History of Computing) (MIT Press 1986).

[26] Collen, The origins of informatics, 1(2) J. Am. Med. Informatics Ass'n 91–107 (Mar.–Apr. 1994).

[27] Collen, The origins of informatics, 1(2) J. Am. Med. Informatics Ass'n 91–107 (1994).

[28] Augarten, Bit by Bit: An Illustrated History of Computers (Houghton Mifflin Co. 1984).

[29] Bashe, Johnson, et al., IBM's Early Computers: A Technical History (History of Computing) (MIT Press 1986).

[30] Bashe, Johnson, et al., IBM's Early Computers: A Technical History (History of Computing) (MIT Press 1986).

[31] Smits & Millman, A History of Engineering and Science in the Bell System: Electronics Technology (1925–1975) (AT&T Customer Information Center 1985).

[32] Sarasvathy & Dew, Entrepreneurial logics for a technology of foolishness, 21(4) Scandinavian Journal of Management 385–406 (2005).

[33] Wang, Circuits and Systems for Wireless Concurrent Communication (Feb. 26, 2009) (Ph.D dissertation, California Institute of Technology), available at http://thesis.library.caltech.edu/5179/

[34] Murphy, Microcomputers: Trends, Technologies, and Design Strategies, 18(3) IEEE Journal of Solid-State Circuits 236–244 (1983).

Intel's microprocessor in 1971. Intel introduced the 4004 chip, which was thousands of integrated circuits built onto a single silicone chip.[35]

Today, computing technology is evolving at blistering speeds from the introduction of DNA computers to Google Glass™.[36] The famous "Moore's law," which states that over the history of computing hardware, the number of transistors on integrated circuits doubles approximately every 2 years, is still holding true.[37] With this quick pace of computer technology evolution, we recognize that it is impossible for the previous pages to properly cover the entire history of computers.[38]

## 1.3 Bits: The Elemental Hardware Component

Modern day computer hardware represents and manipulates information using bits.[39] The word "bits" is a shortened form of "binary digits."[40] Bits are the smallest unit of information that a computer system can recognize.[41] Bits represent one of two possible states (values): a digital value of 1 (logical value of true) and 0 (logical value of false). A bit is usually represented by an electrical voltage or current pulse with the 1 value containing a more positive voltage relative to 0.[42] When you group

---

[35] Wade, A Community-Level Analysis of Sources and Rates of Technological Variation in the Microprocessor Market, Academy of Management Journal 1218–1244 (1996); see also Cyrix Corp. v. Intel Corp., 846 F. Supp. 522 (E.D. Tex. 1994), aff'd, 42 F.3d 1411 (Fed. Cir. 1994).

[36] *DNA Computing: New Computing Paradigms* is a great book discussing DNA computing in further detail. Paun, Rozenberg & Salomaa, DNA Computing: New Computing Paradigms (Springer 2006). To learn more about Google Glass, one should read the article *Behind the Google Goggles*. See Bilton, "Behind the Google Goggles, Virtual Reality," N.Y. Times, Feb. 23, 2012, at B1.

[37] See generally Gastle & Boughs, Microsoft III 1 and the Metes and Bounds of Software Design and Technological Tying Doctrine 2, 6 Va. J. L. & Tech. 7 (2001).

[38] For further books around the history of computers, we suggest the following: Augarten, *Bit by Bit: An Illustrated History of Computers* (Houghton Mifflin Co. 1984); Ceruzzi, *A History of Modern Computing* (MIT Press. 2003); Cortada, *Second Bibliographic Guide to the History of Computing, Computers, and the Information Processing Industry* (Vol. 2) (Greenwood Publishing Group 1996); Williams, *A History of Computing Technology* (IEEE Computer Society Press 1997); Metropolis, Howlett & Rota, *A History of Computing in the Twentieth Century* (Academic Press 1980).

[39] "Most digital computers perform their computing operations on information in binary form, a system of representation having only two elementary constituents, called 'bits,' indicated by '1' and '0.'" Application of Benson, 441 F.2d 682, 682 (Ct. Customs & Patent App. 1971).

[40] "[A] 'bit' is a 'contraction of the term "binary digit"; a unit of information represented by a zero or a one.'" Rambus Inc. v. Hynix Semiconductor Inc., 642 F. Supp. 2d 970, 984 (N.D. Cal. 2008) (quoting IEEE Standard Dictionary of Electronic and Electrical Terms (4th ed. 1988)).

[41] "[A] bit is the smallest unit of information (data) a computer can process … ." Rambus, Inc., 642 F.Supp. 2d at 985 (quoting Newton's Telecom Dictionary (4th ed. 1991)).

[42] 642 F.Supp. 2d at 984 (quoting IEEE Standard Dictionary of Electronic and Electrical Terms (4th ed. 1988)).

bits together, their possible states increase exponentially. For example, eight bits are commonly called a byte.[43]

The table below provides a more detailed chart defining common names of bit groups.

| Number of bits in group | Maximum possible unique states | Common name for group |
|---|---|---|
| 1 | 2 | Bit |
| 2 | 4 | Two bits |
| 4 | 16 | Nibble |
| 8 | 256 | Byte |
| 16 | 65,536 | Word |
| 32 | 4,294,967,296 | Double word |
| 64 | 18,446,744,073,709,551,616 | Quad word |
| 128 | 340,282,366,920,938,463,463,374,607,431,770,000,000 | Octa word |

The chart demonstrates the power of grouping bits: Each of the unique states can be defined for a specific purpose. Like the number of characters on a license plate limits the unique number of vehicles that can be catalogued in that state, the number of bytes limits the unique number of interpretations that a computer can make about the binary digits.

Early personal computers (PCs) were based on an 8-bit computer chip with a maximum integer value of 256, meaning only 256 unique functions could be performed during any one period of time.[44] Today, most devices containing processors require a minimum of a 16-bit processor.[45] Most laptops and desktops use 32-bit or 64-bit processors.[46] A 64-bit computer can perform integer calculations with an

[43] "A group of bits is called a byte and represents a character–a letter or integer." Universal City Studios, Inc. v. Reimerdes, 111 F. Supp. 2d 294, 305–6 (S.D. N.Y. 2000), judgment entered, 111 F. Supp. 2d 346 (S.D. N.Y. 2000), aff'd, 273 F.3d 429 (2d Cir. 2001) (quoting The New York Public Library, Science Desk Reference 496 (1995)) (citing Tr. (Felten) at 758–59; Scheindlin & Rabkin, Electronic Discovery in Federal Civil Litigation: Is Rule 34 Up to the Task?, 34 B.C. L. Rev. 327, 333–35 (2000)).

[44] For example, the Commodore 64 was a popular 8-bit computer throughout the 1980s. For a brochure on the technical specifications, see http://www.pcmuseum.ca/Brochures/WOCProgram.pdf. For a more extensive history of specific computer brands, see Reimer, Total Share: 30 Years Of Personal Computer Market Share Figures, ARS Technic (Dec 15, 2005), available at http://arstechnica.com/features/2005/12/total-share/4/ (last visited Nov 30, 2012).

[45] Throughout this chapter, the terms processor and chip are used interchangeable to refer to the microchip that comprises the microprocessor.

[46] The VMScluster software is operable on 64-bit or 32-bit architecture computer systems. *See SuperSpeed, L.L.C. v. Int'l Bus. Mach. Corp.*, Civil Action No. 2:07-cv-0089 (E.D. Tex.).

excess of 18 quintillion results.[47] This is sufficient to meet the processing needs of the majority of computer software applications on the marketplace today.[48] A 64-bit processor expands a computer's processing abilities in several ways, including increasing the following:

1. The number of unique memory locations that can be assigned an address for the storage of a byte or group of bytes[49]
2. The number of distinct colors that can be recognized and stored in memory[50]
3. The number of files that can be stored on a storage device[51]
4. The size of a single file[52]
5. The number of unique functions the computer chip can perform on the data in its memory cells (i.e., adding, subtracting, moving, copying, comparing, testing, etc.)[53]
6. The number of different spoken and written languages that the computer chip can utilize[54]

To provide context, consider the first Nintendo™ game console. Nintendo released its first gaming console in the USA in 1981 using an 8-bit chip. It was

---

[47] See Haigh, 64-bit Computing Solves the World's Most Complex Problems, Electro/94 International. Conference Proceedings (Combined Volumes) 599 (May 10–12 1994), available at http://ieeexplore.ieee.org/stamp/stamp.jsp?tp=&arnumber=472665&isnumber=9952 (subscription only) (stating "All major manufacturers of computer systems are promising to deliver 64-bit Super64 RISC systems in the future. Digital's Alpha AXP architecture is a full 64-bit architecture and its systems are full 64-bit implementations.").

[48] A quintillion is a 1 followed by 18 zeros, not to be confused with the British usage of quintillion which is a 1 followed by 30 zeros. See *Merriam Webster Dictionary*, available at: http://www.merriam-webster.com/dictionary/quintillion (last visited July 16, 2013).

[49] See also Danowitz, et al., CPU DB: Recording Microprocessor History, 55(4) Communications of the ACM 55–63 (2012).

[50] See *S3 Inc. v. NVIDIA Corp.*, 259 F.3d 1364, 1370 (Fed. Cir. 2001) ("It is possible to expand the number of possible colors available with a given number of bits per pixel by using a [RAM] … which functions as a 'look-up table.' The RAM looks up the location (sometimes referred to as an … address) corresponding to the pixel data from the video controller … . This arrangement is sometimes referred to as 'indexed color mode.'").

[51] See Preslan, et al., "A 64-bit, Shared Disk Files System for Linux," in Proceedings of the 16th IEEE Symposium on Mass Storage Systems (IEEE 1999).

[52] See Tsuchiya & Watanabe, "DBLK: Deduplication For Primary Block Storage," in Proceedings of the 27th IEEE Symposium on Mass Storage Systems and Technologies 1–5 (May 23–27, 2011).

[53] See Harris & Harris, Digital Design and Computer Architecture 13, 42, 351–357 (Morgan Kaufmann 2012) (providing a survey starting with digital logic gates and progressing to the design of combinational and sequential circuits to the design of an actual MIPS processor and 64-bit chips). MIPS stands for Microprocessor without Interlocked Pipeline Stages and is used to refer to the computer microprocessors developed by MIPS Technologies, Inc. See generally Morris & Ferguson, How Architecture Wins Technology Wars, 71 Harvard Business Review 86 (1993).

[54] See generally Patterson & Hennessy, Computer Organization and Design: The Hardware/Software Interface (4th ed. 2009).

capable of showing only 54 colors.[55] In contrast, the Nintendo Wii™ gaming console uses a 32-bit processor capable of detecting motion in three dimensions and showing over 16 million colors.[56] Storage space, like computer speed, has increased dramatically. The first computers had the primary storage capacity of 2000–4000 "words"; today computers can store hundreds of millions of words.

## 1.4 Bits: The Elemental Hardware Component—Interpreting Bits and Bytes

To further understand how a computer interprets bits and bytes, consider the values in the table below showing how a byte of data is interpreted as an integer.

| | | | | | | | | | |
|---|---|---|---|---|---|---|---|---|---|
| **Column weight &rarr** | 128 | 64 | 32 | 16 | 8 | 4 | 2 | 1 | Value of byte as integer |
| **Bit state &rarr** | 0 | 1 | 0 | 0 | 0 | 0 | 0 | 1 | **65** |

In the above example, the byte of data is interpreted as an integer. Each position dependent column of data is weighted, and that weight is only included in the sum if the bit (in the byte of data) is set to a 1 (or on). In this case, the binary pattern of "01000001" could represent the integer 65 as the columns to be included in the sum are 64 + 1 = 65.

It must be noted here that the binary string of digits can be interpreted as any value. How this data is interpreted depends on the operating system or software program that is running on the computer system.[57] For example, the exact same binary pattern that has been used above, 01000001, can have numerous interpretations based on the respective memory address associated with the data.

The figure below demonstrates this situation:

| Binary memory address | Data in memory cell | Data interpreted as |
|---|---|---|
| 0000 0001 | 0100 0001 | Color (Yellow) |
| 0000 0010 | 0100 0001 | Integer (65) |
| 0000 0011 | 0100 0001 | Text (Capital A) |
| 0000 0100 | 0100 0001 | Command (Halt) |

[55] *See Nintendo of America Inc. v. Bung Enterprises, Ltd.*, 1999 WL 34975007 (C.D. Cal. 1999); Wikimedia Foundation, Nintendo Entertainment System, Nintendo Consoles, at 15.

[56] See Fairman, Wii-mote Head Tracking: A Three Dimensional Virtual Reality Display, (Senior Project, Computer Engineering Dept., California Polytechnic State Univ. 2010), available at http://digitalcommons.calpoly.edu/cgi/viewcontent.cgi?article=1023&context=cpesp (last visited Mar. 18, 2013). A 32-bit display can technically produce 4.2 billion different colors, but usually they show 24-bit 16.7 million colors and use the rest of the memory to buffer. This all depends on the display and graphics card. Finan, Get Hip to the Data Acquisition Scene: Principles of Digital Signal Recording, 20 Perspectives on Speech Science and Orofacial Disorders 6 (2010).

[57] See Silberschatz, Galvin, & Gagne, 4 Operating System Concepts 5th Ed. (Addison-Wesley 1998).

In the above example, any binary value stored in memory location 0000 0001 is interpreted as a color that will be displayed on the monitor. In this case, 0100 0001 equals Yellow. The 8-bit computer in this example has the memory cell located at address 0000 0001 and can store 1 of 256 different colors (as defined by the software developer). Thus, in a memory cell capable of storing 32 bits, the list of recordable colors would expand to over 4 billion because there are over 4 billion memory addresses available.[58]

As previously mentioned, software sends instructions to hardware and is written in several levels of complexity, with the simplest level being binary code (the 1s and 0s). The binary code is the lowest level programming language that hardware understands.[59] The 1s and 0s represent "on" and "off" with respect to the voltage being sent to the resistor hardware.[60] Essentially, the voltage to the resistor hardware is being turned "on" or "off" based on the binary code it receives.[61] If a decimal system were used, there would be ten different voltages. The wider the array of voltages,

---

[58] Silberschatz, Galvin, & Gagne, Operating System Concepts 5th Ed. 49 (Addison-Wesley 1998); Daugman, How Iris Recognition Works, in 1 International Conference on Image Processing Proceedings, pp. I–33 (IEEE 2002).

[59] The "lowest" level computer programming language is machine language, which is a binary language written in "bits." *See Lotus Dev. Corp. v. Paperback Software Intern.*, 740 F. Supp. 37, 43 (D. Mass. 1990). The third, or lowest level computer language, is machine language, a binary language using two symbols, 0 and 1, to indicate an open or closed switch (e.g., "01101001" means, to the Apple, add two numbers and save the result). *Apple Computer, Inc. v. Franklin Computer Corp.*, 714 F.2d 1240, 1243, 70 A.L.R. Fed. 153 (3d Cir. 1983). Programming languages' ability to deliver a result rests in part on how the programming language defines terms. See generally Definitional Method to Increase Precision and Clarity of Information, U.S. Patent Application 13/418541 (filed Mar. 13, 2012).

[60] "Transistors are simply on and off switches." Nilles, Copyright Protection for Programs Stored in Computer Chips: Competing with IBM and Apple, 7 Ham. L. Rev. 103, 104 n. 4 (1984) (*citing Apple Computer, Inc. v. Franklin Computer Corp.*, 714 F.2d 1240, 1248, 70 A.L.R. Fed. 153 (3d Cir. 1983); Midway Mfg. Co. v. Strohon, 564 F. Supp. 741, 750 (N.D. Ill. 1983); Breyer, The Uneasy Case For Copyright: A Study of Copyright in Books, Photocopies, and Computer Programs, 84 Harv. L. Rev. 281, 342 (1970); see generally Bennett & Evert, What Every Engineer Should Know About Microcomputers (1980); Hnatek, A User's Handbook Of Semiconductor Memories (1977); Microelectronics (a collection of articles), Scientific American (1977); Koenig, Software Copyright: The Conflict Within CONTU, 27 Bull. Copyright Soc'y 340, 366–67 (1980)).

[61] Technically the voltage does not turn completely on or off but is a high and low voltage. *See Chamberlain Grp, Inc. v. Lear Corp.*, 516 F.3d 1331 (Fed. Cir. 2008) (stating, "In other words, microprocessors and memory devices use low and high voltages to manipulate, transmit, receive, and store vast amounts of data. A low voltage represents a 0, while a high voltage represents a 1."); In re Mouttet, 686 F.3d 1322 (Fed. Cir. 2012) (stating, "By altering the resistance, each crosspoint can be programmed to be in a high resistance (low conduction) state or low resistance (high conduction) state. The two states can represent the binary values '0' and '1' and thus store digital data.").

the more you open the system up to malfunctioning.[62] While it is possible to create a computer based on a nonbinary number system, to ensure the best performance of the computer and the least amount of risk for malfunction, binary is used.[63]

## 1.5 Motherboard: The Proverbial Nervous System of the Computer

Computers are made up of many electronic components such as the central processing unit (commonly referred to as the CPU),[64] memory chips, graphics cards, etc. In order to interconnect these components, they are placed on a single large circuit board. In computers, such a circuit board is called a motherboard. Most, but not all, electronic devices require a motherboard.[65] For example, the computer program that runs the timer and automatic shutoff on a coffeepot does not have a motherboard, but a smartphone does.

The motherboard is a fiberglass board that connects the hardware components in a device.[66] On a personal computer, the processor, memory, graphics cards, and internal modem are connected to the motherboard.[67] The Universal Serial Bus

[62] See Meiring de Villiers, *Virus Ex Machina Res Ipsa Loquitur*, 2003 Stan. Tech. L. Rev. 1, 134 (2003) (Power fluctuations or static electricity may alter data stored in memory).

[63] See Air Force Manuals, No. 91-119 (Safety Design and Evaluation Criteria for Nuclear Weapon Systems Software), Chapter 2, Design Criteria for Nuclear Weapon Systems Software, ENFLEX MILITARY 000292, 20XX WL 4838527 (stating that a specific binary data pattern of "ones" and "zeros" (not all "ones" or all "zeros") will reduce the likelihood of hardware or software malfunctions because data patterns will be selected such that a single bit flip will not result in a valid command or data word.).

[64] "The CPU is generally where most of the logical functions or calculations are performed." *Telex Corp. v. Int'l Business Machines Corp.*, 367 F. Supp. 258, 275 (N.D. Okla. 1973), judgment rev'd, 510 F.2d 894 (10th Cir. 1975).

[65] Patterson & Hennessy, Computer Organization and Design: The Hardware / Software Interface 10 (4th ed. 2009).

[66] *See Intel Corp. v.* VIA *Technologies, Inc.*, 174 F. Supp. 2d 1038, 1040 (N.D. Cal. 2001), judgment aff'd, 319 F.3d 1357 (Fed. Cir. 2003) ("By way of background, the components of a computer system include separate chips mounted on a circuit board known as the motherboard. The system memory, microprocessor, chipset, and various input/output devices, such as modems, are all distinct components."). See also Patterson & Hennessy, Computer Organization and Design: The Hardware/Software Interface 18 (4th ed. 2009).

[67] "A motherboard is the main board which holds a computer's key electronics such as the microprocessor, the memory, and other peripheral devices like the keyboard, mouse and monitor." *Gateway 2000, Inc. v. Livak*, 19 F. Supp. 2d 748, 750 (E.D. Mich. 1998).

(USB) and audio ports on the computer also connect to the motherboard, allowing external hardware components to interact with the internal ones.[68]

Motherboards have three components: form factor, chipset, and built-in components.[69] The form factor defines the parameters of the motherboard such as its dimensions, power supply, location of mounts, and number of ports. The chipset on the motherboard creates the completed electronic circuit that coordinates data transfers between the computer components, which in turn determines the built-in components the motherboard supports.[70] The chipset also determines the functionality capabilities of the motherboard, such as its graphic capability and speed, as well as the core functionality of the system.

## 1.6 Motherboard: The Proverbial Nervous System of the Computer—Form Factor

A motherboard's form factor defines the type and location of different components on the motherboard itself. There are various motherboard form factors, and each of them defines a different set of components, sets forth a different layout for the components, and delineates a different specification for the motherboard. While motherboards vary by manufacturer, the physical size and shape of a motherboard is based on a loose set of industry standards, with names such as AT (a.k.a. Advanced Technology), ATX (a.k.a. Advanced Technology eXtended), and BTX (a.k.a. Balanced Technology eXtended) otherwise known as various "form factors."[71] These pseudo-standardized "form factors" allow different hardware manufacturers to create different components that go into a single computer.[72]

The first pseudo-industry standard form factor was the "AT form factor." It was one of the earliest standardized motherboards in the 1990s and is now obsolete.[73] The next generation of motherboards had a different physical layout that improved

[68] See Intel Universal Serial Bus (USB) Specifications, http://www.intel.com/content/www/us/en/io/universal-serial-bus/universal-serial-bus-specifications.html

[69] *See Intel Corp. v.* VIA *Technologies, Inc.*, 174 F. Supp. 2d 1038, 1040 (N.D. Cal. 2001), judgment aff'd, 319 F.3d 1357 (Fed. Cir. 2003) ("By way of background, the components of a computer system include separate chips mounted on a circuit board known as the motherboard. The system memory, microprocessor, chipset, and various input/output devices, such as modems, are all distinct components.").

[70] A chipset is a component in providing communications between the central processing units and main memory means. *LG Electronics, Inc. v. Hitachi, Ltd.*, 655 F. Supp. 2d 1036, 1043 (N.D. Cal. 2009).

[71] See Saltzer & Kaashoek, Principles of Computer System Design: An Introduction, Part I (Morgan Kaufmann 2009).

[72] See Foley, Computer Graphics: Principles and Practice (Addison-Wesley Professional 1996).

[73] See Foley, Computer Graphics: Principles and Practice (Addison-Wesley Professional 1996).

air circulation, acoustics, heat dissipation, and physical size.[74] One of these new motherboards was the "ATX form factor," which came into wide use in the mid-1990s. Within the ATX form factor, there are subvarieties based on a difference in size (expressed in millimeters), for example, micro-ATX (also written with the Greek symbol for micro as "µATX") has a maximum size of 244 mm × 244 mm.[75]

Another form factor is ITX, which is a smaller form factor which has, in turn, spurred the creation of even smaller form factors such as Mini-ITX, Nano-ITX, and Pico-ITX.[76] The nano-ITX and pico-ITX are commonly used for highly specialized devices, such as routers.[77] The form factor for a particular device will depend on the size of the device and the functionality needed for that device.[78] A motherboard for a server will need different capabilities than a motherboard for a smartphone.

## 1.7 Motherboard: The Proverbial Nervous System of the Computer—Chipset

The chipset on a motherboard is a critical component and refers to chips that work closely with the processor, often referred to as the CPU. The chipset is a circuit that coordinates data transfers between the computer components, more specifically between the CPU and the main memory means.[79] The chipset determines the type of processor the motherboard accepts, the type and capacity of RAM, and the internal

[74] "The repositioning of the riser card purportedly permits unimpeded airflow across the computer's internal components [i.e. motherboard] thereby improving the cooling efficiency of the computer's fan." Tulip Computers, Int'l B.V. v. Dell Computer Corp., 236 F. Supp. 2d 364, 367–68 (D. Del. 2002).

[75] An ATX motherboard can be designed so that it contains up to six memory slots for RAM types, support BIOS-controlled power management, SATA controllers, AMD or Intel CPU sockets, and support for USB and IEEE 1394. See generally Casbeer, Kenny, et al., History of 64-bit Computing: AMD64 and Intel Itanium Processors CS-350-1 1-2 (Computer Organization Spring 2004), available at http://www.academia.edu/376174/History_of_64-bit_Computing_AMD64_and_Intel_Itanium_Processors_CS-350-1_Computer_Organization_Spring_2004

[76] Kaneko, Kanehiro, et al., "Cybernetic Human HRP-4C," in 9th IEEE-RAS International Conference on Humanoid Robots: 7–14, available at http://ieeexplore.ieee.org/xpl/articleDetails.jsp?tp=&arnumber=5379537 (last visited Mar. 18, 2013).

[77] See Urness, "Teaching Computer Organization/Architecture by Building a Computer," in Proceedings of the 2007 ACM Workshop on Computer Architecture Education: 72–76, available at http://www.ncsu.edu/wcae/ISCA2007/p72-urness.pdf

[78] Urness, "Teaching Computer Organization/Architecture by Building a Computer," in Proceedings of the 2007 ACM Workshop on Computer Architecture Education: 72–76, available at http://www.ncsu.edu/wcae/ISCA2007/p72-urness.pdf

[79] *LG Electronics, Inc. v. Hitachi, Ltd.*, 655 F. Supp. 2d 1036, 1043 (N.D. Cal. 2009).

and external devices that the motherboard accepts.[80] Depending on its type, the chipset can provide functionality otherwise fulfilled by external components such as audio processing, network interface, and even video.[81]

## 1.8 Motherboard: The Proverbial Nervous System of the Computer—Components (Integrated and Acquired)

Motherboard components fall into two basic groups—integrated components and acquired components—that can be added on or modified later.[82] Integrated components on the motherboard include the clock, CMOS, battery, BIOS, expansion bus, and the system bus:

- The clock is a circuit that synchronizes system signals by giving off pulses. The number of pulses, or *timer ticks* as they are often called, is measured in megahertz (MHz).[83] The higher the number of pulses per second (i.e., the higher the MHz), the more information the system can process.
- The CMOS (pronounced *see-moss*) stands for complementary metal-oxide semiconductor,[84] and it saves the time, system date, and other essential system settings when the computer is powered down. A battery located on the motherboard powers CMOS.

[80] Thus, a gaming console will need a more robust chipset to handle the faster processor and larger amount of RAM, whereas a netbook that only needs basic functionality and web browsing capabilities can have a less robust chipset. See Dempsey, The New Compact, 4(2) Engineering & Technology 40–41 (Jan. 31-Feb. 13, 2009).

[81] Baum, Clarke & Taunton, *A Multimedia Chipset for Consumer Audio-Visual Applications*, 43(3) IEEE Transactions on Consumer Electronics 646–48 (Aug. 1997).

[82] See TM Patents, *L.P. v. Int'l Business Machines Corp.*, 72 F. Supp. 2d 370, 381 (S.D. N.Y. 1999), decision supplemented, 77 F. Supp. 2d 480 (S.D. N.Y. 1999) (citing McGraw Hill Dictionary of Scientific and Technical Terms (3d. ed.1984)) (using the term "integrated" to describe elements with a single semiconductor substrate or deposited on the substrate by a continuous series of compatible processes and capable of performing at least one complete electronic circuit function.); Expert Report of Robert G. Wilhelm in *Fisher-Rosemount Sys., Inc. v. Control Sys. Int'l, Inc.*, 2006 WL 5908522 (S.D.Tex.) ("In my opinion, the term "integrates" means functionally unites or functionally combines.").

[83] See Stanley, Computer Systems 655 (Jones & Bartlett Learning 2009).

[84] *See Agere Sys., Inc. v. Broadcom Corp.*, 2004 Markman 1658530, 2004 WL 1658530 (E.D. Pa. 2004), subsequent determination, 2004 WL 1737495 (E.D. Pa. 2004); *see also Oki America, Inc. v. Advanced Micro Devices, Inc.*, 2006 WL 335369 (N.D. Cal. 2006); Andantech L.L.C. v. C.I.R., T.C. Memo. 2002-97, at *34, T.C.M. (RIA) P 2002-097 (2002), decision aff'd in part and remanded, 331 F.3d 972 (D.C. Cir. 2003).

- BIOS, meaning basic input/output system, is the built-in software program used to interface between the operating system, the motherboard, and the attachments to the motherboard, such as the keyboard and monitor.[85]
- Expansion bus is comprised of expansion slots and the accompanying wires and support chips. The expansion slots allow for later modifications and increased functionality of the device. Just as there are many versions of standardized motherboards, there are many types of standardized expansion slots. These include Peripheral Component Interconnect (PCI),[86] Accelerated Graphics Port (AGP) specifically for video cards,[87] PCI Extended (PCI-X) for applications requiring a lot of power and/or speed, Mini-PCI for laptops, and PCI Express (PCIe), which is currently the fastest expansion slot available.[88]

Acquired components in the context of motherboards consist of sockets that enable various other key components of a computer such as the CPU, memory, or graphics cards. These components are discussed below in further detail.

## 1.9 Motherboard: The Proverbial Nervous System of the Computer—Firmware

The communication between the motherboard and other hardware occurs through small programs consisting of only a few lines of code.[89] This code and the hardware the code is on are collectively called firmware.[90] Firmware is hardware

---

[85] *See* Saltzer & Kaashoek, Principles of Computer System Design: An Introduction (Part I) (Morgan Kaufmann 2009).

[86] See Tooley, PC Based Instrumentation and Control 77 (Routledge 2012).

[87] A video card is a hardware device that creates output for the display. Some video cards are large boards that contain powerful graphics processors dedicated to generating 2D and 3D images along with dedicated memory and cooling fans. Other computers, such as netbooks, smartphones, and tablets, have less powerful graphics processors soldered directly to the motherboard. See generally Magallón, Hopf & Ertl, "Parallel Volume Rendering Using PC Graphics Hardware," in IEEE Ninth Pacific Conference on Computer Graphics and Applications 384–89 (2001).

[88] See Anzt, Heuveline, et al., "Power Consumption of Mixed Precision in the Iterative Solution of Sparse Linear Systems," in IEEE International Symposium on Parallel and Distributed Processing Workshops and Ph.D Forum (IPDPSW) 829–36 (2011).

[89] See generally Culler, Singh, & Gupta, Parallel Computer Architecture: A Hardware/Software Approach (Morgan Kaufmann 1999).

[90] Krikhaar, et al., Enabling System Evolution Through Configuration Management on the Hardware/Software Boundary, 12 Systems Engineering 233 (2009), available at http://www.few.vu.nl/~NP.Veerman/research/KMVV2009.pdf, stating that:

Firmware is another term that is causing confusion, which can also be read in the IEEE definition for firmware: "The combination of a hardware device and computer instructions and data that reside as read-only software on that device." The confusion surrounding this term has led to suggestions that it be avoided altogether. Firmware is used to refer to software load modules in on-board, nonvolatile memory devices, such as a PROM (Programmable Read-Only Memory), or in instructions written in microcode[91] that generally are changed infrequently during the lifetime of the device.[92] Firmware in almost all cases lives on the read-only memory chip, more commonly known as the ROM chip.[93] The ROM chip, unlike the volatile RAM chip (discussed further in §1:16), is a nonvolatile form of memory that is not erased when the computer is powered down.[94] Until the early 1990s, ROM (and the firmware on it) was unchangeable without actually removing the hardware and replacing it with hardware that contained a different set of instructions.[95] With the development of flash ROM, firmware on the ROM chip can now be updated.[96]

---

peripheral memory devices, such as hard-drives. On-board memory devices used to be read-only, but have evolved and can be reprogrammed. Examples are the EPROM, short for Erasable PROM, or flash memory. As such devices are no longer read-only, the definition of firmware seems to be outdated as well. Also, as load modules can be stored on hard-drives and from there loaded into the on-board memory during run-time by the main system software, the confusion increases: When the load module is on the hard-drive, it is considered to be software, but as soon as it is stored in a PROM, it turns into firmware.

[91] *NEC Corp. v. Intel Corp.*, 645 F. Supp. 590, 595 (N.D. Cal. 1986) (The court defined microcode to be "…a set of statements or instructions used directly or indirectly in a computer to bring about a certain result."); Lotus Development Corp. v. Paperback Software Intern., 740 F. Supp. 37 (D. Mass. 1990) (Court defined "[m]icrocode is a set of encoded instructions … that controls the fine details of the execution of one or more primitive functions of a computer. Microcode serves as a substitute for certain elements of the hardware circuitry that had previously controlled that function." Samuelson, CONTU Revisited: The Case Against Copyright Protection for Computer Programs in Machine-Readable Form, 1984 Duke L.J. 663, 677.).

[92] "Machine language, though different for each model of computer and tedious to use, is readily available to the skilled programmer for writing ordinary programs. By contrast, microinstruction sets generally are unavailable for the writing of standard user-oriented programs, although this is theoretically possible." Ross, III, The Patentability of Computer "Firmware," 59 J. Pat. Off. Soc'y 731 n.140 (1977) (citing Kline, Digital Computer Design 362–68 (Prentice Hall 1977); Agrawala & Rauscher, Foundations of Microprogramming, 20, 30 (Academic Press 1976)).

[93] See Aufrichtig, Copyright Protection for Computer Programs in Read Only Memory Chips, 11 Hofstra L. Rev. 329, 370 n. 3 (1982). *See Intel Corp. v. Silicon Storage Tech., Inc.*, 20 F. Supp. 2d 690, 692 (D. Del. 1998) (describing read-only memory as ROM "a type of computer memory that retains its contents even when the computer's power is turned off.").

[94] See generally Murray, & Buchan, A User's Guide to Non-Volatile, On-Chip Analogue Memory, 10(2) Electronics & Communication Engineering Journal 53–63 (Apr. 1998); *see also Apple Computer, Inc. v. Franklin Computer Corporation Puts the Byte Back into Copyright Protection for Computer Programs*, 14 Golden Gate U. L. Rev. 281, 286 (1984).

[95] "A generalized example of firmware would be a 'small, easily replaceable part which is pre-punched or wired in such a way that when activated … cause[s] a particular sequence of computer operations to take place … .'" Ross, III, The Patentability of Computer "Firmware," 59 J. Pat. Off. Soc'y 731, 737 (1977) (quoting Koller, Computer Software Protection: Report of an Institute Clinic, 13 Idea 351, 358 (Spring 1969), reprinted in 13 Pat. Trademark & Copy. J. Res. & Ed. 351 (1969–1970)).

[96] *See generally State v. Chun*, 194 N.J. 54, 943 A.2d 114 (2008), subsequent determination, 2013 WL 5226717 (N.J. 2013) (noting that firmware in Alcotest devices constantly changes).

## 1.10 Central Processing Unit and Microprocessors

The heart of any computer system is the central processing unit, or more commonly the "CPU chip."[97] The CPU chip has many command and control responsibilities. It is the traffic cop that keeps activities in synchronization as the data is read, written, tested, compared, copied, moved, or modified within memory, as well as the CPU chip itself.

CPU chips typically contain seven primary internal components: (1) microcode, (2) cache memory, (3) clock, (4) registers, (5) program counter, (6) the arithmetic logic unit (ALU), and (7) input/output functions. The more complex functions of registers, program counters, and arithmetic logic units will be left for another day. Below is an overview of the remaining internal components.

## 1.11 Central Processing Unit and Microprocessors—Microcode Low-Level Instructions Given to CPU, or Microprocessors

Microcode is the low-level instructions given to microprocessors.[98] Computer chips have the ability to initiate various types of actions as they have been preprogrammed to respond to these binary commands by their developers.[99] For example, a computer chip might be designed such that it adds two integers in two adjoining memory cells, placing the results in a third memory cell, when it sees the binary pattern 0100 0010 presented as a command.[100] In low-end computer chips, the microcode is hard-wired into the design of the chip. In high-end computer chips, the microcode may be programmable, allowing for downstream problems to be fixed without replacing any hardware.[101]

---

[97] *See Quanta Computer, Inc. v. LG Electronics, Inc.*, 553 U.S. 617, 128 S. Ct. 2109, 2113, 170 L. Ed. 2d 996 (2008) (stating, "The main functions of a computer system are carried out on a microprocessor, or central processing unit, which interprets program instructions, processes data, and controls other devices in the system.").

[98] See generally Mislow, Computer Microcode: Testing the Limits of Software Copyrightability, 65 B.U. L. Rev. 733 (1985). *See also Apple Computer, Inc. v. Franklin Computer Corp.*, 545 F. Supp. 812 (E.D. Pa. 1982), judgment rev'd on other grounds, 714 F.2d 1240, 70 A.L.R. Fed. 153 (3d Cir. 1983) at n. 14 (stating, "The microcode controls the actual circuits … . Indeed, the physical machine responds only to microcode. It was microcode, at bottom, that caused [the computer] to translate [the division symbol] into microcode.").

[99] *See NEC Corp. v. Intel Corp.*, 645 F. Supp. 590 (N.D. Cal. 1986); Steinberg, *NEC v. INTEL: The Battle over Copyright Protection for Microcode*, 27 Jurimetrics J. 173 (1986).

[100] See generally Hinckley, NEC v. Intel: *Will Hardware Be Drawn into the Black Hole of Copyright*, 3 Santa Clara Computer & High Tech. L.J. 23, 48 (1987).

[101] For example, see Description of the Microcode Update Device, Microsoft, Article ID: 288302, available at: http://support.microsoft.com/kb/288302; Hewlett-Packard, Microcode Update for HP 786F BIOS Family Computers with Intel Processors, available through searching for title in HP's Business Support Center at http://h20000.www2.hp.com/bizsupport/TechSupport/Home.jsp

## 1.12 Central Processing Unit and Microprocessors—Cache Memory

Computer chips have internal memory, called cache memory, which is designed to be very fast.[102] The function of internal memory is to act as a buffer between the slower main memory (like the hard drive) and the speed of the computer chip itself.[103] An example of a slower function is when a computer writes information to a hard drive, and an example of a faster function is when a computer reads and writes to working memory. The main purpose of cache memory is to anticipate what the computer chip is going to need next and pre-fetch that information from the slower main memory before it is needed; alternatively, recently written values are kept there in case they are needed again soon.[104]

## 1.13 Central Processing Unit and Microprocessors—Clock

The clock controls how fast the computer components work.[105] All the components of a computer are tied directly to the clock at some level. Most clocks are designed to emit electrical pulses at the nanosecond level.[106] For the CPU to process a command, a voltage must be applied to the clock wire, which issues a pulse, or clock

[102] *See Quanta Computer, Inc. v. LG Electronics, Inc.*, 553 U.S. 617, 622, 128 S. Ct. 2109, 170 L. Ed. 2d 996 (2008) (stating, "Frequently accessed data are generally stored in cache memory, which permits faster access than main memory and is often located on the microprocessor itself.").

[103] *See Storage Tech. Corp. v. Cisco Sys., Inc.*, 329 F.3d 823, 826 (Fed. Cir. 2003) (describing cache memory as "a small, usually temporary, memory that can be accessed quickly, often used to store a copy of instructions or data obtained from main memory."); Silicon Graphics, Inc. v. n Vidia Corp., 58 F. Supp. 2d 331, 335 (D. Del. 1999) (describing cache memory as "a smaller and faster memory that stores small amounts of data at a location away from the main memory.").

[104] *See also Intergraph Hardware Technologies Co. v. Toshiba Corp.*, 508 F. Supp. 2d 752, 755–756 (N.D. Cal. 2007) (stating, "In order to compensate for [the main memory's] slow speed, computer systems include a "cache memory" located within the microprocessor. The cache memory is smaller than the main memory and communicates with the CPU much faster than the main memory. Due to its smaller size, only a portion of the data in the main memory is stored in the cache memory at any given time. By allowing the CPU to communicate principally with the cache memory rather than the main memory, the overall speed and performance of the computer system increases dramatically.").

[105] See also Anacker, Affordable Hardware, A.B.A. J., Nov. 1 1986, at 90 ("The primary purpose of the CPU clock is not to keep track of time, but to synchronize the operation of all the computer circuits. The faster the clock rate, the faster the computer can process information.").

[106] See Anacker, Affordable Hardware, A.B.A. J., Nov. 1 1986, at 90 ("Without power pulses, the memory chips in PCs can only remember data for a fraction of a second. The clock rate must be fast enough to refresh those chips. But it must be slower than the fastest speed at which the circuits and components in the computer and its peripheral can operation.").

cycle.[107] A CPU can perform a simple command in a single cycle or a more complex command over the course of multiple cycles.[108] The maximum number of clock cycles a CPU can process in a given period of time defines the clock speed.[109] Clock speed is measured in Hertz (Hz)[110]:

- 1 hertz (1 Hz) = one cycle per second
- 1 megahertz (1 MHz) = one million cycles per second
- 1 gigahertz (1 GHz) = one billion cycles per second

The faster the clock runs, the faster the computer works.[111] Today, a typical desktop computer chip performs a different action three billion times per second.[112]

## 1.14 Central Processing Unit and Microprocessors—Input/Output Function Controls Which Processes Can Provide the CPU Chip with Data

In a CPU chip, the input/output function (the I/O function) controls which processes can provide the CPU chip with data and which processes can receive data from the CPU chip.[113] The CPU chip receives, via the I/O function, commands in binary.[114] As mentioned earlier, the number 1 means that electricity is being transmitted, or

---

[107] See *Microprocessor Enhancement Corp. v. Texas Instruments Inc.*, 520 F.3d 1367 (Fed. Cir. 2008) (stating, "To execute an instruction, a microprocessor must perform a series of tasks, and each task is completed on a fixed time interval defined by the system clock—a clock cycle.").

[108] See *Cornell Univ. v. Hewlett-Packard Co.*, 654 F. Supp. 2d 119 (N.D. N.Y. 2009) (describing a patent allowing "technology for issuing multiple and out-of-order computer processor instructions in a single machine clock cycle.").

[109] See *Barbara's Sales, Inc. v. Intel Corp.*, 227 Ill. 2d 45, 316 Ill. Dec. 522, 879 N.E.2d 910 (2007) (stating "One historical measure of speed is called 'clock speed,' which is measured in hertz.").

[110] "Frequency" is measured in "hertz" or cycles per second. *Watson Indus., Inc. v. Murata Electronics North America, Inc.*, 2003 Markman 23272375, 2003 WL 23272375, *8 (W.D. Wis. 2003).

[111] See *Barbara's Sales, Inc. v. Intel Corp.*, 227 Ill. 2d 45, 316 Ill. Dec. 522, 879 N.E.2d 910, 913 (2007) ("A principal measure of performance for the common consumer is speed. As the speed of a processor increases, the more instructions a processor can process, resulting in less time a computer requires to open software applications, refresh screens, and depict ever more realistic video game characters. One historical measure of speed is called 'clock speed,' which is measured in hertz.").

[112] A common laptop processor is now measured in gigahertz, equal to 1 million hertz.

[113] See Blundell, Computer Hardware 54–58 (Delmar 2008).

[114] See generally Williams, *An Introduction to Computing Infrastructure: Hardware and Operating Systems* 34 (Que Education & Training 1997).

"on," and the number 0 means no transmission of electricity, or "off."[115] The binary commands are transmitted to the CPU via the external data bus (EDB).[116]

The primary components of the CPU chip are connected to a data path that links components on the EDB.[117] The EDB is a multilane path where each bit gets a path. Binary data is transferred among components across this path.[118] The path is extended to external input/output ("I/O") devices so that data from an external hard drive, for example, can be read by the CPU chip and manipulated. However, since these external I/O devices are not in sync with the internal CPU clock, they must be managed so that their actions are brought into sync with the CPU chip.[119] This monitoring and control function is the responsibility of the I/O function of the CPU chip.[120]

## 1.15 Memory Volatile or Nonvolatile

Computer systems store data in memory, with the two most common types of memory being volatile and nonvolatile memory.[121] Volatile and nonvolatile memory cells are differentiated based on what happens when the power to the memory cell is turned off.[122] Nonvolatile memory maintains information even when the power is off.[123] Volatile memory, by comparison, is memory that is refreshed constantly, and once the power is shut off, all information is lost.[124]

---

[115] See Hilton, Survey of Computers, Software, and Information Processing, 31 Idea 67 (1990); *U.S. Philips Corp. v. Atmel Corp.*, 2004 Markman 736810, 2004 WL 736810 (S.D. N.Y. 2004).

[116] See Takahashi, Yamada, et al. A High Performance 32-Bit Microcontroller For Realtime Applications, 74(11) IEICE Transactions on Electronics, 3766–3774 (Nov. 20, 1991).

[117] See Sammes & Jenkinson, Forensic Computing: A Practitioner's Guide 68–78 (Springer 2000).

[118] See Godbole Operating systems 24 (Tata McGraw-Hill Education 2005).

[119] See Godbole Operating systems 145 (Tata McGraw-Hill Education 2005).

[120] Alexander, Robertson, et al., *Corporate Business Servers: An Alternative to Mainframes for Business Computing*, 45 Hewlett Packard Journal, available at http://www.hpl.hp.com/hpjournal/94jun/jun94a1.pdf (last visited Mar. 19, 2013).

[121] See Patterson & Hennessy, *Computer Organization And Design: The Hardware/Software Interface* A-39 (4th ed. 2009).

[122] See *TV/Com Intern., Inc. v. Mediaone of Greater Florida, Inc.*, 2001 Markman 36169709, 2001 WL 36169709, *24 n.10 (M.D. Fla. 2001).

[123] See *TV/Com Intern., Inc. v. Mediaone of Greater Florida, Inc.*, 2001 Markman 36169709, 2001 WL 36169709, *24 n.10 (M.D. Fla. 2001).

[124] See *David L. Aldridge Co. v. Microsoft Corp.*, 995 F. Supp. 728, 732 (S.D. Tex. 1998).

## 1.16 Memory Volatile or Nonvolatile—Volatile Memory

Volatile memory is commonly known as random access memory (RAM).[125] The CPU needs to be able to read and write data to the memory.[126] Memory also enables the CPU to access data within the clock cycle speed of the CPU.[127] Computers use RAM to enable this operation.[128] There are two main types of RAM: dynamic random access memory (DRAM)[129] and static random access memory (SRAM, pronounced *s-ram*).[130]

SRAM maintains the data in a constant state unless the power is shut off.[131] SRAM is typically more expensive than DRAM, so it is used in smaller applications, such as toys, small appliances, and smaller parts of personal computers.[132]

DRAM is a solid chip that can access any point of data stored inside without delay, allowing the processor to access data and programs very quickly.[133] There are many types of DRAM available, with the most common form in personal computers being Synchronous Dynamic Random Access Memory ("SDRAM"),[134] a faster

[125] See *Quanta Computer, Inc. v. LG Electronics, Inc.*, 553 U.S. 617, 128 S. Ct. 2109, 2113, 170 L. Ed. 2d 996 (2008) ("The data processed by the computer are stored principally in random access memory, also called main memory.") (*citing* Webster's New World Dictionary of Computer Terms 334, 451 (8th ed. 2000)).

[126] See Patterson & Hennessy, *Computer Organization and Design: The Hardware/Software Interface* 537–39 (4th ed. 2009).

[127] See Patterson & Hennessy, *Computer Organization and Design: The Hardware/Software Interface* 17–22 (4th ed. 2009).

[128] See Part I, Saltzer & Kaashoek, *Principles of Computer System Design: An Introduction* (Morgan Kaufmann 2009).

[129] See *NEC Corp. v. Hyundai Electronics Industries Co.*, Ltd., 30 F. Supp. 2d 546, 548 (E.D. Va. 1998).

[130] See In re *Static Random Access memory (SRAM) Antitrust Litigation*, 264 F.R.D. 603, 606 (N.D. Cal. 2009).

[131] SRAM is a type of memory device that cannot retain stored data absent a source of power. In re SRAM Antitrust Litigation, 264 F.R.D. at 606; see also The Tech Terms Computer Dictionary, available at http://www.techterms.com/definition/sram (first published, 2005, last visited Nov 21, 2012).

[132] See Patterson & Hennessy, *Computer Organization And Design: The Hardware/Software Interface 17* (4th ed. 2009).

[133] See N*EC Corp. v. Hyundai Electronics Industries Co., Ltd.*, 30 F. Supp. 2d 546, 548 (E.D. Va. 1998).

[134] Synchronous dynamic random access memory (SDRAM) is dynamic random access memory (DRAM) that has a synchronous interface with the computer systems bus. See *Rambus, Inc. v. Infineon Technologies AG*, 164 F. Supp. 2d 743, 747 (E.D. Va. 2001), aff'd in part, vacated in part, rev'd in part on other grounds, 318 F.3d 1081 (Fed. Cir. 2003) ("In a SDRAM, the central processing unit, or CPU, sends and receives information from the memory device according to the 'tick' of a 'clock' contained within the memory system. In DDR SDRAMs, the rate of the transfer of information is doubled because information is sent on both the 'tick' and the 'tock' of the clock.").

version of DRAM.[135] But a computer cannot rely solely on DRAM for storage.[136] Like SRAM, DRAM is nonpermanent and will lose all of its contents as soon as the power is cut.[137] In the average personal computer, the memory is in the form of DRAM.[138]

## 1.17 Memory Volatile or Nonvolatile—Nonvolatile Memory

In comparison, NVRAM, or nonvolatile random access memory, maintains the data in the memory cell when power is removed.[139] This benefit is countered by the fact that NVRAM is slow and expensive. NVRAM is typically found in thumb drives and memory cards and, more recently, in solid-state disk drives.[140] As a means of storing large quantities of information in nonvolatile states, a computer will use various hard drives and data storage devices to overcome the problems associated with volatile memory devices.[141]

The following figure shows data in memory at the binary level. Each of the possible binary states is converted to the equivalent of a light switch. If the light switch is in the off state, the light bulb is considered to be in the "0" state. If the light switch is on, the bulb is considered to be in the "1" state. In this case, our previous integer diagram would look like this:

---

[135] SDRAM increases the speed at which a central processing unit (CPU) can read or write memory by synchronizing itself with the CPU's clock speed. *Rambus Inc. v. Infineon Technologies Ag*, 318 F.3d 1081, 1085 (Fed. Cir. 2003); see also The Tech Terms Computer Dictionary, available at http://www.techterms.com/definition/dram (first published, 2005, last visited Nov 21, 2012). For further discussion of DRAM and SDRAM, see Preliminary Expert Report of Joseph C. McAlexander Regarding Invalidity of Rambus Patents, in Rambus, Inc. v. Hynix Semiconductor Inc. et al., No. 05CV00334, 2008 WL 5424984 (N.D. Cal. Nov. 14, 2008).

[136] See Preliminary Expert Report of Joseph C. McAlexander Regarding Invalidity of Rambus Patents, in *Rambus, Inc. v. Hynix Semiconductor Inc.* et al., No. 05CV00334, 2008 WL 5424984 (N.D. Cal. Nov. 14, 2008) (explaining that Dynamic Random Access Memory (DRAM), which is the main memory for temporary storage, is distinct from the hard drive, which permits long-term "nonvolatile" storage.).

[137] Patterson & Hennessy, *Computer Organization and Design: The Hardware/Software Interface* 21 (4th ed. 2009).

[138] Patterson & Hennessy, *Computer Organization and Design: The Hardware/Software Interface* 18 (4th ed. 2009).

[139] For a discussion on volatile and nonvolatile memory, see *Mettler-Toledo, Inc. v. Fairbanks Scales Inc.*, 551 F. Supp. 2d 576 (E.D. Tex. 2008), aff'd, 671 F.3d 1291 (Fed. Cir. 2012).

[140] See *Fast Memory Erase, LLC v. Spansion, Inc.*, 2010 Markman 363498, 2010 WL 363498 (N.D. Tex. 2010).

[141] The medium for storing software includes hard disks, floppy disks, and magnetic tapes. *Advent Systems Ltd. v. Unisys Corp.*, 925 F.2d 670, 674, 13 U.C.C. Rep. Serv. 2d 669 (3d Cir. 1991). A nonvolatile memory is fixed and, unlike a volatile memory, does not need an electrical current to be saved. Aufrichtig, Copyright Protection for Computer Programs in Read Only Memory Chips, 11 Hofstra L. Rev. 329, 370 n. 8 (1982).

| **Column weight &rarr** | 128 | **64** | 32 | 16 | 8 | 4 | 2 | **1** | Value of byte as integer |
|---|---|---|---|---|---|---|---|---|---|
| **Bit state &rarr** | Off | **On** | Off | Off | Off | Off | Off | **On** | **65** |

If this hypothetical scenario is taken and the light switch is replaced with a single transistor, it results in the initial makings of a memory chip. Memory chips typically contain billions of transistors, each one representing a single bit of information.[142] In addition to storing bytes of data, memory chips must also be able to access this data on demand. This task is accomplished by making the memory chip addressable.[143]

The amount of addressable memory in a computer system is a function of the total number of bits it can recognize.[144] As in our earlier example, an 8-bit computer could only recognize 256 unique memory cells,[145] while a 32-bit computer can recognize 4 billion unique memory cells.[146] Thus, the more unique memory cells a computer has, the more information it can store and access faster and more smoothly.

## 1.18 Mass-Storage Devices: Hard-Disk Drives, Solid-State Drives, and Redundant Array of Independent Disks (RAIDs)

Digital devices, such as computers, need more than just volatile memory for storing programs and data.[147] In most personal computers, that additional storage is provided by a hard drive, which is a mass-storage device that provides cheap and nonvolatile data storage.[148] A hard drive is electronic hardware that stores information

[142] See Patterson & Hennessy, *Computer Organization and Design: The Hardware/Software Interface* 44–47 (4th ed. 2009).

[143] See *Wiener v. NEC Electronics, Inc.*, 102 F.3d 534, 539 (Fed. Cir. 1996) (abrogated on other grounds by, *Cybor Corp. v. FAS Technologies, Inc.*, 138 F.3d 1448 (Fed. Cir. 1998)).

[144] Saltzer & Schroeder, The Protection of Information in Computer Systems, 63(9) Proceedings of the IEEE 1278–1308 (Sept. 1975); see also Pagiamtzis & Sheikholeslami, *Content-Addressable Memory (CAM) Circuits and Architectures: A Tutorial and Survey*, 41(3) IEEE Journal of Solid-State Circuits 712–27 (Mar. 2006).

[145] An 8-bit memory cell holds a number that has a value between 0 and 255. The 8-bit ASCII standard assigns a number to each of a set of 256 characters, $2 \times 2 \times 2 \times 2 \times 2 \times 2 \times 2 \times 2 = 256$. Contained within the 256 characters are English, German, Spanish, and Greek letters, symbols, and punctuation symbols. S3 Inc. v. NVIDIA Corp., 259 F.3d 1364, 1366 (Fed. Cir. 2001).

[146] A 16-bit machine can directly generate only about 65,000 unique numbers for its storage system. A 32-bit machine, however, can directly generate some 4.3 billion different numbers. See Kidder, *The Soul of a New Machine* (Back Bay Books 2011).

[147] See *David L. Aldridge Co. v. Microsoft Corp.*, 995 F. Supp. 728, 732 (S.D. Tex. 1998) (explaining the difference between volatile RAM and nonvolatile ROM).

[148] See U.S. v. Barth, 26 F. Supp. 2d 929, 932 (W.D. Tex. 1998) ("The hard-drive is the large, non-removable mass storage component of a computer or computer network."); *State v. Grenning*, 142

and supports the sending and retrieving of information over a hardware interface using a protocol.[149]

## 1.19 Mass-Storage Devices: Hard-Disk Drives, Solid-State Drives, and Redundant Array of Independent Disks (RAIDs)—Hard-Disk Drives

Hard-disk drives store information much like memory cells, but unlike with memory, magnetic patterns are used.[150] There is a sequential address that gets you to the location of the data and a reliable technique for storing the data on the surface of the hard-drive platter.[151]

In the table below, note that the hard drive converts the state of the light switch to one of two magnetic patterns—north and south.[152]

| **Column weight &rarr** | 128 | **64** | 32 | 16 | 8 | 4 | 2 | **1** |
|---|---|---|---|---|---|---|---|---|
| **Bit state &rarr** | Off | **On** | Off | Off | Off | Off | Off | **On** |
| **Surface of hard drive &rarr** | South | **North** | South | South | South | South | South | **North** |

Hard drives are designed to mimic the state of DRAM, but instead of ones and zeros, it writes out magnetic patterns.[153] So, to use our example from above, if searching a hard drive for the occurrence of a Capital "A," the computer would be looking for the magnetic pattern SNSS SSSN somewhere on the surface of the hard-disk platter.

Wash. App. 518, 174 P.3d 706, 713 (Div. 2 2008), aff'd, 169 Wash. 2d 47, 234 P.3d 169 (2010) ("Hard-drives store permanent, static, and unchanging data.").

[149] The hard drive can store anything that can be stored electronically: executable programs, source code, documents, images, presentations, database entries, or any other text or numeric data. Generally, hard drives store information in files and files are usually managed by a file system, which defines how the files are organized in the storage media.

[150] See *David L. Aldridge Co. v. Microsoft Corp.*, 995 F. Supp. 728, 732 n.2 (S.D. Tex. 1998); see generally Grochowski & Halem, Technological Impact of Magnetic Hard Disk Drives on Storage Software, 42 IBM Systems J. 338 (2003).

[151] See *generally* Grochowski & Halem, *Technological Impact of Magnetic Hard Disk Drives on Storage Software*, 42 IBM Systems J. 338 (2003).

[152] For a detailed technical discussion about magnetic features of hard drives, see *McFadyen, Fullerton & Carey, State of the Art Magnetic Hard Disk Drives*, 31 MRS Bulletin 379 (May 2006), available at http://physics.ucsc.edu/~galers/class/Reference/MR-materials.pdf (last visited Nov 30, 2012).

[153] See Morley & Parker, *Understanding Computers 2009: Today and Tomorrow* 109–112 (Cengage Learning 2009).

The hard drive consists of multiple disks coated in a magnetic material and a moving arm.[154] The moving arm hovers over the surface of the disks, and a device on the end of the arm, called a "read/write head," can read and write data to the disks.[155] Hard drives store data in magnetic fields,[156] which means even a tiny dust particle on a platter would act like a mountain in the way of the read/write heads and would cause damage to the drive.[157] To keep the air clean inside the drive, most hard drives use a device to keep the air pressure equalized between the interior and the exterior of the drive.[158] Hard drives run at a set spindle speed counted in revolutions per minute (RPM).[159] The faster the spindle speed, the faster the controller can store and access data from the hard drive.[160] Turning on a computer takes time, in part, because a hard drive must spin up before the read/write heads can retrieve and load data into the computer's RAM.[161]

Hard drives divide into two major groups: (1) those with moving parts[162] and (2) those without moving parts.[163] Most hard drives consist of individual disks, each

---

[154] Plaintiff's Opening Claim Construction Brief, in Rembrandt Data Storage, *LP v. Seagate Technology LLC*, No. 10CV00693, 2011 WL 3223048, *6 (W.D. Wis. June 24, 2011).

[155] See Morley & Parker, *Understanding Computers 2009: Today and Tomorrow* 94–99 (Cengage Learning 2009).

[156] See Morley & Parker, *Understanding Computers 2009: Today and Tomorrow 97* (Cengage Learning 2009).

[157] Easily installable removable integrated hard disk and controller, U.S. Patent No. 5,233,594 (issued Aug. 3, 1993) ("External contaminants such as smoke and dust can destroy a hard disk because the read/write heads float extremely near to the platter surfaces [...]").

[158] See generally Morley & Parker, *Understanding Computers 2009: Today and Tomorrow* 51–63 (Cengage Learning 2009).

[159] Schroeder & Gibson, "Disk Failures in the Real World: What Does an MTTF of 1,000,000 Hours Mean to You?," in Proceedings of the 5th USENIX Conference on File and Storage Technologies (FAST) Art. No. 1 (USENIX Ass'n Berkeley 2007).

[160] See Anderson, Dykes & Riedel, "More Than an Interface—SCSI vs. ATA," in Proceedings of the 2nd USENIX Conference on File and Storage Technologies (FAST'03) 245–57 (Mar. 2003).

[161] See S*torage Computer Corp. v. Veritas Software Corp.*, 2003 Markman 203068, 2003 WL 203068 (N.D. Tex. 2003); see Patterson, Gibson & Katz, "A Case for Redundant Array of Inexpensive Disks (RAID)," in Proceedings of the ACM SIGMOD International Conference on Management of Data (June 1988); U.S. v. Stierhoff, 477 F. Supp. 2d 423, 439 n.7 (D.R.I. 2007), aff'd, 549 F.3d 19 (1st Cir. 2008); *Sun Microsystems Inc. v. Network Appliance*, 2009 WL 1513384 (N.D. Cal. 2009); Jun, Zhiming, & Zhiping, A Key Technology Of Design In RAID System, 1 Computer and Peripherals 001 (2000) (Chinese).

[162] See Morley & Parker, *Understanding Computers 2009: Today and Tomorrow* 108–110 (Cengage Learning 2009).

[163] See generally Morley & Parker, *Understanding Computers 2009: Today and Tomorrow* 101 (Cengage Learning 2009).

with read/write heads on actuator arms controlled by a servo motor.[164] Most hard drives, whether with or without moving parts, are enclosed in a sealed case that prevents contamination by outside air.[165]

## 1.20 Mass-Storage Devices: Hard-Disk Drives, Solid-State Drives, and Redundant Array of Independent Disks (RAIDs)—Solid-State Drives

Another mass-storage device is the solid-state drive, which uses integrated circuit assemblies as memory to store data persistently. Solid-state drives do not employ any moving mechanical components. Instead of moving platters, they use memory chips to store data.[166] Solid-state drives have been available for 30 years, if you could afford them. It was not until the introduction of iPad, iPhone, and similar smartphone devices that the prices declined to allow for widespread adoption. As mentioned, hard-disk drive uses a head mounted on a mechanical actuator to access rotating magnetic storage media, but a solid-state drive uses nonvolatile memory as its storage media. This means that solid-state drives use silicon and lack moving parts. Fewer parts and different materials make solid-state drives more robust than hard-disk drives. Today, solid-state drives are commonplace in smartphones, digital cameras, and high-end laptops.[167]

Solid-state drives and hard-disk drives are members of a storage class termed "block devices." Both of these storage devices use logical addressing to access data and abstract the physical media using small, fixed, contiguous segments of bytes as the addressable unit.[168] Both of these block devices consist of three major parts: storage media, a controller for managing the media, and a host interface for accessing the media.[169]

---

[164] *Sumitomo Corp. of America v. U.S.*, 18 Ct. Int'l Trade 501, 855 F. Supp. 1283, 1284 (1994) (stating that "The read/write heads function in conjunction with actuators, [1] which in turn are part of a positioning system that moves the heads to precise locations in order to access a particular track on the computer disk."). The term "actuator" is defined to be "any of various electric, hydraulic, or pneumatic mechanisms by means of which something is moved or controlled indirectly instead of by hand. …" 855 F. Supp. at 1284 n. 1 (*citing* Webster's Third New International Dictionary 22 (1st ed. 1986)).

[165] Garrie & Spernow, *Legally Correct But Technologically Off the Mark*, 9 Nw. J. Tech. & Intell. Prop. 1 (2010).

[166] See generally Morley & Parker, *Understanding Computers 2009: Today and Tomorrow* 101 (Cengage Learning 2009).

[167] Secure digital (SD) and compact flash (CF) memory cards, often used in digital cameras, are smaller and scaled back versions of solid-state drives because a digital camera's need for storage is substantially less than a laptop or server.

[168] Cornwell, McKusick, et al., *Anatomy of a Solid-State Drive*, 55(12) Communications of the ACM 59–63 (2012).

[169] Cornwell, McKusick, et al., *Anatomy of a Solid-State Drive*, 55(12) Communications of the ACM 59–63 (2012).

## 1.21 Mass-Storage Devices: Hard-Disk Drives, Solid-State Drives, and Redundant Array of Independent Disks (RAIDs)

A RAID, or redundant array of independent disks, is an array, or group, of multiple independent physical drives that provide high performance and fault tolerance.[170] A RAID drive group appears to the host computer as a single storage unit or as multiple virtual units.[171] A RAID essentially spreads data across several disks, using techniques such as disk striping (RAID level 0)[172] and disk mirroring (RAID level 1)[173] to achieve redundancy, lower latency, and/or higher bandwidth for reading and/or writing and data recoverability. A RAID drive group is a group of physical drives that are managed in partitions known as virtual drives.[174]

RAID configurations are often referred to by levels and describe the disk configuration for the particular system. There are different RAID configurations, or levels, based on the needs of the computing environment referred to as "RAID levels."[175] There are seven different RAID levels that are in widespread use today.[176] RAID levels vary based on the degree of redundancy and performance that is required from the storage for the system.

A RAID can be implemented as a software utility or as hardware.[177] Software RAID is more economical, but it sacrifices speed for a lower price.[178] Hardware RAID uses multiple hard drives in combination with a dedicated controller card to accomplish the mirroring or striping.[179]

---

[170] RAID is generally used for administering large storage, although traditional RAIDs have only one or two fault tolerances, which is not sufficient for constructing large storage. Matsumoto & Uehara, "N-nary RAID: 3-resilient RAID Based on an N-nary Number," in International Conference on Advanced Information Networking and Applications 249–255 (May 26–29, 2009).

[171] Patterson, Gibson & Katz, *A Case for Redundant Arrays of Inexpensive Disks (RAID)*, 17(3) ACM SIGMOD Record 109–116 (June 1988).

[172] Chen & Lee, *Striping In A RAID Level 5 Disk Array*, 23(1) ACM SIGMETRICS Performance Evaluation Review 136–45 (May 1995).

[173] Thomasian & Blaum, *Mirrored Disk Organization Reliability Analysis,* 55(12) IEEE Transactions on Computers 1640–1644 (Dec. 2006).

[174] Patterson, Gibson & Katz, *A Case for Redundant Arrays of Inexpensive Disks (RAID)*, 17(3) ACM SIGMOD Record 109–116 (June 1988).

[175] See, e.g., Patterson, Gibson & Katz, *A Case for Redundant Arrays of Inexpensive Disks (RAID)*, 17(3) ACM SIGMOD Record 109–116 (June 1988); Kim, Kim, & Shin, "Volume Management In SAN Environment," in Proceedings of Eighth International Conference on Parallel and Distributed Systems 500–505 (2001); Method and Apparatus for Assigning RAID Levels, U.S. Patent No. 6,718,434 (issued Apr. 6, 2004).

[176] See, e.g., Patterson, Gibson & Katz, *A Case for Redundant Arrays of Inexpensive Disks (RAID)*, 17(3) ACM SIGMOD Record 109–116 (June 1988). This article provides an overview of RAID and the article also discusses the different level configurations.

[177] See Patterson, Gibson & Katz, *A Case for Redundant Arrays of Inexpensive Disks (RAID)*, 17(3) ACM SIGMOD Record 109–116 (June 1988).

[178] See Kant, *RAID Hard Disk Arrays* (Milwaukee Sch. of Engineering, Feb. 2, 2005).

[179] See Chen, Lee, et al., *RAID: High-Performance, Reliable Secondary Storage,* 26(2) ACM Computing Surveys (CSUR) 145–185 (June 1994).

## 1.22 Other Data Storage Devices: CD, DVD, Blu-Ray, and Flash Memory

Compact discs ("CDs") and digital versatile discs ("DVDs") are other popular forms of data storage for computers.[180] Both CDs and DVDs are optical discs.[181] Optical discs work by encoding data in a spiral on the surface of a shiny disc, by either leaving the surface flat or pushing it down to form a "pit."[182] A laser bouncing off the surface then scans the surface of the disc.[183]

Prior to the invention of the DVD, CD capacity held firm at 700 MB of data, or about 80 minutes of video. The lowest capacity of a DVD is 4.37 GB of data, or about 2 hours of video. The highest capacity DVD is currently at 16GB of data, or about 8 hours of video. DVDs are able to hold more data because they use smaller pits than CDs and the pits are closer together.[184] This allows for a larger total pit number. DVDs can also be double sided, allowing the user to flip the disk over and write to the other side.[185] Finally, DVDs can be in a single-layer or dual-layer format. The dual-layer format uses two pitted layers on each side.

Following closely on the heels of DVDs are Blu-ray Discs™. Blu-ray discs offer more capacity than DVDs, up to 50 GB on dual-layer discs.[186] The blue-violet laser that gives the disc its name is more precise than the red laser technology used to read DVDs.[187] This means that more information can be accurately written and read off

---

[180] See, e.g., *Universal City Studios, Inc. v. Corley*, 273 F.3d 429, 435 (2d Cir. 2001) (noting the difference between CDs and DVDs); *Princo Corp. v. Inter'l Trade Com'n,* 616 F.3d 1318, 1322 (Fed. Cir. 2010), cert. denied, 131 S. Ct. 2480, 179 L. Ed. 2d 1209 (2011) (describing CD, CD-R, and CD-RW); *U.S. v. Denton*, 487 F. Supp. 2d 1180, 1183 (D. Or. 2007).

[181] In general, an optical disk is a storage medium, such as a compact disk (CD) or a digital versatile disk (DVD). *Kamatani v. Benq Corp., 2005 Markman* 6217424, 2005 WL 6217424 (E.D. Tex. 2005); see also In re *Optical Disk Drive Antitrust Litigation*, 2011 WL 3894376 (N.D. Cal. 2011).

[182] Optical discs are a non-deletion mass-storage technology. Copeland, *What If Mass Storage Were Free?*, 15(2) ACM SIGIR Forum 1–7 (Mar. 1980).

[183] Milster, *Horizons for Optical Data Storage*, 16(3) Optics And Photonics News 28–33 (2005).

[184] "Because high-resolution video requires more data to be stored, the development of the DVD optical disc was driven by the need to store a large amount of data. The differences require smaller pits spaced more closely together, and a re-tuned laser to read the data." NISSIM CORP., *Plaintiff, v. CLEARPLAY, INC.*, Matthew Jarman, Lee Jarman, and William Aho, Defendants., 2005 WL 6750830 (S.D. Fla. 2005); see also Birkett, The Chemistry of Optical Discs, 79(9) J. of Chem. Educ. 1081 (Sept. 2002).

[185] See Satoh, Isao, et al. "Key technology for high density rewritable DVD (DVD-RAM)," 34(2) IEEE Transactions on Magnetics 337–42 (1998). For the uninitiated, digital versatile disk (DVD) is a high density type of compact disk which stores a minimum of 4.37 gigabytes of information on a single sided, single-layer disk. DVDs may also be double sided or "reverse spiral" dual layered to store even more data. Fulton, Courtroom Technology: DVD, Digital, Settlement Brochures in a Tort Liability Case, 1 Ann.2001 ATLA-CLE 755.

[186] See Tsukuda, Ito, et al., "50 GB Read Only Memory Disc With Dual Layer Structure," in Proceedings of the International Symposium on Optical Memory and Optical Data Storage Topical Meeting 10–12 (2002).

[187] See Watson, How Blu-ray Discs Work, https://electronics.howstuffworks.com/blu-ray.htm

the disk. Blu-ray can also manage high definition video better than DVD, which leads to a better viewing experience. Writing to different types of media generally requires specific types of hardware.[188]

A final popular form of data storage is flash memory.[189] Flash memory is a solid chip like DRAM, but it stores data permanently.[190] Smartphones and some laptops use flash memory for data storage. Secure data cards, which are discussed above with solid-state drives, are used in digital cameras and are another form of flash memory. All of these forms of data storage plug into the motherboard and hold data until accessed by the computer, at which point the data is transferred to DRAM for faster access.[191]

## 1.23 Input and Output Devices

Another important category of computer hardware is input and output devices.[192] The keyboard, mouse, and computer monitor are common types of input and output devices.[193]

Input devices are physical devices that can be used to insert data into a computer or other computational device.[194] An input device provides data or instruction to a

[188] *Universal City Studios, Inc. v. Corley*, 273 F.3d 429 (2d Cir. 2001).

[189] Flash memory is also widely used in mobile phones, laptops, digital audio players, and digital cameras. *Fast Memory Erase, LLC v. Spansion, Inc.*, 2010 WL 5093945, *1 n.1 (N.D. Tex. 2010), report and recommendation adopted, 2010 WL 5093944 (N.D. Tex. 2010), aff'd, 423 Fed. Appx. 991 (Fed. Cir. 2011).

[190] See Kennedy, *Solid! SSDS Can Bring Magic to Your Computer,* A.B.A. J., (December 2011), at 23 (describing flash memory as a nonvolatile solid-state drive).

[191] See Rangaswami, Dimitrijević, et al., "MEMS-Based Disk Buffer for Streaming Media Servers," in Proceedings of the 19th International Conference on Data Engineering 619–30 (Mar. 5–8, 2003).

[192] For example, if you are running a word processor, then the keyboard is the input and the screen is the output. The Tech Terms Computer Dictionary, http://www.techterms.com/definition/io (first published 2005, last visited, Nov. 21, 2012). See generally Intergraph Hardware Technologies Co. v. Toshiba Corp., 508 F. Supp. 2d 752 (N.D. Cal. 2007); *Superspeed Software, Inc. v. Oracle Corp.*, 447 F. Supp. 2d 672, 692 (S.D. Tex. 2006); see also *St. Clair Intellectual Property Consultants, Inc. v. Apple, Inc.*, 2012 Markman 3238252, 2012 WL 3238252 (D. Del. 2012).

[193] See Asentinel LLC v. Cass Information Systems, Inc., 2012 WL 1097337, *13 (W.D. Tenn. 2012), report and recommendation adopted, 2012 WL 1097336 (W.D. Tenn. 2012) (citing Sauer Decl. ¶22(2)); see also *Fujitsu Ltd. v. Belkin Intern., Inc.*, 2012 Markman 368574, 2012 WL 368574 (N.D. Cal. 2012) (listing keyboards, monitors, or a mouse as input/output devices); U.S. v. Alexander, 2007 WL 2712043 (W.D. Mo. 2007), judgment aff'd, 574 F.3d 484 (8th Cir. 2009) (listing as peripheral input-output devices, mouse, keyboard, printers, fax machine, digitizing tablet, stylus, scanner, video display monitor, head mounted displays, optical readers, and reproducing devices capable of interfacing with computers and related communications devices that can be used to transmit or receive information to or from a computer).

[194] See, e.g., *Apple, Inc. v. Samsung Electronics Co.*, Ltd., 876 F. Supp. 2d 1141 (N.D. Cal. 2012); *Smith v. Wacker Neuson Corp.*, Prod. Liab. Rep. (CCH) P 18842, 2012 WL 1555114 (S.D. Ill. 2012); *Tomita Technologies USA, LLC v. Nintendo Co.*, Ltd., 855 F. Supp. 2d 33 (S.D. N.Y. 2012),

computer for display, processing, outputting, storing, or transmitting. Input devices do not receive data[195] but instead are used to convert user actions (e.g., keystrokes) or analog data into digital signals that are processed by a computer.

Input devices include the following:

Keyboard
Mouse
Microphone
Scanner

Output devices, like input devices, are also connected to a computer. However, output devices are used to transmit data out of the computer usually in the form of text, image, sound, or some other form.[196] An output device is a device that is capable of transmitting information from a computer to some outward form such as printers, monitors, and synthesizers to name a few.[197]

Output devices include the following:

- Monitor or other digital display—a visual interface that displays pixelated images.[198] Monitors range from standard computer monitors, to handheld gaming console monitors, to the monitors on the back of a digital camera.
- Printer—a device used to create a physical version of an electronic file.[199] Printers have advanced to allow for 3D printing of objects.[200]
- Speaker—a device used to output sound.[201] Speakers can be internal or external.

---

rev'd in part on other grounds, 594 Fed. Appx. 657 (Fed. Cir. 2014); *Motorola Mobility, Inc. v. TiVo, Inc.*, 2012 Markman 6087792, 2012 WL 6087792 (E.D. Tex. 2012); *Federal Home Loan Mortg. Corp. v. Graff/Ross Holdings LLP*, 893 F. Supp. 2d 28 (D.D.C. 2012), aff'd, 604 Fed. Appx. 930 (Fed. Cir. 2015).

[195] *Realtime Data, LLC v. Realtime Data, LLC*, 2012 Markman 4627246, 2012 WL 4627246 (E.D. Tex. 2012).

[196] See, e.g., Systems and Methods for Presenting and/or Converting Messages, U.S. Patent No. 6,801,793 (Issued Oct. 5, 2004).

[197] Examples of computer output devices are printer, video screen, and magnetic disk drive. Sugden & Simmond, Computer Mathematics using Pascal, 2d Edition, Bond University, Information Technology papers, School of Business 1, available at http://epublications.bond.edu.au/cgi/viewcontent.cgi?article=1060&context=infotech_pubs (last visited July 16, 2013).

[198] "Since the beginning of the digital era, users have needed a way to view the results of the programs they run on a computer—but the manner in which computers have spit out data has changed considerably over the last 70 years." Edwards, A Brief History of Computer Monitors, PC World Nov. 1, 2010, at 1.

[199] See generally Meyer, Printing Technologies and Systems, Chapter 23 in Whitaker, Microelectronics (2d ed 2006).

[200] "Additive manufacturing (3D printing) is commonly used to produce physical models for a wide variety of applications, from archaeology to design." Calì, Calian, et al., 3D-Printing of Non-Assembly, Articulated Models, 31(6) ACM Transactions on Graphics (TOG) 130 (2012).

[201] See generally Carter & Lunt, Podcasting and Copyright: The Impact of Regulation on New Communication Technologies, 22 Santa Clara Computer & High Tech. L.J. 187 (2005).

## 1.24 Graphics Cards

The images that display on a computer monitor are made up of pixels.[202] A computer places these pixels, usually numbering over several million, when creating an image.[203] This conversion of binary data from the CPU into a picture is achieved through the use of a graphics card, also known as a video card.[204] Some computers have a built-in graphics card housed on the motherboard, but many modern computers have an expansion port that houses the graphics card separate from the motherboard.[205]

A graphics card receives data about the image from the CPU and software applications. The graphics card then determines how to order these pixels on the screen to create the image. Finally, the graphics card transmits the image to the monitor via a cable.[206]

Graphics cards accomplish this task using four main components:

1. A motherboard—this connection provides data and power.[207]
2. A processor—commonly called a graphics processing unit (GPU). It is markedly similar to a CPU but is designed especially for performing complex calculations associated with graphics rendering.[208] The GPU can be as fast as a CPU, thus generating a great deal of heat necessitating housing near a cooling system.[209]

---

[202] "Pixels are the smallest unit of color that can appear on a computer screen." *Silicon Graphics, Inc. v. n Vidia Corp.*, 58 F. Supp. 2d 331 (D. Del. 1999).

[203] "Digital images are, in fact, thousands of pixels arranged in arrays of rows and columns." *Research Corp. Technologies, Inc. v. Microsoft Corp.*, 627 F.3d 859 (Fed. Cir. 2010).

[204] "[Graphics cards] plays an important role in displaying information or images on a monitor or screen." *Internet Machines LLC v. Alienware Corp.*, 2011 Markman 2551295, 2011 WL 2551295, *1 (E.D. Tex. 2011).

[205] "A motherboard will have at least one slot intended for use by a *video card*. The older board uses an AGP slot for that purpose, and the newer board uses a long PCIe x16 slot for video." Jean Andrews, A+ Guide to Managing and Maintaining Your PC 190 (2009).

[206] To make a 3D image, the graphics card first creates a wire frame out of straight lines. Then, it rasterizes the image (fills in the remaining pixels). It also adds lighting, texture, and color. For fast-paced games, the computer has to go through this process about 60 times per second. Without a graphics card to perform the necessary calculations, the workload would be too much for the computer to handle. "[T]o display a document on a computer screen, a CPU must send information about what the document looks like from the computer's memory to the computer's video card." *Internet Machines LLC v. Alienware Corp.*, 2011 Markman 2551295, 2011 WL 2551295, *1 (E.D. Tex. 2011).

[207] See §§1:5 et seq. for further discussion on the components and functionality of motherboards.

[208] Owens, Houston, et al. GPU computing, 96(5) Proceedings of the IEEE 879–99 (May 2008); see, e.g., *In re Graphics Processing Units Antitrust Litigation*, 253 F.R.D. 478 (N.D. Cal. 2008).

[209] For GPUs, the temperature can range from 100–145?C (212–293?F). Yang & Ma, "Cooling High-Speed Chips Using Intelligent Control Technology," in Proceedings of the IEEE International Conference on Automation and Logistics 1330–34 (Aug. 5–7, 2009).

3. Memory—this provides a temporary storage place for completed pictures and holds information about each pixel.[210]
4. A monitor connection—for viewing the final result via a cable to the monitor.

The quality of the graphics rendered to the monitor is determined by the quality of these components in conjunction with the speed of the connection between the graphics card and the motherboard. Faster transfer rates translate directly into better quality graphics.[211] While this is rapidly evolving with the rise of smartphones, tablets, and other hardware, it is beyond the scope of this chapter to explore how graphics work with these new devices.

[210] See generally Morley & Parker, *Understanding Computers 2009: Today and Tomorrow*, 40 (Cengage Learning 2009).

[211] See generally Morley & Parker, *Understanding Computers 2009: Today and Tomorrow.* 69 (Cengage Learning 2009); Costi-Kowolik & Gutierrez-Mazon, "A First Approach Towards a High-Speed PCI-Based Data Acquisition Card for Industrial Applications," in IEEE 24th Convention of Electrical and Electronics Engineers in Israel 426–29 (Nov. 2006).

# Chapter 2
# Software

## 2.1 Computer Software

> He saw a calf being born, and he was amazed when the tiny animal struggled up within minutes and began to walk. "It was not something she had learned, but it was instead hard-wired into her," he recalled. "A human baby couldn't do that. I found it remarkable, even though no one else did." He put it in hardware-software terms: "It was as if something in the animal's body and in its brain had been engineered to work together instantly rather than being learned."—Walter Isaacson[1]

Computer software is a set of instructions that runs on a computer.[2] It does not consist solely of programming language.[3] Rather, from a technical perspective, software is defined as a program of all the associated information and materials needed to support its installation, operation, repair, and enhancement.[4] It also includes written programs, procedures, rules, and associated documentation pertaining to the

[1] Isaacson, Steve Jobs (Simon & Schuster 2011).

[2] The Federal Circuit defines software as the "set of instructions, known as code that directs a computer to perform specified functions or operations." Fantasy Sports Properties, Inc. v. Sportsline.com, Inc., 287 F.3d 1108, 1118 (Fed. Cir. 2002).

Any software referenced in this chapter or in this book is not to be considered as an endorsement of that software or a recommendation that said software is better or worse than any other software in the marketplace.

[3] *See* Evolution, Inc. v. SunTrust Bank, 342 F. Supp. 2d 943, 947 n.3 (D. Kan. 2004) (explaining software code may be source code or object code: "'Source code' refers to human-readable software code used by programmers to develop a software program. 'Object code' is machine-readable code that is a series of 1s and 0s. Source code is converted into object code through a process called 'compiling.'"). For a technically accurate discussion of source and object code in the legal literature, see Samuelson, CONTU Revisited: The Case Against Copyright Protection for Computer Programs in Machine-Readable Form, 1984 Duke L.J. 663, 764–69 (1984).

[4] Squires & Preece, Predicting Quality in Educational Software: Evaluating for Learning, Usability and the Synergy Between Them, 11(5) Interacting with Computers 467–83 (May 1999).



D. B. Garrie et al., *Uncovering Digital Evidence*,
https://doi.org/10.1007/978-3-031-68118-9_2

operation of a computer system, which are stored within digital medium.[5] Indeed, because computer software instructs a computer how to perform actions, in the broadest sense, it includes everything that is not hardware.[6] Put another way, computers are, in effect, incomplete machines when manufactured and acquire functionality only after being coupled with software.[7]

In this chapter, we begin by providing a quick survey of the history of software and programming languages. Following that is an overview of the three different levels at which programming languages operate. Then, readers are offered a brief introduction to algorithms and data structures and why understanding these two constructs is critical to understanding how computer software operates. Following this discussion is an overview of two key pieces of computer software: the operating system and virtual machines. Finally, we provide readers with a review of the concepts underlying computer software design, development, and testing.

## 2.2 History of Computer Software

The history of computer software starts in 1804 in Europe where two inventors created a loom that performed tasks through punched cards.[8] This technical insight eventually led John Von Neumann, who in 1945 works at the Institute for Advanced Study, to propose two key concepts. The first concept, *shared-program technique*,[9] is that computer hardware should be simple and not require hardwiring for each program. Instead, complex instructions should control the hardware, allowing the hardware to be reprogrammed.[10] The second concept, *subroutines*, is the use of instruction sets designed to perform frequently used operations.[11]

---

[5] See *also* Frank, Critical Issues in Software 22 (1983) (only 20% of the cost of program development goes into coding); see, e.g., Law Research Service, Inc. v. General Automation Inc., 494 F.2d 202, 204 n.3 (2d Cir. 1974); Sherin v. State of Tennessee, 601 F.2d 590 (6th Cir. 1979) (unpublished); Massachusetts v. Microsoft Corp., 373 F.3d 1199 (D.C. Cir. 2004).

[6] Garland, Value & Cents: The Valuation of Computer Software, 18–1 A.B.I.J. 24 (Robert F. Reilly ed., Feb. 1999).

[7] See Patterson and Hennessy, Computer Organization and Design: The Hardware/Software Interface (Morgan Kaufmann 2009).

[8] See Guarnieri, The Roots of Automation Before Mechatronics [Historical], 4(2) IEEE Industrial Electronics Magazine 42–43 (June 2010); Heide, Punched-Card Systems and the Early Information Explosion, 1880–1945 (Johns Hopkins University Press 2009).

[9] See Introduction to Software History, The History of Computing Project 17 (C. Robat, ed. 2006). This technique stated that the actual computer hardware should be simple and not need to be hand-wired for each program. Instead, complex instructions should be used to control the simple hardware, allowing it to be reprogrammed much faster.

[10] See Eigenmann and Lilja, "Von Neumann Computers," in Wiley Encyclopedia of Electrical and Electronics Engineering (Jan. 30, 1998).

[11] See Weikum and Vossen, Transactional Information Systems: Theory, Algorithms, and the Practice Of Concurrency Control and Recovery (Morgan Kaufmann 2001).

The next instrumental step toward the development of modern software arose from Claude Shannon's thesis published in 1948 describing how binary logic could be used to program computers.[12] Approximately a year later, the first computer language, Short Code, appeared. It was the first computer language for electronic devices and required the programmer to change the language statements into 0s and 1s by hand.[13] Software further evolved in 1951 with the development of the compiler. A compiler is a program that turns language statements into 0s and 1s for a computer to understand.[14] This development allowed for quicker programming, because the programmer no longer had to perform the complex and tedious process of manually turning language statements into 0s and 1s.[15]

In 1957, IBM created FORTRAN for scientific computing.[16] While not widely used today, at the time, it was a huge step forward.[17] FORTRAN allowed developers to create software that enabled a computer to perform a repetitive task from a single set of instructions by using loops.[18] Westinghouse Electric Corporation is thought to have produced the first commercially viable FORTRAN software program.[19]

After FORTRAN, a team of computer programmers backed by a consortium of businesses and the Pentagon created COBOL, Common Business Oriented Language.[20] COBOL increased the readability of computer software code and allowed software to run on any computer with a COBOL compiler, requiring only

[12] See Kahn, A Tribute to Claude E. Shannon (1916–2001) [Society News], 39(7) IEEE Communications Magazine 18–22 (2001).

[13] Hunt, Programming Languages, 15(4) Computer 70–88 (1982) (offering a great survey of the history of programming languages).

[14] Backus, "The history of Fortran I, II, and III," in IEEE Annals of the History of Computing (Oct.–Dec. 1998), original 1978 article available at http://www.softwarepreservation.org/projects/FORTRAN/paper/p165-backus.pdf (providing overview of FORTRAN and a robust history of how the compiler came to be).

[15] See Introduction to Software History, The History of Computing Project 17 (C. Robat, ed. 2006).

[16] Hunt, Programming Languages, 15(4) Computer 70–88 (1982) (offering a robust survey of the history of programming languages).

[17] Hunt, Programming Languages, 15(4) Computer 70–88 (1982) (offering a robust survey of the history of programming languages).

[18] Hunt, Programming Languages, 15(4) Computer 70–88 (1982) (offering a robust survey of the history of programming languages); see also Backus, Beeber, et al., "The FORTRAN Automatic Coding System," in Proceedings of the ACM Western Joint Computer Conference, Los Angeles, California 188–98 (February 26–28, 1957) (offering a more in-depth discussion of the FORTRAN programming language).

[19] See Campbell-Kelly, Not All Bad: An Historical Perspective on Software Patents, 11 Mich. Telecomm. & Tech. L. Rev. 191 (2004).

[20] See generally Sammet, The early history of COBOL, ACM History of Programming Languages I (1978) (offering a great overview of the history of computer programming up until the 1970s).

minimal modifications.[21] Today, COBOL is still used to create computer software, and skilled COBOL programmers are in demand.[22]

In 1968, Niklaus Wirth created Pascal, yet another software language, to be used as a teaching tool.[23] It attempted to combine many of the best features of the languages in use at the time: COBOL, FORTRAN, and ALGOL.[24] While Pascal showed promise, it was eventually replaced by C, a computer language developed in 1972 by Dennis Ritchie, then an employee at Bell Labs in New Jersey.[25] One of the major languages of today, C shares many similarities with Pascal.[26] C grew rapidly because it fixed most of Pascal's speed issues.[27] Today, C is used by programmers to create computer software that runs on operating systems such as UNIX, Windows, MacOS, and Linux.[28]

The next major computer software milestone occurred in 1983 with the introduction of object-oriented programming (OOP).[29] Prior to OOP, software executed tasks using subroutines, essentially a recipe for executing repetitive tasks.[30] With

---

[21] See generally Hoare, An Axiomatic Basis for Computer Programming, 12(10) Communications of the ACM 576–80 (1969).

[22] See Clayton, COBOL, The Computer Language that Refused to Die, Tech Europe, The Wall Street Journal (Nov. 16, 2011), available at: http://blogs.wsj.com/tech-europe/2011/11/16/cobol-the-computer-language-that-refused-to-die/ (last visited Dec. 11, 2012).

[23] "PASCAL is supposed not to contain the features and constructs of other languages that are hard to explain and are said to be an 'insult to minds trained in systematic reasoning.' Contrary to this statement we will see that on the one hand some useful constructs of other languages that are not hard to explain have been left out of PASCAL, whereas PASCAL, on the other hand, has features that are hard to explain and hinder the user in systematic programming." Habermann, Critical comments on the programming language PASCAL, Paper 1736 (Carnegie-Mellon University, Computer Science Dept. 1973), available at http://repository.cmu.edu/cgi/viewcontent.cgi?article=2735&context=compsci

[24] See Wirth, Recollections About the Development of Pascal, ACM History of Programming Languages II (1996).

[25] See Ritchie, The Development of the C Language, 28(3) ACM SIGPLAN Notices 201–08 (1993).

[26] See Ritchie, The Development of the C Language, 28(3) ACM SIGPLAN Notices 201–08 (1993); Pohl & Edelson, A to Z: C Language Shortcomings, 13(2) Computer Languages 51–64 (1988).

[27] Habermann, Critical comments on the programming language PASCAL, Paper 1736 (Carnegie-Mellon University, Computer Science Dept. 1973), available at http://repository.cmu.edu/cgi/viewcontent.cgi?article=2735&context=compsci

[28] See Chen, Dios, et al., An Empirical Study of Programming Language Trends, 22(3) IEEE Software 72–79 (May–Jun. 2005).

[29] See Stefik & Bobrow, Object-Oriented Programming: Themes and Variations, 6(4) AI Magazine, 40 (AAAI 1985), available at http://www.aaai.org/ojs/index.php/aimagazine/article/view/508/444 (last visited Mar. 20, 2013).

[30] Cary, Shasharina, et al., Comparison of C++ and Fortran 90 for Object-Oriented Scientific Programming, 105(1) Computer Physics Communications, at 20–36 (Sept. 1997). Essentially, in object-oriented programming, one develops objects that represent certain concepts or entities from the problem domain and then embodies these abstractions in computer code. 105(1) Computer Physics Communications, at 20–36. Every single one of these objects consists of both the internal data representation and methods, both for internal use by the object itself and for external use, for

OOP, the subroutines are upgraded to fully functioning independent operations that can send and receive information to other operations.[31]

In 1995, Sun Microsystems released Java, which has since become the most popular computer programming language.[32] The reason for Java's widespread popularity is a subject of some debate. Some people argue that it was just good timing.[33] Other possible reasons include the following: (i) Java is a free computer language unlike similar languages[34]; (ii) Java is platform independent, meaning that once you write an application in Java it can be run in many different environments[35]; (iii) Java standard libraries handle multithreading,[36] memory management, and network operations rather adeptly[37]; and (iv) Java has built-in support for using computer networks, with the ability to execute code from remote sources "securely."

Whatever the reason, Java was built from the ground up to use object-oriented programming methodology.[38] Object-oriented programming encourages modular design and software.[39] Object-oriented programming can be characterized by routines for manipulating data structures that incorporate easily into either a higher-level object or a final program.[40]

---

interacting with that data. 105(1) Computer Physics Communications, at 20–36. Essentially, by hiding the data and internal methods from the user, a technique known as encapsulation, the software developer of an object can change the internal representation without breaking software that uses the object. 105(1) Computer Physics Communications, at 20–36. By the delivery of a fixed interface between objects, one achieves code modularity and flexibility, and one greatly simplifies the task of building a program in stages or programming in teams, since program components are naturally separated. 105(1) Computer Physics Communications, at 20–36.

[31] Cary, Shasharina, et al., 105(1) Computer Physics Communications, at 20–36; Pierce & Turner, Simple Type-Theoretic Foundations for Object-Oriented Programming, 4(2) Journal of functional programming 207–247 (1993).

[32] See generally Szyperski, Gruntz, & Murer, Component Software: Beyond Object-Oriented Programming (Addison-Wesley 2002) (provides a guide to object-oriented programming and the associated software and explains how to use such tools and examines the key components of object-oriented software design and construction).

[33] Tyma, Why Are We Using Java Again?, 41(6) Communications of the ACM 38–42 (June 1998).

[34] Badros, Javaml: A Markup Language for Java Source Code, 33(1) Computer Networks: The International Journal of Computer and Telecommunications Networking 159–77 (June 2000).

[35] Gosling, The Java Language Specification (Prentice Hall 2000).

[36] "Multithreading is defined to be the execution of a multithreaded program on a processor that is able to exploit the existence of multiple threads in increasing performance." Loikkanen & Bagherzadeh, "A Fine-Grain Multithreading Superscalar Architecture," in Proceedings of the 1996 Conference on Parallel Architectures and Compilation Technique 163–68 (Oct. 1996).

[37] Watt & Brown, Programming Language Processors in Java: Compilers and Interpreters (Pearson Education 2000). *See also* TiVo, Inc. v. EchoStar Communications Corp., 516 F.3d 1290 (Fed. Cir. 2008).

[38] Szyperski, Gruntz & Murer, Component Software: Beyond Object-Oriented Programming (Addison-Wesley 2002).

[39] Snyder, Encapsulation and Inheritance in Object-Oriented Programming Languages, 21(11) ACM SIGPLAN Notices 38–45 (June 1986).

[40] Hollaar, Justice Douglas Was Right: The Need for Congressional Action on Software Patents, 24 AIPLA QJ 283 (1996); Nygaard, Basic Concepts in Object Oriented Programming, ACM SIGPLAN Notices 128–32 (Oct. 1986).

One programming language, whether it be Java, C, C#, or Pascal, is not better than another because it has something the other lacks. Rather, the value of a programming language is a function of the features a particular programming language offers and whether these features are sufficient to achieve the objectives of the software program.

## 2.3 Hierarchy of Software Programming Languages: Machine Language, Assembly Language, and (Many) High-Level Languages

Software programs are written using computer programming languages that are classified into one of the three broad groups: machine language, assembly language, or a high-level language.[41] Machine language is a series of instructions written in the language a computer can follow. Assembly language is one level of abstraction above machine language, with each assembly language statement usually corresponding to a single machine language instruction.[42] "High-level languages are closer to natural language than low-level languages which direct the functioning of the computer."[43] Software programs written in either assembly language or a high-level language must be converted to machine language for the computer to follow.[44] Computer code or coding is the process of writing detailed in-depth instructions using a programming language that essentially speaks to the computer and tells it what to do.[45] Computer code accomplishes single or multiple tasks and

[41] See Dun & Bradstreet Software Services, Inc. v. Grace Consulting, Inc., 307 F.3d 197, 201 n.2 (3d Cir. 2002) (*citing* Note, Copyright Protection of Computer Program Object Code, 96 Harv. L. Rev. 1723, 1725 (1983)); Apple Computer, Inc. v. Franklin Computer Corp., 714 F.2d 1240, 1243, 70 A.L.R. Fed. 153 (3d Cir. 1983).

[42] "[L]ower level assembly language corresponds directly to object code on a one-to-one basis." Cogdell, Comment: Copyright Protection for Computer Programs, 10 N.C. J. Int'l L. & Com. Reg. 667, 669 (1985).

[43] Bernstein v. U.S. Dept. of State, 974 F. Supp. 1288, 1311 (N.D. Cal. 1997), aff'd, 176 F.3d 1132 (9th Cir. 1999), reh'g granted, opinion withdrawn, 192 F.3d 1308 (9th Cir. 1999).

[44] See Bernstein v. U.S. Dept. of State, 974 F. Supp. 1288, 1311 (N.D. Cal. 1997), aff'd, 176 F.3d 1132 (9th Cir. 1999), reh'g granted, opinion withdrawn, 192 F.3d 1308 (9th Cir. 1999); *see generally* Dun & Bradstreet Software Services, Inc. v. Grace Consulting, Inc., 307 F.3d 197 (3d Cir. 2002); Data General Corp. v. International Business Machines Corp., 93 F. Supp. 2d 89 (D. Mass. 2000).

[45] After each necessary module is identified and designed and its relationship to the other modules has been laid out conceptually, the resulting program structure must be embodied in a written language that the computer can read. See Computer Associates Intern., Inc. v. Altai, Inc., 982 F.2d 693, 37 Fed. R. Evid. Serv. 348, 119 A.L.R. Fed. 741 (2d Cir. 1992). This process is called "coding" and requires two steps. Whelan Associates, Inc. v. Jaslow Dental Laboratory, Inc., 797 F.2d 1222, 1230, 21 Fed. R. Evid. Serv. 571 (3d Cir. 1986). The first step requires the programmer to transpose the program's structural blueprint into a source code. This step has been described as "comparable to the novelist fleshing out the broad outline of his plot by crafting from words and

often is reused and edited to further future software changes or upgrades.[46] The programming language that is used to write the code is a communication technique for expressing instructions to a computer, and it provides a set of syntactic and semantic rules used to define computer programs. Programming languages allow software developers to identify what data a computer will act upon or how the data is stored or transmitted, as well as to dictate the conditions under which to perform specific actions.[47] Some programming languages are designed for broad use, and others are designed for a singular purpose, e.g., telecommunication or supercomputing.[48]

Machine language, also known as object code,[49] is the lowest level and the only programming language level that computer hardware understands or executes.[50] Machine language is written using binary code, i.e., 0s and 1s.[51] In machine language, the "0" and "1" symbols are called bits and indicate the presence or absence of an electrical charge, e.g., an open or closed gate.[52] For example, the binary figure "'01101001'" orders the Apple computer to add two numbers and save the result.[53]

---

sentences the paragraphs that convey the ideas." Kretschmer, Note: Copyright Protection For Software Architecture: Just Say No!, 1988 Columb. Bus. L. Rev. 823, 824–27 (1988); *see also* Englund, Note, Idea, Process, or Protected Expression? Determining the Scope of Copyright Protection of the Structure of Computer Programs, 88 Mich. L. Rev. 866, 867–73 (1990); Menell, An Analysis of the Scope of Copyright Protection for Application Programs, 41 Stan. L. Rev. 1045, 1051–57 (1989); Spivack, Comment, Does Form Follow Function? The Idea/Expression Dichotomy In Copyright Protection of Computer Software, 35 U.C.L.A. L. Rev. 723, 729–31 (1988). Source code can be written in any of a number of different computer languages, such as C, C++, COBAL, FORTRAN, etc., changing based on the target computer the program is being written. Whelan, 797 F.2d at 1230. After the source code is written, the next step is to compile into object code, which is the binary language comprised of zeros and ones through which the computer directly receives its instructions. 797 F.2d at 1230–31; *see generally* Englund, 88 Mich. L. Rev. at 867–73.

[46] See Cohen & Lemley, Patent Scope and Innovation in the Software Industry, 89 Calif. L. Rev. 1, 41 (2001) (depicting software innovation's incremental character as akin to most inventions patented).

[47] See Wooldridge, An Introduction to Multiagent Systems (Wiley 2002).

[48] Spinellis, Notable Design Patterns for Domain-Specific Languages, 56(1) Journal of Systems and Software 91–99 (Feb. 1, 2001).

[49] See Solomon, The Copyrightability of Computer Software Containing Trade Secrets, 63 Wash. U. L.Q. 131, 153 (Spring 1985). *See* Note, Copyright Protection of Computer Program Object Code, 96 Harv. L. Rev. 1723, 1724–26 (1983).

[50] See Dun & Bradstreet, 307 F.3d at 197, 201 n.2.

[51] See Aycock, A Brief History of Just-In-Time, 35(2) ACM Computing Surveys (CSUR) 97–113 (June 2003).

[52] Midway Mfg. Co. v. Strohon, 564 F. Supp. 741, 750 (N.D. Ill. 1983); *see also* Skrien, CPU Sim 3.1: A Tool For Simulating Computer Architectures for Computer Organization Classes, 1(4) Journal on Educational Resources in Computing (JERIC) 46–59 (Dec. 2001) (providing an overview of the basics of computer architecture).

[53] Apple Computer, Inc. v. Franklin Computer Corp., 714 F.2d 1240, 1243, 70 A.L.R. Fed. 153 (3d Cir. 1983).

It is also important to note that machine language is unique to each processor family.[54]

The next level of programming language is assembly language.[55] Assembly languages are mid-level computer languages that function as a middleman between the machine language and high-level programming languages.[56] The machine program language uses only 0s and 1s; programming in assembly language uses the alphabet, typically in abbreviated words.[57] An example of a program written in assembly language is as follows:

```
    mov ax, 15 // load 15 into ax
    add ax, 3 // add 3 to the contents of ax, so ax now
contains 18
    inc ax // add 1 to ax, so ax now contains 19
    dec ax // subtract 1 from ax, so ax now contains 18
```

Assembly language is one level of abstraction above machine language, with each assembly language statement usually corresponding to a single machine language instruction.[58] Software programs written in assembly language use a program called an assembler to translate assembly language statements into the target computer's machine language.[59] Generally, computer programs developed in assembly

[54] See Lotus Development Corp. v. Paperback Software Intern., 740 F. Supp. 37, 43–44 (D. Mass. 1990).

[55] See Apple Computer, Inc. v. Formula Intern., Inc., 562 F. Supp. 775, 778–780 (C.D. Cal. 1983), judgment aff'd, 725 F.2d 521 (9th Cir. 1984) (stating "[t]he source code form is often translated into letters, numbers, and symbols sometimes called assembly language. Then the source code or assembly language is finally translated to what is called 'object code' which is machine language useable by the machine. Then, as a final step, the object code is imprinted onto the silicon chip or diskette by photochemical process or electrically."); *see also* Stern, Another Look at Copyright Protection of Software: Did the 1980 Act Do Anything for Object Code, 3 Computer L.J. 1 (1981).

[56] See, e.g., Dun & Bradstreet, 307 F.3d at 201 n.2; Apple v. Franklin, 714 F.2d at 1243.

[57] See Dun & Bradstreet, 307 F.3d at 201 n. 2 (stating, "Computers can 'understand' (that is, execute) only programs in 'machine language'—the lowest level. A machine language is a cluster of '0' and '1' symbols called 'bits,' which are the only symbols recognized by digital computers.").

[58] "[L]ower level assembly language corresponds directly to object code on a one-to-one basis." Cogdell, Comment: Copyright Protection for Computer Programs, 10 N.C. J. Int'l L. & Com. Reg. 667, 669 (1985).

[59] As the Third Circuit explained in *Dun & Bradstreet*:

To make it easier for humans to read and write programs, two "higher" levels of languages exist. The first level is "assembly language." Assembly language instructions consist of alphanumeric labels rather than bits. To be executed by the computer, the alphanumeric instructions must be translated into their corresponding clusters of bits by another computer program known as an "assembler." At the next level are "high-level" computer languages, such as FORTRAN or COBOL, that employ English-like words and syntax and are therefore easier to use and understand than assembly or machine language. Each high-level instruction is the equivalent of several assembly or machine language instructions. A computer program known as a "compiler" translates high-level programs into the corresponding object code. Programs written in assembly or high-level languages are referred to as "source programs" or "source code".

language are for a particular computer architecture and are thus not very portable. While it is relatively easier to write programs in assembly language than in machine language, assembly language programs are still quite difficult to write and understand.[60]

The high-level programming language group is the third level of computer programming languages.[61] High-level programming languages enable programmers to write programs that are much more independent of a particular type of computer than either assembly or machine programming languages.[62] High-level programming languages more closely resemble human language, using English words and symbols to indicate a command.[63]

Below is an example of a program written using a high-level language:

```
public class HelloWorld &lcub;
public static void main(String[] args)&lcub;
System.out.println("Hello, World");
&rcub;
&rcub;
```

To create this program, the programmer must first download and install Java on a computer and make sure the computer has a text editor and a terminal window, which is the default on most Windows computers. The programmer opens the text editor, types the text, and saves it as HelloWorld.java. The program now needs to be compiled using the *javac HelloWorld.java.* Once this is completed, the software program can be executed by typing in "java HelloWorld."[64]

In the above example, the text editor is used to create high-level software code, which is a sequence of characters. The software program above uses a compiler, which is an application that translates the Java language to machine language. So, in the above example, the Java compiler takes the text file with the ".java" extension

Dunn & Bradstreet, 307 F.3d at 201 n.2, *citing* Note, Copyright Protection of Computer Program Object Code, 96 Harv. L. Rev. 1723, 1725 (1983).

[60] Cady, Copyrighting Computer Programs: Distinguishing Expression from Ideas, 22 Temp. Envtl. L. & Tech. J. 15, 23 (Fall, 2003).

[61] See generally Paciaroni, Copyright Law-Computer Programs, 23 Duq. L. Rev. 457 (1984).

[62] See generally Duvanel, The Evolution and Enforcement of Computer Software Copyright in the Peoples Republic of China, 16 N.Y.L. Sch. J. Int'l & Comp. L. 337 (1996).

[63] See Cassell, Introduction to Computers and Information Processing 265, 300 (1980). Machine language is translated higher-level language into binary digits, a form readable by the computer. Cassell, Introduction to Computers and Information Processing at 443. See, e.g., Apple v. Franklin, 714 F.2d at 1243; Lotus v. Paperback Software, 740 F. Supp. at 44.

[64] See Oracle America, Inc. v. Google Inc., 872 F. Supp. 2d 974, 977 n.2 (N.D. Cal. 2012) (stating "…the term 'Java' means the Java platform, sometimes abbreviated to 'J2SE,' which includes the Java development kit (JDK), javac compiler, tools and utilities, runtime programs, class libraries (API packages), and the Java virtual machine.").

as input and produces a file with a ".class" extension.[65] The software, once compiled, can be run by the computer, which means the computer follows the instructions of the computer program.[66] In this case, the software writes the string *Hello World*.

A single command in a high-level language may be the equivalent of several commands in assembly or machine language.[67] The text files that contain computer programs, or strings of commands written in assembly or high-level languages, are referred to as being source code files.[68] One of the advantages of using a high-level programming language is that it is easier to read, write, and maintain, relative to assembly or machine programming languages.[69]

The first high-level programming languages were designed in the 1950s.[70] Today, there are dozens of such programming languages used, including Ada, Algol, BASIC, COBOL, C, C++, FORTRAN, LISP, Pascal, and Prolog.[71] To demonstrate the differences between the programming languages, consider the following

---

[65] See Sun Microsystems, Inc. v. Microsoft Corp., 21 F. Supp. 2d 1109, 1112–1113 (N.D. Cal. 1998), order vacated 188 F.3d 1115 (9th Cir. 1999) and reinstatement granted, 87 F. Supp. 2d 992 (N.D. Cal. 2000) (stating that "[t]he Java runtime environment comprises the Java class libraries and the Java runtime interpreter. A system platform or browser program that implements the Java runtime environment can execute application programs developed using the Java programming environment.").

[66] In *Sun Microsystems, Inc. v. Microsoft Corp.*, the court defined Sun's Java Technology to be a collection of programming components that create a standard, platform-independent programming and runtime environment. Sun's Java Technology has two basic elements: the Java programming environment and the Java runtime environment. Sun Microsystems, Inc., 21 F. Supp. 2d at 1112. The court further recognized that the Java programming environment allows software developers to create a single version of program code that is capable of running on *any platform* which possesses a compatible implementation of the Java runtime environment. 21 F. Supp. 2d at 1113. The Java programming environment comprises (1) Sun's specification for the Java language, (2) Sun's specification for the Java class libraries, and (3) the Java Compiler. 21 F. Supp. 2d at 1113.

[67] Hinsen, The Molecular Modeling Toolkit: A New Approach to Molecular Simulations, 21(2) Journal of Computational Chemistry 79–85 (Jan. 2000) "Programs written in high-level languages are significantly shorter than programs using the common machine-oriented languages (Fortran, C, C++, Pascal, etc.). This means shorter development times, fewer mistakes, and code that is easier to understand."

[68] See, e.g., Lotus v. Paperback Software, 740 F. Supp. at 44; Apple v. Franklin, 714 F.2d at 1243.

[69] See Albert, Alternative Approach to Computer Pirating Disputes, the Mnookin-Jones Settlement: IBM v. Fujitsu, An, 3 Temp. Int'l & Comp. L.J. 113 (1989) (programming language may be in binary form, (object or machine code), or in an easier to read language, (high-level language)).

[70] See Zittrain, The Generative Internet, 119 Harv. L. Rev. 1974 (2006).

[71] See Bernstein v. U.S. Dept. of Justice, 176 F.3d 1132 (9th Cir. 1999), reh'g granted, opinion withdrawn, 192 F.3d 1308 (9th Cir. 1999) ("[s]oftware engineers generally do not create software in object code—the series of binary digits (1s and 0s)—which tells a computer what to do because it would be enormously difficult, cumbersome, and time-consuming. Instead, software engineers use high-level computer programming languages such as "C" or "Basic" to create source code as a shorthand *1148 method for telling the computer to perform a desired function. In this respect, lines of source code are the building blocks or the tools used to create an encryption machine."). See also Herndon Jr. & Berzins, The Realizable Benefits of a Language Prototyping Language, 14(6) IEEE Transactions on Software Engineering 803–09 (June 1988).

example: Assume that you would like to take the value “B,” divide that by the value “C,” and then add the result to “A.” Here is how that command would look in the various languages:

In machine (binary),

“0010000000010001; 1000000011010010; 1101000000010000.”

In assembly,

“LOAD B; DIV C; ADD A”[72]

In a high-level language,

“(A) + (B / C)”

Computer software written in assembly language is assembled into object code by an assembler, which is a program that processes assembly language into object code.[73] Computer software written using high-level programming languages are either compiled or manually interpreted into machine language object code.[74]

Software, such as Google’s Chrome™ browser, is made up of a sequence of millions of these very simple machine code instructions. The computer central processing unit (CPU) runs the machine code instructions using a “fetch execute” cycle where the CPU acquires the first instruction in the sequence, executes it, and then gets the next instruction or directs the CPU to perform a different instruction sequence as defined in the software program file. Software, such as Chrome, contains the bytes of machine code that represent the software. Each machine code instruction is 4 bytes, and the whole program, in this case Chrome, is effectively a gigantic sequence of instructions. In our example, when a user runs the software Chrome, it is launched by the operating system. The operating system is a special software program that is responsible for making sure the software can operate (e.g., allocate an area of random access memory (RAM) for Chrome, the software program), loading Chrome into the memory, and instructing the CPU to run the Chrome program, computer software machine code instructions.

---

[72] See Abbot, Reverse Engineering of Software: Copyright and Interoperability, 14 J. L. & Inf. Sci. 7 (2003).

[73] See Asset Marketing Systems, Inc. v. Gagnon, 542 F.3d 748, 755 n.5 (9th Cir. 2008). The case explains that explaining that source code is compiled into object code, which the computer can understand.

[74] See also Dun & Bradstreet, 307 F.3d at 197, 201 n.2. Each compute and language combination requires a new compiler or interpreter so the language can be correctly translated into the right set of instructions for the CPU.

## 2.4 Data Structures and Algorithms

Data structures are used to describe a collection of values. For example, a **database** is a data structure and so is a grocery list. On the other hand, **algorithms** define a sequence of steps and decisions which can be employed to solve a problem.[75] These distinct concepts are arguably the most critical components employed in developing software. In fact, nearly every programming language allows for the **creation of data structures** and **inherently supports the development of algorithms**.[76] The secret sauce for a large portion of the software in the marketplace today is either the algorithms or the data structures.[77]

A. **What Is an Algorithm? How Are Algorithms Used in Software?**
   Algorithms are the "how" of computer programming.[78] When using a computer language to write a software program, you are telling the computer what to

---

[75] Examples of several common data structures are arrays, linked lists, queues, stacks, binary trees, and hash tables. See generally Lewis & Chase, Java Software Structures: Designing and Using Data Structures (Addison-Wesley 2009).

[76] See Whelan Associates, Inc. v. Jaslow Dental Laboratory, Inc., 797 F.2d 1222, 21 Fed. R. Evid. Serv. 571 (3d Cir. 1986) (seeming to regard data structures as copyrightable); Matter of Application of Bradley, 600 F.2d 807 (C.C.P.A. 1979), judgment aff'd, 450 U.S. 381, 101 S. Ct. 1495, 67 L. Ed. 2d 311 (1981) (data structure for microcode function held patentable); see also In re Lowry, 32 F.3d 1579 (Fed. Cir. 1994) (holding data structure patentable subject matter); In re Warmerdam, 33 F.3d 1354 (Fed. Cir. 1994) (allowing to find the claim for the machine implementation of the data structure was patentable).

[77] See Chap. 9.

A few of the recent cases involving software algorithms include the following EdiSync Systems, Inc. v. Centra Software, Inc., 2012 Markman 2196047, 2012 WL 2196047 (D. Colo. 2012); Tarkus Imaging, Inc. v. Adobe Systems, Inc., 2012 Markman 1669598, 2012 WL 1669598 (D. Del. 2012); de Silva v. Cinquegrani, 2012 WL 1230763 (N.D. Ill. 2012); Alere Inc. v. Church & Dwight Co., Inc., 2012 WL 1098420 (D. Mass. 2012); NDSL, Inc. v. Patnoude, 914 F. Supp. 2d 885 (W.D. Mich. 2012); Asentinel LLC v. Cass Information Systems, Inc., 2012 WL 1097336 (W.D. Tenn. 2012).

Some of the recent cases involving data structures: Bancorp Services, L.L.C. v. Sun Life Assur. Co. of Canada (U.S.), 687 F.3d 1266 (Fed. Cir. 2012); Synopsys, Inc. v. Sabharwal, No. 3: 12-cv-05334-RS (N.D. Cal. Oct. 18, 2012); Apple, Inc. v. Samsung Electronics Co., Ltd., No. 11-CV-01846-LHK (N.D. Cal. Sept. 7, 2012); Intellectual Ventures I LLC v. Check Point Software Technologies Ltd., 2012 Markman 6200337, 2012 WL 6200337 (D. Del. 2012); Magna Carta Holdings, LLC v. Nextgen Healthcare Information Systems, Inc., 2012 Markman 787505, 2012 WL 787505 (N.D. Ill. 2012); Versata Software, Inc. v. Internet Brands, Inc., 902 F. Supp. 2d 841 (E.D. Tex. 2012), aff'd, 550 Fed. Appx. 897 (Fed. Cir. 2014); Research in Motion, Ltd. v. Eastman Kodak Co., 2012 Markman 4512415, 2012 WL 4512415 (N.D. Tex. 2012); SmartPhone Technologies LLC v. Research in Motion Corp., 2012 Markman 3150756, 2012 WL 3150756 (E.D. Tex. 2012); SmartGene, Inc. v. Advanced Biological Laboratories, SA, 852 F. Supp. 2d 42 (D.D.C. 2012), judgment aff'd, 555 Fed. Appx. 950 (Fed. Cir. 2014).

[78] "An algorithm is simply a series of steps telling a processor how to perform a given task." Swinson, Copyright or Patent or Both: An Algorithmic Approach to Computer Software Protection, 5 Harv. J. L. & Tech. 145, 146 (Fall 1991).

do.[79] Designing software programs involves instructing the computer on how you want it to accomplish the tasks. This instruction makes use of algorithms.[80]

An algorithm is a method or a process followed to solve a specific problem.[81] In the simplest form, it is a means of getting from A to B. Consider the following nontechnical example: The grass in your yard is very tall (Point A). The grass needs to be less tall, given the community rules in your neighborhood (Point B). How you get from Point A to Point B can happen in a variety of ways. You can mow the grass yourself, you can pay someone to mow it, you can spray chemicals on the grass and kill it, or you can plant a garden so you no longer have any grass. Each of these solutions will take you from Point A to Point B, but each has its own idiosyncratic steps that are, in effect, an algorithm to solve the problem.[82] While the above example demonstrates a problem can be solved by many different algorithms,[83] note that a given algorithm solves only one problem (e.g., making the grass shorter).[84] Similarly, programmers use algorithms to determine how software takes each step.[85]

B. **Data Structures: Linear and Nonlinear**

A data structure is the framework and the physical implementation for organizing and representing information used by a program.[86] Data structures can take

---

Most text books provide an overview of several dozen basic data structures and several dozen basic algorithms. See, e.g., Cormen et al., An Introduction to Algorithms (1990) (1,100+ page book describing a wide variety of data structures and algorithms); Knuth, Sorting and Searching (4th ed. 1975) (multivolume series on algorithms).

[79] "Users use command terms to tell the computer what to do." Lotus Development Corp. v. Borland Intern., Inc., 49 F.3d 807, 815 (1st Cir. 1995), judgment aff'd, 516 U.S. 233.

[80] "The expression of the method of solution is known as an algorithm." Gemignani, Product Liability and Software, 8 Rutgers Comp. Tech. L.J. 173 n. 27 (1981).

[81] "Applications programs are, generally speaking, problem solving programs." Gemignani, 8 Rutgers Comp. Tech. L.J. at n. 275.

[82] See Shaffer, Data Structures and Algorithm Analysis (Prentice-Hall 2013).

[83] "[T]wo programmers may use different algorithms and interfaces, but write programs that accomplish identical goals." Swinson, Copyright or Patent or Both: An Algorithmic Approach to Computer Software Protection, 5 Harv. J. L. & Tech. 145, 149 (Fall 1991).

[84] See, e.g., Diamond v. Diehr, 450 U.S. 175, 186("The term 'algorithm' is subject to a variety of definitions ... [Petitioner's] definition is significantly broader than the definition this Court employed in *Benson* and *Flook*."); *accord* Parker v. Flook, 437 U.S. 584, 98 S. Ct. 2522, 57 L. Ed. 2d 451 (1978); Gottschalk v. Benson, 409 U.S. 63; In re Schrader, 22 F.3d 290, 293 n.5 (Fed. Cir. 1994). The Court of Appeals, Federal Circuit, also held that any step-by-step process, be it electronic, chemical, or mechanical, involves an "algorithm" in the broad sense of the term. See State Street Bank & Trust Co. v. Signature Financial Group, Inc, 149 F.3d 1368, 1374–75 (Fed. Cir. 1998) (abrogated on other grounds by, In re Bilski, 545 F.3d 943 (Fed. Cir. 2008)); see also Benson, 409 U.S. at 65, 93 S.Ct. 253 (describing a mathematical algorithm as a "procedure for solving a given type of mathematical problem").

[85] See Shaffer, Data Structures and Algorithm Analysis (Prentice-Hall 2011).

[86] "In the most general sense, a data structure is any data representation and its associated operations." See generally Shaffer, Data Structures and Algorithm Analysis 4 (Prentice-Hall 2011). The IEEE Standard Computer Dictionary defines the phrase "data structure" as "[a] physical or logical relationship among data elements, designed to support specific data manipulation functions." IEEE

different forms but nearly all software utilizes data structures, which are usually encapsulated in a module within the software.[87] Common data structures used in computer software generally divide into linear and nonlinear data structures.[88]

1. *Linear data structures*
   Linear data structures traverse the data elements sequentially, such that only one data element can be reached directly.[89] The data elements in a linear data structure are accessed in sequential fashion, applying a queue concept. The linear data structure queue concept follows the first-in first-out principle, meaning the first person in line is the first to leave the line.
2. *Nonlinear data structures such as a tree*
   Nonlinear data structures are those where the data elements are not accessed in a sequential fashion.[90] An example of a nonlinear data structure is the tree data structure,[91] which consists of a set of nodes called vertices and a set of edges which links the vertices.[92] Every data item in a tree is attached to one or more other nodes, but in a way that reflects a relationship. An example of

Standard Computer Dictionary 155. *See also* Santisi, Note: In re Warmerdam: When is a Software Process Too Abstract to Merit Patent Protection?, 13 J. Marshall J. Comp. & Info. L. 667, 670 n. 24 (Summer, 1995).

[87] In short, the US Court of Appeals, Federal Circuit held in In re Lowry that data structures are physical entities that provide increased efficiency in computer operations. In re Lowry, 32 F.3d 1579 (Fed. Cir. 1994); *see also* Apple, Inc. v. Samsung Elecs. Co., 2012 WL 3283478 (N.D. Cal. 2012), rev'd and remanded on other grounds, 107 U.S.P.Q.2d 2048, 2013 WL 4487610 (Fed. Cir. 2013) (description of "the algorithms used by each constituent module" and description that "identifies the functions, input and output variables, and data structures used by each module" are trade secrets); Beacon Wireless Solutions, Inc. v. Garmin Intern., Inc., 894 F. Supp. 2d 727, 730, ("technical details of the plaintiffs' fleet management system (e.g., the underlying source code, algorithms, protocols, or formats) qualify as trade secrets").

[88] See Stern & Naish, Animating Recursive Algorithms, 4(2) Interactive Multimedia Electronic Journal of Computer-Enhanced Learning (Wake Forest Univ. 2002); see generally Clapes, Lynch and Steinberg, Silicon Epics and Binary Bards: Determining the Proper Scope of Copyright Protection for Computer Programs, 34 U.C.L.A. L. Rev. 1493, 1527 (1987) (discussing how data structures operate in software programs); see also Tarjan, 14 Data structures and network algorithms (Society for Industrial and Applied Mathematics 1983).

[89] See Dixit, Mastering Data Structures Through C Language10–25 (Laxmi Publications, Ltd. 2010).

[90] Graph data structures are abstract data structures that are meant to implement the graph concept from mathematics, and a tree is a graph without loops. See National Instruments Corp. v. EnSoft Corp., 815 F. Supp. 2d 1054 (S.D. Iowa 2011) (discussing patent dispute that involves real-world application of graph data structures).

[91] See generally Munro, Raman & Storm, "Representing Dynamic Binary Trees Succinctly," in Proceedings of the Twelfth Annual ACM-SIAM Symposium on Discrete Algorithms 529–36 (Jan. 2001). (stating "the standard representation of a tree, with a pointer or two per parent-child relationship, is easy to navigate and update. Furthermore, the structure can be easily augmented so that operations such as determining subtree size can also be supported in constant time.").

[92] Binary trees are a special class of trees where the max number of nodes permitted is two. Lucas, Baronaigien & Ruskey, On Rotations and the Generation of Binary Trees, 15(3) J. Algorithms 343–66 (Nov. 1993).

a tree data structure is in the diagram below.[93] Other types of trees include directory trees, family trees, company organization chart, table of contents, rooted tree, or a free tree. Other nonlinear data structures include multidimensional arrays, tables, graphs, and sets.

3. *Hash table data structure*
   Another common data structure found in software is the hash table.[94] The hash table is a data structure that can perform lookups in near-constant time.[95] A hash table stores key/value pairs, and hash tables can be quickly searched by its key. As a result, hash tables provide for relatively fast lookup, reasonably fast insertion, and efficient use of memory. In more concrete terms, a hash table is an abstraction of an array that allows any value to be used as an index. The index is called the key, and the content of the array element of that index is called the value.[96]

## 2.5 Operating Systems

Software can be categorized in many different ways; however, one distinct group in software is the operating system.[97] An operating system (hereinafter "OS") is software that provides a mechanism to manage a computer's hardware and applications.

---

[93] See Frakes & Baeza-Yates, Information Retrieval: Data Structures and Algorithms (1992); Vaucher, Pretty-Printing of Trees, 10(7) Software: Practice and Experience 553–61 (1980).

[94] See, e.g., Northeastern University v. Google, Inc., 2010 Markman 4511010, 2010 WL 4511010, *9 (E.D. Tex. 2010) ("the Court construes "hash table" to mean "a table that associates hash values with other data" and "local hash table" to mean "a hash table containing at least the hash values and data associated with said first portion of said hashed query fragment.").

[95] In addition, hash tables map keys to values without traversing a data structure over all the keys. See Dixit, Mastering Data Structures Through C Language 10–25 (Laxmi Publications, Ltd. 2010); Shaffer, Data Structures and Algorithm Analysis (3d ed. 2012). See, e.g., Agrawal & Srikant, "Fast Algorithms for Mining Association Rules," in Proceedings of the 20th Int'l. Conference on Very Large Data Bases 487–499 (Morgan Kaufmann Sept. 1994).

[96] However, perfect hashing, for example, uses more memory to allow expected rapid table construction and constant time lookup, while open-address hashing allows some lookups and insertions to be slow while using little memory. See generally Dietzfelbinger, Karlin, et al., Dynamic Perfect Hashing: Upper and Lower Bounds, 23(4) SIAM Journal on Computing 738–61 (1994).

[97] See Computer Associates Intern., Inc. v. Altai, Inc., 775 F. Supp. 544, 550 (E.D. N.Y. 1991), aff'd in part, vacated in part, 982 F.2d 693, 37 Fed. R. Evid. Serv. 348, 119 A.L.R. Fed. 741 (2d Cir. 1992) ("[o]perating systems are the programs that manage the resources of the computer and allocate those resources to other programs that need them. For example, operating system software might perform, among others, these functions: channeling information entered at a keyboard to the proper application program; sending information from an application program to a display screen; providing blocks of memory to an application program that requires them; and allocating processing time among several application programs running on the computer at the same time."); see also Shontz, Computer Software: Time to Pay a Fair Share, 68 Taxes 162 (1990).

It serves as the primary user interface.[98] The OS is the functional equivalent of a "software platform," since other software is constructed to operate within the parameters of the particular OS.[99] The platform itself contains application program interfaces (hereinafter "APIs") that provide software vendors instruction on how to access useful modules of code built into the platform.[100] Such modules include the Windows API, informally WinAPI, which contains a core set of APIs available in the Microsoft Windows operating systems that developers can use to develop software to work on Microsoft Windows platform.

The APIs and the OS's underlying code allow software developers to create software in a more expeditious fashion.[101] Windows API, for example, contains a multitude of APIs that can be accessed by software operating on the OS, such as word processing programs, multimedia applications, and games.[102]

The operating system platform is both a resource allocator[103] and a control program. As a resource allocator, an operating system manages the CPU time, memory space,[104] file-storage space,[105] and I/O devices[106] and allocates them to programs for

[98] See Silberschatz, Galvin, et al., Operating System Concepts 4 (Wiley 1998); Summers, An Overview of Computer Security, 23(4) IBM Systems Journal 309–25 (1984); Carrier, File System Forensic Analysis, Vol. 3 (Addison-Wesley 2005).

[99] Two of the standard text books, used to teach introduction to operating systems: Silberschatz, Galvin, et al., Operating System Concepts 4 (Wiley 1998); Palmer & Walters, Guide to Operating Systems (Course Technology Ptr. 2011).

[100] Dun & Bradstreet Software Services, Inc. v. Grace Consulting, Inc., 307 F.3d 197 (3d Cir. 2002); see also Convole, Inc. v. Compaq Computer Corp., 2005 Markman 1902921, 2005 WL 1902921, *10 (S.D. N.Y. 2005) (defining an API to be "an advanced programming interface (API) which allows one software program to 'interface' with another."); Karjala, Copyright Protection of Operating Software, Copyright Misuse, and Antitrust, 9 Cornell J.L. & Pub. Pol'y 161, 169–70 (1999).

[101] See U.S. v. Microsoft Corp., 253 F.3d 34, 53 (D.C. Cir. 2001) (finding that operating systems function as a vehicle for software applications and have two distinct functions: allocate memory and control peripherals).

[102] See Bresnahan, "New Modes of Competition," in Competition, Innovation and the Microsoft Monopoly: Antitrust in the Digital Marketplace 155, 159 (Jeffrey A. Eisenach & Thomas M. Lenard eds. 1999) (defining a platform as "a shared, stable set of hardware, software, and networking technologies on which users build and run computer applications").

[103] The resource allocator is responsible for assigning resources to different tasks running in the system. See generally Ngolah, Wang & Tan, Implementing Task Scheduling and Event Handling In RTOS+, 3 Canadian Conference on Electrical and Computer Engineering 1523–26 (May 2–5, 2004).

[104] See Stuart, Principles of Operating Systems: Design & Applications 284 (Cengage Learning EMEA, Jan 10, 2008).

[105] Storage Management System with File Aggregation and Space Reclamation Within Aggregated Files, U.S. Patent No. 6,021,415 (filed Oct. 29, 1997) (issued Feb. 1, 2000).

[106] See Tandy Corp. v. Personal Micro Computers, Inc., 524 F. Supp. 171, 173 (N.D. Cal. 1981) (defining an input-output routine as "… a computer program which tells the computer how to take the information which is put into the computer by an operator in one computer language and translate that information into a more simplified "machine" language which the computer can understand. For obvious reasons, this program is crucial to the operation of the computer, and it is this

executing tasks.[107] As a control program, an operating system controls the execution of programs to prevent errors and ensure the machine operates properly.[108]

Traditionally, operating systems are seen as a program that is always running on the computer. In essence, the operating system hides the hardware resources behind abstractions to provide an environment that is more user-friendly and allows programs to operate more efficiently.[109] For example, Windows tends to be a single graphical user interface (e.g., the home screen, with or without windows open), whereas other OSs (e.g., Linux) can have several different interfaces.[110] In a program like Windows, the visual components on the graphical interface (i.e., those with which the user interacts) can change, while the underlying operating system remains the same.[111]

Today, when a computer is first powered up, the hardware runs a tiny "boot loader" program, which examines the available hardware and allows the user to select what operating system to start.[112] The operating system starts up, sets up

---

program which is the subject of the lawsuit."). See generally Engineering Dynamics, Inc. v. Structural Software, Inc., 26 F.3d 1335 (5th Cir. 1994), opinion supplemented on denial of reh'g, 46 F.3d 408 (5th Cir. 1995); PC Connector Solutions LLC v. SmartDisk Corp., 406 F.3d 1359 (Fed. Cir. 2005); Universal City Studios, Inc. v. Reimerdes, 111 F. Supp. 2d 294 (S.D. N.Y. 2000), judgment entered, 111 F. Supp. 2d 346 (S.D. N.Y. 2000), aff'd, 273 F.3d 429 (2d Cir. 2001); Telex Corp. v. International Business Machines Corp., 367 F. Supp. 258 (N.D. Okla. 1973), judgment rev'd on other grounds, 510 F.2d 894 (10th Cir. 1975) (disapproved of by, Memorex Corp. v. International Business Machines Corp., 555 F.2d 1379 (9th Cir. 1977)) and (disapproved of by, Memorex Corp. v. International Business Machines Corp., 555 F.2d 1379 (9th Cir. 1977)) (disapproved of on other grounds by, Memorex Corp. v. International Business Machines Corp., 555 F.2d 1379 (9th Cir. 1977)).

[107] "A primary aim of an operating system is to share a computer installation among many programs making unpredictable demands upon its resources. A primary task of its designer is therefore to construct resource allocation (or scheduling) algorithms for resources of various kinds (main store, drum store, magnetic tape handlers, consoles, etc.)." Hoare, Monitors: An Operating System Structuring Concept, 17(10) Communications of the ACM 549–57 (1974).

[108] See generally Novell, Inc. v. Microsoft Corp., 505 F.3d 302, 316–17 (4th Cir. 2007) (finding that "[a]n operating system is software that controls the computer's resources, including memory, disk space, keyboards, and the central processing unit. An operating system also facilitates communication between the computer's resources and software applications, including word-processing and spreadsheet applications."), citing to U.S. v. Microsoft Corp., 253 F.3d 34, 53–55, 60, 74 (D.C. Cir. 2001) (en banc); U.S. v. Microsoft Corp., 84 F. Supp. 2d 9, 12 (D.D.C. 1999).

[109] Engler & Kaashoek, "Exterminate All Operating System Abstractions," in Proceedings of the Fifth IEEE Workshop on Hot Topics in Operating Systems 78–83 (May 4–5, 1995).

[110] Silberschatz, Galvin, et al., 4 Operating System Concepts (Addison-Wesley 1998).

[111] See Computer Associates Intern., Inc. v. Altai, Inc., 982 F.2d 693, 698, 37 Fed. R. Evid. Serv. 348, 119 A.L.R. Fed. 741 (2d Cir. 1992); Mitel, Inc. v. Iqtel, Inc., 124 F.3d 1366 (10th Cir.1997) (defining "[a]n "operating system" is itself a program that manages the resources of the computer, allocating those resources to other programs as needed.").

[112] "Booting is the process of starting or resetting a computer. The computer boot process on a typical IBM-compatible computer using either a DOS or Windows operating system proceeds as follows. When the computer is first turned on, it loads and executes the 'basic input/output system' ("BIOS"). The BIOS transfers control to a "boot loader" that loads the first sector of the first track of the hard drive. This sector contains a software program, the master boot record ("MBR"), that

housekeeping, and typically launches a file viewer program to show the user the file systems available.[113] However, not all computers have operating systems; for example, most of the computers in refrigerator ice machines do not have an operating system, as it is a fairly straightforward task to create ice when buttons are pushed or minimal ice levels are detected.[114]

Currently, operating systems generally fall into one of the following four categories:

- The first category of operating systems is *real time*, which is an operating system program that provides an abstraction[115] for the underlying hardware for the user.[116] It also provides a reliable platform to software programs to execute task

---

controls the computer until it loads the operating system. The MBR contains a small database called a "partition table" that specifies the location and type of partitions on the disk. The MBR examines the partition table to determine which of the partitions to load and execute. The computer code, including the operating system, in the partition identified as "bootable" by the MBR is then loaded. After that code is loaded and executed, the computer is 'booted' and ready for operation by the user." Altiris, Inc. v. Symantec Corp., 318 F.3d 1363, 1366–67 (Fed. Cir. 2003); *see also* Apple, Inc. v. Psystar Corp., 673 F. Supp. 2d 931 (N.D. Cal. 2009), aff'd, 658 F.3d 1150 (9th Cir. 2011), cert. denied, 132 S. Ct. 2374, 182 L. Ed. 2d 1017 (2012); Digital Privacy, Inc. v. RSA Security, Inc., 195 F. Supp. 2d 771 (E.D. Va. 2002).

[113] Karjala, The Protection of Operating Software under Japanese Copyright Law, 29 Jurimetrics J. 43 (1988). This article states that the operating software relieves the programmer of the most mundane of these housekeeping chores and permits programming at a higher level.

[114] Mokube & Adams, "Honeypots: Concepts, Approaches, and Challenges," in Proceedings of the 45th Annual ACM Southeast Regional Conference 321–26 (Mar. 2007); Nelson, Prasad, et al., "An Embedded Architectural Framework for Interaction Between Automobiles and Consumer Devices," in Proceedings of the Tenth IEEE Real-Time and Embedded Technology and Applications Symposium 192–99 (May 25–28, 2004); Alexander, Wijesinha, & Karne "An Evaluation of Secure Real-Time Transport Protocol (SRTP) Performance for VoIP," in Proceedings of the Third IEEE International Conference on Network and System Security 95–101 (Oct. 19–21, 2009).

[115] Sets of routines in software that provide programs with access to hardware resources through programming interface. Abstraction in programming/coding decreases the complexity and increases the efficiency of the coding by hiding unnecessary details about the object or system. With abstraction, the programmer/coder tries to ensure the programming/coding in a manner that makes sense by including all the relevant aspects of the programming/coding are included and none of the extraneous ones.

[116] Lee & Lin, Embedded Processor Core Design to Support Real-Time Operating Systems, (Technical Report Part IV, University of Auckland, Faculty of Engineering 2003). *See also* Microware Systems Corp. v. Apple Computer, Inc., 126 F. Supp. 2d 1207, 53 Fed. R. Evid. Serv. 1618 (S.D. Iowa 2000), aff'd, 238 F.3d 989 (8th Cir. 2001) (stating real-time computer software "enables a full range of high-tech or 'smart' devices from cellular telephones and wireless communication devices to antilock brakes to function properly. Collectively, the RTOS software and the sophisticated devices that are run by it are known in the computer industry as 'embedded systems.' Microware competes directly with other RTOS developers in the embedded systems market."); see also QNX Software Systems GmbH & Co. KG v. Netrino, LLC, 2010 WL 4941985 (D. Md. 2010); Computer Associates Intern., Inc. v. Computer Automation, Inc., 678 F. Supp. 424 (S.D. N.Y. 1987).

scheduling and multitasking and guarantees worst case performance to meet task deadlines.[117] A real-time operating system can also provide services such as task synchronization and memory management.[118]

- The second category of operating systems is *single-user, single-task operating systems*, which are programs that allow a computer or electronic device to run only one application at a time.[119]
- The third category of operating systems is *single-user multitasking*, which is an operating system that runs multiple software processors at the same time.[120] This is a rather common type of operating system, formerly used by Microsoft Windows 98 and Apple Macintosh. For example, these computers can play a video file, download a PDF from the Internet, and edit a Word file simultaneously.
- The fourth category of operating systems is *multiuser operating system*, which allows multiple users to use the system resources simultaneously.[121] The multiuser operating system is responsible for ensuring that the requirements of multiple users are balanced and that each of the programs being used has sufficient and separate resources to avoid the situation where one user can affect all the users.[122] Linux, UNIX, VMS, and MVS are examples of multiuser operating systems.[123]

---

[117] Labrosse, MicroC/OS-II. The Real-Time Kernel (1999); Jung, Meyer & Milutinovic, Flexible Register Window Structure for Multi-Tasking, in Proceedings of the Twenty-Fourth Annual Hawaii International Conference on System Sciences, Vol. 1, 110–116 (Jan. 8–11, 1991).

[118] Quammen, Miller & Tabak, "Register Window Management for a Real-Time Multitasking," in Proceedings of the Twenty-Second Annual Hawaii International Conference on System Sciences (Jan. 6–9-1989).

[119] MS-DOS is a single-user, single-task operating system designed for Intel 8086/8088 chip personal computers. See generally Schulman, Undocumented DOS: A Programmers Guide to Reserved MS-DOS Functions and Data Structures 2nd ed. (Addison-Wesley 1993). "The most significant weakness of MS-DOS is its inability to provide the multitasking environment required to fully use the processing power of 80,386 [32-bit] machines. Because it was designed for a single-user, single-task processing environment, it can only run one application (process) at a time. MS-DOS applications are also limited to 640K of RAM which is not sufficient for many new applications, especially graphics and computer assisted design/computer assisted manufacturing (CAD/CAM) products." See Nealon, Technology Assessment of Operating Systems (No. ASQBG-I-89-023) (Army Inst. for Research in Management Information and Computer Science, Atlanta, Ga. 1989).

[120] Elmasri, Carrick & Levine, Operating systems: A Spiral Approach (McGraw-Hill 2009); Simon, An Embedded Software Primer (Addison-Wesley 1999).

[121] Burgess, Principles of Network and System Administration (Wiley 2004). See also Step-Saver Data Systems, Inc. v. Wyse Technology, 939 F.2d 91, 15 U.C.C. Rep. Serv. 2d 1 (3d Cir. 1991); Arizona Retail Systems, Inc. v. Software Link, Inc., 831 F. Supp. 759, 22 U.C.C. Rep. Serv. 2d 70 (D. Ariz. 1993).

[122] Sagar, "Embedded Operating Systems for Real-Time Applications," in M. Tech. credit seminar report, Electronic Systems Group, EE Dept, IIT Bombay (Submitted in November 2002).

[123] See generally MacKinnon, The Linux Operating System: Debian GNU/Linux, 14(4) Journal of Applied Econometrics 14(4), 443–52 (1999); Burgess, Principles of Network and System Administration (Wiley 2004).

It is worth noting that while operating systems such as the former Windows 2000 and Windows XP can support hundreds or thousands of networked users, they are not true multiuser operating systems.[124] The system administrator is the only user for Windows XP or Windows 2000, and all the remote user logins are really being run by a computer program because neither of these operating systems allow for access privileges or allow for concurrent access. By comparison [to a multiuser operating system such as Linux, Unix, etc.], a computer software application, such as Google's Chrome, is effectively a file of machine code instructions that when triggered, be it by a mouse click, a finger to the screen, or an audio command, launches the computer software. This means the operating system loads the initial section of machine code into memory and instructs the CPU to start executing the computer software and finally directing the CPU to start running the machine code.

## 2.6 Software Development Design and Models

Software development is defined as the profession concerned with specifying, designing, developing, and maintaining software applications by applying technologies and practices from computer science, project management, and other fields.[125] The field of software development has seen complex and rapid growth in the last decade and is now considered a mainstream industry.

A. **Software Design**
   Software engineers design the basis, or architecture, of the software.[126] The computer program is built by software developers.[127] Software developers take the architectural design documents and write code based on these design

[124] See generally Burgess, Principles of Network and System Administration (Wiley 2004).

[125] The term software engineer is thought to have first been coined at the NATO Science Committee in Garmisch, West Germany, in October of 1968. Scaling Up: A Research Agenda for Software Engineering, 33 Comm. of the ACM 281, 24 & n.7 (Mar. 1990) (excerpts from a report on software development by the Computer Science and Technology Board). Software engineering has been defined as: "The practical application of scientific knowledge in the design and construction of computer programs and the associated documentation required to develop, operate, and maintain them." Boehm, Software Engineering, Classics in Software Engineering 325, 326 (Edward N. Yourdon ed. 1979).

[126] See Chung & do Prado Leite, "On Non-Functional Requirements in Software Engineering," in Conceptual Modeling: Foundations and Applications 363–79 (Springer-Verlag 2009). See also Plains Cotton Co-op. Ass'n of Lubbock, Texas v. Goodpasture Computer Service, Inc., 807 F.2d 1256 (5th Cir. 1987); Sony Computer Entertainment, Inc. v. Connectix Corp., 203 F.3d 596, 599, 180 A.L.R. Fed. 655 (9th Cir. 2000) ("[s]oftware engineers designing a product that must be compatible with a copyrighted product frequently must "reverse engineer" the copyrighted product to gain access to the functional elements of the copyrighted product."); E.F. Johnson Co. v. Uniden Corp. of America, 623 F. Supp. 1485 (D. Minn. 1985).

[127] See, e.g., Bentley, Writing Efficient Programs (Prentice Hall 1982).

documents.[128] They write source code and this output is commonly referred to as a source program.[129] Because software developers almost always write computer software in something other than machine language, the code needs to be translated into machine language before it can be executed.[130] The actual program that is executed by a computer is usually referred to as an object program, as this machine language program is ready to be run by the computer (or digital device). An object program is frequently referred to as an "executable." Although it is difficult to identify the point at which the process of "designing" software ends and the process of "implementing" or "coding" software begins,[131] execution provides a reasonable basis for distinguishing between software design and source code.[132]

---

[128] See *also* Brooks, Jr., No Silver Bullet: Essence and Accidents of Software Engineering, IEEE Computer, Apr. 1987, at 10, 12 (describing the complexity of conforming a program to other systems' interfaces). The software engineering community views the technical design process as the basic building block for the future of well-engineered, reliable software products. Kapor, "A Software Design Manifesto," in Bringing Design to Software 1–9 (Winograd, ed. Addison-Wesley 1996). Software starts with the designer conceptualizing a problem and coming up with a solution based on applied techniques and logically applied principles. Kapor, A Software Design Manifesto.

[129] See, e.g., Computer Associates Intern., Inc. v. Altai, Inc., 982 F.2d 693, 37 Fed. R. Evid. Serv. 348, 119 A.L.R. Fed. 741 (2d Cir. 1992); Apple Computer, Inc. v. Franklin Computer Corp., 714 F.2d 1240, 70 A.L.R. Fed. 153 (3d Cir. 1983); U.S. v. Microsoft Corp., 253 F.3d 34 (D.C. Cir. 2001) ("Microsoft observes that software developers do write applications for other operating systems, pointing out that at its peak IBM's OS/2 supported approximately 2500 applications. ... This misses the point. That some developers write applications for other operating systems is not at all inconsistent with the finding that the applications barrier to entry discourages many from writing for these less popular platforms. Indeed, the District Court found that IBM's difficulty in attracting a larger number of software developers to write for its platform seriously impeded OS/2's success.").

[130] The Copyright Act defines a computer program as "a set of statements or instructions to be used directly or indirectly in a computer in order to bring about a certain result." 17 U.S.C. §101. In writing these directions, the programmer works "from the general to the specific." Whelan Associates, Inc. v. Jaslow Dental Laboratory, Inc., 797 F.2d 1222, 1229, 21 Fed. R. Evid. Serv. 571 (3d Cir. 1986). *See generally* Englund, Note, Idea, Process, or Protected Expression?: Determining the Scope of Copyright Protection of the Structure of Computer Programs, 88 Mich. L. Rev. 866, 867–73 (1990) (hereinafter "Englund"); Menell, An Analysis of the Scope of Copyright Protection for Application Programs, 41 Stan. L. Rev. 1045, 1051–57 (1989); Kretschmer, Note, Copyright Protection For Software Architecture: Just Say No!, 1988 Colum. Bus. L. Rev. 823, 824–27 (1988); Spivack, Comment, Does Form Follow Function? The Idea/Expression Dichotomy in Copyright Protection of Computer Software, 35 U.C.L.A. L. Rev. 723, 729–31 (1988).

[131] This issue is long-standing in both the subject field of inquiry and legal scholarship. See, e.g., Arsenault, Comment: Software Without Source Code: Can Software Produced by a Computer Aided Software Engineering Tool Be Protected?, 5 Alb. L.J. Sci. & Tech. 131, 164 (1994) ("Object-oriented representations, rapid prototype tools, and fourth-generation languages blur the line between design and code, and provide other high-level representations of software.").

[132] See, e.g., Plotkin, Computer Programming and the Automation of Invention: A Case for Software Patent Reform, 2003 U.C.L.A. J. L. Tech. 7, n. 29 (2003) (citing Hamlet & Maybee, The Engineering of Software: Technical Foundations for the Individual 211–12 (Addison-Wesley 2001): "Despite the similarities between the processes of designing and coding, there is one tremendous distinction between the end results: code can be executed on hardware—a design cannot.").

B. **Software Development Models**

The software development methods used to create software influence the actual fruition of the software, ranging from the architecture to the programming languages.[133] Although software development methods have been subdivided into as many as 19 developmental subtypes, this section examines four more common software development models:

The particular software development model a team elects to utilize varies as a factor of the team's goals, timeline, budget constraints, and extent to which the team has used a particular model previously.[134] Frequently, software projects combine features from these four models, adjusting for the constraints of the particular project.

1. **Waterfall Software Development Model**

The waterfall model is a structured system for software development that has been around since the early 1970s. The model is a time-ordered list of steps/stages to be used to develop software. In the waterfall model, as the name suggests, the software production cycle progresses sequentially in the following five stages:

- **Phase 1—system conceptualization:** The system conceptualization step seeks to define the functionality and process underlying the software and ascertain how these system pieces interrelate.[135]
- **Phase 2—system analysis:** In the system analysis step, the team gathers the system requirements from the end users and establishes how these system requirements will be included in the system.[136] This process hinges on extensive communication between the customer and developer.[137]
- **Phase 3—system design:** The system design phase focuses on the system's data requirements, interface construction, and software development. In this phase, the software development team creates a blueprint of the system being constructed to ensure that it performs all necessary tasks in an efficient manner.

[133] For an overview of software development methodologies, see Chemuturi & Cagley, Jr, Mastering Software Project Management: Best Practices, Tools and Techniques (J. Ross Publishing 2010).

[134] See Von Mayrhauser & Von Mayrhauser, Software Engineering: Methods and Management (Academic Press 1990).

[135] Gasson, Human-Centered vs. User-Centered Approaches, 5(2) Journal of Information Technology Theory and Application 29–46 (2003).

[136] Davis, Bersoff, & Comer, A Strategy for Comparing Alternative Software Development Life Cycle Models, 14(10) IEEE Transactions on Software Engineering 1453–61 (1988).

[137] See generally Davis, Bersoff, & Comer, A Strategy for Comparing Alternative Software Development Life Cycle Models, 14(10) IEEE Transactions on Software Engineering 1453–61 (1988). Because of this dependency, third parties are often retained to facilitate communication between the customers and the system developer to ensure that the product satisfies all of the customer's needs.

- **Phase 4—implementation (or coding):** The implementation (coding) phase is where the software is actually created.[138] In this step, the requirements and system's specifications from the system design phase are translated into source code, resulting in an executable machine code.
- **Phase 5—testing (stabilization):** As the software is created and added to the computer hardware, it is tested to ensure that the system is operating properly.[139] Testing is performed throughout a product's developmental cycle to ensure that it works correctly, efficiently, and according to specifications.[140] There are two types of testing: internal and external. Programmers perform internal testing to ensure that the code is efficient and consistent throughout the program.[141] External testing is used to ensure that the software meets the system design requirements and all necessary details associated with those processes.[142]

One benefit of using the waterfall model is that it facilitates departmentalization and managerial control,[143] which in turn allows managers to delegate specific tasks to different groups/members and establish detailed schedules for each stage of development, thereby allowing for on-time delivery of the product.[144] Nevertheless, the waterfall model used today has been modified to address several shortcomings.[145] Among these shortcomings is the often substantial time lapse between the collection of requirements and the delivery of software, during which time the requirements usually change, leaving the designer with software that does not meet the end users' needs.[146]

[138] *See generally* Basil & Turner, Iterative Enhancement: A Practical Technique for Software Development, 4 IEEE Transactions on Software Engineering 390–96 (1975).

[139] See generally Curtis, Krasner, & Iscoe, A Field Study of the Software Design Process for Large Systems, 31(11) Communications of the ACM 1268–87 (1988).

[140] Adrion, Branstad, & Cherniavsky, Validation, Verification, and Testing of Computer Software, 14(2) ACM Computing Surveys (CSUR) 159–92 (1982).

[141] Beizer, Software Testing Techniques (Dreamtech Press, 2002); Pressman & Ince, 5 Software Engineering: A Practitioner's Approach (McGraw-Hill, 1992).

[142] Testing tends to be a labor-intensive process because it is iterative by nature when done in the waterfall model. Jones, Variations In Software Development Practices, 20(6) IEEE Software 22–27 (Nov.–Dec. 2003).

[143] Davis, Bersoff, & Comer, A Strategy for Comparing Alternative Software Development Life Cycle Models, 14(10) IEEE Transactions on Software Engineering 1453–61 (1988).

[144] Davis, Bersoff, & Comer, A Strategy for Comparing Alternative Software Development Life Cycle Models, 14(10) IEEE Transactions on Software Engineering 1453–61 (1988).

[145] Another criticism of the waterfall model is that it lacks a set of detailed activities that are prescribed for actual software development work. Hoog, Jong & Vries, Constraint-Driven Software Design: An Escape from the waterfall model, 7(3) Performance Improvement Quarterly 48–63 (1994). The waterfall model has also been criticized as being too rigid and unrealistic for developing products that meet a customer's expectations. Chemuturi, Software Estimation Best Practices, Tools & Techniques: A Complete Guide for Software Project Estimators (J. Ross Publishing 2009).

[146] Málaga Chocano, A Comparative Study of Iterative Prototyping vs. Waterfall Process Applied to Small And Medium Sized Software Projects (doctoral dissertation, Massachusetts Institute of Technology 2004), available at http://hdl.handle.net/1721.1/34801 (last visited Mar. 27, 2013).

2. **Iterative Software Development Model**
   The iterative model is a software development model that divides a software production project into small steps (a.k.a. iterations).[147] The iterative software development model was created to address some of the waterfall model shortcomings. Since the iterative model allows software teams to deliver software incrementally, it allows developers to capitalize on information garnered from incremental versions of the system.[148]

   By using small steps for design, implementation, and testing, the software team can quickly derive lessons from prior iterations and make modifications to address shifting requirements.
3. **Agile Software Development Model**
   The agile model provides the customer with deliverables as the project progresses, as opposed to a single software application at the end of the project.[149] The agile model relies on a series of quick iterative planning and development cycles that allows the software team to evaluate constantly the product and obtain immediate feedback from stakeholders. This approach allows the team to improve quickly both the product and the team's internal working with the iteration. Usually when software teams use the agile model, they streamline the requirements definition and solution design phases prior to the launch of the full project, with more details evolving during the iterations that follow.[150]

   The agile model generally requires a full time project team that includes a customer or end user to be involved in the development cycles.[151] Often, the agile model is used by small teams with a core of two developers that code (often in pairs), the customer, a software architect, a business analyst, and a project manager.[152] The agile model relies on oral communication rather than formal documents; this is a major difference between this model and the other models discussed above, where a great deal of energy and resources is devoted to documenting the software requirements prior to software development.[153]

---

[147] With Iterative Development, a project is divided into small parts, which allows the development team to demonstrate results earlier on in the process and obtain valuable feedback from system users. See Munassar & Govardhan, A Comparison Between Five Models Of Software Engineering, 7(5) International Journal of Computer Science Issues 94–101 (2010).

[148] See generally Garrie, The Legal Status of Software, 23 J. Marshall J. Computer & Info. L., 711 (Summer, 2005).

[149] Fowler & Highsmith, The Agile Manifesto, 9(8) Software Development 28–35 (2001).

[150] Boehm, Get Ready for Agile Methods, With Care, 35(1) Computer 64–69 (Jan. 2002).

[151] Koch, Agile Software Development: Evaluating the Methods for Your Organization (Artech house 2005).

[152] Conboy & Fitzgerald, "Toward a Conceptual Framework of Agile Methods: A Study of Agility in Different Disciplines," in Proceedings of the ACM Workshop On Interdisciplinary Software Engineering Research 37–44 (2004).

[153] Beck, Beedle, et al., Manifesto for Agile Software Development (Agile Alliance 2001), available at http://www.agilealliance.org/the-alliance/the-agile-manifesto/ (last visited Mar. 25, 2013).

4. **Ad Hoc Software Development Model**
   The ad hoc model is used when the software requirements are not predefined; usually, the software is developed in tandem with the requirements.[154] The ad hoc model can be used for an entire project or for a subset of development (e.g., small projects).[155] When using the ad hoc model, it can be difficult to determine schedules, budgets, and product functionality,[156] which, in turn, makes using this model challenging when developing large software projects. Moreover, the success of a software project done using the ad hoc model rests largely on the capabilities of the development team, so for medium and large software projects, where coordination and discipline become necessary tools for goal attainment, the ad hoc model does not often deliver adequate results.[157]

C. **Software Development Best Practices**
   The quality of a software application can, and normally does, vary widely. However, the International Organization for Standardization has provided a standard set of characteristics that allows a user to ascertain the quality of the software. Examples of these characteristics include the following:

   - *Reliability*: The standard definition for software reliability is the probability of execution without failure for some defined interval, called the mission time.[158]
   - *Stability*: Software stability is usually measured based on its coupling structure, but it is possible that some part of the system is highly coupled, but not subject to any environmental changes, resulting in a stable design with a low stability value.[159]
   - *Portability*: Software is portable if it can operate in different environments.[160]

---

[154] Chemuturi & Cagley, Jr., Mastering Software Project Management: Best Practices: Tools and Techniques 25 (2010) (discussing the negative aspects of ad hoc development).

[155] Muffatto, Open Source: A Multidisciplinary Approach 73 (Imperial College Press 2006).

[156] Chemuturi, Requirements Engineering and Management for Software Development Projects 9 (Springer 2013).

[157] See Paulk et al., Key Practices of the Capability Maturity Model, Version 1.1 (Software Engineering Institute, Feb. 1993).

[158] See Musa, Iannino, & Okumoto, Software Reliability (McGraw-Hill, 1987); Musa, A theory of software reliability and its application, 3 IEEE Transactions on Software Engineering 312–27 (Jan. 1975).

[159] See Sethi, Cai, et al., "From Retrospect to Prospect: Assessing Modularity and Stability From Software Architecture," in Joint Working IEEE/IFIP Conference on Software Architecture & European Conference on Software Architecture 269–72 (Sept. 14–17, 2009).

[160] See Mooney, "Portability and Reusability: Common Issues And Differences," in Proceedings of the 23rd ACM Annual Conference on Computer Science 150–56 (Feb. 1995). From a theoretical perspective, software portability is a model of the computing environments in which our programs will be expected to operate. Brown & Hall, "Fortran Portability Via Models and Tools," in Proceedings of Workshop on Portability of Numerical Software 158–64 (Springer-Verlag 1977).

- *Maintainability*: Software is maintainable when it is defined as an integrated measure of multiple characteristics of the software, like readability of source code, documentation quality, and understandability of the software.[161]
- *Usability*: Software usability is a function of the manner in which the software supports the user in performing specific tasks and thus software developers need to acquire a sound knowledge of user's roles, tasks, culture, and work environment to ensure the software being developed is "usable."[162]

For a more complete listing of the international standard for the evaluation of software quality, one should consult ISO 9126.[163]

## 2.7 Software Testing

Software testing is the process used to identify the completeness and quality of computer software.[164] Technically speaking, testing can never establish the absence of errors in a particular software program.[165] Testing methodologies can only find defects, not prove that there are none. Testing methodologies range from the most informal, ad hoc testing to formally specified and controlled methods such as automated testing and unit testing.[166] Software testing as a subject matter generally refers to a practice used to improve upon a software application. Software testing generally occupies a substantial amount of the overall time and money during development. While software testing is less glamorous, it is a critical component to delivery of software. Imagine the failure of the software operating the battery temperature

161 See Aggarwal, Singh & Chhabra, "An Integrated Measure of Software Maintainability," in Proceedings Annual IEEE Reliability and Maintainability Symposium 235–41 (2002); Zhuo, Lowther, et al., "Constructing and Testing Software Maintainability Assessment Models" in Proceedings of First International IEEE Software Metrics Symposium 61–70 (May 21–22, 1993).

162 See Fitzpatrick & Higgins, "Usable Software and Its Attributes: A Synthesis of Software Quality, European Community Law and Human-Computer Interaction," in People and Computers XIII, Proceedings of HCI '98, 3–21, at 10 (Springer, 1998); O'Neill, "Task Model Support for Cooperative Analysis," in 13(18) ACM Conference Companion On Human Factors In Computing Systems 259–260 (1996).

163 The international ISO/IEC standard 9126 defines a general quality model for software products. Abran, Khelifi, et al., Usability Meanings and Interpretations in ISO Standards, 11(4) Software Quality Journal 325–38 (Nov. 2003).

164 "Why do we test? The two main reasons are: to make a judgment about quality or acceptability and to discover problems." Jorgensen, Software Testing: A Craftsman's Approach 3 (2nd ed.) (2002).

165 Dijkstra, Notes on Structured Programming (1970), available at http://www.cs.utexas.edu/users/EWD/ewd02xx/EWD249.PDF (last visited Mar. 25, 2013).

166 Dijkstra, Notes on Structured Programming (1970), available at http://www.cs.utexas.edu/users/EWD/ewd02xx/EWD249.PDF

in an airplane[167] or the software responsible for administering radiation in chemotherapy treatment; the results can be drastic.[168]

A. **Five Levels of Software Testing: Unit Testing, Integration Testing, System Testing, Acceptance Testing, and Regression Testing**

Software testing generally falls into one of the following buckets: unit testing, integration testing, system testing, acceptance testing, and regression testing.[169]

1. ***First Level of Software Testing: Unit Testing***

The unit testing phase involves taking the smallest piece of testable software in the application, isolating it from the remainder of the code, and determining whether it behaves exactly as you expect.[170] Unit testing is often performed early or during the software development process.[171] Generally, unit testing requires that each unit be tested independently prior to integration into modules, and it is done by software developers or white-box software QA team members.[172]

Unit testing is performed by authoring and running unit tests that ensure the source code delivers against the design requirements and operates as intended. Unit tests can be written by hand or be part of an integrated software testing platform.[173] Irrespective of the manner in which the unit tests are developed, there are two types of unit testing: drive unit testing (black-box testing) and program-based unit testing (white-box testing).[174] Drive unit testing focuses on ensuring the functionality is being delivered, and program-

---

[167] Halpert, From a Plane Crash to the Conviction of an Innocent Person: Why Forensic Science Evidence Should Be Inadmissible Unless It Has Been Developed as a Safety-Critical System, 32 Hamline L. Rev. 65 (2009).

[168] Wolpert, Product Liability and Software Implicated in Personal Injury, 60 Def. Counsel J. 519 (1993).

[169] Wolpert, Product Liability and Software Implicated in Personal Injury, 60 Def. Counsel J. 519 (1993). This article discusses how software testing occurs in the software development process. Wahl, When "Oops!" Isn't Enough: Responsibility for Unreliable Software, in Social and Ethical Effects of the Computer Revolution 171 (J.M. Kizza ed. MacFarland & Co. 1996).

[170] See generally Unit Testing topic: Visual Studio NET 2003, available at http://msdn.microsoft.com/en-us/library/aa292197(v=vs.71).aspx (last visited Jan. 27, 2013); Cheon & Leavens, A Simple and Practical Approach to Unit Testing: The JML and Junit Way, ECOOP 2002—Object-Oriented Programming 1789–1901 (2006); Zhao, "Data-Flow-Based Unit Testing of Aspect-Oriented Programs," in Proceedings of 27th Annual IEEE International Conference on Computer Software and Applications 188–197 (Nov. 2003).

[171] Sen, Marinov & Agha, CUTE: A Concolic Unit Testing Engine for C, 30(5) ACM SIGSOFT Software Engineering Notes 263–72 (Sept. 2005).

[172] Zhu, Hall & May, Software Unit Test Coverage and Adequacy, 29(4) ACM Computing Surveys 366–427 (December 1997).

[173] Cheon & Leavens, A Simple and Practical Approach to Unit Testing: The JML and JUnit Way (2006).

[174] Runeson, A Survey of Unit Testing Practices, 23(4) IEEE Software 22–29 (2006).

based unit testing is focused more on verifying the source code is performing properly.[175]

2. ***Second Level of Software Testing Is Integration Testing***
   The software integration testing phase focuses on testing how the pieces of the software (modules) pass data, function, or interact. Integration testing is usually done by the software developer and occurs after unit testing and before validation testing. Generally, integration testing is administered by a test plan, and the software developers develop integration test cases using the design documents to determine that the software functional, performance, and reliability requirements are being delivered.

   Integration testing seeks to validate that the individual source code units operate properly when combined into a larger code base. When source code is integrated, errors can arise. For example, a software team developing a missile could find that the GPS and fuel modules operate independently flawlessly, but when integrated, the GPS module does not transmit sufficient location data to the fuel module, making it possible the missile could run out of fuel midflight or confuse Paris, California with Paris, France. Integration tests focus on the software module interfaces and flow of data, or information, between the modules and not on the individual module, or unit, which is done in the unit testing phase.

   Finally, software integration testing can often prove to be the most time-consuming and expensive part of testing.[176] It is common to find software development projects with 50–70% of effort on testing and 50–70% of the testing effort on integration testing.

3. ***Third Level of Software Testing Is System Testing***
   System testing is a form of black-box testing that focuses on validating the computer software accuracy and completeness in performing the purposes as designed.[177] System testing focuses on simulating real-world scenarios that test the various functions of the system required to perform in the "real world." System testing completes once the actual results align with the expected results, the differences can be explained, or the users find the differences to be permissible. System testing usually begins after unit and integration testing. It is good practice for the software quality assurance team to review the previous test results prior to system testing, and this review should be performed pre- and postdelivery of a computer software program.[178] For example, a software QA team responsible for testing a complex web-based

[175] See generally Steven & Cohen, Encyclopedia of Software Engineering (Taylor & Francis 2012).

[176] Tsai, Bai, et al., "End-To-End Integration Testing Design," in 25th Annual International Computer Software and Applications Conference 166–71 (2001). IEEE.

[177] Lewis, Software Testing and Continuous Quality Improvement (Auerbach Pubs 2004).

[178] See, e.g., Somers v. Converged Access, Inc., 454 Mass. 582, 584–585, 911 N.E.2d 739 (2009); eBusiness Application Solutions, Inc. v. Gupta, 2009 WL 960774 (Cal. App. 6th Dist. 2009), unpublished/noncitable; Lewis, Software Testing and Continuous Quality Improvement (Auerbach Pubs 2004).

healthcare customer relationship management platform might test the search engine component, which should only accept a string of numbers representing the customer's healthcare identification card, by seeing how the search engine component responds to incorrect input such as a string of letters. In this system testing example, the software QA team is validating that the healthcare customer relationship management software platform will respond as expected and not allow a user to input malformed data into the system.[179]

4. ***Fourth Level of Software Testing Is Acceptance Testing***
In software development, acceptance testing is a test that is conducted to determine if the requirements of a specification or contract are met.[180] The extent of acceptance testing in the context of software can include a range of actions including simulation tests and performance tests.

Acceptance testing can involve black-box testing being performed on software; however, software developers divide acceptance testing into acceptance testing performed by the software providers, or creator, and acceptance testing by the customer, the user, or client, prior to handover or transfer of ownership.[181] Acceptance testing performed by the customer is also referred to as a user acceptance testing (UAT), end user testing, or field testing.[182] The intent of this test is to ascertain the software's compliance with the business requirements and determine if it is acceptable for delivery to the customer.

Acceptance testing that is performed by the software provider, or creator, of the software is done in conjunction with the client. Usually, the client plays a critical role in this step, because the client needs to certify that the system conforms to the agreed upon requirements.[183]

Generally, acceptance testing occurs near the end of testing and prior to the software provider moving the software to market or production. The focus of the testing is to validate the end-to-end business; it is not focused on cosmetic errors, typos, or system testing.[184] Acceptance testing is generally

---

[179] Lewis, Software Testing and Continuous Quality Improvement (Auerbach Pubs 2004). Generally, the Software QA team performs system testing and not the software development team. Lewis, Software Testing and Continuous Quality Improvement (Auerbach Pubs 2004).

[180] See Indiana Bell Tel. Co., Inc. v. McCarty, 362 F.3d 378, 390 (7th Cir. 2004) (stating that "[t]he purpose of the acceptance test is to ensure the line is error-free, resulting in better quality and reliability for customers.").

[181] See, e.g., Market America, Inc. v. Google, Inc., 2010 WL 3156044 (D. Del. 2010); Liberty Bay Credit Union v. Open Solutions, Inc., 905 F. Supp. 2d 389 (D. Mass. 2012); Mecklenburg County v. Nortel Government Solutions Inc., 2008 WL 906319 (W.D. N.C. 2008); Assistmed, Inc. v. Conceptual Health Solutions, Inc., 2006 WL 3691003 (N.D. Tex. 2006), amended on denial of reconsideration, 2007 WL 900969 (N.D. Tex. 2007).

[182] See Edwards v. Toys "R' Us, 527 F. Supp. 2d 1197 (C.D. Cal. 2007).

[183] Verma, Yadav & Tiwari, Software Testing Techniques for Finding Errors, 1(2) International Journal of Research Review in Engineering Science and Technology 89 (Sept. 2012).

[184] Verma, Yadav & Tiwari, Software Testing Techniques for Finding Errors, 1(2) International Journal of Research Review in Engineering Science and Technology 89 (Sept. 2012).

carried out in a separate environment with production-like data to simulate the operational environment.[185]

Most often, acceptance testing is performed by the users of software, and it usually occurs at the client location. The steps involved in acceptance testing vary, but generally they include the following:

- Create test scenarios, or cases, by analyzing the business requirements and other software development documents.
- Develop an acceptance test plan that outlines the strategy that will be used to validate that the software meets the business requirements; the test plan usually defines with greater specificity the test scenarios and may also include a timeline for administering the test scenarios.[186]
- Run the test scenarios using data, ideally live data for purposes of validation, anonymizing data to mitigate privacy concerns where appropriate.
- Record the results of the acceptance tests and report bugs, if any, and then retest once the bugs are fixed.
- Obtain sign-off from the customer.[187]

- When performing acceptance testing, the deliverables may include a test plan, test cases, test results, and a bug or defect log. The extent and time required for acceptance testing varies based on several factors, including the complexity of the software, the amount of data the software uses, and the availability of the end users.

5. ***Fifth Level of Software Testing Is Regression Testing***
   Regression testing refers to the act of retesting the components of the software that are not altered when new features are added or the code base is tweaked to address a bug. Generally, the software QA team performs the regression testing, and often they re-execute test cases to validate that prior functionality of the software has not been altered, meaning that the software modifications did not introduce new bugs. Regression testing can be done on

[185] Verma, Yadav & Tiwari, Software Testing Techniques for Finding Errors, 1(2) International Journal of Research Review in Engineering Science and Technology 89 (Sept. 2012); Ray, "Acceptance Tests of Distributed Processing Orientated Supervisory Control and Data Acquisition (SCADA) Systems for Offshore Platforms," in Proceedings of the 1st IEEE European Test Conference 221–28 (Apr. 12–14, 1989).

[186] The purpose of this step is to formalize a method to analyze, verify, and generate test scenarios in a systematic manner before proceeding with the actual acceptance testing. See, e.g., Hsia, Kung & Sell, Software Requirements and Acceptance Testing, 3(1) Annals of Software Engineering 291–317 (1997).

[187] The final acceptance decision is made by the customer. Albeanu & Vladicescu, "Total Quality for Software Engineering Management," in Handbook of Reliability Engineering 567–84 (Springer 2003).

a new software build, when new functionality is added to existing software or simply when there is a bug patch applied. While regression testing is most often done after the completion of verification that the bug was remedied or the functionality is operating, it is not always the case, as sometimes a software release can take months to finish. When there is an extended timeframe for a software project, regression tests may be incorporated into the daily or weekly test cycles.

Generally, regression testing is limited only to retesting of existing software that has been altered to add new features or mitigate bugs or for one of several other reasons. The software is being tested to ensure that no other previously working functions have flunked as a result of the fixtures and that newly added features have not produced problems with previous versions. Software regression testing best practices are initiated after a software developer has attempted to fix a distinguished problem or has added a source code to a program that may have unwittingly introduced errors.[188] In other words, it is a quality control measure to ensure that the freshly modified piece of a code still abides with its specified requirements and nonmodified code has not been impacted by the maintenance activity.

Regression testing is also known as verification testing because regression testing is initiated after remediation of a software bug to validate that new source code did not inadvertently introduce errors.[189] The intent of regression testing is to provide a measure of quality control to ensure that the newly modified code still complies with its specified requirements and that unmodified code has not been affected by the maintenance activity.[190] Today, a great deal of regression testing is automated using regression testing software.[191]

[188] Onoma, Tsai, et al., Regression Testing in an Industrial Environment, 41(5) Communications of the ACM 81–86 (May 1998). The frequent and extensive use of regression testing has resulted in several firms, mainly software, to develop in-house regression testing tools to automate the process.

[189] West & Aiken, Multiple Regression: Testing and Interpreting Interactions (Sage Publications, Inc. 1991).

[190] Rothermel, Untch, et al., Prioritizing Test Cases For Regression Testing, 27(10) IEEE Transactions on Software Engineering 929–48 (Oct. 2001).

[191] Examples of regression testing software include TBrun™, made by LDRA; TestComplete™, made by AutomatedQA; TestWorks™, made by Software Research; Vermont HighTest Plus™, made by Vermont Creative Software; AppsWatch™, made by NRG; GJTester™, made by TreborSoft; JUnit™, made by junit.org; QEngine™, made by AdventNet; QF-Test™, made by QFS; Netvantage Functional Tester™, made by Netvantage Technologies; Rational Robo™, made by Rational Software; and vTest™, made by Verisium.

B. **Common Software Test Methods Used in the Five Different Levels of Testing**
Within each of these testing buckets, there are a variety of testing methodologies such as control flow testing, statement coverage, data flow testing, functional testing,[192] code reading,[193] and structural tests.[194]

1. ***Most Software Test Methods Are Either a White-Box or Black-Box Test Method or Technique***
While many software test methods, or techniques, exist, it is possible to classify most methods as either white-box[195] or black-box methods.[196]

White-box methods, or techniques, operate as software code verification. White-box test methodologies construct test cases from the source code of the program and generally focus on addressing particular features of the software program's structure. White-box testing focuses on probing the computer software execution to discover bugs, or errors, with the computer software itself. Examples of white-box testing are control flow testing,[197]

---

192 "In functional testing, which is a 'black-box' approach, a programmer constructs test data from the program's specification through methods such as equivalence partitioning and boundary value analysis. The programmer then executes the program and contrasts its actual behavior with that indicated in the specification." Basili & Selby, Comparing the Effectiveness of Software Testing Strategies, SE-13(12) IEEE Transactions on Software Engineering 1278–96 (Dec. 1987) (internal citations omitted).

193 "In code reading by stepwise abstraction, a person identifies prime subprograms in the software, determines their functions, and composes these functions to determine a function for the entire program. The code reader then compares this derived function and the specifications (the intended function)." Basili & Selby, Comparing the Effectiveness of Software Testing Strategies, SE-13(12) IEEE Transactions on Software Engineering 1278–96 (Dec. 1987) (internal citations omitted).

194 "In structural testing, which is a 'white-box' approach, a programmer inspects the source code and then devises and executes test cases based on the percentage of the program's statements or expressions executed (the 'test set coverage')." Basili & Selby, Comparing the Effectiveness of Software Testing Strategies, SE-13(12) IEEE Transactions on Software Engineering 1278–96 (Dec. 1987) (internal citations omitted).

195 Examples of white-box software include TBrun™, made by LDRA, and WebKing™, made by ParaSoft.

196 Examples of black-box software include eggplant™, made by TestPlant; TBrun™, made by LDRA; and WebKing™, made by ParaSoft.

197 Control flow testing means that different paths according to the control flow of the component are tested. A representation that is often used for the control flow of a component is a flow graph, which abstracts the execution of the component into a graph-like structure. Toroi, Jäntti, et al., How to Test Software (University of Kuopio 2002). The purpose of control flow testing is to ensure that the JUT behaves as specified by the finite state machine (FSM) representation of the protocol. Zhou, A New Approach to Generating and Selecting Test Sequences for Conformance Testing, (Dissertation, The University of British Columbia, 1992).

data flow testing,[198] branch testing,[199] statement coverage,[200] and condition coverage.[201]

Black-box methods, or techniques, serve primarily as a validation technique that determines if the software meets the customer needs. Black-box testing methods, or techniques, are derived from the design, or specifications, of the software program itself.[202] Black-box testing presumes the software program is a "black box" where the inner workings of the software program are unknown. Examples of black-box testing are functional testing,[203] equivalence partitioning,[204] cause-effect,[205] and robustness testing.[206]

---

[198] Data flow testing methods explore the events related to the status of variables during component's execution. See Toroi, Jäntti, et al., How to Test Software (University of Kuopio 2002); Frankl & Weyuker, An Applicable Family of Data Flow Testing Criteria, 14(10) IEEE Transactions on Software Engineering 1483–98 (Oct. 1988).

[199] Branch testing is a structural strategy which asks that each branch (transfer of control) in the program be exercised. Ntafos, "An Evaluation of Required Element Testing Strategies," in Proceedings of the 7th International IEEE Conference on Software Engineering 250–56 (Mar. 1984).

[200] Statement coverage testing requires that each statement is executed at least once in the testing process. See Toroi, Jäntti, et al., How to Test Software (University of Kuopio 2002); Frankl & Weyuker, An Applicable Family of Data Flow Testing Criteria, 14(10) IEEE Transactions on Software Engineering 1483–98 (Oct. 1988); Netisopakul, White, et al., "Data Coverage Testing of Programs for Container Classes," in Proceedings of the 13th International IEEE Symposium on Software Reliability Engineering 183–94 (2002).

[201] Condition coverage testing requires that each statement is executed at least once and each condition in a decision takes on all possible outcomes at least once. See Toroi, Jäntti, et al., How to Test Software (University of Kuopio 2002); Frankl & Weyuker, An Applicable Family of Data Flow Testing Criteria, 14(10) IEEE Transactions on Software Engineering 1483–98 (Oct. 1988). Complete condition coverage does not necessarily imply complete branch coverage. Toroi, Jäntti, et al., How to Test Software (University of Kuopio 2002); Frankl & Weyuker, An Applicable Family of Data Flow Testing Criteria, 14(10) IEEE Transactions on Software Engineering 1483–98 (Oct. 1988). Condition coverage testing is a family of testing techniques that are based on the logical flow of control through a program. Offutt & Voas, Subsumption of Condition Coverage Techniques by Mutation Testing, ISSE-TR-96–01 (Jan. 1996).

[202] Black-box testing tools are mainly record and playback tools. These tools are used for regression testing to check whether new build has created any bug in previous working application functionality. These record and playback tools record test cases in the form of scripts like TSL, VB script, JavaScript, and Perl.

[203] Howden, Theory and Practice of Functional Testing, 2(5) IEEE Software 6–17 (1985).

[204] The basic assumption of equivalence partitioning is that if the program functions correctly for one test case selected from an equivalence class, then it will function correctly for any case from the equivalence class. Teasley, Leventhal, et al., Why Software Testing Is Sometimes Ineffective: Two Applied Studies of Positive Test Strategy, 79(1) Journal of Applied Psychology 142 (1994); *see also* Kaner & Padmanabhan, "Practice and Transfer of Learning in the Teaching of Software Testing," in 20th Conference on Software Engineering Education & Training 157–66 (July 2007).

[205] Cause-effect testing is a test methodology that explores all the combinations of input conditions; in practice, however, the complexity of the method and the large test suite it requires mean it is difficult to be applied for most projects. See Liu and Kuan Tan, Covering Code Behavior on Input Validation in Functional Testing, 51(2) Information and Software Technology 546–53 (2009).

[206] Robustness testing is a testing methodology to detect the vulnerabilities of a component under unexpected inputs or in a stressful environment. Lei, Li, et al., Robustness Testing for Software Components, Robustness Testing for Software Components, 75(10) Science of Computer Programming 879–97 (Oct. 1, 2010).

2. ***Example: Demonstrating Differences Between White-Box and Black-Box Testing***
   Below we look at data flow testing, a white-box method, and functional testing, a black-box method, to demonstrate the differences between white-box and black-box methods.

   *Data flow testing example*: Data flow testing is a white-box testing technique, which focuses on detecting the misuse of data value, generally arising from software coding errors made by the software developers. For example, a software developer for a nuclear reactor control module might create a software variable without ever defining it, or the software developer might define a variable in the emergency shutdown module but fail to initialize the variable before using the variable. Example of this in Java is as follows:

```
    // declare a variable called "shutdownvalue"
    int shutdownvalue;
    // check to see value of the variable and if it
equals 1000
    if (shutdownvalue == 1000)&lcub;
    // shutdown the nuclear reactor
    shutdownreactor();
    &rcub;};
```

   In the above example, *shutdownvalue* has been declared with a data type of "int," but the programmer did not initialize it or give it a value, which means it will not call *shutdownreactor*. Data flow testing traces the sequences of events related to a specific data item with the objective to detect incorrect sequences, as shown in the above example.[207]

   *Functional test example:* Functional testing is a type of black-box testing that utilizes test cases derived from the software specifications being tested. The testing team evaluates functions by providing them input and reviewing the output to ensure the application is operating as proposed. The objective is to validate the software program against the design documents and usually follows five steps:

   1. Identify core functions the software is performing.
   2. Provide input based on the parameters of the function.
   3. Establish the output that function will provide.
   4. Perform the test.
   5. Compare the output with the expected outputs.
      Functional testing focuses on ensuring that the computer software meets the requisite performance and efficiency needs as set forth by the

[207] Data flow testing can be enhanced by using data flow graph tools, which generates graphical representations of the sequences of events related to a variable of interest.

consumers of the computer software.[208] For example, a software team has delivered a complex car navigation system, and the software QA team assigns an individual to functionally test the address book application. This individual would then perform a series of checks that include, create, save, and edit addresses. In our example, the functional testing focuses on the functionality of the address book component of the car navigation software. The actual nuts and bolts of the address book component and the car navigation software itself are not considered, meaning the functional tests affirm that the address book software does what the users expect it to do—create, edit, and save addresses.

C. **The Resolution of Bugs, or Errors, Identified During the Software Testing Is Referred to as Software Debugging**
Irrespective of the software method being deployed, when performing the act of software testing, a tester is seeking to remedy errors or bugs. This act is known as "debugging."[209] Debugging is the art of identifying, locating, and remedying bugs or errors in computer software code or hardware devices. The general steps applied when debugging software programs are (1) defining the problem or error, (2) isolating the source of the problem, (3) remedying the problem, and (4) confirming resolution of the problem. When a developer or software QA engineer applies one of the software test methods discussed in this section and identifies a bug or error, they are debugging the software program.[210]

In conclusion, software testing should be performed throughout the lifetime of the software program. Good software testing practices increase maintainability of software by guarding against any regressions during the addition of new functionality or changes to existing functionality. Moreover, software testing is a critical and central component to the software development process and should not be overlooked.

---

[208] Functional testing varies from system testing, as system testing focuses on testing against the user requirements, where functional testing a software program focuses on testing against written computer software design documents or written specifications. Howden, Theory and Practice of Functional Testing, 2(5) IEEE Software 6–17 (1985).

[209] "Debugging is a two-step process that begins when you find an error as a result of a successful test case. Step 1 is the determination of the exact nature and location of the suspected error within the program. Step 2 consists of fixing the error." Myers, Sandler & Badgett, The Art of Software Testing, 112 (Wiley 2011).

[210] Debugging is only as effective as the process and the engineers driving the process, but it is a critical process when developing new software or hardware. Individuals that are debugging software have access to a suite of debugging tools, which assist in identifying software code errors. These debugging tools are sometimes incorporated into the programming language themselves.

# Chapter 3
# The Internet

## 3.1 Introduction

> The Internet is the first thing that humanity has built that humanity doesn't understand, the largest experiment in anarchy that we have ever had.—Eric Schmidt, Executive Chairman of Google

What is the Internet? The Internet is a global network connection of computers.[1] It is a public network, neither controlled nor owned by any single person or entity.[2] There is no central storage location of information transmitted via the Internet, nor is there a universal channel of communication.[3] Instead, each separate computer or network "independently … exchange[s] communications and information with other computers."[4] Essentially, it is "a vast collection of computer networks which form and act as a single huge network for transport of data and messages … ."[5]

---

[1] See Inset Systems, Inc. v. Instruction Set, Inc., 937 F. Supp. 161, 163, 155 A.L.R. Fed. 745 (D. Conn. 1996) ("[t]he Internet is a global communications network linked principally by modems which transmit electronic data over telephone lines. Worldwide there are approximately 20 to 30 million users of the Internet."); Dibbell, "The Shadow Web," 306(3) Scientific American, at 60–65.

[2] Krasovec, Cyberspace: The Final Frontier, for Regulation?, 31 Akron L. Rev. 101, 103 (1997); McIvor, McHugh, & Cadden, Internet Technologies: Supporting Transparency in the Public Sector, 15(3) International Journal of Public Sector Management 170–87 (2002).

[3] Remondino & Chen, 35 Years of Internet, 10 Years of ISPRS Online, available at http://www.isprs.org/proceedings/XXXV/congress/comm6/papers/690.pdf (last visited April 8, 2013).

[4] Remondino & Chen, 35 Years of Internet, 10 Years of ISPRS Online, available at http://www.isprs.org/proceedings/XXXV/congress/comm6/papers/690.pdf (last visited April 8, 2013). *See also* Dem, The Internet Guide for New Users (1994); Gromov, The Roads and Crossroads of Internet History: Internet History with a Human Face (1995, updated 1998, 2005, 2012), available at http://www.internetvalley.com/intval.html (last accessed Apr. 8, 2013).

[5] See Slater III, Internet History and Growth, Internet Society (PowerPoint presentation 2002), available at http://www.internetsociety.org/sites/default/files/2002_0918_Internet_History_and_Growth.ppt (Sept. 2002); Brian, Media Technology and Society: A History from the Telegraph to



D. B. Garrie et al., *Uncovering Digital Evidence*,
https://doi.org/10.1007/978-3-031-68118-9_3

The Internet comprises a "unique … medium of worldwide human communication."[6] To understand the Internet, we begin with an abbreviated history that reflects the tandem developments in networking, the World Wide Web, and email. Next, we will examine the infrastructure underlying the Internet, with particular focus on its physical design, devices for routing information over the Internet, and how both the design and devices work together to enable Internet connectivity. Then, we discuss how the Internet is managed and controlled globally and within different countries. Next, we discuss how data moves across the Internet via software known as protocols and includes detailed examples of how these protocols impact email and web pages. Finally, there are two important appendices to this chapter. The first focuses on Internet tracking technologies and reviews the growing number of ways and means to track an individual's use of the Internet on their home, work, and mobile devices. The second provides an in-depth explanation of Voice Over Internet Protocol (VoIP), the means by which users can make telephone calls over the Internet instead of using a cellular or landline.

## 3.2 History of the Internet

Sixty years ago, communication between New York and Shanghai would have taken months, if the post mail worked at all.[7] Today, it takes seconds to communicate over immense distances with little or even no cost.[8]

### *Internet Network*

The Internet was originally created for the Department of Defense ("DOD") in 1969,[9] as an experimental project of the Advanced Research Project Agency ("ARPA").[10] The DOD funded this project for the purpose of building a redundant

---

the Internet (1998); Hauben, Netizens: On the History and Impact of Usenet and the Internet (Wiley-IEEE Computer Society Press 1997).

[6] See also Leiner, et al., A Brief History of the Internet, 39(5) Computer Communication Review 22 (2009); Krasovec, Cyberspace: The Final Frontier, for Regulation?, 31 Akron L. Rev. 101, 103 (1997).

[7] Christensen, 32(3) Review of the History of Information Security: A Comprehensive Handbook 284–94 (de Leeuw & Bergstra, ed. 2008).

[8] Rao & Reiley, The Economics of Spam, 26(3) The Journal of Economic Perspectives 87–110 (2012). According to Rao & Reiley, the cost to send SPAM is no more than of $0.0001 per message.

[9] See, e.g., Segaller, Nerds 2.0.1: A Brief History of the Internet (1998); Hafner, Where Wizards Stay Up Late: The Origins of The Internet (1998).

[10] See Salus, The Net: A Brief History of Origins, 38 Jurimetrics 161, 161–167 (1998) (for a brief history of the Advanced Research Project Agency's role in creating the Internet). ARPA was renamed the Defense Advanced Research Projects Agency (DARPA) in 1972.

communications network.[11] The network was known as the Advanced Research Project Agency Network ("ARPANET"),[12] and it provided a series of redundant telephone lines between the DOD, defense contractors, and defense research universities.[13] Subsequently, ARPANET expanded to encompass corporations, universities, and, lastly, the general public. "ARPANET" came to be called the "DARPA Internet" and, finally, just the "Internet."[14] Since its creation in the late 1960s, the Internet continued to evolve through the efforts of a relatively small network of individuals,[15] which expanded it to government and research universities through the use of local-area networks.[16]

This widespread implementation of local-area networks and personal computers helped the Internet establish itself as a new means of communication.[17] In 1980, the now common protocol Transmission Communication Protocol/Internet Protocol (TCP/IP) was adopted.[18] TCP/IP is important because it standardized the way computers communicated to each other. This combination of a hardware platform and a software platform allowed the Internet to grow from a research exchange to the community and commercial center we know today.[19]

---

[11] Abbate, Inventing the Internet 37 (MIT Press 2000).

[12] See American Civil Liberties Union v. Reno, 929 F. Supp. 824, 831 (E.D. Pa. 1996), judgment aff'd, 521 U.S. 844, (offering a succinct history of the Internet).

[13] See Antolin-Jenkins, Defining the Parameters of Cyberwar Operations: Looking for Law in All the Wrong Places?, 51 Naval L. Rev. 132, 135–36 (2005). "[N]ow internet communications travel through all available communication mediums: telephone lines, microwave relays, satellite uplinks and downlinks, fiber optic cables." Antolin-Jenkins, 51 Naval L. Rev. at 135–36. See, e.g., Cate, Privacy in the Information Age 9–11 (1997); Salus, 38 Jurimetrics at 163 (the defense research universities included the University of California Los Angeles, Stanford, University of California Santa Barbara, and the University of Utah).

[14] Reno, 929 F. Supp. at 831.

[15] See generally Leiner, Cerf, et al., The Past and Future History of the Internet, 40(2) Communications of the ACM 102–108 (Feb. 1997).

[16] 40(2) Communications of the ACM at 104.

[17] Ibid, 102–108.

[18] Ibid. See §3:5 on Protocols infra for more information.

[19] Segal, A Short History of Internet Protocols at CERN (CERN IT-PDP-TE, April 1995), available at http://ben.home.cern.ch/ben/TCPHIST.html (last accessed Apr. 8, 2013); 40(2) Communications of the ACM at 102–108.

## *The World Wide Web Revolutionizes Public Interaction with the Internet*

In 1990, Tim Berners-Lee, a researcher at the European Organization for Nuclear Research (CERN),[20] created "a WWW browser-editor which read Hypertext Markup Language (HTML) documents from Uniform Resource Locator (URL) addresses."[21] This invention sparked a widespread ability for users to easily interact with the Internet over a standardized means. In 1993, this became known as the World Wide Web ("WWW").

Today, the WWW is one of the most used Internet services.[22] The WWW allows users to access electronic data, via a web browser, in the form of web pages that are stored on other computers connected to the Internet through a network.[23] Web pages typically "contain text, graphics, pictures, sound, video, [or] other computer software that is used to create special effects for a particular [w]eb page."[24] Internet users have the ability to view web pages "no matter where in the world [the] [w]eb page is located."[25]

---

[20] Remondino & Chen, 35 Years of Internet, 10 Years of ISPRS Online, available at http://www.isprs.org/proceedings/XXXV/congress/comm6/papers/690.pdf (last accessed Apr. 8, 2013); Hughes, Entering the World-Wide Web: A Guide to Cyberspace (Honolulu Community College Oct. 1993), available at http://info.eps.surrey.ac.uk/SCS/manuals/WWW-Guide/ (last accessed June 18, 2013).

[21] Ibid.

[22] See American Civil Liberties Union v. Reno, 217 F.3d 162 (3d Cir. 2000), vacated, 535 U.S. 564, 122 S. Ct. 1700, 152 L. Ed. 2d 771 (2002) ("[t]he World Wide Web is a publishing forum consisting of millions of individual "Web sites" each containing information such as text, images, illustrations, video, animation or sounds provided by that site's creator."); Yahoo!, Inc. v. La Ligue Contre Le Racisme et L'Antisemitisme, 169 F. Supp. 2d 1181, 1194 (N.D. Cal. 2001), rev'd on other grounds, 379 F.3d 1120 (9th Cir. 2004), on reh'g en banc, 433 F.3d 1199 (9th Cir. 2006) and rev'd and remanded, 433 F.3d 1199 (9th Cir. 2006) ("[t]he World Wide Web is a publishing forum consisting of millions of individual websites that contain a wide variety of content."); Morrison & Foerster, LLP v. Wick, 94 F. Supp. 2d 1125 (D. Colo. 2000); American Civil Liberties Union v. Gonzales, 478 F. Supp. 2d 775 (E.D. Pa. 2007), order aff'd, 534 F.3d 181 (3d Cir. 2008); Malarkey-Taylor Associates, Inc. v. Cellular Telecommunications Industry Ass'n, 929 F. Supp. 473, 476 n.1 (D.D.C. 1996) ("[t]he World Wide Web is a method for communicating over the Internet that permits the user to locate a document by its address and then jump to other documents that are linked to the first document").

[23] Wille, Personal Jurisdiction and the Internet--Proposed Limits on State Jurisdiction over Data Communications in Tort Cases, 87 KY. L.J. 95, 193 (1999).

[24] Kleinrock, An Early History of the Internet, 48(8) IEEE Communications Magazine 26–36 (2010); see also Leiner, et al., A Brief History of the Internet (2003), available at http://www.internetsociety.org/internet/what-internet/history-internet/brief-history-internet (last visited Apr. 8, 2013).

[25] Kleinrock, An Early History of the Internet, 48(8) IEEE Communications Magazine 26–36 (2010); see also Leiner, et al., A Brief History of the Internet (2003), available at http://www.internetsociety.org/internet/what-internet/history-internet/brief-history-internet (last visited Apr. 8, 2013).

The WWW has evolved from a unidirectional service, with users all accessing a relatively small set of web pages, to what is now known as Web 2.0, where users contribute content to websites in real time that other users can access.[26] Following closely on the heels of Web 2.0 is Web 3.0. While still in the nascent stages, Web 3.0 is loosely defined as Web 2.0 augmented to include semantic tagging of data.[27] In practical terms, this translates to the Internet functioning as a personal assistant. A user might ask "Where can I find Mexican food in New York City?", and the results returned will include a list of restaurants merged with data on where you have been before, what you liked, what you disliked, and your current location.[28]

## *Email Fundamentally Changes Modern Communication*

Early email and instant messaging were employed on timesharing computers in the 1960s. In 1971, Ray Tomlinson created an email application for ARPANET, which is still the baseline model for email applications today.[29] A combination of hardware and software is required to send information across the Internet. From a software perspective, this is done through the use of protocols. One of the early protocols was the *file transfer protocol*, commonly known by its acronym FTP.[30] FTP was created as a reliable and efficient means to transfer files and remotely access computers.[31] FTP was the primary means of transmitting information over the Internet until the advent of *Simple Mail Transfer Protocol*, or SMTP, in the early 1980s. Where FTP focused on sending a single file across the Internet, SMTP is the primary means to send email. As communication over the Internet changed from exchanging commands and files to communicating via email, the SMTP protocol became part of the foundation of the modern Internet. SMTP formed the basis for sending emails as we recognize them today.[32] SMTP remains the standard means to send an email from one computer to another.[33]

---

[26] Examples of this include Wikipedia (http://www.wikipedia.org), photo-sharing websites such as Flickr (http://www.flickr.com), and the layers that users can add on Google Earth that are viewable to other users. For an in-depth review of recent Internet see, Goodchild, Editorial: Citizens as Voluntary Sensors: Spatial Data Infrastructure in the World of Web 2.0, 2 International Journal of Spatial Data Infrastructures Research 24032 (2007).

[27] Hendler, Web 3.0 Emerging, 42(1) Computer 111–13 (2009).

[28] Strickland, How Web 3.0 Will Work (2008), http://www.howstuffworks.com/web-30.htm (last visited Apr. 8, 2013).

[29] Leiner, et al., A Brief History of the Internet, 39(5) Computer Communication Review 22 (2009).

[30] Stevens & Wright, 1 TCP/IP Illustrated: The Protocols (Addison-Wesley Professional 1994).

[31] Postel & Reynolds, File Transfer Protocol (FTP), RFC 959, Internet Engineering Task Force: Network Working Group (Oct. 1985), available at http://tools.ietf.org/html/rfc959 (last visited Apr. 8, 2013).

[32] Leiner, et al., A Brief History of the Internet, 39(5) Computer Communication Review 22 (2009).

[33] Klensin, Simple Mail Transfer Protocol, RFC 5321, Internet Engineering Task Force (Oct. 2008), available at http://tools.ietf.org/html/rfc5321 (last visited Apr. 8, 2013).

Widespread use of email did not begin until the late 1980s, when universities began to connect to the Internet.[34] A few short years later, large Internet service providers (ISPs) such as America Online (AOL) were offering email services to customers using SMTP.[35]

## 3.3 The Design and Hardware of the Internet

This section discusses the physical hardware components that connect computers, devices, cars, phones, etc. to the Internet. As mentioned in the start of this chapter, the Internet is a conglomeration of thousands of independently operating devices.[36]

### *Physical Design of the Internet*

The Internet is an informal hierarchy of network operators divided into three tiers.[37] The first level, or Tier 1, encompasses Internet access providers who connect with one another.[38] The providers interact with each other over large fiber optic lines known as "backbones."[39] Maintained by large telecommunications companies, the

[34] Ray Tomlinson is credited for inventing email. Specifically, he was the first to send messages to users who did not share the same computer. See Crocker, Email History, http://www.livinginternet.com/e/ei.htm (last visited Apr. 8, 2013); Hardy, The Evolution of ARPANET Email, at 11 (May 13, 1996) (unpublished thesis, University of California at Berkeley); Peter, The History of Email, http://www.nethistory.info (last visited Apr. 8, 2013).

[35] Odlyzko, Internet Pricing and the History of Communications, 36(5) Computer Networks 493–517 (2001). See also About AOL: Overview, available at: http://corp.aol.com/about-aol/overview (discussing history and evolution of the company).

[36] "The Internet is not a physical or tangible entity, but rather a giant network which interconnects innumerable smaller groups of linked computer networks. It is thus a network of networks…." CompuServe Inc. v. Cyber Promotions, Inc., 962 F. Supp. 1015, 1018 (S.D. Ohio 1997) (quoting American Civil Liberties Union v. Reno, 929 F. Supp. 824 (E.D. Pa. 1996), judgment aff'd, 521 U.S. 844).

[37] Hoβfeld, Hausheer, et al., An Economic Traffic Management Approach to Enable the Triplewin for Users, ISPs, and Overlay Providers 24–34 (IOS Press Books Online 2009).

[38] See Cohen, Broadband Internet: Access, Regulation and Policy 10 (2007) (AT&T, Verizon, Sprint-Nextel, Level3, and Quest are all Tier 1 service providers that own "backbone" cables).

[39] See Clarke & Knake, Cyber War: The Next Threat to National Security and What To Do About It 281 (2010) (Internet backbones are comprised of national fiber optic cables operated by large Tier 1 Internet Service Providers); see also Hoβfeld, Hausheer, et al., An Economic Traffic Management Approach to Enable the Triplewin for Users, ISPs, and Overlay Providers 24–34 (IOS Press Books Online 2009); Calvert, Doar, & Zegura, Modeling Internet Topology, 35(6) IEEE Communications Magazine 160–163 (1997); Hahn & Wallsten, The Economics of Net Neutrality, 3(6) The Economists' Voice (2006); Valancius, et al., How Many Tiers? Pricing in the Internet Transit Market, 41(4) SIGCOMM-Computer Communication Review 194 (2011).

backbones facilitate the transmission of large amounts of data simultaneously to various regions.[40] The backbones are then connected internationally to network access points ("NAPs"). The NAPs are the gateways through which international Internet traffic flows: "each individual entity, whether a government entity, a communications company, or a corporation with a large intranet, agrees to intercommunicate with one another through the NAPs."[41]

While the Tier 1 backbones span the globe, they do not go to all the major cities in the world. Tier 1 networks connect at NAPs. These connection points are both costly and not available to the ordinary consumer.[42] Tier 1 providers do not charge one another to interconnect.

The second level, or Tier 2, consists of substantial Internet service providers (ISPs) that generally have their own smaller networks that are limited to a specific geographical region. Tier 2 providers rely partially on Tier 1 companies to deliver worldwide access, which Tier 2 providers obtain by buying some level of traffic using a transit agreement. The price point varies based on the traffic rules that are in place, which in turn means price can vary based on different criteria such as amount of inbound traffic or the difference between inbound and outbound traffic.[43]

The third and final level, Tier 3, constitutes all ISPs that are solely resellers of Internet access services. They rely on interconnection agreements with Tier 2 providers to gain access to the Internet. Generally, Tier 3 providers are more localized—the Tier 3 ISPs are purely resellers of Internet access services.[44] An end user can purchase services from an ISP, which sits on any of the tiers, although it is less common to purchase directly from a Tier 1 provider.[45]

---

[40] See Cohen, Broadband Internet: Access, Regulation and Policy 10 (2007).

[41] Antolin-Jenkins, Defining the Parameters of Cyberwar Operations: Looking for Law in All the Wrong Places, 51 Naval L. Rev. 132 (2005).

[42] "To facilitate the transition, NSF designated four regional aggregation points, called network access points (NAPs), where private carriers could interconnect their back-bone networks to create a fully compatible nationwide data network." Townsend, The Internet and the Rise of the New Network Cities, 1969–1999, 28(1) Environment and Planning B 39–58 (2001).

[43] See Reynolds, Mitchell, et al., Economic Study on IP Interworking [White paper] (Mar. 2007).

[44] "Tier 3 ISPs are purely resellers of internet access services." Reynolds, Mitchell, et al., Economic Study on IP Interworking [White paper] (Mar. 2007).

[45] For an in-depth discussion of Internet Service Provider topology and price see, Reynolds, Mitchell, et al., Economic Study on IP Interworking, [White paper] (Mar. 2007).

## *Physical Devices for Routing Information over the Internet*

The tiers discussed above form the foundation for the Internet. Actual data is transmitted over this structure through the use of routers, which facilitate the transmission of data packets over the Internet.[46] The router receives and forwards packets through the subnetworks (the tiers discussed above) and autonomous systems that constitute the Internet.[47]

The Internet consists of a large number of autonomous regions of administrative control (a.k.a. autonomous systems or routing domains).[48] These routing domains usually consist of a network service provider, large company, or organizational unit.[49] Each of these routing domains interconnects a series of subnetworks; they use a distinct routing policy that connects to one or more remote routing domains at neutral, private, or public exchange points.[50]

A router makes routing decisions based on its knowledge of the "topology," the conditions on the network, and routing policies as specified by network administrators within their domain.[51] To do this, routers exchange path and topology information primarily using two special purpose routing protocols:[52] (i) an inter-domain (or exterior) routing protocol used to exchange information between peer routers in different autonomous systems[53] and (ii) an intra-domain (or interior) routing protocol, which passes information between routers within a routing domain.[54]

---

[46] Song & Perrig, "Advanced and Authenticated Marking Schemes for IP Traceback," in 2 Proceedings of Twentieth Annual Joint Conference of the IEEE Computer and Communications Societies 878–886 (2001).

[47] Yau, Lui, et al., Defending Against Distributed Denial-Of-Service Attacks with Max-Min Fair Server-Centric Router Throttles, 13(1) IEEE/ACM Transactions on Networking (TON) 29–42 (Feb. 2005).

[48] Labovitz, Malan & Jahanian, Internet Routing Instability, 27(4) ACM SIGCOMM Computer Communication Review 115–26 (Oct. 1997).

[49] Paxson, End-To-End Routing Behavior in the Internet, 26(4) ACM SIGCOMM Computer Communication Review 25–38 (Aug. 1996).

[50] Labovitz, Ahuja, et al., Delayed Internet Routing Convergence, 30(4) ACM SIGCOMM Computer Communication Review 175–87 (Aug. 2000).

[51] Petersen & Aase, A Comparison of Picking, Storage, and Routing Policies in Manual Order Picking, 92(1) International Journal of Production Economics 11–19 (Nov. 8, 2004).

[52] Petersen & Aase, A Comparison of Picking, Storage, and Routing Policies in Manual Order Picking, 92(1) International Journal of Production Economics 11–19 (Nov. 8, 2004).

[53] Fuller, Yu & Varadhan, Classless Inter-Domain Routing (CIDR): An Address Assignment and Aggregation Strategy, RFC 1519, 1993 RFC Editor, available at http://www.ietf.org/rfc/rfc1519.txt (last visited Apr. 9, 2013).

[54] Faloutsos, Banerjea & Pankaj, QoSMIC: A Quality of Service Sensitive Multicast Internet Protocol, 28(4) ACM SIGCOMM Computer Communication Review 144–53 (Oct. 1998).

Each router, in turn, connects to multiple other routers, forming a large interwoven communications network that offers multiple communication paths to the same point.[55] For example, if David in Seattle, Washington, sends a message to his friend Mary in Tel Aviv, Israel, the message should traverse the shortest path between David and Mary.[56] However, if the entire Pacific Northwest experiences a power outage, and the Internet backbones in every state from Washington to Arizona go down, then David's message would be rerouted to nodes that still operate, thereby demonstrating the redundant and resilient nature of the Internet. The example also illustrates the decentralized and interconnected nature of the Internet.[57] This interwoven design provides data packets with redundant pathways, or alternative routes, which mitigates the impact if a router goes down.[58]

## *The Evolving Technology of Internet Connectivity*

Depending on geographic location and available technology, Internet connectivity is achieved through a variety of different media. These include analog dial-up; ISDN (integrated services digital network) dial-up; dedicated lines, including DSL,

---

[55] See Iannaccone, Gianluca, et al., Feasibility of IP Restoration in a Tier 1 Backbone, 18(2) IEEE Network 13–19 (2004); Labovitz, Ahuja, et al, "Experimental Study of Internet Stability and Backbone Failures," in IEEE Twenty-Ninth Annual International Symposium on Fault-Tolerant Computing 278–85 (1999).

[56] However, if an ISP goes down, it can present huge problems for the Internet and while rare, it does happen. For example, in April 25, 1997, a misconfigured router maintained by a small Virginia service provider injected an incorrect routing map into the global Internet, indicating that the network provided optimal connectivity to all Internet destinations. Fraleigh, Moon, et al., Packet-Level Traffic Measurements from the Sprint IP Backbone, 17(6) IEEE Network 6–16 (Nov.-Dec. 2003). The Internet providers that relied on this map diverted their traffic to the Virginia provider, creating a gigantic log jam that grounded the major Internet backbones to a halt for nearly 2 hours. While this problem is unlikely to repeat today because of additional controls and routing technology, it is still possible that if the backbone goes down, the Internet would likely grind to a halt.

[57] The Internet is a decentralized, self-maintained networking system that links computers and computer networks around the world and is capable of quickly transmitting communications. See American Libraries Ass'n v. Pataki, 969 F. Supp. 160, 164 (S.D. N.Y. 1997); American Civil Liberties Union v. Reno, 31 F. Supp. 2d 473, 481 (E.D. Pa. 1999), aff'd, 217 F.3d 162 (3d Cir. 2000), vacated, 535 U.S. 564, ("Reno III").

[58] See Labovitz, Ahuja, et al, "Experimental Study of Internet Stability and Backbone Failures," in IEEE Twenty-Ninth Annual International Symposium on Fault-Tolerant Computing 278–85 (1999).

cable, fiber optic, and local-area networks (LANs); cellular wireless;[59] WiMax wireless;[60] and satellite.

Analog dial-up was the most common way to connect to the Internet in the USA when the Internet first began gaining widespread usage in the early 1990s.[61] Analog dial-up uses a telephone line, modem, and software to manage the connection.[62] A traditional telephone line (or "landline") uses an analog signal, while a computer operates digitally. A modem translates between these two asynchronous systems.

From its beginning, the entire telephone line system was analog. Over time, however, telephone companies began to upgrade their *trunk lines*, the lines that connected each of the central telephone offices. Today, the only analog telephone lines are those that run from an end user to the central office, and oftentimes these have been upgraded to digital, as well.[63] A modem translates data between analog and digital, and vice-versa, when sending data, to allow computers to talk to one another over the Internet.[64] The software on this system acts as the intermediary between the Internet service provider (ISP) and the computer.[65] This includes prompting the user for a username and password, as well as providing an interface, such as a web

---

[59] "A cellular phone operates as a two-way radio that transmits and receives signals throughout a cellular network. The design of a cellular network is divided into 'geographic coverage areas called 'cells,'" arranged in the pattern of a hexagonal grid or honeycomb. The point where three cells meet is called the cell site (or cell tower). The number of antennas operating on the cell site, the height of the antennas, topography of the surrounding land, and obstructions (both natural and man-made) determine the size of each cell's coverage area. Blank, The Limitations and Admissibility of Using Historical Cellular Site Data to Track the Location of a Cellular Phone, 18 Rich. J.L. & Tech. 3 (2011).

[60] Worldwide Interoperability for Microwave Access, or WiMax, is a wireless standard that can cover large geographic areas. It operates like wireless over radio waves but can cover areas up to 30 miles, compared to a wireless router's cover of around 100 feet. It is comparable to DSL and cable Internet in terms of speed, making it slightly faster than wireless. Faust& Hafner, WiMAX-Accessing Academic Content Wherever Learners and Researchers Locate (2011); Chakraborty & Bhattacharyya, Overview of End-to-End WiMAX Network Architecture," in WiMax Security And Quality Of Service, Ch. 1 (2010).

[61] "In January 1999, 65% of Internet users were using analog dial-up modems with an average speed of access of 33 kbps." Broadband Today, Federal Communications Commission, Staff Report (1999), available at http://www.fcc.gov/Bureaus/Cable/Reports/broadbandtoday.doc

[62] See Ainscough, The Internet for the Rest of Us: Marketing on the World Wide Web, 13(2) Journal of Consumer Marketing 36–47 (1996).

[63] See Comcast Cablevision of Broward County, Inc. v. Broward County, Fla., 124 F. Supp. 2d 685, 687 (S.D. Fla. 2000); Downes, Electronic Communications and the Plain View Exception: More "Bad Physics," 7 Harv. J. L. & Tech. 239 (19931994).

[64] "A modem translates computer text and numeric data into an audio signal that can be passed back and forth" Manning, Plugging in to Computer Bulletin Boards. ERIC Digest" (1986), http://www.ericdigests.org/pre-925/computer.htm (last visited Apr. 16, 2013). "A modem translates analogue information into digital." Carpenter, Analogous: Digital/Analogue Metaphors," Digitalis Newspaper Catalogue (Oct. 2011), available at: http://eprints.gold.ac.uk/6738/1/Ele_Carpenter_Analogous_FINAL.pdf (last visited Apr. 9, 2013).

[65] See Batzel v. Smith, 333 F.3d 1018 (9th Cir. 2003) (describing what kind of entity constitutes an ISP).

browser, to access the Internet. After analog, the evolution of connective technologies has rapidly advanced.

Next came the integrated services digital network, commonly referred to as ISDN,[66] a form of digital dial-up that is much faster than analog dial-up. ISDN requires special equipment at the central telephone office. ISDN allowed for faster Internet speeds, up to 128 Kbps, which is still slow by modern standards. ISDN requires a digital line from end to end.[67]

A digital subscriber line (DSL) connection also uses standard (digital) telephone lines, but special equipment on each end increases the speeds up to 768 Kbps upload speed and approximately 3 Mps download speeds. DSL connections require a special DSL modem and router.[68]

Cable Internet operates over television cable lines[69] and can operate at 10 Mps upload speeds and100+ Mps download speeds.[70] The cable connection operates through the cable line, which then connects to cable modems and routers (for wireless) or an Ethernet connection (for direct wired connection).[71]

Local-area networks (LANs) are typically Ethernet networks that connect multiple computers via Ethernet cables to a centralized router(s).[72]

---

[66] See U S West Communications, Inc. v. Wyoming Public Service Com'n, 989 P.2d 616 (Wyo. 1999) (discussing the nature of ISDN service).

[67] Shelanski, The Speed Gap: Broadband Infrastructure and Electronic Commerce, 14 Berkeley Tech. L.J. 721 (1999) (discussing different forms of connecting infrastructure technology).

[68] Shelanski, 14 Berkeley Tech. L.J. at 725 (discussing different forms of connecting infrastructure technology).

[69] See National Cable & Telecommunications Ass'n v. Brand X Internet Services, 545 U.S. 967, 975, 125 S. Ct. 2688, 162 L. Ed. 2d 820, 32 A.L.R. Fed. 2d 651 (2005) (describing the nature of cable internet and the accompanying technology). See generally Esbin, Internet Over Cable: Defining the Future in Terms of the Past (OPP Working Paper Series), Federal Communications Commission (Aug. 1998), available at http://transition.fcc.gov/Bureaus/OPP/working_papers/oppwp30.pdf (last visited Apr. 9, 2013) (describing the assent of cable Internet service over prior forms of connectivity).

[70] Horrigan, Home Broadband Adoption 2006 (Pew/Internet & American Life Project 1 (May 28, 2006), available at http://www.pewinternet.org/Reports/2006/Home-Broadband-Adoption-2006.aspx (last visited Apr. 9, 2013); Press Release, Neilsen//Netratings, Two-Thirds of Active U.S. Web Population Using Broadband, Up 28 Percent Year-Over-Year to an All-Time High (Mar. 14, 2006), available at http://www.nielsennetratings.com/pr/pr_060314.pdf (last visited Apr. 9, 2013); Organisation for Economic Co-operation & Development, OECD Broadband Statistics to June 2006 (2006), http://www.oecd.org/internet/broadband/oecdbroadbandstatisticstodecember2006.htm; see Committee on Broadband Last Mile Technology, Computer Science and Telecommunications Board, National Research Council, Broadband: Bringing Home The Bits ch. 3 (The National Academies Press 2002), available at http://www.nap.edu/openbook.php?record_id=10235&page=82; Crawford, Internet Think, 5 J. on Telecomm. & High Tech. L. 467 (2006); see also National Cable & Telecommunications Ass'n v. Brand X Internet Services, 545 U.S. 967, 125 S. Ct. 2688, 162 L. Ed. 2d 820, 32 A.L.R. Fed. 2d 651 (2005).

[71] See Lemley & Lessig, End of End-to-End: Preserving the Architecture of the Internet in the Broadband Era, 48 UCLA L. Rev. 925 (Apr. 2001).

[72] See Bell Communications Research, Inc. v. Vitalink Communications Corp., 55 F.3d 615, 616 (Fed. Cir. 1995) (describing how LAN operate). See also Kueser, This LAN Is My LAN, This LAN

Wireless networks connect end users to the Internet in a variety of ways. Wireless routers convert signals from a cable Internet connection to local devices under the IEEE 802.11 wireless Ethernet standard.[73] Bluetooth technology and Infrared Data Association (IrDa) protocol are also commonly used wireless networks.[74]

Cellular networks are networks provided by cellular providers.[75] This service has gone through iterations of speed, including 3G, 4G, and LTE-Advance most recently.[76] Chapter 5 provides more information on these networks.

## 3.4 Controlling Physical Access to the Internet

The Internet is comprised of a series of decentralized networks, such that "[n]o single entity—academic, corporate, governmental, or non-profit—administers the Internet."[77] It was designed to be decentralized, so that a message could be rerouted if one or more networks were damaged or unavailable.[78] "This redundant system of linked computers was designed to allow vital research and communications to continue even if portions of the network were damaged, say, in war."[79]

Viewed from a network perspective, the Internet is a "giant network which interconnects innumerable smaller groups or linked computer networks. It is thus a network of networks."[80] This means that an outside actor is able to control the Internet only to the extent it can control the ISPs.[81] Today, a country can utilize various

Is Your LAN: The Case for Extending Private Property Rights to Wireless Local Area Networks, 72 UMKC L. Rev. 787 (2003–2004).

[73] *See* In the Matter of Appropriate Regulatory Treatment for Broadband Access to the Internet Over Wireless Networks, 22 F.C.C.R. 5901, 2007 WL 1288052 (F.C.C. 2007). See generally Broadcom Corp. v. Qualcomm Inc., 543 F.3d 683 (Fed. Cir. 2008); NTP, Inc. v. Research In Motion, Ltd., 418 F.3d 1282 (Fed. Cir. 2005) (discussing the use of wireless technology).

[74] See generally Madni, "Bluetooth Technology for Next Generation," in 10th Research Seminar Series Workshop, School of Engineering, Design & Technology, University of Bradford (Apr. 13, 2011).

[75] See Chap. 5 for more information on cellular network advancements.

[76] See Chap. 5 for more information on cellular network advancements.

[77] American Civil Liberties Union v. Reno, 929 F. Supp. 824, 832 (E.D. Pa. 1996), judgment aff'd, 521 U.S. 844.

[78] Reno, 929 F. Supp. at 831.

[79] 929 F. Supp. at 831.

[80] 929 F. Supp. at 830. Because the Internet is comprised of several networks, a user must connect to an Internet service provider (ISP) to access the Internet. See Antolin-Jenkins, 51 Naval L. Rev. at 136 ("By connecting to the ISP, the computer becomes part of the network, and it may be utilized in the process of sending messages.").

[81] See generally IANA, Internet Assigned Numbers Authority, http://www.iana.org/; ICANN, The Internet Corporation for Assigned Names and Number, http://www.icann.org/; ISC, Internet Software Consortium, http://www.isc.org/; Zittrain & Edelman, Internet Filtering in China, 7(2) IEEE Internet Computing 70–77 (Mar.-Apr. 2003); Chadwick & May, Interaction Between States

mechanisms to turn the Internet "off" ranging from turning off the power to backbone routers to altering the routing tables, but with the widespread use of mobile devices, it is much more difficult to control access to the information that is transmitted over the Internet.[82]

However, many countries manage to maintain control of the Internet through a variety of more advanced means. For example, during the revolution in Egypt in 2011, officials were able to effectively shut off the Internet because a single entity, TeleCom Egypt, was the only portal for ISPs to connect to the Internet in and out of the country.[83] Further, there were only ten ISPs operating in Egypt at the time, allowing government officials to force an expeditious shutdown.[84]

China has a more complex system in place for monitoring, blocking, and shutting down the Internet.[85] Unlike Egypt, China maintains an ongoing infrastructure with the sole purpose of monitoring Internet use and blocking individual sites deemed unfavorable.[86] This allows Chinese officials to monitor individual users and websites and block only the material they deem inappropriate, instead of shutting down the entire Internet.[87]

---

and Citizens in the Age of the Internet: "e-Government" in the United States, Britain, and the European Union, 16(2) Governance 271–300 (2003).

[82] See generally Yook, Jeong, & Barabasi, 2001: Modeling the Internet's Large-Scale Topology, available at http://arxiv.org/abs/condmat/0107417

[83] PBS Newshour, Transcript (Feb. 16, 2011), available at http://www.pbs.org/newshour/bb/world/jan-june11/egypt2_02-16.html

[84] PBS Newshour, Transcript (Feb. 16, 2011), available at http://www.pbs.org/newshour/bb/world/jan-june11/egypt2_02-16.html

[85] Khazan, What it's like to use the internet in China, Worldviews (Nov. 8, 2012 10:58 a.m.), available at http://www.washingtonpost.com/blogs/worldviews/wp/2012/11/08/what-its-like-to-use--the-internet-in-china/ (last visited July 17, 2013).

[86] Bradsher, China Toughens Its Restrictions on Use of the Internet, N.Y. Times, Dec. 28, 2012, available at http://www.nytimes.com/2012/12/29/world/asia/china-toughens-restrictions-on-internet-use.html (last visited July 17, 2013).

[87] Shirky, The Political Power of Social Media: Technology, the Public Sphere, and Political Change, 90 Foreign Aff. 28 (2011); Sklerov, Solving the Dilemma of Sate Responses to Cyberattacks: A Justification for the Use of Active Defenses against States Who Neglect Their Duty to Prevent, 201 Mil. L. Rev. 1 (2009); Liang & Lu, Internet Development, Censorship, and Cyber Crimes in China, 26 Journal of Contemporary Criminal Justice 103 (2010); Rashid, "Bahrain Restricts Internet Traffic, Blocks YouTube in Crackdown on Protests," eWeek Mobile, February 18, 2011, available at http://www.eweek.com/c/a/Security/Bahrain-Restricts-Internet-Traffic-Blocks-YouTube-in-Crackdown-on-Protests-386152/ (last visited Apr.9, 2013).

## 3.5 Protocols: The Software That Runs the Internet

The more than one billion devices communicating over the Internet do so through the use of a shared set of protocols that functions as a universal language.[88] A protocol is a uniform set of rules that governs the way users communicate and the way machines treat data. These standards enable two devices to connect and transmit data to one another—they define how data is transmitted between computing devices and over networks.[89] Internet protocols include TCP/IP (Transfer Control Protocol/ Internet Protocol), HTTP (Hypertext Transfer Protocol), FTP (File Transfer Protocol), and SMTP (Simple Mail Transfer Protocol), among many others.

Each protocol acts like a conveyor belt carrying a packet of information from one point to another, with each protocol performing a different operation on the data. As the Supreme Court well-described in *Reno v. ACLU*:[90]

> Any message or file to be transmitted is broken into smaller pieces, called packets. Each packet contains the Internet Protocol (IP) address of the destination … a small portion of data from the original document, and an indication of the data's place in the original document. The packets are routed along the web-like network of interconnected computers. Not all packets from the same transmission necessarily follow the same path. Along the way, computers called routers determine the shortest-in-time route for each packet from source to destination. Each packet therefore takes a stepping-stone path through the network of connected computers, subject to re-routing along the way if there is congestion, an outage, or any other error in any part of the path. At the destination computer, the packets are reassembled according to instructions they contain into the original file or message. If any packets are missing, the destination computer may request they be resent from the source computer.

Thus, each protocol has a specific job to perform on the transmitted data before that data is handed off to the next protocol. For example, after one drafts an email and presses send, protocols are tasked with taking the binary 1s and 0s comprising the message and splitting them into small packets of data. Another protocol assigns an address to the packets. A separate protocol transmits those packets. Then, on the receiving end, the packets are reassembled into the correct sequence and displayed as an incoming email message.

These protocols are housed in a larger abstraction often referred to as the TCP/IP model. This model uses four abstraction layers, each having their own distinct protocols.[91] These four abstraction layers in ascending order are as follows: (1) the network layer, (2) the Internet layer (where IP sits), (3) the transport layer (where

---

[88] "Internet communication relies on … a set of standard operating and transmission protocols that structure the Internet's operation." In re DoubleClick Inc. Privacy Litigation, 154 F. Supp. 2d 497, 501 (S.D. N.Y. 2001).

[89] White, Data Communications and Computer Networks: A Business User's Approach (Course Technology 2010).

[90] Reno v. American Civil Liberties Union, 521 U.S. 844, 849, (internal quotations and citations omitted).

[91] See Information technology–Open Systems Interconnection–Basic Reference Model: The Basic Model, ISO/IEC 7498–1 (June 15, 1996), available at http://standards.iso.org/ittf/

TCP sits), and (4) the application layer.[92] The "layers" of the TCP/IP model at the top (the application and transport layers) are logically closer to the user application, while those near the bottom (the network and Internet layers) are logically closer to the physical transmission of the data (i.e., the network).[93] In practical terms, this means the TCP/IP model insulates users and developers from having to understand the underlying network. Instead, developers can build programs to work on the top application layer, confident that this layer will function with the lower layers automatically.[94]

The application layer manages the assembling of a message or file into smaller packets that are transmitted over the Internet and received by the transport layer that reassembles the packets into the original message.[95] The Internet layer handles the address part of each packet so that it gets to the right destination.[96] Each gateway computer on the network checks this address to see where to forward the message.[97] Even though some packets from the same message are routed differently than others, they will be reassembled at the destination in the correct sequence.[98] The network layer determines how data is moved physically across the network.[99]

PubliclyAvailableStandards/s020269_ISO_IEC_7498-1_1994(E).zip (last visited Dec. 14, 2012) (hereinafter "ISO/IEC 7498-1").

[92] See ISO/IEC 7498-1.

[93] "The bottom layers, [...] handle the physical transmission of data." Hsing, Evolutionary Design of Local Area Networks (Master's thesis, Naval Postgraduate School, Monterey Ca. 1996), available at http://www.dtic.mil/cgi-bin/GetTRDoc?Location=U2&doc=GetTRDoc.pdf&AD=ADA318349 (last visited Apr. 13, 2013).

[94] See generally Comer, Internetworking with TCP/IP Vol. 1: Principles, Protocols, and Architecture (4th ed. 2000).

[95] "OSI has both the session layer and the presentation layer, whereas TCP/IP combines them into the application layer." Sicker & Blumensaadt, Misunderstanding the Layered Model(s), 4 J. on Telecomm. & High Tech. L. 299 (2005).

[96] "Finally, the network access layer forms the lowest layer in the TCP/IP model being responsible for transmitting and receiving IP datagrams." Koufopavlou, Tantawy & Zitterbart, "Analysis of TCP/IP for high performance parallel implementations," in Proceedings of the 17th IEEE Conference on Local Computer Networks (1992).

[97] "Every packet is sent first to a 'Gateway Computer,' which is reading the destination address and send the packet to another 'Gateway.'" Simian, Georgiev, & Simian, "A Search Optimization Model in a Network Having Broken Packages," in Proceedings of the 12th WSEAS International Conference on Computers (2008).

[98] "Routers do more than forward packets: they compute checksums, fragment and re-assemble packets." Milgrom, Mitchell, & Srinagesh, Competitive Effects of Internet Peering Policies (MIT Press 2000).

[99] See generally Comer, Internetworking with TCP/IP Vol. 1: Principles, Protocols, and Architecture (4th ed. 2000).

## 3.6 Protocols: The Software That Runs the Internet—Application Layer

The application layer has the higher-level protocols, which are used by most applications for network communication.[100] Some of the more commonly known application layer protocols include the Internet Message Access Protocol (IMAP),[101] a protocol for retrieving email messages, and the Hypertext Transfer Protocol (HTTP),[102] a networking protocol for distributed, collaborative, hypermedia information systems.[103] HTTP acts as a request and response mediator. For example, when one computer requests information from another computer, the HTTP protocol is what mediates that interaction.[104] Data encoded with application layer proto-

---

[100] Stevens, W. Richard, and Gary R. Wright. 1 TCP/IP Illustrated: The Protocols 3 (Addison-Wesley Professional 1994).

[101] "The IMAP service is an application layer protocol which allows a client to access his/her e-mails stored on a remote server over a TCP/IP connection. IMAP stands for Internet Message Access Protocol." Makanju, et al., "Logview: Visualizing Event Log Clusters," in Proceedings of Sixth Annual Conference on Privacy, Security and Trust (Oct. 1–3, 2008).

[102] The Court in *ACLU v. Reno* explained this thusly:

> The Web links together disparate information on an ever growing number of Internet-linked computers by setting common information storage formats (HTML) and a common language for the exchange of Web documents (HTTP). Although the information itself may be in many different formats, and stored on computers which are not otherwise compatible, the basic Web standards provide a basic set of standards which allow communication and exchange of information. Despite the fact that many types of computers are used on the Web, and the fact that many of these machines are otherwise incompatible, those who "publish" information on the Web are able to communicate with those who seek to access information with little difficulty because of these basic technical standards.

929 F. Supp. 824, 837–838 (E.D. Pa. 1996).

Some additional technical resources include the following: Berners-Lee & Fielding, Hypertext Transfer Protocol--HTTP/1.0 (1996); Fielding, Gettys, et al., Hypertext Transfer Protocol--HTTP/1.1,RFC 2616, Network Working Group, The Internet Society (June 1999), available at http://www.hjp.at/doc/rfc/rfc2616.html (last visited Dec. 14, 2012; Krishnamurthy & Rexford, Web Protocols and Practice: HTTP/1.1, Networking Protocols, Caching, and Traffic Measurement (Addison-Wesley Professional 2001).

[103] "The Hypertext Transfer Protocol (HTTP) is an application-level protocol for distributed, collaborative, hypermedia information systems. HTTP has been in use by the World-Wide Web global information initiative since 1990." Fielding, Gettys, et al., Hypertext Transfer Protocol--HTTP/1.1 §1.3, available at: http://www.hjp.at/doc/rfc/rfc2616.html#sec_1.3 (last visited Dec 14, 2012).

[104] Williams, Battle & Cuadrado, Protocol Mediation for Adaptation in Semantic Web Services, in Proceedings of the Third European Conference on the Semantic Web: Research and Applications 635–649 (Springer-Verlag 2006); Lu, Hong, et al., Pollock: Automatic Generation of Virtual Web Services From Web Sites, In Proceedings of the ACM Symposium on Applied Computing, 1650–55 (Mar. 2005); Bose & Stirpe, "System, method and applications real-time messaging over HTTP-based protocols," U.S. Patent Application No. 09/824,541 (filed Apr. 2, 2001).

cols are subsequently encapsulated into the transport layer protocols (such as TCP or UDP), which in turn uses the Internet and network layer protocols to transfer the data.[105]

## 3.7 Protocols: The Software That Runs the Internet—Transport Layer

The transport layer provides a uniform networking interface for programmers to access; the focus of the transport layer is on opening and maintaining connections between Internet hosts.[106] The transport layer is responsible for providing the nuts and bolts around the transmission of the data independent of the underlying network, error and flow control,[107] congestion control,[108] segmentation,[109] and application addressing.[110]

In the transport layer, the Transmission Control Protocol (TCP) ensures the data packets are reorganized in the proper order upon reaching their destination.[111] TCP, along with the Internet Protocol (IP), function as the most important protocols for transmitting data across the Internet. TCP and IP provide the basic software structure for communication across most modern networks.[112] In addition to acting as an

---

[105] "When an application sends data using TCP, the data is sent down the protocol stack, through each layer, until it is sent as a stream of bits across the network." Stevens & Wright, 1 TCP/IP Illustrated: The Protocols 9 (Addison-Wesley Professional 1994).

[106] "The transport layer provides a flow of data between two hosts, for the application layer above." Stevens & Wright, 1 TCP/IP Illustrated: The Protocols 9 (Addison-Wesley Professional 1994).

[107] Flow control manages the rate of data transmission between the sender and receiver. Iren, Amer, & Conrad, The Transport Layer: Tutorial and Survey, 31(4) ACM Computing Surveys (CSUR) 360–404 (1999); Doshi, Johri, et al., Error and Flow Control Performance of a High Speed Protocol, 41(5) IEEE Transactions on Communications (May 1993).

[108] Congestion control relates to how fast packets leave the sender and enter the network to avoid overwhelming the network and receiver. There are a variety of methods to implement congestion control. See Mathis & Mahdavi, Forward Acknowledgement: Refining TCP Congestion Control, 26(4) ACM SIGCOMM Computer Communication Review 281–91 (Oct. 1996).

[109] Segmentation refers to the separation of data units prior to sending onto the network. Xylomenos, et al., TCP Performance Issues Over Wireless Links, 39(4) IEEE Communications Magazine 52–58 (Apr. 2001).

[110] Application addressing refers to port number addressing. Bortoluzzi, Cunha & Specialski, "An Extended Model for TCP/IP Architecture," in Proceedings of the Ninth International Conference on Communications Systems (Sept. 7, 2004).

[111] Stevens & Wright, 1 TCP/IP Illustrated: The Protocols 9 (Addison-Wesley Professional 1994).

[112] "TCP/IP is the underlying protocol used for web page transfers, e-mail transmissions, file transfers, and peer-to-peer networking over the Internet." Dunkels, "Full TCP/IP For 8-Bit Architectures," in Proceedings of the First International ACM Conference on Mobile Systems, Applications and Services (2003). The Open System Interconnection Model is another model that breaks the TCP/IP Model layers into modules. See, e.g., Hunt, TCP/IP Network Administration 85–98 (1992) (with no universal agreement about how to describe the layers of the TCP/IP model, it is generally

addressing system, TCP/IP provides the framework for the movement of data over the Internet[113] and to programmers seeking to develop applications.[114] TCP/IP also serves as a communication protocol in a private network behind a firewall or router.[115]

## 3.8 Protocols: The Software That Runs the Internet—Internet Layer

The Internet layer has multiple jobs: (1) routing, (2) providing a single network interface to the higher layer protocols, and (3) providing an address for the data.[116] Without the Internet layer, programmers would have to write additional code for every single one of their applications for each network layer protocol.[117] Beyond creating a programming nightmare, that would result in different versions of each application—one for Ethernet, another one for Token Ring, and so on[118]—thereby greatly limiting the functionality and utility of the Internet. So, the Internet layer is critical because it provides one single network interface for the protocols in the

viewed as composed of fewer than seven layers); Lessig, Code and Other Laws of Cyberspace, at 101 (2000) (most descriptions of the TCP/IP suite define three to five functional layers). See Information technology--Open Systems Interconnection--Basic Reference Model: The Basic Model, ISO/IEC 7498-1 (Jun 15, 1996), available at http://standards.iso.org/ittf/PubliclyAvailableStandards/s020269_ISO_IEC_7498-1_1994(E).zip (last visited Dec 14, 2012) (hereinafter "ISO/IEC 7498-1").

[113] In *Vonage Holdings Corp. v. Minnesota Public Util.*, the court states:

> Voice communication using the Internet has been called Internet Protocol ("IP") telephony, and rather than using circuit switching, it utilizes "packet switching," a process of breaking down data into packets of digital bits and transmitting them over the Internet.

Vonage Holdings Corp. v. Minnesota Public Utilities Com'n, 290 F. Supp. 2d 993 (D. Minn. 2003) (citing Kiser & Collins, Regulation On The Horizon: Are Regulators Poised To Address the Status of IP Telephony?, 11 CommLaw Conspectus 19, 20–21 (2003)).

[114] See Comer, Internetworking with TCP/IP Vol. 1: Principles, Protocols, and Architecture (4th ed. 2000).

[115] Wong & Garrie, Regulating Voice Over Internet Protocol: An EU/US Comparative Approach, 22 Am. U. Int'l L. Rev. 549 (2007); see also Four Seasons Hotels and Resorts B.V. v. Consorcio Barr, S.A., 267 F. Supp. 2d 1268 (S.D. Fla. 2003), aff'd in part, rev'd in part on other grounds, 138 Fed. Appx. 297 (11th Cir. 2005).

[116] "The *network* layer (sometimes called the *Internet* layer) handles the movement of packets around the network. Routing of packets, for example, takes place here. IP (Internet Protocol), ICMP (Internet Control Message Protocol), and IGMP (Internet Group Management Protocol) provide the network layer in the TCP/IP protocol suite." Stevens & Wright, 1 TCP/IP Illustrated: The Protocols 3 (Addison-Wesley Professional 1994).

[117] Koufopavlou, Tantawy, & Zitterbart, "Analysis of TCP/IP for High Performance Parallel Implementations," in 17th IEEE Conference on Local Computer Networks (Sept. 13–16, 1992).

[118] See Murhammer, TCP/IP Tutorial and Technical Overview (Prentice Hall 1999).

application and transport layers.[119] Various protocols operate at the Internet layer, including Internet Protocol (IP),[120] Internet Control Message Protocol (ICMP),[121] Address Resolution Protocol (ARP),[122] and Reverse Address Resolution Protocol (RARP).[123] The Internet Protocol is essentially the Internet layer, and all the other protocols exist to support this IP layer.[124]

In the Internet layer, the Internet Protocol address identifies the computer and the network on which it resides.[125] The IP component acts as the transportation director, providing routing (via the IP address) from the local computer to the global Internet.[126] IP addresses consist of four sets of numbers, separated by a period, e.g., 214.36.195.98. This is referred to as a dotted decimal notation that a computer translates to binary form.[127] Each one of the four decimal numbers corresponds to a byte of the address.[128]

The current Internet protocol, referred to as IP version 4 or IPv4, utilizes a 32-bit address, which provides for 4 billion unique addresses.[129] All IP addresses are distributed in a hierarchical manner by a central registry, the Internet Assigned Numbers Authority (IANA).[130] This organization allocates huge blocks of numbers to five regional IP address registries: AfriNIC (African region), APNIC (Asia-Pacific

---

[119] See Atkinson & Kent, Security Architecture for the Internet Protocol, RFC 2401, Network Working Group, Internet Engineering Task Force (Nov. 1998), available at http://www.ietf.org/rfc/rfc2401.txt (last visited Apr. 15, 2013).

[120] Stevens & Wright, 1 TCP/IP Illustrated: The Protocols 3 (Addison-Wesley Professional 1994).

[121] "The Internet control message protocol (ICMP). ICMP is used for two important diagnostic programs; ping and traceroute. Packets sent by ping are returned by computers that are connected to the Internet. Ping is used to establish whether particular IP addresses have computers associated with them and whether those computers respond. Traceroute functions in a slightly more complicated fashion, but its function is to return a list of every IP address that is used to route data in between the source and destination IP address. Traceroute is used to identify and diagnose networks." Preston, Finding Fences in Cyberspace: Privacy and Open Access on the Internet, 6 J. Tech. L. & Pol'y 57 (2001).

[122] ARP maps an IP address to a specific machine. Miller, Internet Technology Handbook (Wiley-Interscience 2004).

[123] Translates hardware addresses into IP addresses. Finlayson, Mann, et al., A Reverse Address Resolution Protocol, RFC 903, Network Working Group, Internet Engineering Task Force (June 1984), available at http://www.ietf.org/rfc/rfc903.txt (last visited Apr. 15, 2013).

[124] See generally Goralski, The Illustrated Network: How TCP/IP Works in a Modern Network (2009).

[125] "[A]n IP address identifies both a destination computer and the subnet it is attached to." Agrawal and Sreenan, Get wireless: a mobile technology spectrum, 1(4) IT Professional 18–23 (1999).

[126] Stevens & Wright, 1 TCP/IP Illustrated: The Protocols (Addison-Wesley Professional 1994).

[127] Ibid.

[128] Ibid.

[129] Stallings, IPv6: The New Internet Protocol, 34(7) IEEE Communications Magazine 96–108 (July 1996); Lampson, Srinivasan & Varghese, IP Lookups Using Multiway and Multicolumn Search, 7(3) IEEE/ACM Transactions on Networking 324–334 (June 1999).

[130] Childress, Cathey & Dixon, The Adoption of IPv6, 18(4) Journal of Computing Sciences in Colleges 153–58 (Apr. 2003).

region), ARIN (North America, parts of the Caribbean, and Antarctica), LACNIC (Latin American and Caribbean region), and RIPE NCC (Europe, Russia, Central Asia, and the Middle East regions).[131] These five regional centers allocate smaller blocks to large Internet service providers, who in turn allocate these blocks to other entities, all the way to individual machines.[132]

With the rapid growth in the past 10 years, there was a concern that we would exhaust IPv4.[133] This has largely been avoided by the adoption of Network Address Translation (NAT), which simplified and conserves network addresses.[134] NAT enables networks to utilize a single IP address for many hundreds of Internet-connected machines.[135] NAT has experienced some implementation issues, including problems relating to the routing of Internet packets.[136] It also violates the "end-to-end" design principle that Internet machines in the middle should only deliver packets, never altering them in any way.[137]

---

[131] "While all requests for new top-level domains must be sent to the Internic (at mailto:hostmaster@internic.net), the regional registries are often enlisted to assist in the administration of the DNS, especially in solving problems with a country administration. The contact mailboxes for these regional registries are: INTERNIC (mailto:hostmaster@internic.net); APNIC (mailto:hostmaster@apnic.net); RIPE NCC (mailto:ncc@ripe.net)." Postel, Domain Name System Structure and Delegation (1994).

[132] Postel, Domain Name System Structure and Delegation (1994). The court in *PGMedia, Inc. v. Network Solutions, Inc.*, stated:

The IP numbering system was established in 1983 as part of a network system software called Transmission Control Protocol/Internet Protocol (TCP/IP"). (Id. &pp;6, 13.) The NSF supported many of the original technical studies that developed the Internet Protocol. (Pl.'s 56.1 Stmnt. &p;7.) Over time, more and more institutions and sites desired to be connected to the network (Id. &p;8.) and those that did connect were required to operate in accordance with TCP/IP and other consensus-based network standards. (Id. &p;10.) The Internet Engineering Task Force (supra, note 5) began in 1986 and received NSF support. (Id. &p;11.)

PGMedia, Inc. v. Network Solutions, Inc., 51 F. Supp. 2d 389, 393 (S.D. N.Y. 1999), judgment aff'd, 202 F.3d 573 (2d Cir. 2000).

[133] Childress, Cathey & Dixon, The Adoption of IPv6, 18(4) Journal of Computing Sciences in Colleges 153–58 (Apr. 2003).

[134] Memik, Mangione-Smith & Hu, "Netbench: A Benchmarking Suite for Network Processors," in Proceedings of IEEE/ACM International Conference on Computer Aided Design 39–42 (2001).

[135] Memik, Mangione-Smith & Hu, "Netbench: A Benchmarking Suite for Network Processors," in Proceedings of IEEE/ACM International Conference on *Computer Aided Design* 39–42 (2001).

[136] Wood, Clerget, et al., IP Routing Issues in Satellite Constellation Networks, 19(1) International Journal of Satellite Communications 69–92 (2001).

[137] "The end to end arguments are a set of design principles that characterize (among other things) how the Internet has been designed. These principles were first articulated in the early 1980s, and they have served as an architectural model in countless design debates for almost 20 years. The end to end arguments concern how application requirements should be met in a system. When a general purpose system (for example, a network or an operating system) is built, and specific applications are then built using this system (for example, e-mail or the World Wide Web over the Internet), there is a question of how these specific applications and their required supporting services should be designed. The end to end arguments suggest that specific application-level functions usually cannot, and preferably should not, be built into the lower levels of the system--the core of the network." Blumenthal & Clark, Rethinking the Design of the Internet: The End-To-End Arguments

To further avoid IPv4 address famine, a new version of the Internet protocol has been developed by the Internet Engineering Task Force called IPv6.[138] It uses 128-bit addresses, instead of the current 32-bit.[139] IPv6 creates an unimaginably huge expansion of the IP address space, allowing the Internet to handle the coming swell of users from the developing world.[140]

## 3.9 Protocols: The Software That Runs the Internet—Network Layer

The network layer is the physical layer and, as such, the lowest in the hierarchy.[141] It is responsible for the nuts and bolts of transmitting information from one place to another on a network.[142] Most consumer Internet applications connect to the Internet via the application layer protocols, including World Wide Web (HTTP and HTTPS), email (POP3, IMAP, and SMTP), Telnet and SSH, and FTP/SFTP.[143]

TCP and IP were developed by a Department of Defense research project to connect a number of different networks designed by different vendors.[144] Anticipating

---

vs. The Brave New World, 1(1) ACM Transactions on Internet Technology 70–109 (2001); *see also* Kodialam, Lakshman, et al., Oblivious Routing of Highly Variable Traffic in Service Overlays and IP Backbones, 17(2) IEEE/ACM Transactions on Networking 459–472 (Apr. 2009).

[138] The Court in *PGMedia, Inc. v. Network Solutions, Inc.*, stated:

Computers on the Internet do not actually find each other using domain names like usdcsdny.gov. Instead, they use a number known as an Internet Protocol or IP number. Each entity connected to the Internet has one or more unique IP numbers, separated by periods; the overall IP 391*391 number can be no longer than 12 digits. (Strawn &p;13.) When the Internet was first developing, the IP numbers were assigned and maintained by the late Dr. Jon Postel at the University of Southern California; this effort later became known as the Internet Assigned Numbers Authority ("IANA"), which still allocates IP numbers today. (Strawn Decl. &p;14.)

PGMedia, Inc. v. Network Solutions, Inc., 51 F. Supp. 2d 389, 392 (S.D. N.Y. 1999), judgment aff'd, 202 F.3d 573 (2d Cir. 2000).

[139] IPv4 provides only for 4,294,967,296 IPv4 addresses. Kabachinski, IPv4 and the Promise of IPv6: Part I, 38(1) Biomedical Instrumentation & Technology 39–42 (Jan.–Feb. 2004).

[140] See Goncalves & Niles, IPv6 Networks (McGraw-Hill, Inc. 2001); Rowe & Gallaher, Could IPv6 Improve Network Security-And, If So, at What Cost, 2 I/S: J. L. & Pol'y for Info. Soc'y 231 (2005).

[141] "Finally, the network access layer forms the lowest layer in the TCP/IP model being responsible for transmitting and receiving IP datagrams." Koufopavlou, Tantawy & Zitterbart, "Analysis of TCP/IP for High Performance Parallel Implementations," in Proceedings of the 17th IEEE Conference on Local Computer Networks 576–85 (Sept. 13–16, 1992).

[142] Paul, Yates, et al., "The Cache-and-Forward Network Architecture for Efficient Mobile Content Delivery Services in the Future Internet," in Proceedings of First ITU-T Kaleidoscope Academic Conference on Innovations in NGN: Future Network and Services, (May 12–13, 2008).

[143] Kurose & Ross, Computer Networks: A Top Down Approach Featuring the Internet (Pearson Addison-Wesley, 2006).

[144] Weinberg, ICANN and the Problem of Legitimacy, Duke L.J. 187 (2000).

that communications networks could be damaged in hostilities,[145] the DOD designed TCP/IP to be robust and automatically recover from any node or phone line failure.[146] To achieve this goal, the DOD created a protocol that labels each packet of data and allows the packets to be reassembled when they reach the receiving device.[147] This design allows the construction of very large networks with less central management. The downside of automatic recovery is that network problems can go undiagnosed and uncorrected for long periods of time.

One of the purposes of the TCP/IP is to provide end-to-end connectivity, which in turn defines how data is formatted, addressed, transmitted, routed, and received.[148] TCP/IP uses the client/server model of communication in which a computer user (a client) requests a service (such as sending a web page) by another computer (a server) in the network.[149]

TCP/IP communication is point-to-point, meaning each communication is from one point (or host computer) in the network to another point or host computer.[150] TCP/IP, and the higher-level applications that use it, are collectively said to be "stateless" because each client request is considered a new session unrelated to any previous one (unlike ordinary phone conversations that require a dedicated connection for the call duration).[151] Being stateless frees network paths so that everyone can use them continuously.[152]

With the above information on the hardware and protocols that underlie the Internet communication, we now examine how the most familiar tasks of sending email and surfing the World Wide Web are performed.

---

[145] This damage can include data that is lost, duplicated or delivered out of order by the Internet Protocol. For an exhaustive discussion on TCP/IP, see http://www.faqs.org/rfcs/rfc793.html

[146] Frischmann, Privatization and Commercialization of the Internet Infrastructure: Rethinking Market Intervention into Government and Government Intervention Into the Market, 2 Colum. Sci. & Tech. L. Rev. 1 (2000).

[147] Jaware, Sonawane, et al., Implementation of Hardware Stack TCP/IP using Virtex-2 Pro FPGA (Nov. 2009), available at http://www.techrepublic.com/whitepapers/implementation-of-hardware-stack-tcpip-using-virtex-2-pro-fpga/1726321 (last visited Apr. 15, 2013); see also Cerf, Burleigh, et al., Delay-Tolerant Networking Architecture, RFC 4838, Network Working Group, Internet Engineering Task Force (Apr. 2007), available at http://tools.ietf.org/html/rfc4838 (last visited Apr. 15, 2013).

[148] See generally Comer, Internetworking with TCP/IP Vol. 1: Principles, Protocols, and Architecture (4th ed. 2000).

[149] See generally Stevens & Wright, 1 TCP/IP Illustrated: The Protocols (Addison-Wesley Professional 1994).

[150] Stevens & Wright, 1 TCP/IP Illustrated: The Protocols (Addison-Wesley Professional 1994).

[151] "[S]tateless (i.e., processes each received packet independently of previously received packets)." Samaraweera, & Fairhurst, "High speed Internet Access Using Satellite-Based DVB Networks," in Proceedings of the IEEE International Networks Conference (Sept. 1998).

[152] The transport layer itself is not stateless as far as any one message is concerned. Its connection remains in place until all packets in a message have been received. See generally Comer, Internetworking with TCP/IP Vol. 1: Principles, Protocols, and Architecture (4th ed. 2000).

## 3.10 Protocols: The Software That Runs the Internet—Email

Email, as we know it, came about in 1971, when the first email was sent using the "@" symbol.[153] A great deal happens behind the scenes to enable a message to travel from point A to point B.[154] The key to any email is an address in the following form: mailto:user@domain.ext. Once an email has an address, it is transmitted to an outgoing mail server, most often via Simple Mail Transfer Protocol (SMTP).[155] The SMTP server operates like the post office and determines where to send the mail by contacting a Domain Name System (DNS) server.[156] The DNS server translates domains to IP addresses and then determines if the specific domain has any mail exchange servers and records this information.[157] Once the SMTP server receives the appropriate information, the message is sent to the target domain's mail exchange server via a Mail Transfer Agent (MTA).[158] The MTA determines where to put the

---

[153] See Crocker, Email History, http://www.livinginternet.com/e/ei.htm (last visited Apr. 15, 2013); Hardy, The Evolution of ARPANET Email 11 (May 13, 1996) (unpublished thesis, University of California at Berkeley), http://www.livinginternet.com/References/Ian%20Hardy%20Email%20 Thesis.txt (last visited Apr. 15, 2013); Peter, The History of Email, http://www.nethistory.info/ History%20of%20the%20Internet/email.html (last visited Apr. 15, 2013); see Hafner & Lyon, Where Wizards Stay Up Late: The Origins of the Internet 212 (1996); Hafner & Lyon, Talking Headers, Wash. Post Mag., Aug. 4, 1996, at 14; Chapman, The History of the Internet in a Nutshell (Nov. 15, 2009), http://sixrevisions.com/resources/the-history-of-the-internet-in-a-nutshell/ (last visited July 17, 2013).

[154] Intel Corp. v. Hamidi, 30 Cal. 4th 1342, 1 Cal. Rptr. 3d 32, 71 P.3d 296 (2003); CompuServe Inc. v. Cyber Promotions, Inc., 962 F. Supp. 1015, 1018 (S.D. Ohio 1997) (stating "However, there is no per-message charge to send electronic messages over the Internet and such messages usually reach their destination within minutes. Thus electronic mail provides an opportunity to reach a wide audience quickly and at almost no cost to the sender.").

[155] SMTP transmits commands and replies over lines via a transmission channel (see J. Klensin, Simple Mail Transfer Protocol Memo, RFC 5322, Network Working Group, Internet Engineering Task Force, at 14 (Oct. 2008), available at http://tools.ietf.org/html/rfc5321 (last visited Nov. 21, 2012). To complete the transmission, SMTP utilizes "a numeric completion code (indicating failure or success) [for program use] usually followed by a text string [for human users]" (*id.*).

[156] Petroliam Nasional Berhad v. GoDaddy.com, Inc., 2010 WL 3619780 (N.D. Cal. 2010) ("In response to the entry of a domain name, the user's computer communicates back and forth with the Domain Name System ('DNS'), a set of servers that allow the user to locate the IP Address for the computer that hosts the desired website. The DNS does not provide any website content, but instead functions as the Internet's equivalent of 'directory assistance.' The fundamental building block of the DNS is the 'nameserver,' which is a database of IP Addresses.").

[157] See, e.g., TracFone Wireless, Inc. v. Bitton, 278 F.R.D. 687, 693 (S.D. Fla. 2012); U.S. Commodity Futures Trading Com'n v. Aliaga, 272 F.R.D. 617, 621 (S.D. Fla. 2011) (due process satisfied by email addresses recently used to send messages to customers); Chanel, Inc. v. Zhixian, 2010 WL 1740695 (S.D. Fla. 2010) (due process satisfied when emails did not bounce back). But see Chanel, Inc. v. Lin, 2009 WL 1034627 (S.D. Fla. 2009) (denying service via email because, although an email address was active, the court had doubts that the defendant himself was specifically sending and receiving emails on the account).

[158] Moonesamy & Levine, Mail Header Trace Fields (2012)

mail. Once this step is completed, the recipient fetches the email using an email client that works via POP or IMAP.[159]

The following hypothetical demonstrates this process in further detail:

- Sarah is in Shanghai, China, on vacation with her husband and she wants to send her dad, Bob, an email whose address is mailto:bob@email.com. Sarah is at a cybercafé with her iPad connected to the Internet via the wireless router.
- The first thing Sarah's iPad must do is acquire an IP address from the local network. Once she connects to the wireless router, Sarah's iPad automatically requests an IP address from the Linux gateway server at the cafe, using a protocol called DHCP.[160] The gateway server is connected to a local ISP provider, MookieCookie, via a 20MB per second cable model. The gateway server has a unique IP address assigned by MookieCookie DHCP server: 173.223.0.110.
- The gateway server uses Network Address Translation (NAT)[161] to assign a temporary nonpublic IP address to each device at the cafe, including Sarah's iPad. This means that Sarah's iPad thinks it has the IP address 98.138.253.109, but the outside world thinks Sarah's iPad has the IP address of the gateway server, 173.223.0.110.[162]
- When Sarah hits send, her iPad chops the email into small packets and sends them to a mail server with instructions to deliver to Bob's email address via the

[159] See supra 3:6 (in footnotes) for a discussion of IMAP. Garfinkel, Spafford & Schwartz, Practical UNIX and Inernet Security 348 (O'Reilly Media 2011); see also Zhang, Deng, et al., "Research of the Email Account Maintaining Technology for Mail Gateway," in Proceedings of the 2012 IEEE International Conference on Computer Distributed Control and Intelligent Environmental Monitoring 547–550 (Mar. 2012).

[160] See generally Droms, Dynamic Host Configuration Protocol, RFC 1531, Network Working Group, Internet Engineering Task Force (Oct. 1993), available at http://tools.ietf.org/html/rfc1531 (last visited Apr. 15, 2013); Innovative Communications Technologies, Inc. v. Vivox, Inc., 2012 Markman 5331573, 2012 WL 5331573 (E.D. Va. 2012) (stating that DHCP supports three mechanisms for IP address allocation. In "automatic allocation," DHCP assigns a permanent IP address to a host. In "dynamic allocation," DHCP assigns an IP address to a host for a limited period of time (or until the host explicitly relinquishes the address). In "manual allocation," a host's IP address is assigned by the network administrator, and DHCP is used simply to convey the assigned address to the host. A particular network will use one or more of these mechanisms, depending on the policies of the network administrator.); U.S. v. Larson, 2011 WL 3841078 (W.D. Mo. 2011).

[161] For definitions and case law use of Network Address Translation, see Verizon Services Corp. v. Vonage Holdings Corp., 503 F.3d 1295, 1315 (Fed. Cir. 2007); Tener v. Cremer, 89 A.D.3d 75, 931 N.Y.S.2d 552 (1st Dep't 2011).

[162] The gateway server is the translator from public IP to nonpublic IP address and distributes packets to the appropriate devices at the cafe that requested the specific packets, assigned by the gateway server via DHCP.

designated mail server. Sarah's iPad is running Sparrow, a standard Apple program that supports various email protocols: SMTP, POP3,[163] and IMAP.[164]

- While Sparrow is intelligent enough to format the message into valid commands, it relies on the MAC operating system, the TCP/IP stack, to translate the message into valid IP packets. Sarah's packets go through the connection to the cybercafé gateway server, then through a modem or phone line to the MookieCookie server, and through a gateway machine at MookieCookie.
- In the following second, the packets take a journey through 26 machines in China, Kohsamui, Ankara, Naxos, London, Reykjavik, Miami, Quito, Cusco, and Santiago. These 26 computers are routers whose task is to move packets from machine to machine in the right direction, processing tens of millions of packets a minute.[165] The routers contain a routing table which tells the router the next place to forward the packets based on the final destination of the packet.
- Machine #26 is the last machine in the chain, the mail server for Bob's email. Unlike the routers on the network, this machine does more than forward packets; in fact, it operates as a mail server, a piece of software that receives incoming email and distributes it to users and sends outgoing email to other mail servers.
- When Sarah's packets are received by the mail server, Machine #26 notices that Sarah's email is addressed to Bob and needs to be transmitted to the mail server named email.com, so the mail server sends IP packets to mailto:email.com. Every single IP packet representing Sarah's iPad email has to go from the cybercafé to mailto:email.com. This connection spans 12 computers and 5 networks and takes under 1/20th of a second. The mail server is a small piece of a larger server owned by Rackspace. This larger server provides web, FTP, and mail services to dozens of different domains. The mail server on the Rackspace machines receives email from Sarah and appends it to a "spool file," and the mail server on the Rackspace machine is done. Once the email is received by Bob's mail server, email.com, the email sits there until Bob retrieves it via "Checking your email."

---

[163] U.S. v. Szymuszkiewicz, 622 F.3d 701 (7th Cir. 2010), as amended, (Nov. 29, 2010); American Boat Co., Inc. v. Unknown Sunken Barge, 567 F.3d 348, 351 (8th Cir. 2009) ("POP" stands for Post Office Protocol, a protocol used to pull mail from one server to another server or to a desktop email program such as Microsoft Outlook.); Oracle Corp. v. Parallel Networks, LLP, 588 F. Supp. 2d 549 (D. Del. 2008), judgment vacated, 375 Fed. Appx. 36 (Fed. Cir. 2010).

[164] The IMAP is another TCP/IP protocol which is described in detail in "Internet Message Access Protocol-Version 4revl," RFC 2060, Network Working Group, Internet Engineering Taskforce, available at http://www.ietf.org/rfc2060; U.S. v. Szymuszkiewicz, 622 F.3d 701 (7th Cir. 2010), as amended, (Nov. 29, 2010); Intermec Technologies Corp. v. Palm Inc., 811 F. Supp. 2d 973 (D. Del. 2011); Miller, Vandome & McBrewster, Gmail (Alphascript Publishing 2009).

[165] See §3:5, Part B for more information on routers.

## 3.11 Protocols: The Software That Runs the Internet—Web Pages

In order to explain how a web page works, we need to define the following:

- *HTML*: A computer programming language that describes how a web page is rendered to a screen.[166]
- *Web page(s)*: A text file that contains text, including HTML tags which the web browser interprets to determine how to render text on the screen.[167]
- *Web browser*: A computer software application able to find and request a web page stored on a web server and interpret HTML tags on the page to render an image.[168]
- *Web server*: A computer software application that can respond to a web browser's request for a page and send the page to the web browser through the Internet.[169]

A user with a web browser can view a web page. When a user requests to view a web page on the Internet, they are requesting the page from a web server. For example, when a user types the Uniform Resource Locator or URL (for instance, http://www.whitehouse.gov), the web browser on your computer requests the page from the web server, and the web server sends the page back, as shown in the diagram. Using the above terms, this picture and example are a high-level overview of how a web page is rendered to a web browser:

- The web browser on your computer needs to know to which IP address the website http://www.whitehouse.gov resolves. If your web browser does not contain this information in its memory cache, it requests the information from at least

[166] American Civil Liberties Union v. Reno, 929 F. Supp. 824 (E.D. Pa. 1996), judgment aff'd, 521 U.S. 844, 117 S. Ct. 2329, 138 L. Ed. 2d 874 (1997) (describing HTML as a formatting language used to develop web pages).

[167] Panavision Intern., L.P. v. Toeppen, 141 F.3d 1316, 1319 (9th Cir. 1998) (holding modified on other grounds by, Yahoo! Inc. v. La Ligue Contre Le Racisme Et L'Antisemitisme, 433 F.3d 1199 (9th Cir. 2006)) (defining a web page to be a "computer data file that can include names, words, messages, pictures, sounds, and links to other information. Every web page has its own website, which is its address, similar to a telephone number or street address. Every website on the Internet has an identifier called a 'domain name.' The domain name often consists of a person's name or a company's name or trademark."); Marobie-FL, Inc. v. National Ass'n of Fire Equipment Distributors, 983 F. Supp. 1167, 1171 (N.D. Ill. 1997) (stating that a "Web Page is a collection of electronic documents which may include text, graphics, sound, or video."); Zippo Mfg. Co. v. Zippo Dot Com, Inc., 952 F. Supp. 1119 (W.D. Pa. 1997).

[168] Reno v. American Civil Liberties Union, 521 U.S. 844, 852; U.S. v. Tucker, 305 F.3d 1193, 1197 (10th Cir. 2002) (finding that a "[w]eb browser is computer software that allows a user to view Web pages."); U.S. v. Microsoft Corp., 84 F. Supp. 2d 9 (D.D.C. 1999) (stating that a "'Web browser' is a type of Web client that enables a user to select, retrieve, and perceive resources on the Web.")

[169] Automated Business Companies v. ENC Technology Corp., 2009 Markman 3190448, 2009 WL 3190448 (S.D. Tex. 2009), amended on reconsideration in part, 2009 Markman 3674507, 2009 WL 3674507 (S.D. Tex. 2009) (defining as a server that hosts web pages.)

one Domain Name Server (DNS) server (via the Internet), and the DNS server tells the browser the specific IP address for the website.[170]

- Once the web browser knows the IP address for the particular website, it requests the full URL from the web server.[171]
- The web server responds by sending back the requested page and returns an error message if the page does not exist. If the requested page exists, the web browser receives the page from the web server and displays it for the user.[172] A web server generally contains multiple websites with each website assigned a unique IP address, which is what the DNS server uses to resolve the domain name.[173]

Proxy servers are another component of the Internet and computer networks.[174] A proxy server is a server computer program that acts as an intermediary for requests from clients seeking resources from other servers.[175] A client connects to the proxy server requesting some service, such as a file, connection, web page, or other resource available from a different server, and the proxy server evaluates the request as a way to simplify and control their complexity.[176]

---

[170] Caswell & Ramanathan, Using Service Models for Management of Internet Services, 18(5) IEEE Journal on Selected Areas in Communications 686–701 (Sept. 2006).

[171] See generally Collin, Setting Up a Web Server, (Elsevier 1997); Rooney, Introduction to IP Address Management (Wiley-IEEE Press 2010).

[172] Wise v. State, 364 S.W.3d 900, 904 (Tex. Crim. App. 2012) (finding that "[w]hen a computer user views a webpage, the web browser stores a copy of the page on the computer's hard drive in a folder or directory."); Del Gallo, III, Who Owns the Website: The Ultimate Question When a Hiring Party Has a Falling-Out with the Website Designer, 16 J. Marshall J. Computer & Info. L. 857, 859 (1998) ("A website is comprised of computer software sitting on one computer terminal ready to be accessed by the World Wide Web similarly to the way software is made available to many computers on a LAN contained within a single office.").

[173] Often web browsers are referred to as a client and the web server as a server. While beyond the scope of this book, it is possible to configure multiple websites using a single IP address using ports or headers.

[174] For example, CERN has a proxy server, available at http://www.w3.org/Daemon/User/Proxies/Proxies.html

[175] Luotonen & Altis World-wide web proxies, 27(2) Computer Networks and ISDN Systems 147–54 (Nov. 1994).

[176] eBay, Inc. v. Bidder's Edge, Inc., 100 F. Supp. 2d 1058 (N.D. Cal. 2000); Cook v. Martin, 71 S.W.3d 677, 679 (Mo. Ct. App. W.D. 2002) (defining "[a] proxy server is a specialized computer or similar device that enables multiple computers to utilize a single Internet connection. A proxy server may be configured such that it appears that only one computer is utilizing the connection (concealing that multiple machines may actually be connecting through the proxy server).").

## Appendices

### *Appendix A: Internet Tracking Technologies*

Unfortunately, web surfing generates a massive amount of personal information about a user each time he or she goes online. Users often operate under an illusion of anonymity in cyberspace. However, the reality of the Internet is much different: Prying eyes can identify individual users and track online activity by monitoring and examining "clickstreams."

A "clickstream" is the aggregation of the electronic information generated as a web user communicates with other computers and networks over the Internet.[177] The name "clickstream" refers to the series of mouse clicks users make as they travel the web. Each click translates into digital data, which is then sent by the surfer's computer to other computers on the Internet telling them what information to return to the user.[178] Since online movement requires the user to send or request certain information from other computers on the web, every step in cyberspace inevitably becomes part of the clickstream record.[179] This data can be shockingly revealing, providing a record of the entirety of one's online experience, including movements among web sites, geographical location, the type of computer and Internet browser in use, and any transactions or comments made at individual websites.[180]

"Clickstream data provide information about the sequence of pages or the path viewed by users as they navigate a website."[181] Clickstream data captures the users's activity on the Internet, "including every Web site and every page of every website that the user visits, how long the user had a page or site open, in what order the pages were visited, any newsgroups that the user participates in, and even the email addresses to and from which the user sends and receives mail."[182]

Clickstream data was initially used to garner basic information from a web user,[183] such as the type of computer an individual used to access the Internet, the

---

[177] See In re DoubleClick Inc. Privacy Litigation, 154 F. Supp. 2d 497, 507 (S.D. N.Y. 2001).

[178] See Garrie, Armstrong & Harris, Voice Over Internet Protocol and the Wiretap Act: Is Your Conversation Protected, 29 Seattle U. L. Rev. 97 (2005).

[179] See Wong & Garrie, Demystifying Clickstream Data: A European and US Perspective, 20 Emory Int'l L. Rev. 563 (Fall 2006).

[180] See Jenab, Will the Cookie Crumble?: An Analysis of Internet Privacy Regulatory Schemes Proposed in the 106th Congress, 49 Kan. L. Rev. 641 (2001).

[181] Montgomery, Li, et al, Modeling Online Browsing and Path Analysis Using Clickstream Data, 23(4) Marketing Science 579–595 (2004).

[182] Bucklin & Sismeiro, A Model of Web Site Browsing Behavior Estimated on Clickstream Data, 40 Journal of Marketing Research 249–267 (2003). See Evans, Monitoring Technology in the American Workplace: Would Adopting English Privacy Standards Better Balance Employee Privacy and Productivity?, 95 Cal. L. Rev. 1115 (2007).

[183] Skok, Establishing a Legitimate Expectation of Privacy in Clickstream Data, 6 Mich. Telecomm. & Tech. L. Rev. 61 (1999).

type of Internet browser utilized, and the identification of each site or page visited.[184] As technology evolved, however, so did clickstream data.[185] Today, when an individual discloses certain information during a visit to a website via their iPhone, cell phone, tablet, laptop computer, iPod, or desktop computer, it is possible that the website will be collecting clickstream data of a much more personal nature.[186]

Clickstream data is used because centralized web server technologies cannot store and sort the vast amounts of data required to deliver the respective web solutions to each individual user to a site or to authenticate a user.[187] Thus, websites off-load certain information to the end user's device where it is stored in special text files called "cookies."[188]

In the mid-1990s, web portals began to use cookie technology. This enabled companies to deliver user-specific solutions for each machine that accessed their web pages.[189] These cookies provide the website with a mechanism through which they collect and store data on the storage device of the end user's machine,[190] which then retransmits information back to the server each time the browser accesses a

---

[184] See Gonul, "Stereotyping Bites the Dust; Marketers No Longer Focusing On Demographic Profiling," Pittsburgh Post-Gazette (Pennsylvania), Sooner Edition February 26, 2002, at B3; Dearne, "You are Being Monitored Online," The Australian, September 24, 2002, at Features 31.

[185] Lin, Prioritizing Privacy: A Constitutional Response to the Internet, 17 Berkley Tech. L.J. 1085, 1104 (2002) (clickstream data is a trail of information that a user leaves behind while browsing on the Web). See generally Edelstein, "Pan for Gold in the Clickstream," March 12, 2001 available at http://www.informationweek.com/828/prmining.htm (last visited Apr. 15, 2013); Winn & Wrathall, Who Owns the Consumer? The Emerging Law of Commercial Transactions in Electronic Consumer Data, 56 Bus. Law. 213, 234–35 (2000).

[186] See In re Pharmatrak, Inc., 329 F.3d 9, 15 (1st Cir. 2003) (this information could be in the form of passwords, email addresses, credit card numbers, medication, stock trades, and other sensitive information that your machine stores).

[187] See Moeller, Distributed Data Warehousing Using Web Technology, American Management Association (AMACOM New York, 2001).

[188] See Berry & Linoff, Mastering Data Mining: The Art and Science of Customer Relationship Management (Wiley 2000); Colin, The CRISP-DM Model: The New Blueprint for Data Mining, 5 Journal of Data Warehousing 4, 13–22 (Fall 2000).

[189] See Berman & Mulligan, Privacy in the Digital Age: Work in Progress, 23 Nova. L. Rev. 551, 554 (1999) ("The data trail, known as transactional data, left behind as individuals use the Internet is a rich source of information about their habits of association, speech, and commerce. Transactional data, click stream data, or 'mouse droppings,' as it is alternatively called, can include the Internet protocol address ('IP address') of the individual's computer, the browser in use, the computer type, and what the individual did on previous visits to the Web site, or perhaps even other Web sites."). See also Jenab, Comment, Will the Cookie Crumble?: An Analysis of Internet Privacy Regulatory Schemes Proposed in the 106th Congress, 49 Kan. L. Rev. 641, 667–68 (2001); Solove, Privacy and Power: Computer Databases and Metaphors for Information Privacy, 53 Stan. L. Rev. 1393, 1458–60 (2001); Zimmerman, Note, The Way the "Cookies" Crumble: Internet Privacy and Data Protection in the Twenty-First Century, 4 N.Y.U. J. Legis. & Pub. Pol'y 439, 459–60 (2000).

[190] Once a user has accessed a website that uses cookie technology or an affiliated site, the embedded cookie on the hard drive begins collecting data about the user's web activities. In the following four reported cases, cookie technology was used by websites to mine personal information from the users' machines. In re Pharmatrak, Inc., 329 F.3d 9, 12 (1st Cir. 2003); In re Intuit Privacy Litigation, 138 F. Supp. 2d 1272, 1274 (C.D. Cal. 2001); In re DoubleClick Inc. Privacy Litigation,

specific server's web page, thereby enabling a website to record, track, monitor, and generate customized dynamic pages reflecting the stored data.[191]

The functionality of the data mining industry and most web portals would be severely limited, if not rendered useless, in the absence of clickstream data or cookies.[192] Although it is possible for authentication processes to be retooled so they require users to log in or to consent affirmatively to monitoring by cookies or clickstream data tracking, it is highly unlikely that fully informed end users would interact with sites that track, monitor, and perhaps sell personally identifiable information.[193]

Internet companies currently rely heavily on tracking clickstream data to deliver customized services and advertisements to Internet users.[194] For example, DoubleClick, an Internet advertising company, had stockpiled over 100 million user profiles by the year 2002.[195]

Since then, the technology and ability to profile has greatly improved, and Internet companies now rely on clickstream data more than ever before.[196] Cell phones, PDAs, Web TVs, Xboxes™, laptops, desktops, and other web-enabled applications utilize clickstream data in either a direct or derivative form.[197] Thus, if the courts construe the Wiretap Act to protect clickstream data as it protects other electronic communications, both the business world and government functions would be disrupted.[198] To demonstrate this expansive reliance on cookie technologies, simply view the cookies stored on your own computer.[199]

---

154 F. Supp. 2d 497, 502–03 (S.D. N.Y. 2001); Chance v. Avenue A, Inc., 165 F. Supp. 2d 1153, 1155 (W.D. Wash. 2001).

[191] See Spencer, Reasonable Expectations and the Erosion of Privacy, 39 San Diego L. Rev. 843, 910 (2002); see Walker, The Costs of Privacy, 25 Harv. J.L. & Pub. Pol'y 87, 113–117 (2001). Han & Kamber, Data Mining: Concepts and Techniques (Morgan-Kaufmann Academic Press 2001); Rajagopalan & Krovi, Benchmarking Data Mining Algorithms, 13(1) Journal of Database Management 25–36 (Jan.–Mar. 2001).

[192] A sampling of websites that would be impacted are as follows: http://www.yahoo.com; http://www.google.com; http://www.chase.com; http://www.schwab.com; and http://www.ibm.com. Adjoining these websites are a slew of intranet and web applications that utilize cookies and clickstream data for authentication. Not only will business be impacted but also a large number of government enabled web applications.

[193] See Kang, Information Privacy In Cyberspace Transactions, 50 Stan. L. Rev. 1193 (1998).

[194] See Verga, Cloudburst: What Does Cloud Computing Mean to Lawyers, 5 J. Legal Tech. Risk Mgmt. 41 (2010).

[195] See In re Pharmatrak, Inc., 329 F.3d 9, 21 (1st Cir. 2003); In re DoubleClick Inc. Privacy Litigation, 154 F. Supp. 2d 497, 505 (S.D. N.Y. 2001); Chance v. Avenue A, Inc., 165 F. Supp. 2d 1153, 1155–57 (W.D. Wash. 2001).

[196] See generally In re DoubleClick Inc. Privacy Litigation, 154 F. Supp. 2d 497 (S.D. N.Y. 2001).

[197] See Garrie, The Legal Status of Software, 23 J. Marshall J. Computer & Info. L. 711 (Summer 2005).

[198] Garrie, Blakley & Armstrong, Legal Status of Spyware, 59 Fed. Comm. L.J. 157 (Dec. 2006).

[199] Garrie, Introduction: Creating Legitimate Digital Privacy Rights for Internet Users, 3 Rutgers J. L. & Urb. Pol'y 149 (2006).

## *Appendix B: Voice over Internet Protocol*

In comparison with traditional telephone networks, the Voice over Internet Protocol (VoIP) is an extremely efficient means of relaying voice communications.[200] Since Internet traffic has been placed into packets,[201] there is no need for a phone conversation to occupy a circuit for the full duration of an exchange.[202] In fact, it is possible to use the circuit for the milliseconds required to transmit the data packet containing the oral communication.[203] Since each data packet has a unique source and destination address embedded in the header,[204] simultaneous conversations can exist serially on the same circuit without interfering with one another.[205] This means that on the same piece of copper carrying a phone call, hundreds of email exchanges can occur in the same period of time. It also means that it is possible via VoIP to enable real-time telephone conversations over the Internet. This is possible because the computer places the oral communications in packets and compresses the voice traffic. This allows VoIP to provide up to six voice circuits in the same bandwidth of a traditional telephone line (56 kbps).[206]

VoIP is a technology by which oral communications can be transferred from circuit-switched networks to (or over) Internet Protocol networks, and vice versa.[207] VoIP transforms standard oral telephone signals into compressed data packets that are sent over the Internet.[208] The audio signal at this point is captured either by way of a microphone or received from line input.[209] This analog representation is then converted to a digital representation at the audio input device.[210] The resulting

[200] See El-Bakry & Mastorakis, Fast Detection of Specific Information in Voice Signal Over Internet Protocol, 8(5) WSEAS Transactions on Communications 483–94 (May 2009).

[201] See §3:5 for a discussion of packets.

[202] See Das, Parulkar, & McKeown, Unifying Packet and Circuit Switched Networks, IEEE GLOBECOM Workshops (Nov. 30–Dec. 4, 2009).

[203] See Das, Parulkar, & McKeown, Unifying Packet and Circuit Switched Networks, IEEE GLOBECOM Workshops (Nov. 30–Dec. 4, 2009).

[204] See §3:5 for a discussion of packet routing.

[205] See Wang, Guohui, et al., Your Data Center Is a Router: The Case for Reconfigurable Optical Circuit Switched Paths (Carnegie-Mellon Univ., Computer Science Department, at 62 (Oct. 2009).

[206] See Bai & Cheng, "A Simple Method for Estimating the Service Quality of VoIP," in Proceedings of the Fifth IEEE Consumer Communications and Networking Conference 596–97 (Jan. 10–12, 2008).

[207] See Bota, Florin, et al., "Comparison of energy efficiency in PSTN and VoIP systems," in Proceedings of the Third International ACM Conference on Future Energy Systems: Where Energy, Computing and Communication Meet (May 9–12, 2012).

[208] See generally Ganguly & Bhatnagar, VoIP: Wireless, P2P and New Enterprise Voice Over IP (Wiley Publishing, 2008.

[209] See ITUT (International Telecommunications Union) Recommendation H.225.0, Call Signaling Protocols and Media Stream Packetization for packet Based Multimedia Communication Systems (1998).

[210] Iossifov, Totev, & Tochatschek, "Experiences in VoIP Telephone Network Security Policy at the University of Applied Sciences (FHTW) Berlin," in Proceedings of the International ACM

digital samples are copied into a memory buffer (identified as a "socket") as blocks of digital data.[211] Here, a silence detector decides whether the block is silence or a portion of speech.[212] Once this is completed, the communication is transmitted to another VoIP terminal.[213] This terminal parses the header information, and the block of audio is decoded applying the same codec and the samples written into a buffer.[214] Next, the block of samples is copied from the buffer to the audio output device.[215] The audio output device makes the digital-to-analog conversion and outputs the signal.[216]

VoIP can be used with either a telephone or a PC as the user terminal.[217] This gives different modes of operation: PC to PC, PC to telephone, telephone to PC, and telephone to telephone (via the Internet).[218] All VoIP protocols are application layer protocols.[219]

Wiretapping dangers increase considerably in the VoIP world.[220] People have known about the possibilities for wiretapping on regular telephone lines, but the public itself views such threats to be limited to corporate espionage and criminal activities.[221] To eavesdrop over the switched circuit telephone network generally

Conference On Computer Systems and Technologies (2007).

211 See Garrie & Armstrong, Voice Over Internet Protocol and the Wiretap Act: Is Your Conversation Protected?, 29 Seattle Univ. L. Rev. 97 (2005), available at http://digitalcommons.law.seattleu.edu/cgi/viewcontent.cgi?article=1849&context=sulr (last visited Apr. 15, 2013).

212 For a discussion on silence suppression technology, see Ahson & Ilyas, VoIP Handbook: Applications, Technologies, Reliability, and Security §3.2.1 (CRC Press 2008).

213 See Ahson & Ilyas, VoIP Handbook: Applications, Technologies, Reliability, and Security §3.2.1 (CRC Press 2008).

214 See Carden, Building Voice Over IP, Network Computing, May 8, 2000.

215 "The voice packets travel through the data network to the receiver where an important component called the playback buffer is places for the purpose of absorbing variations or jitter in delay and for providing a smooth playback. Packets are then delivered to the depacketizer and eventually to the decoder, which reconstructs the original voice signal." Ahson & Ilyas, VoIP Handbook: Applications, Technologies, Reliability, and Security §1.2.1 (CRC Press 2008).

216 Ahson & Ilyas, VoIP Handbook: Applications, Technologies, Reliability, and Security §1.2.1 (CRC Press 2008).

217 "A terminal is an end user device, which can be a simple telephone or PC/workstation." Li, et al., QoS Enabled Voice Support In the Next Generation Internet: Issues, Existing Approaches and Challenges, 38(4) IEEE Communications Magazine 54–61 (Apr. 2000).

218 See Jang, Kim, et al., "Performance Analysis of Media Gateway for Voice Service," in Revised Papers from International Conference on Information Networking, Wireless Communications Technologies and Network Applications 28–39 (Springer-Verlag 2002).

219 See Marjalaakso, Security Requirements and Constraints of VoIP, Department of Electrical Engineering and Telecommunications, Helsinki University of Technology §2.1 (2001), available at http://www.tml.tkk.fi/Opinnot/Tik-110.501/2000/papers/marjalaakso/voip.html (last visited Apr. 15, 2013).

220 See Landau, Security, Wiretapping, and the Internet, 3(6) IEEE Security & Privacy 26–33 (Nov.–Dec. 2005).

221 See Adrian, VoIP On Tap: Whether the FCC Should Apply Wiretapping Standards to Voice Over Internet Protocol, 57 Admin. L. Rev. 647 (2005).

requires access to some type of hardware device that may or may not be very sophisticated.[222] The equipment or software needed to eavesdrop on VoIP is much more sophisticated, but well within the reach of a 16-year-old hacker.[223] Data sniffing tools[224] are readily available, and these tools will soon be enhanced to become aware of the new VoIP protocols.[225] Because in an office environment, VoIP traffic travels over a data network that is used by all of the regular users of the corporate LAN,[226] any or all of the conversations traversing a network could theoretically be compromised by anyone with a regular connection on the network.[227] VoIP packets could be identified and stored for reassembly to be played back at a later time.[228] Privacy for oral traffic could be vastly enhanced by the use of encryption.[229]

Gatekeeper or call manager type devices, which authenticate users and establish connections, can physically reside on any server on the network.[230] This is really a double-edged sword. Logging information about user calls may be useful for billing or tracking purposes, but these logs can also become targets for hackers.[231] If this type of information becomes compromised, it can create serious concerns for organizations or individuals.[232] In addition, hacking efforts can bring down a VoIP system, unlike a hardwired telephone system.[233]

---

[222] See Karabian, The Case Against Wiretapping, 1 Pac. L.J. 133 (1970).

[223] See Singleton, Big Brother Hears You, But Can He Understand What He Hears--The Problematic Application of CALEA to VoIP Communications in the Age of Encryption, 15 Tul. J. Comp. & Int'l L. 283 (2007); Jong & Gligor, "Discovering Records of Private VoIP Calls without Wiretapping," in Proceedings of the Seventh ACM Symposium on Information, Computer and Communications Security 67–68 (2012).

[224] "Data-sniffing tools enable the attacker to examine transmission content." Ransbotham & Mitra, Choice and Chance: A Conceptual Model of Paths to Information Security Compromise, 20(1) Information Systems Research 121–39 (Mar. 2009).

[225] See Wong & Garrie, Privacy in Electronic Communications: The Regulation of VoIP in the EU and the United States, 15 Computer and Telecomm. L.R. 139 (2009).

[226] See Werbach, Using VoIP to Compete, 83(9) Harvard Business Review 140–47 (2005).

[227] See Walsh & Kuhn, Challenges in Securing Voice Over IP, 3(3) IEEE Security & Privacy 44–49 (2005).

[228] See Me & Verdone, "An Overview of Some Techniques to Exploit VoIP Over WLAN," in Proceedings of the International Conference on Digital Communications 67 (IEEE Computer Society 2006).

[229] See Walsh & Kuhn, Challenges In Securing Voice Over IP, 3(3) IEEE Security & Privacy44–49 (2005).

[230] See Saxena, Sanjay & Sharma, Impact of VoIP and QoS on Open and Distance Learning, 7(3) Turkish Online Journal of Distance Education 28 (July 2006), available at http://tojde.anadolu.edu.tr/tojde23/pdf/article_2.pdf (last visited Apr. 15, 2013).

[231] See Slay & Simon, Voice Over IP: Privacy and Forensic Implications, 1(1) International Journal of Digital Crime and Forensics 89–101 (2009); Androulidakis, On the Importance of Securing Telephony Systems, 8(1) WSEAS Transactions On Communications 102–11 (2009).

[232] See Slay & Simon, Voice Over IP: Privacy and Forensic Implications, 1(1) International Journal of Digital Crime and Forensics 89–101 (2009).

[233] See Almeida, & Lourenço, Security Issues in Unified Communications, 2(2) International Journal of Research and Reviews in Computer Science 403–09 (Mar. 2011).

# Chapter 4
# Cloud Computing

## 4.1 Overview of Cloud Computing

While there are many definitions of "cloud computing," the key thesis is that instead of storing data in-house, the data and data applications are stored remotely, with access to the data provided via the Internet (the "cloud" in "cloud computing").[1] A more technical definition follows:

> [C]loud computing is a model for enabling ubiquitous, convenient, on-demand network access to a shared pool of configurable computing resources (e.g., networks, servers, storage, applications and services) that can be rapidly provisioned and released with minimal management effort or service provider interaction.[2]

[1] See Brad Smith, Senior Vice President and General Counsel, Microsoft, Keynote Address at the Brookings Institution: Cloud Computing for Business and Society (Jan. 20, 2010), available at http://www.brookings.edu/events/2010/01/20-cloud-computing (last visited May 23, 2013); Geelan, Twenty-One Experts Define Cloud Computing. Virtualization (Jan. 24, 2009), Virtualization Journal, http://virtualization.sys-con.com/node/612375 (last visited May 23, 2013); Kennedy, Working in the Cloud (Aug. 1, 2009), A.B.A. Journal, http://www.abajournal.com/magazine/article/working_in_the_clouds/ (last visited May 23, 2013).

[2] According to the official National Institute of Standards and Technology definition, "cloud computing is a model for enabling ubiquitous, convenient, on-demand network access to a shared pool of configurable computing resources (e.g., networks, servers, storage, applications and services) that can be rapidly provisioned and released with minimal management effort or service provider interaction." See Mell & Grance, The NIST Definition of Cloud Computing, NIST Special Publication, 800-145 (U.S. Dept. of Commerce, Computer Security Div. Sept. 2011), available at http://csrc.nist.gov/publications/nistpubs/800-145/SP800-145.pdf; Armbrust, Fox, et al., A View of Cloud Computing, 53(4) Communications of the ACM 50–58 (2010).



D. B. Garrie et al., *Uncovering Digital Evidence*,
https://doi.org/10.1007/978-3-031-68118-9_4

The origin of the name "cloud" is not Latin but derives from an IT architecture metaphor for the distant location of hardware and software accessed by a customer through a cloud service provider.[3]

It is helpful to divide cloud computing systems into two sections: the front end and the back end.[4] These two sections connect via a network, which is most often the Internet. The front end is the customer's computer (or computer network) and the applications necessary to access the cloud.[5] The back end is composed of the various computers, servers, and data storage systems that create the cloud.[6]

The cloud is composed of software applications, delivered as services over the Internet,[7] and servers in datacenters.[8] A customer can put virtually any computer program in the cloud, from medical surgery software[9] to the newest Microsoft Xbox game.[10] The cloud allows customers to elastically provision computing resources in

---

[3] See, e.g., Rearden LLC v. Rearden Commerce, Inc., 597 F. Supp. 2d 1006, 1021 (N.D. Cal. 2009), vacated and remanded, 683 F.3d 1190 (9th Cir. 2012) (stating that cloud computing is "a term used to describe a software-as-a-service (SAAS) platform for the online delivery of products and services"); FTC Complaint of Electronic Privacy Information Center at 4, In re Google, Inc. & Cloud Computing Servs. (Mar. 17, 2009) ("Cloud Computing Services are an emerging network architecture by which data and applications reside on third party servers, managed by private firms, that provide remote access through web-based devices."), available at http://epic.org/privacy/cloudcomputing/google/ftc031709.pdf (last visited July 17, 2013); Gellman, World Privacy Forum, Privacy In The Clouds: Risks To Privacy And Confidentiality From Cloud Computing 4 (Feb. 23, 2009), available at http://www.worldprivacyforum.org/pdf/WPF_Cloud_Privacy_Report.pdf (last visited May 23, 2013) ("[C]loud computing involves the sharing or storage by users of their own information on remote servers owned or operated by others and accessed through the Internet or other connections.") (emphasis omitted).

[4] For a discussion on front-end and back-end servers, see Weiss, Computing in the Clouds, 11(4) netWorker 16–25 (Dec. 2007).

[5] See Wee & Liu, "Client-Side Load Balancer Using Cloud," in Proceedings of the ACM Symposium on Applied Computing 399–405 (ACM 2010); Moreno-Vozmediano, Montero & Llorente, "Elastic Management of Cluster-Based Services in the Cloud," in Proceedings of the 1st Workshop on Automated Control for Datacenters and Clouds 19–24 (ACM 2009).

[6] Rimal, Choi & Lumb "A Taxonomy and Survey of Cloud Computing Systems," Fifth International Joint Conference on INC, IMS and IDC (2009); Weiss, Computing in the Clouds, 11(4) netWorker 16–25 (Dec. 2007).

[7] See Chap. 3 for an in-depth discussion of how the Internet started, the physical topology of connected networks, and the software programs that allow end users the ability to connect with almost anyone in the world.

[8] Although this book is designed as a reference source, with chapters serving as stand-alone guides, it may be useful to understand how hardware and software work together to fully grasp how cloud services function. The chapters on Hardware (Chap. 1) and Software (Chap. 2) offer a thorough background which will more than adequately prepare one for the material in this chapter.

[9] For a comprehensive article discussing how cloud uses medical imaging, see Umamakeswari, Vijayalakshmi & Renugadevi, Storage and Retrieval of Medical Images Using Cloud Computing, 5(4) J. of Artificial Intelligence 207–13 (2012).

[10] See Fouquet, Niedermayer & Carle, "Cloud Computing for the Masses," in Proceedings of the 1st ACM Workshop on User-provided Networking: Challenges and Opportunities 31–36 (ACM 2009).

a manner that is commensurate with demand.[11] For example, Amazon Web Services allows for auto-scaling using customer defined triggers such as "Add 10 instances when CPU usage exceeds 75% for 5 minutes."[12] The cloud does not require customers to make substantial computer hardware expenditures beyond the front-end computers or devices used to access the cloud.[13]

The cloud is deployed via one of three models: public, private, or hybrid. Within this rubric, the cloud delivers services that generally fall into three categories: Infrastructure as a Service (IaaS), Platform as a Service (PaaS), and Software as a Service (SaaS). The following sections will discuss each of these in turn.

## 4.2 Cloud Computing Service Models

The service deployed by the cloud dictates to some extent the amount of control a customer has over the computational environment. Businesses have rapidly adopted cloud computing in the three models mentioned above. In fact, cloud technology is being used across sectors including medical, finance, and entertainment.[14]

## 4.3 Cloud Computing Service Models: Infrastructure as a Service (IaaS)

Cloud providers using the Infrastructure as a Service (IaaS) model deliver computing resources, including processing, storage, and networking.[15] IaaS alleviates the need for the customer to purchase, house, and manage basic hardware and software

---

[11] See Mao, Li & Humphrey, "Cloud Auto-Scaling With Deadline and Budget Constraints," in 11th IEEE/ACM International Conference on GRID Computing 41–48 (Oct. 25–28, 2010).

[12] See Decandia, Hastorun, et al., "Amazon's Highly Available Key-Value Store," in Proceedings of 21st ACM SIGOPS Symposium on Operating Systems Principles 205–20 (ACM 2007); Buyya, Yeo et al., Cloud Computing and Emerging IT Platforms: Vision, Hype, and Reality for Delivering Computing as the 5th Utility, 25(6) Future Generation Computer Systems 599–616 (June 2009). For a discussion of the central processing unit (CPU), please refer to Sect. 1.10 in Chap. 1.

[13] Erdogmus, Cloud Computing: Does Nirvana Hide Behind The Nebula?, 26(2) IEEE Software 4–6 (2009).

[14] Shimrat, Technology Matters: Cloud Computing and Healthcare, San Diego Physician 26, Apr.2009, available at: http://www.himss.org/files/HIMSSorg/content/files/Code%2093_Shimrat_CloudComputingandHealthcare_2009.pdf. For a discussion of how a business in the financial services industry may implement a cloud service, see an example offering from Microsoft: Microsoft Cloud Services for the Financial Services Industry, http://download.microsoft.com/download/7/E/E/7EEB8F76-A08D-4F74-AD3C-7C73B85AF368/Cloud%20Computing%20for%20Financial%20Services.pdf (PDF download, last accessed June 20, 2013).

[15] Vaquero, Merino et al., A Break in the Clouds: Towards a Cloud Definition, 39(1) ACM SIGCOMM Computer Communication Review 2009.

infrastructure components for the IT department.[16] IaaS provides these resources as a metered service similar to water, gas, or electricity.[17] Take data storage as an example: When a customer uses the storage service of an IaaS cloud provider, the customer pays for what they consume without purchasing any hard drives or knowing where their data is stored.[18]

An example of IaaS is Amazon Web Services (AWS). NASA used AWS to manage the networking, processing, and storage necessary to broadcast feedback from the Mars rover, Curiosity.[19] The predicted surge in traffic to the NASA website during the landing of Curiosity would have been unmanageable given the infrastructure that NASA had in place to support its public outreach programs.[20] AWS allowed scalable levels of Internet traffic that ensured Curiosity's landing was viewable around the world via a live feed, and that costs to NASA were kept to a minimum during off-peak viewing time by lowering the capacity of the website. Now, NASA maintains all the live images and metadata captured by Curiosity on AWS.[21]

Although most services are managed by the cloud provider using IaaS, security provisions that extend beyond the basic infrastructure are carried out mainly by the

---

[16] Armbrust, Fox, et al., A View of Cloud Computing, 53(4) Communications of the ACM 50–58 (Apr. 2010).

[17] IaaS can be delivered by an Internet service provider (ISP). In *American Civil Liberties Union v. Reno*, the court defined ISP as follows: Individuals can also access the Internet through commercial and noncommercial "Internet service providers" that typically offer modem telephone access to a computer or computer network linked to the Internet. Many such providers—including the members of plaintiff Commercial Internet Exchange Association—are commercial entities offering Internet access for a monthly or hourly fee. Some Internet service providers, however, are nonprofit organizations that offer free or very low cost access to the Internet. For example, the International Internet Association offers free modem access to the Internet upon request. Also, a number of trade or other nonprofit associations offer Internet access as a service to members.

American Civil Liberties Union v. Reno, 929 F. Supp. 824 (E.D. Pa. 1996), judgment aff'd, 521 U.S. 844 (1997). See also Verizon Commc'ns, Inc. v. F.C.C., 535 U.S. 467, 489–490 (2002) (describing the physical structure of a local telephone exchange).

[18] ISPs using an IaaS model offer customers computing, storage, and networking infrastructure, charging customers in accordance with the resources utilized. Vázquez, Huedo, et al., Evaluation of a Utility Computing Model Based on the Federation of Grid Infrastructures, Euro-Par 2007 Parallel Processing (Lecture Notes in Computer Science, Vol. 4641) 372–81 (2007); see also Khan, "Apps.gov": Assessing Privacy in the Cloud Computing Era, 11 N.C. J. L. & Tech. 259 (2010). See In the Matter of Federal-State Joint Board on Universal Service, 13 F.C.C.R. 11501, 13 F.C.C.R. 11830, 1998 WL 166178 (F.C.C. 1998); see also Kuster, Cloud Computing Services (CCS): A Threat for Internet Neutrality?, Internet Economics VI, 117 (2012), available at http://www.csg.uzh.ch/teaching/hs11/inteco/extern/IFI-2012.02.pdf#page=117 (last visited June 20, 2013).

[19] AWS Case Study: NASA Tells The World About Mars With AWS, Amazon Web Services, http://aws.amazon.com/solutions/case-studies/nasa-jpl-curiosity/ (last visited Apr. 18, 2013).

[20] AWS Case Study: NASA Tells The World About Mars With AWS, Amazon Web Services, http://aws.amazon.com/solutions/case-studies/nasa-jpl-curiosity/ (last visited Apr. 18, 2013).

[21] AWS Case Study: NASA Tells The World About Mars With AWS, Amazon Web Services, http://aws.amazon.com/solutions/case-studies/nasa-jpl-curiosity/ (last visited Apr. 18, 2013).

customer.[22] For example, to secure data sent over the Internet and stored on a cloud, the customer ensures that the data is encrypted and the encryption is not done by the cloud provider.[23] Although no cloud provider is impervious to security breaches, the security the cloud provider offers is likely to be a great deal more compelling than what an individual organization will be able to muster, given that securing computer systems is not likely their core business.[24]

## 4.4 Cloud Computing Service Models: Platform as a Service (PaaS)

Cloud providers that supply Platform as a Service (PaaS) manage the computing infrastructure for the customer and support a set of programs that interface to cloud applications.[25] PaaS providers usually offer software development tools and an application execution environment. Some examples of PaaS include the following:

- Azure, the Microsoft Windows cloud service, which allows customers to create and run applications from within the hosted service.[26]
- Google App Engine, which enables customers to build and host web applications on Google's cloud service.[27]
- Eccentex cloud service, which allows customers to establish and manage enterprise case management solutions both in a public and private cloud environment.[28]

---

[22] Allen et al., Security for Information Technology Service Contracts, CMU/SEI-SIM-003, Software Engineering Institute, Carnegie Mellon University, Jan. 1988, available at http://www.sei.cmu.edu/reports/98sim003.pdf (last visited Jan. 11, 2013).

[23] Alpeyev, Galante, Yasu, Amazon.com Server Said to Have Been Used in Sony Attack, Bloomberg (May 14, 2011), http://www.bloomberg.com/news/2011-05-13/sony-network-said-to-have-been-invaded-by-hackers-using-amazon-com-server.html (last visited Jan. 12, 2013).

[24] Google was forced to make an embarrassing apology in February when its Gmail service collapsed in Europe, while Salesforce.com is still smarting from a phishing attack in 2007, which duped a staff member into revealing passwords. See Binning, Top Five Cloud Computing Security Issues (Apr. 24, 2009), http://www.computerweekly.com/Articles/2010/01/12/235782/Top-five-cloud-computing-security-issues.htm (last visited Jan. 12, 2013).

[25] Pham, E-Discovery in the Cloud Era: What's a Litigant To Do?, 5 Hastings Sci. & Tech. L.J. 139, 147 (Winter 2013).

[26] For further information discussing Microsoft Windows Azure, see http://www.windowsazure.com.

[27] For further information discussing Google App Engine—Google Developer, see https://developers.google.com/appengine/.

[28] For further information discussing Eccentex, see http://www.eccentex.com.

Typically, cloud providers offering PaaS target businesses and not individual consumers.[29] PaaS allows customers to leverage the PaaS provider's resources to run custom applications. For example, a cloud provider using the PaaS model is able to deliver operating systems and associated services over the Internet without requiring downloads or installation by the customer and allowing the customer to build custom applications that utilize the PaaS provider's resources.[30] It is possible, though not necessary, that SaaS applications can be built on top of PaaS, or a private data center.[31]

In a PaaS environment, the customer does not manage or control the underlying cloud infrastructure.[32] However, the customer does control the applications deployed and the settings relating to the applications they deployed in the PaaS environment. Companies shifting to a PaaS environment should be mindful of the hefty migration costs that can arise if they seek to migrate to an alternative PaaS provider, since most applications deployed have custom code written to capitalize on proprietary services unique to the particular PaaS provider.[33] While SaaS, which is discussed in the next section, is arguably the best known model, developers and organization are leveraging PaaS because it allows developers to create applications quickly and easily without the complexity of buying and maintaining the software and infrastructure underneath it.[34]

[29] Rimal, Choi, & Lumb, "A Taxonomy and Survey of Cloud Computing Systems," in Proceedings of the Fifth International Joint Conference on INC, IMS and IDC 44–51 (IEEE Computer Society 2009).

[30] Buyya, Yeo et al., Cloud Computing and Emerging IT Platforms: Vision, Hype, and Reality for Delivering Computing as the 5th Utility, 25(6) Future Generation Computer Systems 599–616 (June 2009).

[31] See Liu, Tong, et al., NIST Cloud Computing Reference Architecture, NIST Special Publication 500–292 (U.S. Dept. of Commerce, Sept. 2011), available at http://www.nist.gov/customcf/get_pdf.cfm?pub_id=909505 (last visited July 18, 2013) http://www.cloudcredential.org/images/pdf_files/nist_reference_architecture.pdf.

[32] Cheng, PaaS-onomics: A CIO's Guide to using Platform-as-a-Service to Lower Costs of Application Initiatives While Improving the Business Value of IT, White Paper for LongJump.com (2008).

[33] A good example demonstrating these risks can be found in Cellary & Strykowski, "E-Government Based on Cloud Computing and Service-Oriented Architecture," in Proceedings of the 3rd International Conference on Theory and Practice of Electronic Governance 5–10 (ACM Nov. 2009).

[34] PaaS is sometimes called "cloudware" because of the migration of technical resources from privately owned computers into the Cloud. Bojanova & Samba, "Analysis of Cloud Computing Delivery Architecture Models," in IEEE Workshops of International Conference on Advanced Information Networking and Applications 453–58 (Mar. 2011).

## 4.5 Cloud Computing Service Models: Software as a Service (SaaS)

Cloud providers using the Software as a Service (SaaS) model offer applications that are accessible to customers over a network, usually the Internet.[35] The following examples of SaaS show the diverse use and implementation of this deployment model:

- Microsoft Office 365 is a cloud version of Microsoft Office. It includes access to Office programs such as Word and Excel from virtually any device in any location.[36]
- SalesForce CRM is a software program that allows users to track all aspects of the client relationship, including accounts, contacts, forecasting, analytics, leads, and opportunities.[37]
- GoToMeeting, an online conference calling service, is a SaaS model deployed over the Internet.[38]
- Google Apps is a productivity suite that allows users to access their email, documents, calendar, and online storage of data, as well as share files with connected users.[39]
- NetSuite is a collection of tools that enables users to manage their customers, sales, marketing, and accounting from any computer or device at any time.[40]

Today, SaaS platforms compete with traditional desktops, laptops, and smartphones that run applications directly on devices.[41] While the delivery of software applications over the network is not a new idea, in the past, it failed to reach the level of an industry platform.[42] In fact, SaaS has been around since the 1960s, but it

---

[35] Greschler & Mangan, Networking Lessons in Delivering 'Software as a Service'—Part I, 12(5) Int'l J. of Network Management 317–21 (2002); see also Soma, Gates, et al., Chasing the Clouds without Getting Drenched: A Call for Fair Practices in Cloud Computing Services, 16 J. Tech. L. & Pol'y 193 (2011); Johnson, It's Electric: An Argument for Certainty and Parity in Regulation to Welcome the New Age of Broadband Delivery—Broadband Over Power Lines, 39 Ga. L. Rev. 1401 (2004).

[36] For more information on Microsoft Office 365, see http://office.microsoft.com/en-us/business/what-is-office-365-for-business-FX102997580.aspx (last visited Apr. 24, 2013).

[37] For more information on SalesForce CRM, see http://www.salesforce.com/crm/ (last visited Apr. 24, 2013).

[38] For more information about GoToMeeting, see http://www.gotomeeting.com (last visited Apr. 16, 2013).

[39] For more information on Google Apps, see http://www.google.com/intl/en/enterprise/apps/business/ (last visited Apr. 16, 2013).

[40] For more information on NetSuite, see http://www.netsuite.com/portal/products/netsuite/main.shtml (last visited Apr. 16, 2013).

[41] Cusumano, Cloud Computing and SaaS as New Computing Platforms, 53(4) Communications of the ACM 27–29 (2010).

[42] Armbrust, Fox, et al., A View of Cloud Computing, 53(4) Communications of the ACM 50–58 (2010).

was not until the late 1990s and early 2000s when companies started to package software applications and offer them via the web that SaaS really started to take off.[43] These applications range from email to calendars and many other consumer applications.[44]

SaaS vendors have evolved further and now have opened their cloud infrastructure to other product companies, thus becoming an industry platform.[45] For example, SalesForce.com initially created a customer relationship management (CRM) platform and delivered it over servers and through a browser.[46] At this point, SalesForce.com had built an in-house platform for the delivery of SaaS to their customers.[47] SalesForce expanded with the introduction of AppExchange, an integration platform that allowed other application firms to build products that leveraged SalesForce CRM. SalesForce extended this open platform concept with Force.com, a development and deployment environment that leverages SalesForce's SaaS infrastructure.[48] This example demonstrates how modern SaaS platforms are competing with traditional software. The SaaS ecosystem is evolving, and today there are SaaS application vendors, which are companies that develop the applications that are offered as a service by SaaS providers.[49]

## 4.6 Public, Private, and Hybrid Cloud Deployment Models

In addition to choosing a service model, customers can choose how their cloud service model is deployed. The three models of deployment offer differing levels of access, security, and cost-efficiency, which all must be weighed to determine which model best fits the customer's needs:

---

[43] Velte, Velte & Elsenpeter, Cloud Computing, A Practical Approach (McGraw-Hill, Inc. 2009).

[44] Martens, Poeppelbuss & Teuteberg, Understanding the Cloud Computing Ecosystem: Results from a Quantitative Content Analysis, Wirtschaftsinformatik 16 (Feb. 2011).

[45] Zhang, Cheng & Boutaba, Cloud Computing: State-Of-The-Art and Research Challenges, 1(1) Journal of Internet Services and Applications 7–18 (2010).

[46] Cusumano, Cloud Computing and SaaS as New Computing Platforms, 53(4) Communications of the ACM 27–29 (2010).

[47] Nambisan & Sawhney, A Buyer's Guide to the Innovation Bazaar, 85 Harv. Bus. Rev. 109 (2007); Marston, Li, et al., Cloud Computing—The Business Perspective, 51(1) Decision Support Systems 176–189 (2011).

[48] Hagel, Brown & Davison, Shaping Strategy in a World of Constant Disruption, 86 Harv. Bus. Rev. 80 (2008); Mathur & Nishchal, "Cloud Computing: New Challenge to the Entire Computer Industry," 1st International Conference on Parallel Distributed and Grid Computing 223–28 (IEEE Oct. 28–30, 2010); Singh, Gupta & Mukherjee, A Survey on Cloud Computing and its Services, 1(5) Int'l J. of Advanced Research in Computer Science and Electronics Engineering121 (2012).

[49] Mietzner, Leymann & Papazoglou, "Defining Composite Configurable SaaS Application Packages Using SCA, Variability Descriptors and Multi-Tenancy Patterns," in Third International Conference on Internet and Web Applications and Services 156–61 (June 8–13, 2008).

- *Public cloud*: when a cloud is made available in a pay-as-you-go manner to the general public.[50]
- *Private cloud*: when a cloud is made available via an internal datacenter of a business or other organizations—not made available to the general public.[51]
- *Hybrid cloud*: When a public and private cloud are connected to allow for sharing of data and applications while taking advantage of the characteristics of both.[52]

## 4.7 Public, Private, and Hybrid Cloud Deployment Models: Public Cloud

A public cloud is one in which the infrastructure and computational resources that it comprises are made available to the general public over the Internet.[53] It is owned and operated by a cloud provider delivering cloud services to customers and, by definition, is external to the customers' organizations.[54]

An example of a public cloud is Amazon Elastic Compute Cloud (EC2).[55] The European counterpart to NASA, the European Space Agency (ESA), uses EC2 in its Data User Elements program, which collects data points relating to the current state

[50] See Armbust, Fox, et al., Above the Clouds: A Berkeley View of Cloud Computing, Technical Report No. UCB/EECS-2009-28 (Feb. 10, 2009), available at http://www.eecs.berkeley.edu/Pubs/TechRpts/2009/EECS-2009-28.pdf (last visited May 24, 2013) (examining both public and private cloud computing environments).

[51] See Armbust, Fox, et al., Above the Clouds: A Berkeley View of Cloud Computing, Technical Report No. UCB/EECS-2009-28 (Feb. 10, 2009), available at http://www.eecs.berkeley.edu/Pubs/TechRpts/2009/EECS-2009-28.pdf (last visited May 24, 2013) (examining both public and private cloud computing environments).

[52] Owens Jr., Is the Future of Internet Gambling in the Cloud?, 14 Gaming L. Rev. and Economics 235 (2010) (defining hybrid clouds to be "unique clouds bound together by standardized or proprietary technology that allows them to share data and applications, as that sharing becomes advantageous").

[53] For a discussion of service providers and public cloud security issues, see Jansen & Grance, Guidelines on Security and Privacy in Public Cloud Computing, NIST Special Publication 800-144 (2011).

[54] Peng, Zhang, et al., "Comparison of Several Cloud Computing Platforms," in Proceedings of the 2009 Second International Symposium on Information Science and Engineering 23–27 (IEEE Computer Society 2009). See also Mell & Grance, The NIST Definition of Cloud Computing, NIST Special Publication, 800-145 (U.S. Dept. of Commerce, Computer Security Div. Sept. 2011), available at http://csrc.nist.gov/publications/nistpubs/800-145/SP800-145.pdf (last visited July 18, 2013).

[55] For more information about Amazon EC2, see http://aws.amazon.com/ec2/ (last visited Apr. 22, 2013).

of the Earth.[56] While much of the work is done by satellites, ESA uses EC2 to manage a statistical system for measuring program usage.

## 4.8 Public, Private, and Hybrid Cloud Deployment Models: Private Cloud

At the other end of the spectrum sit private clouds.[57] A private cloud is one in which the computing environment is operated exclusively for a single customer.[58] It can be managed by the customer or by a third party and may be hosted within the customer's data center or outside of it.[59]

A private cloud has the potential to allow a customer greater control over the infrastructure and computational resources than is possible with a public cloud.[60] The customization and unshared infrastructure of a private cloud permit a more secure environment, which may be ideal for government agencies, doctors, lawyers, and technology innovators.[61]

## 4.9 Public, Private, and Hybrid Cloud Deployment Models: Hybrid Clouds

A hybrid cloud combines on-site (a private cloud) and off-site (a public cloud) data hosting enabling customers to segregate sensitive data or migrate their systems from a local office to a company-wide cloud solution.[62] Each cloud remains a distinct entity but is bound to the other cloud(s) through standardized or proprietary technology that allows application and data portability between the clouds.[63]

---

[56] More information about this program is available at https://aws.amazon.com/solutions/case-studies/european-space-agency/ (last visited Apr. 22, 2013).

[57] Grossman, The Case for Cloud Computing, 11(2) IT Professional 23–27 (2009).

[58] Armbrust, Fox, et al., A View of Cloud Computing, 53(4) Communications of the ACM 50–58 (2010).

[59] Mell & Grance., Effectively and Securely Using the Cloud Computing Paradigm, NIST, Information Technology Lab (2009).

[60] Peng, Zhang, et al., Comparison of Several Cloud Computing Platforms, Second International IEEE Symposium on Information Science and Engineering 23–27 (Dec. 26–28, 2009).

[61] Kaufman, Can Public-Cloud Security Meet Its Unique Challenges?, 8(4) IEEE Security & Privacy 55–57 (2010).

[62] Furht, Cloud Computing Fundamentals, in Handbook of Cloud Computing 3–19 (2010); Hofmann & Woods, Cloud Computing: The Limits of Public Clouds for Business Applications, 14(6) IEEE Internet Computing 90–93 (2010).

[63] Sotomayor, Montero, et al., Virtual Infrastructure Management in Private and Hybrid Clouds, 13(5) IEEE Internet Computing 14–22 (2009).

Hybrid cloud computing allows a private cloud to realize the benefits of a public cloud.[64] For example, a private cloud can utilize a public cloud component to perform work that is not easily run in the private cloud or when there is a workload surge on the private cloud.[65] One company that uses hybrid cloud computing is SoftCom.[66] SoftCom retains a private cloud for sensitive research activities relating to the development of new image-processing systems and data-mining algorithms and uses CloudX, a hybrid cloud provider, for other, nonsensitive services.[67]

## 4.10 Public, Private, and Hybrid Cloud Deployment Models: Virtualization

Virtualization is the ability to run an application across a number of computers simultaneously.[68] Virtualization is a component of all cloud deployment models. It allows applications to be stored on a server and accessed by each computer on the network.[69] For example, the customer simply needs a keyboard, a screen, and an Internet connection, and they can run Windows or Office without noticing that the software is stored on another machine.[70]

Virtualization can be implemented through any of the service offerings of a cloud provider, so that a customer can pay for the cloud provider to manage the hardware

---

[64] Khan & Malluhi, Establishing Trust in Cloud Computing, 12(5) IT Professional 20–27 (2010).

[65] Armbrust, Fox, et al., A View of Cloud Computing, 53(4) Communications of the ACM 50–58 (2010).

[66] Khan & Malluhi, Establishing Trust in Cloud Computing, 12(5) IT Professional 20–27 (2010).

[67] Khan & Malluhi, Establishing Trust in Cloud Computing, 12(5) IT Professional 20–27 (2010).

[68] The benefit of desktop virtualization is that it allows each computer to have its own operating system subject to tight controls imposed by the limitations of desktop virtualization, assuming the network is properly protected. See Miller & Pegah, "Virtualization: Virtually at the Desktop," Proceedings of the 35th Annual ACM SIGUCCS Fall Conference 255–60 (ACM Oct. 2007). Moreover, due to the time and costs involved in installing and configuring a PC, desktop virtualization is getting more popular as an optimization tool in IT departments. See Hazari & Schnorr, Leveraging Student Feedback to Improve Teaching in Web-Based Courses, 26(11) The Journal 30–38 (1999).

[69] Setting up a new PC is a time-consuming process and using desktop virtualization removes this burden and cost. See Beaty, Kochut & Shaikh, "Desktop to Cloud Transformation Planning," in Proceedings of the International IEEE Symposium on Parallel & Distributed Processing 1–8 (May 23–29, 2009). Desktop virtualization reduces the time taken to provision a workstation from days or weeks to just a few minutes, allowing users to start working productively much quicker.

[70] Miller & Pegah, "Virtualization: Virtually at the Desktop," in Proceedings of the 35th annual ACM SIGUCCS Fall Conference 255–60 (ACM Oct. 2007); Ruest & Ruest, Virtualization, A Beginner's Guide (McGraw-Hill Osborne Media 2009); Bostick, Pie in the Sky: Cloud Computing Brings an End to the Professionalism Paradigm in the Practice of Law, 60 Buffalo L. Rev. 1375 (2012); Katzan, Cloud Software Service: Concepts, Technology, Economics, 1(4) Service Science 256–69 (2009).

and software.[71] In addition to cloud-based virtualization, organizations can run virtualization without the use of a cloud provider.[72] This can be done by setting up a local network and running software off the central servers instead of on each individual user's computer.[73]

## 4.11 Business and Legal Risks Presented by the Cloud

Today, many business and technology stakeholders are steering their companies toward the cloud.[74] While the cloud may make sound business sense, stakeholders, especially those in the legal field, should be cognizant of various legal issues involving such things as control and custody of data,[75] data preservation and collection,[76] data review and production,[77] and attorney-client privilege.[78] Other cloud issues focus around who had access to the data and how quickly the owners of the data can

[71] Rimal, Choi, & Lumb, "A Taxonomy and Survey of Cloud Computing Systems," in Proceedings of the Fifth International Joint Conference on INC, IMS and IDC 44–51 (IEEE Computer Society 2009).

[72] See Clark, Designing Storage Area Networks: A Practical Reference for Implementing Storage Area Networks (Addison-Wesley Longman Publishing 2003).

[73] Hess & Newman, Practical Virtualization Solutions: Virtualization from the Trenches (Prentice Hall 2009).

[74] See Horrigan, Cloud Computing Gains in Currency: Online Americans Increasingly Access Data and Applications Stored in Cyberspace (Pew Research Ctr. 2008), available at http://pewresearch.org/pubs/948/cloud-computing-gains-in-currency (last visited May 24, 2013); see also Fowler & Worthen, The Internet Industry Is on a Cloud—Whatever That May Mean (Mar. 26, 2009), The A-HED, Wall St. J., available at http://online.wsj.com/article/SB123802623665542725.html; Cisco, Cisco Global Cloud Index: Forecast and Methodology, 2010–2015 17 (2011), available at http://www.cisco.com/en/US/solutions/collateral/ns341/ns525/ns537/ns705/ns1175/Cloud_Index_White_Paper.pdf (last visited July 18, 2013).

[75] "Cloud computing has unique attributes that require risk assessment in areas such as data integrity, recovery, and privacy, and an evaluation of legal issues in areas such as e-discovery, regulatory compliance, and auditing." Brodkin, "Gartner: Seven Cloud-Computing Security Risks," (July 2, 2008), http://www.infoworld.com/d/security-central/gartner-seven-cloud-computing-security-risks-853.

[76] Betancourt, A Guide to Protecting Your Online Identity (Apr. 21, 2009), http://mashable.com/2009/04/21/protecting-online-identity/; Rolim, Koch, et al., "A Cloud Computing Solution for Patient's Data Collection in Health Care Institutions," in Proceedings of the 2010 Second International Conference on eHealth, Telemedicine, and Social Medicine 95–99 (IEEE Computer Society 2010).

[77] See Foster, Zhou, et al., "Cloud Computing and Grid Computing 360-Degree Compared" in IEEE Grid Computing Environments Workshop 1–10 (Nov. 12–16, 2008).

[78] See Fleming & Dorrain, Survey of the Law of Cyberspace: Introduction, 66 Bus. Lawyer 155 (2010); Grimes, Jaeger, & Fleischmann, Obfuscatocracy: Contractual Frameworks in the Governance of Virtual Worlds, 13(9) First Monday, volume 13, number 9 (Sept. 1, 2008), https://firstmonday.org/ojs/index.php/fm/article/view/2153/2029 (last visited July 18, 2013).

effect change: be it in the form of a litigation hold, a desire to delete information, or a need to produce information on a deadline.[79]

## 4.12 Business and Legal Risks Presented by the Cloud: Data Custody

Unlike physical possessions, data can be quickly and easily transported around the world in seconds, copied a million times over, deleted in the blink of an eye, and stored in a country 10,000 miles away. Oftentimes, customers of the cloud do not know where their data resides or who has custody of the data and metadata created by the applications that run in the cloud.[80]

Duties and obligations of the cloud provider and the customer are defined on a contract-by-contract basis.[81] As in many contract disputes, the court will often define terms, roles, and responsibilities where the parties have not previously done so.[82] For example, if the cloud provider contract does not stipulate how long data will be kept after the termination of the contract, counsel will be forced to argue their position, which may or may not align with common practices of other cloud providers (who are potentially the only source of "best practices" for data management)[83]—to which the court may respond, *if it is so important now, why didn't you create a contract clause to address it?*[84]

[79] Law Firm Technology 2011: Head for the Cloud?, American Lawyer, http://www.americanlawyer.com/PubArticleTAL.jsp?id=1202520215210&Law_Firm_Technology_2011_Head_for_the_Cloud (last visited July 18, 2013).

[80] Pham, E-Discovery in the Cloud Era: What's a Litigant To Do?, 5 Hastings Sci. & Tech. L.J. 139, 147 (Winter 2013).

[81] It is possible to negotiate a nonstandard contract with a cloud provider. See Create an Account, Google, https://accounts.google.com/NewAccount (last visited Sept. 4, 2012) and Google Apps for Business, http://www.google.com/enterprise/apps/business (discussing a user's ability to customize their services by contacting the sales department).

[82] Goetz & Scott, The Limits of Expanded Choice: An Analysis of the Interactions Between Express and Implied Contract Terms, 73(2) Cal. L. Rev. 261–322 (1985).

[83] Gergen, The Use of Open Terms in Contract, 92(5) Colum. L. Rev. 993, 997–1081 (1992); Baker & Krawiec, Incomplete Contracts in a Complete Contract World, 33 Fla. St. U. L. Rev. 725 (2006).

[84] Hamilton Ins. Serv., Inc. v. Nationwide Ins. Cos., 86 Ohio St. 3d 270, 1999-Ohio-162, 714 N.E.2d 898 (1999) ("There can be no implied covenants in a contract in relation to any matter specifically covered by the written terms of the contract itself."); Skurka Aerospace, Inc. v. Eaton Aerospace, L.L.C., 781 F. Supp. 2d 561, 575 (N.D. Ohio 2011) ("an implied term cannot contradict an express term of a contract [...].").

## 4.13 Business and Legal Risks Presented by the Cloud: Privileged and Confidential Information

The attorney-client privilege is a long-held tenet of the US legal system. For data stored in the USA, the risk of an opposing party viewing privileged or confidential data can be overcome with the usual clawback agreements.[85]

If the data is stored in a country without these protections, and the opposing party is either located in that country or easily has access to information in that country, there is a risk of privileged information being made available.[86] For example, in-house counsel in European jurisdictions may not be afforded the same protections under attorney-client privilege as outside counsel, including their communications to the company's foreign operators.[87]

The risk of privileged and confidential information being made available to opposing parties can be exacerbated when the opposing party is a government, a government-owned entity, or a government proxy. One way to mitigate this risk is to ensure all privileged and confidential data is located on servers in the USA or a country with equivalent rules regarding privileged and confidential data.[88]

---

[85] Walworth, Wetzler, et al., Privilege Law, its Global Application, and the Impact of New Technology 3–5 (ABA Midyear Conf., Feb. 3, 2012), available at http://www.americanbar.org/content/dam/aba/publications/young_lawyer/attorneyclientprivlege.authcheckdam.pdf (last accessed July 18, 2013) (discussing the three jurisdictional approaches to inadvertent waiver). Under HIPAA, a covered entity may not use or disclose protected health information unless as permitted or required by 45 C.F.R. §164.502(a) and must ensure such protected health information is only accessible to those authorized under 45 C.F.R. §164.508. 45 C.F.R. §§164.502, 164.504(e), 164.508. See also Gellman, Privacy in the Clouds: Risks to Privacy and Confidentiality from Cloud Computing 9 (2009), available at http://www.worldprivacyforum.org/pdf/WPF_Cloud_Privacy_Report.pdf ("Before a covered entity may transfer protected health information to a service provider, the entity and the provider must enter into a business associate agreement. While a business associate is not directly subject to the HIPAA rule currently, the agreement between the business associate and the covered entity would essentially require the business associate to comply with the same standards that apply to the covered entity.").

[86] Commission Decisions on the Adequacy of the Protection of Personal Data in Third Countries, European Commission, available at http://ec.europa.eu/justice/data-protection/document/international-transfers/adequacy/index_en.htm (last visited Oct. 26, 2012) (stating the European Union only recognizes the US Department of Commerce's Safe Harbor Privacy Principles and the transfer of Air Passenger Name Record to the US Bureau of Customs and Border Protection as providing adequate protection).

[87] Rosensweig & Thurber, How Global is the Attorney-Client Privilege? (Nov. 2011), New England In-House, http://www.goulstonstorrs.com/portalresource/lookup/wosid/contentpilot-core-6-25502/media.name=/Rosensweig%20and%20Thurber%20global%20privilege%20article.pdf (last visited Apr.15, 2013).

[88] New York State Bar Association, Report of the Privacy Task Force 40–41 (2009), available at http://www.nysba.org/AM/Template.cfm?Section=Privacy_Report (last visited May 24, 2013). The EEA consists of 27 European Union countries as well as Iceland, Liechtenstein, and Norway. Switzerland is not party to the EEA Agreement but is nonetheless bound to comply under an EU agreement. European Union, European Commission, available at http://ec.europa.eu/justice/data-protection/bodies/authorities/eu/index_en.htm (last visited May 24, 2013); EEA Agreement,

Storing private, privileged, or confidential data in the cloud presents greater risks for both a cloud customer (such as a law firm) and the customer's client. Unlike self-hosting data, a cloud customer may be unaware of how a cloud provider backs up data or how long their data is kept after the cloud customer deletes the data.[89] Since each cloud provider is different and has different internal policies regarding backups and deletion,[90] counsel should be aware of the practices and procedures followed for each cloud provider used.[91] For instance, counsel should not assume that the contract terms with Dropbox are similar to the contract terms with Rackspace, especially when it comes to critical decisions such as deletion policies, backup policies, and data privacy and security.[92]

Further, maintaining privacy can become significantly more complicated if the documents are stored in another country.[93] Other countries have confidentiality and

EFTA, http://www.efta.int/eea/eea-agreement.aspx (last visited May 24, 2013). The USA falls short of the EU standard as the privacy laws in the USA limit protection to the data of US citizens. Opinion 6/2002 on Transmission of Passenger Manifest Information and Other Data from Airlines to the United States, at 5 n.16 (Oct. 24, 2002), available at http://ec.europa.eu/justice/policies/privacy/docs/wpdocs/2002/wp66_en.pdf (last visited May 24, 2013).

[89] Lee, Google Explains Gmail Fail that 'Erased' Users' Emails, Disabled Accounts, Huffington Post (Mar. 1, 2011), http://www.huffingtonpost.com/2011/03/01/google-gmail-problems-explained_n_829638.html (last visited July 18, 2013) (discussing how about 40,000 Gmail users lost all their email, which Gmail was able to recover due to their policy of backing up user data on tape).

[90] See Tomlinson v. El Paso Corp., 245 F.R.D. 474, 477 (D. Colo. 2007) (holding statutorily mandated preservation duties could not be delegated to a third party, and thus the responding party maintained control of their documents); Goodman v. Praxair Services, Inc., 632 F. Supp. 2d 494, 515 (D. Md. 2009) ("Rule 34 'control' would not require a party to have legal ownership or actual physical possession of any documents at issue."); Nycomed U.S. Inc. v. Glenmark Generics Ltd., 2010 WL 3173785, *7 (E.D. N.Y. 2010) (holding that documents stored with a third party were still under the control of the responding party); New Jersey Manufacturers Ins. Co. v. Hearth & Home Techs., Inc., 2008 WL 2571227, *7 (M.D. Pa. 2008) (holding, "A plaintiff, particularly one who was represented by counsel prior to the spoliation, is not relieved of this responsibility merely because the plaintiff did not itself act in bad faith and a third party to whom Plaintiff entrusted the evidence was the one who discarded or lost it").

[91] Haslam, Herman, et al., "Practice Safe SaaS: Don't Lose Your Head (Or Data) In The Clouds," 4 Privacy & Data Security L.J. 771 (October 2009); Scheier, What to Do if Your Cloud Provider Disappears, InfoWorld (Apr. 20, 2009), http://www.infoworld.com/d/cloud-computing/what-do-if-your-cloud-provider-disappears-508 (last visited May 24, 2013).

[92] For a discussion of terms and conditions in cloud contracts, see Bradshaw, Millard & Walden, Contracts for Clouds: Comparison and Analysis of the Terms and Conditions of Cloud Computing Services, 19(3) Int'l J. of L. & Tech. 187–223 (2011).

[93] Sunosky, Privacy Online: A Primer on the European Union's Directive and the United States' Safe Harbor Privacy Principles, 9 Currents: International Trade Law Journal 80–88 (2000); Sun Microsystems, 2007. "Sun Modular Datacenter" (12 December), available at http://docs.oracle.com/cd/E19115-01/mod.dc.s20/index.html (last visited May 24, 2013).

privacy laws that can vary greatly from those in the USA.[94] For a more thorough discussion of jurisdiction and the implications of document location, see Sect. 4.15.[95]

## 4.14 Business and Legal Risks Presented by the Cloud: Litigation Hold

Litigation is often unexpected, and promptly enforcing a litigation hold requires all parties to move in a coordinated effort.[96] In the cloud, this becomes more complicated as data can be spread across servers operated by different service providers in different states and different countries.[97] Ensuring that all data remains intact and that regular deletion practices cease can be a momentous effort if litigants are unprepared.[98] Cloud customers should endeavor to contract around this risk by inserting clauses regarding access to data, including specific response time frames that must be met by the service provider.[99]

---

[94] See Linde v. Arab Bank, PLC, 262 F.R.D. 136 (E.D. N.Y. 2009). (The *Linde* Court denied the discovery of documents, which were protected under Israeli confidentiality laws, but ordered production of the remaining materials).

[95] Recently the Italian Court of Cassation, the highest court in Italy, took the case against Google executives for content posted on YouTube. Previously the lower court ruled against Google, but an appeals court acquitted the executives of defamation. For an early discussion of the case, see Hansell, Google Executives Face Jail Time for Italian Video (Feb. 2, 2009), New York Times Blogs, http://bits.blogs.nytimes.com/2009/02/02/google-executives-face-jail-time-for-italian-video/ (last visited July 18, 2013). For a recent account of the case, see Essers, Google Video trial to continue to Italian supreme court, IDG News Service (Apr. 17, 2013), http://www.pcworld.com/article/2035387/google-video-trial-to-continue-to-italian-supreme-court.html (last visited July 18, 2013).

[96] Abadi, "Data Management in the Cloud: Limitations and Opportunities," in Bulletin of the IEEE Computer Society, Technical Committee on Data Engineering 3 (2009), available at ftp://131.107.65.22/pub/debull/A09mar/abadi.pdf. (last visited July 18, 2013) ("Amazon's S3 cloud storage service replicates data across 'regions' and 'availability zones' so that data and applications can persist even in the face of failures of an entire location."). See Fed. R. Civ. P. 26, 37, 45; Dickenson, Third Party Discovery, EDDE Journal, (Spring 2012), at 12–14, available at http://www.americanbar.org/content/dam/aba/administrative/science_technology/2012_spring_v3i2.authcheckdam.pdf (last visited July 18, 2013).

[97] See Cohen, Drawing the Line: How Much Data Access is too Much? Security Concerns Take Center Stage in Our Annual Technology Survey, American Lawyer (Nov. 1, 2011) ("Continuing cost pressure is among the factors leading firms to explore cloud-based technologies-applications that run on a vendor's infrastructure and that are located far off-site …. Nearly two-thirds of firms (63%) report using some type of cloud-based solution").

[98] See, e.g., How Do I Recover Old Versions of Files, Dropbox, https://www.dropbox.com/help/11/en (last visited July 20, 2012) ("[Dropbox] keeps snapshots of every change in your Dropbox folder over the last 30 days (or more with the Pack-Rat feature)").

[99] For assistance or model language, readers can email to Daniel@lawandforensics.com.

## 4.15 Jurisdiction and Cloud Computing

Since cloud computing is relatively new, novel issues concerning jurisdiction may arise.[100] Generally, in civil lawsuits, the customer is charged with producing relevant documents in its "possession, custody, or control."[101] This typically means that the customer is responsible for producing its documents without regard to where the documents are physically stored, provided they are the customer's documents or the customer has control over the documents.[102] However, because the customer using the cloud will place its documents in a different physical location from the office of that customer, several new questions may arise, creating legal issues for which there is little precedent.[103]

Storing documents in a remotely located cloud raises questions regarding consent to jurisdiction for the customer.[104] Courts have yet to decide if the minimum contacts necessary to establish jurisdiction are satisfied merely because documents are there, even if it has no other contacts whatsoever. When documents are stored in the cloud, courts have to decide whether the documents are governed by the law of the state in which they are physically located, by the location of the company which generated the documents, or by the laws of the state where an employee or executive of the company resides.[105]

In criminal law proceedings, jurisdiction is more complicated considering the ability of law enforcement or government regulators to access cloud data. As the use of digital records increases, including email, instant messaging, and cell phone

---

[100] Horrigan, Use of Cloud Computing Applications and Services, Pew Internet and the American Life Project, at http://www.pewinternet.org (last visited Jan. 11, 2011).

[101] Fed. R. Civ. P. 34(a); *see* Flagg v. City of Detroit, 252 F.R.D. 346, 347 (E.D. Mich. 2008) (confirming the obligation to preserve and produce ESI cannot be avoided merely "through the simple expedient of storing it with a third party"); Columbia Pictures Industries v. Bunnell, 2007 WL 2080419, *1 (C.D. Cal. 2007) ("Federal courts have consistently held that documents are deemed to be within a party's possession, custody or control for purposes of Rule 34 if the party has actual possession, custody or control, or has the legal right to obtain the documents on demand."); Cyntegra, Inc. v. Idexx Laboratories, Inc., 2007 WL 5193736, *5 (C.D. Cal. 2007), order aff'd, 322 Fed. Appx. 569 (9th Cir. 2009) ("[C]ourts have extended the affirmative duty to preserve evidence to instances when that evidence is not directly within the party's custody or control so long as the party has access to, or indirect control over, such evidence").

[102] Pham, E-Discovery in the Cloud Era: What's a Litigant To Do?, 5 Hastings Sci. & Tech. L.J. 139, 147 n.100 (Winter 2013), citing Soares, Fox Rothschild LLP, "Applying E-Discovery Best Practices to Cloud Computing," The Legal Intelligencer, Jan. 31, 2012, at 2 (reprinted with permission at http://www.foxrothschild.com/newspubs/newspubsArticle.aspx?id=4294970830).

[103] See Hand, Head in the Clouds, 449(7165) Nature 963 (Oct. 2007).

[104] See In re Air Cargo Shipping Services Antitrust Litigation, 278 F.R.D. 51, 54–55 (E.D. N.Y. 2010) (holding that "France's relatively weak national interest in prohibiting disclosure … [was] outweighed by the more substantial United States interests").

[105] See Gucci America, Inc. v. Curveal Fashion, 2010 WL 808639 (S.D. N.Y. 2010). (A trademark infringement litigation, wherein the court concluded that "the United States interest in fully and fairly adjudicating matters before its courts … outweighs Malaysia's interest in protecting the confidentiality of its banking customers' records").

records, so does law enforcement's use of technology to conduct investigations and establish evidence in cases.[106] If the government wishes to review, or even seize, the records located in the cloud, courts will have to decide if law enforcement has the requisite power. But first, a determination must be made as to which court has the jurisdictional authority to decide. It is important to remember that law enforcement and government agencies may have difficulty using their authorized powers if they are outside of the jurisdictional limits of those powers.

Some of the jurisdictional issues can be addressed in the cloud contract.[107] Agreements can be made concerning the ownership and control of the customer's data and how the particular customer's data will be managed following the termination of the contract. Disputes that involve other entities not party to the cloud agreement may not be subject to the terms of the agreement, which could present additional issues for the company. Accordingly, operating in the cloud presents significant uncertainty and has the potential for future disputes concerning jurisdiction.

## 4.16 Cloud Computing Benefits, Costs, and Risks

The cloud certainly provides software developers and companies, large and small, with the ability to avoid expending large capital outlays in hardware to deploy their service or the human expense to operate it. They need not focus on planning for too little or too much success, foregoing potential customers and revenue. The cloud enables customers with large batch-oriented tasks to get results much faster than ever before by allowing their programs to scale, since using 2000 servers for 1 hour costs the same as using one server for 2000 hours. The cloud allows for elasticity of computing resources, without having to pay a premium for large scale, which is unprecedented in the history of computing. Yet, when a company looks at deploying a cloud, it must carefully weigh the benefits, costs, and risks and thus engage the relevant legal, business, and security personnel in the decision process.[108]

[106] See Hardy, "The Death of Hardware," Forbes, Feb. 11, 2008, available at http://www.forbes.com/technology/forbes/2008/0211/036.html.

[107] DiRomualdo, A., & Gurbaxani, V., "Strategic intent for IT outsourcing," (1998), available at http://escholarship.org/uc/item/7kc4d3p1 (last visited June 20, 2013). Strategic intent for IT outsourcing. Switching cloud providers is not without risk, as cloud users may lose control over their data or their client's data. Additional risks include the cloud provider failing to provide services or the cloud provider being sold to another firm. Martin, Hey! You! Get Off of My Cloud: Defining and Protecting the Metes and Bounds of Privacy, Security, and Property in Cloud Computing, 92(2) Journal of the Patent & Trademark Office Society 283–314 (2011).

[108] See generally Smith, Building Confidence in the Cloud: A Proposal for Industry and Government Action to Advance Cloud Computing (Jan. 20, 2010), available at http://download.microsoft.com/download/C/0/0/C00D24A5-A686-4109-9DB8-14A29E058069/Building_Confidence_in_the_Cloud_White_Paper.doc (last visited July 18, 2013). Describing how cloud computing is purchased and implemented using sophisticated technology services over the Internet on an as-needed

## 4.17 Cloud Computing Benefits, Costs, and Risks: Benefits of Switching to Cloud Computing

Switching to the cloud can provide a host of benefits, such as the following:

- Saving money by lowering the costs of IT labor and data center support.[109]
- Improving performance and scalability of services by limiting up-front capital infrastructure and labor investment based on demand.[110]
- Reducing data storage costs.[111]
- Eliminating the need for cloud computing customers to plan far ahead for equipment provisioning by creating the illusion of infinite computing resources available on demand.[112]
- Allowing for provision of computing resources on an as-needed basis (e.g., processors by the hour and storage by the day), thus enabling customers to pilot new ideas at lower costs.[113]

Companies that migrate to the cloud can achieve major benefits by utilizing better management of the technology life cycle, gaining the ability to scale IT infrastructure capacity to meet increased demand, and lowering the time spent waiting for IT resources.[114] The cloud also provides companies with greater business agility in a changing and uncertain economy by allowing the company to rapidly expand or

---

basis. These services include email, word processing, software development tool, and complex data center operations, just to name a few.

[109] "Cloud computing providers can build large datacenters at low cost due to their expertise in organizing and provisioning computational resources. The economies of scale increase revenue for cloud providers and lower costs for cloud users." Chen, Paxson, & Katz, What's New About Cloud Computing Security?, University of California, Berkeley Report No. UCB/EECS-2010-5 (Jan. 20, 2010).

[110] "Enterprises currently employ Cloud services in order to improve the scalability of their services and to deal with bursts in resource demands." Buyya, Yeo, et al., Cloud Computing and Emerging IT Platforms: Vision, Hype, and Reality for Delivering Computing as the 5th Utility, 25(6) Future Generation Computer Systems 599–616 (June 2009).

[111] See Schadt, Linderman, et al., Computational Solutions to Large-Scale Data Management and Analysis, 11(9) Nature Reviews Genetics 647–57 (2010).

[112] Voorsluys, Broberg & Buyya, "Introduction to Cloud Computing," in Cloud Computing, 1–41 (2011); Rafique, Tareen, et al., "Cloud Computing Economics Opportunities and Challenges" in Proceedings of the 4th IEEE International Conference on Broadband Network and Multimedia Technology 401–406 (2011).

[113] See Buyya, Yeo, & Venugopal, "Market-Oriented Cloud Computing: Vision, Hype, and Reality for Delivering IT Services as Computing Utilities," in Proceedings of 10th IEEE International Conference on High Performance Computing and Communications (2008). "The key observation is that cloud computing's ability to add or remove resources at a fine grain (one server at a time with EC2) and with a lead time of minutes rather than weeks allows matching resources to workload much more closely." Armbrust, Fox, et al., A View of Cloud Computing, 53(4) Communications of the ACM 50–58 (2010).

[114] Olekar & Sreekumar, Cloud Computing: Migration from Traditional Systems to the Cloud, 2(3) International Journal of Advanced Research in Computer Engineering & Technology 1128 (2013).

contract IT capabilities, paying only for what the company consumes. Finally, the cloud enables companies to grow their core business rather than maintain core IT infrastructure.

## 4.18 Cloud Computing Benefits, Costs, and Risks: Costs of Cloud Computing

While these business benefits are certainly meaningful, legal and business costs do exist. Migrating personal or business functions to a cloud is not a trivial task. The steps necessary to making this transition include identifying the current data environment, establishing data formats, reviewing security controls for data, avoiding future legal problems by careful contract language, and verifying that the cloud can support customer needs and training.

The due diligence process to determine the best cloud service and model for an organization can involve a substantial investment in time and money. There are costs to exploring the benefits of the cloud, including selecting a cloud provider, considering the terms of implementation, and negotiating the terms of the cloud contract. The larger the organization and the number of stakeholders, the more costly this process can be.

Once an organization has decided on a model and services to fit their needs, the cost of implementation and customization must be addressed. These costs include training costs, maintenance costs, and troubleshooting. All of these entail a substantial initial investment and a much lower ongoing cost. Even though the cloud provider may be responsible for maintaining the data and fixing problems, the company will still incur some costs. The company cannot, and should not, expect that it can simply tell the cloud provider to "handle it" and that the problem will then go away.

If an organization has chosen a private cloud over a public cloud, they should be aware of losing the economies of scale that come with a public cloud. In a private cloud, the cloud infrastructure is operated solely for an organization, may be managed by the organization or a third party, and may exist on or off premises. A public cloud is a cloud where the infrastructure is made available to the general public or a large industry group and is owned by a cloud provider. However, unlike a private cloud, it is imperative that counsel recognize that public clouds likely have multiple customers and that additional care must be taken to ensure that its data are not being exposed to multiple customers on shared servers.

As a final point of analysis, a company should consider how many litigation matters they are involved in annually and if discovery will be impacted by a relocation of data. The costs of any litigation will include electronic discovery costs, and the company must consider whether these costs will increase or decrease as a result of the cloud and should consider whether any increased costs could potentially offset or mitigate the benefits of using the cloud.[115]

## 4.19 Cloud Computing Benefits, Costs, and Risks: Risks of Cloud Computing

Though difficult to quantify, the risks underlying cloud data storage are very real. For example, loss or damage to data can happen due to equipment failure, weather and power outages, and seizure of corporate assets in bankruptcy proceedings.[116] Provisions should be made to deal with such problems that account for the interruption in the normal flow and use of data.[117]

Accordingly, cloud computing also creates a substantial dependency between the customer and the cloud provider.[118] If data stored on the cloud becomes inaccessible, the customer may be unable to conduct business.[119] The customer should consider the risks that can arise in a situation where the cloud is inaccessible, even if the loss of access is temporary, and develop a coordinated response plan.[120]

Cloud computing could lead to increased risk of litigation over certain types of data, such as a patent litigation, where valuable proprietary information is at stake. If security is not a priority at a cloud provider, or the customer does not take care to

---

[115] Electronic discovery can be defined as the discovery of electronic documents and data including email, web pages, word processing files, computer databases, and virtually anything that is stored on a computer. Technically, documents and data are "electronic" if they exist in a medium that can only be read through the use of computers. Such media include cache memory, magnetic disks (such as computer hard drives or floppy disks), optical disks (such as DVDs or CDs), and magnetic tapes (Kroll Ontrack, Glossary of Terms, http://www.krollontrack.com/glossaryterms).

[116] Caplan, Bankruptcy in the Cloud: Effects of Bankruptcy by a Cloud Services Provider 4 (2010), available at http://ftp.documation.com/references/ABA10a/PDfs/3_3.pdf (last visited July 18, 2013). See also 11 U.S.C.A. §721 (2012) (mandating the business cease operations unless the court has authorized a "trustee to operate the business of the debtor for a limited period, if such operation is in the best interest of the estate and consistent with the orderly liquidation of the estate").

[117] Any solution needs to incorporate guarantees that data owners would be able to gain control of their data in a usable form should their service providers become inoperable. See ABA Legal Technology Resource Center, FYI: Software as a Service (SaaS) for Lawyers, http://www.abanet.org/tech/ltrc/fyidocs/saas.html (last visited Mar. 9, 2010).

[118] A user interacts with an online service through the Internet, and the online service's vendor provides the necessary software applications and remote data storage. ABA Legal Technology Resource Center, FYI: Software as a Service (SaaS) for Lawyers, http://www.abanet.org/tech/ltrc/fyidocs/saas.html (last visited Mar. 9, 2010).

[119] See Open Cloud Manifesto, Mar. 2009, available at http://www.opencloudmanifesto.org/index.htm (last visited July 13, 2013).

[120] ABA Legal Technology Resource Center, FYI: Software as a Service (SaaS) for Lawyers, http://www.abanet.org/tech/ltrc/fyidocs/saas.html (last visited Jan. 10, 2013).

encrypt data, the added risk of losing proprietary information may outweigh the benefits of cloud computing.

For better or worse, the task of evaluating these costs and risks falls primarily upon in-house counsel or their outside counsel.[121] Counsel must review and negotiate the terms of the cloud provider agreement and account for the various legal issues and other problems that can arise.[122]

Counsel should identify how data will be collected and preserved before that data is put on the cloud. A good practice is to record the results of the due diligence in a data map or other litigation readiness tool and store that along with the cloud contract. Should litigation later arise, the customer will be prepared to implement a litigation readiness plan. This may also be useful in the event there is subsequent litigation over the intention of the arrangement.[123]

Companies must be engaged in the entire process as well. While their most important concern should be the handling and treatment of data—how it will be stored, accessed, and used—they will also need to consider the costs.[124] In a large organization, different business units may have very different needs and issues (as well as cost analyses) and store information in different ways.[125] Consequently, each piece will require thoughtful analysis.

---

[121] Gupta, Szego & Jacobs, PLI Electronic Discovery Guidance 2008: What Corporate and Outside Counsel Need to Know (2008) (discussing when the duty to preserve arises and managing compliance with the legal and ethical eDiscovery obligations).

[122] Counsel should ensure that an adequate ESI discovery plan is in place, to avoid confusion in the event of litigation. See Mirbeau of Geneva Lake LLC v. City of Lake Geneva, 2009 WL 3347101 (E.D. Wis. 2009) (the court reprimands both parties for failure to develop meaningful ESI discovery plan).

[123] See Kennedy, Working in the Cloud (Aug. 1, 2009), A.B.A. Journal, http://www.abajournal.com/magazine/article/working_in_the_clouds/ (last visited May 23, 2013). That could create severe liability issues for cloud users because of their contractual responsibilities or because of the damage caused to their clients by a loss of data or system access.

[124] See In re Veeco Instruments, Inc. Securities Litigation, 2007 WL 983987 (S.D. N.Y. 2007). In this matter, the court found that backup tapes were not reasonably accessible where the parties failed to define discovery parameters at the outset. In reaching its decision, the court noted that while the defendant had neglected to identify the backup tapes as an inaccessible source of potentially responsive information, as required by Fed. R. Civ. Pro. 26(b)(2), both parties had overlooked their obligation to discuss discovery parameters and protocols. Finding that the plaintiff could not reasonably assume that the defendant would have undertaken discovery of the backup tapes as a matter of course, the court determined that the backup tapes were not reasonably accessible.

[125] Stanton & Victor, What We See in the Clouds: A Practical Overview of Litigating Against and on Behalf of Organizations Using Cloud Computing, 59 U.S. Attorneys' Bulletin, No. 3, May 2011, at 40 (citing Radian Asset Assur., Inc. v. College of the Christian Bros. of New Mexico, 2010 WL 4928866, *1–2 (D.N.M. 2010) (holding the transfer of data from on-line network storage to near-line storage is a normal business function)), available at http://www.umiacs.umd.edu/~oard/teaching/708x/spring12/readings/stanton2.pdf ("Courts may view cloud computing as a normal business function where the data cannot be made inaccessible when the organization should have known of potential E-Discovery needs when incorporating cloud computing into their systems").

One possible way to divide information is to segregate information by type. For example, the company can treat emails differently than other data, or it may make sense to store sales data, production data, and inventory data in a unique cloud system in order to maximize storage and usage efficiency. Thus, depending on the company, the process of implementing a cloud may involve several different approaches.[126]

In short, the cloud can provide significant competitive advantages in use, storage, and efficiency of data. But these advantages will only be realized if they outweigh the costs and risks associated with the cloud. Careful attention to these costs and risks at the outset—before implementation of the cloud—is the key to its successful use.[127]

[126] Naone, "Computer in the Cloud," Technology Review (Sept. 18, 2007), http://www.technologyreview.com/news/408689/computer-in-the-cloud/ (last visited July 18, 2013).

[127] Thompson, "Storm Warning for Cloud Computing," BBC News (May 27, 2008), http://news.bbc.co.uk/2/hi/technology/7421099.stm (last visited July 18, 2013).

# Chapter 5
# Mobile Phones

## 5.1 Introduction to Mobile Phones

Mobile phones are devices that make and receive communications, most often as telephone calls and text messages, by connecting to a cellular network.[1] Mobile phone services have existed since 1973, allowing people to communicate anywhere without the need for fixed telephone lines.[2] From large, bulky, and expensive equipment carried in briefcases to sleek, pocket-sized devices readily afforded by most people, they have evolved in size, price, and functionality.[3]

Most mobile devices allow you to send, receive, and store information in multiple ways, providing calendars, messaging, Internet access, email, and even full media playback.[4] Mobile phones are not simply for voice-calling—they are telephones, calendars, cameras, entertainment devices, radios, media players, and Dictaphones, all in one.[5] Mobile phones merge oral and data communications and

[1] See generally Berresford, The Impact of Law and Regulation on Technology: The Case History of Cellular Radio, 44 Bus. Law. 721 (1988); McGuigan, Connors & Cannon, Cellular Mobile Radio Telecommunications: Regulating an Emerging Industry, 1983 BYU L. Rev. 305. The first reports of mobile phone inventions go all the way back to 1906, when the *Los Angeles Herald* published a story on wireless telephoning. Los Angeles Herald [microform], May 21, 1906, Page 7, Image 7, available at http://chroniclingamerica.loc.gov/lccn/sn85042462/1906-05-21/ed-1/seq-7/ (last visited May 20, 2013).

[2] Ren, From Cloud Computing to Language Engineering, Affective Computing and Advanced Intelligence, 2(1) International Journal of Advanced Intelligence 1–14 (2010) (stating the first mobile phone was invented by Dr. Martin Cooper, an employee of the Motorola Corporation, in 1973).

[3] Kumar & Zahn, Mobile Communications: Evolution and Impact on Business Operations, 23(6) Technovation 515–20 (2003). See generally Goggin, Cell Phone Culture: Mobile Technology In Everyday Life (Routledge 2012).

[4] See generally Goggin, Cell Phone Culture: Mobile Technology In Everyday Life (Routledge 2012).

[5] See generally Goggin, Cell Phone Culture: Mobile Technology In Everyday Life (Routledge 2012).

 
D. B. Garrie et al., *Uncovering Digital Evidence*,
https://doi.org/10.1007/978-3-031-68118-9_5

represent a new frontier that raises a litany of issues regarding privacy, eavesdropping, data retention, and production.[6]

The following offers readers a quick overview of mobile phone and network technologies:

- *First generation (1G)*—analog cellular radio (voice only)
- *Second generation (2G)*—digital cellular radio (voice and basic data only)
- *Third generation (3G)*—multimedia cellular radio (audio, data, entertainment, images, video clips, voice, etc.)
- *Beyond 3G/fourth generation/(B3G/4G)*—interoperable with other broadband wireless solutions, delivering converged services across different network types and reducing the costs of delivering data to mobile users utilizing data intensive applications

In the USA today, there are more than 320 million active mobile phones.[7] These phones deliver turn-by-turn directions, Internet browsing, dinner reservations, and music ticket purchases.[8]

The remainder of this chapter focuses on the technical underpinnings of mobile phones and networks.[9] First, we discuss the basic software and hardware underlying the mobile phone. Next, we look at the evolved mobile phone. A discussion follows about the now-ubiquitous application (commonly known as an "app") software that increases the functionality of smartphones. We next review the Internet as viewed from a mobile phone. The focus then shifts to the ever-evolving communications platforms that allow for transmission of voice and data content. Finally, we discuss the four different mobile messaging services that underlie text messaging.

## 5.2 What Is a Mobile Phone? How Does It Work?

A mobile phone is a digital device that transmits audio signals through mobile hardware using analog or digital frequencies. Mobile phones are actually radios, albeit rather sophisticated radios.[10] The telephone was invented by Alexander Graham

---

[6] Discussion of the convergence of oral and written communications is beyond the focus of this chapter. See generally Cohen, Examined Lives: Informational Privacy and the Subject as Object, 52 Stan. L. Rev. 1373, 1374 (2000); Richards, The Information Privacy Law Project, 94 Geo. L.J. 1087, 1117–19 (2006). See also Garrie, Armstrong & Harris, Voice Over Internet Protocol and the Wiretap Act: Is Your Conversation Protected?, 29 Seattle U. L. Rev. 97 (Fall 2005).

[7] CTIA The Wireless Association, Wireless Quick Facts (stating there are 321.7 million wireless subscriber connections as of June 2012), available at http://www.ctia.org/advocacy/research/index.cfm/aid/10323 (last visited May 20, 2013).

[8] For a sampling of features, see http://en.wikipedia.org/wiki/Mobile_phone_feature (last visited Mar. 28, 2013).

[9] This chapter does not discuss the more advanced components of mobile phones such as computer vision with mobile devices.

[10] Marvin, When Old Technologies Were New (Oxford University Press 1988).

Bell in 1876.[11] The radio was invented by Nikolai Tesla in the 1880s.[12] The combination of these inventions ultimately led to the modern mobile phone.

Before the iPhone and before mobile phones that did not require a briefcase came about, mobile communications were achieved via radio-telephones, such as CB radios.[13] The radio-telephone system required at least one central antenna tower in a city.[14] These towers had 25 channels available for users to communicate, which obviously limited the number of users that could use radio-telephones.[15] The central antenna was a transmitter with an approximate range of 50 miles.[16] The advent of the cellular phone system meant that numerous cell towers were built to divide the city into small cells, or quadrants.[17] This exponentially increased the number of channels available for users to transmit communication. Now, a mobile phone can communicate on over 1500 channels.

Most mobile phones can receive or transmit signals within a 3–15-mile range.[18] However, in practical terms, terrain obstructions and voice relay delays limit this distance drastically.[19] Mobile phones are full-duplex devices (as opposed to half-duplex devices such as walkie-talkies), meaning one frequency is used for talking and the other frequency is used for listening.[20] The cell tower transmission range varies subject to topography, buildings, and other obstructions, which can all disrupt the transmission.[21] Because there are numerous cell towers, a cell phone can use a low-powered transmitter to reach the closest tower.[22] Low-power usage also means

---

[11] Agar, Constant Touch: A Global History of the Mobile Phone (Icon Books, Ltd., 2013).

[12] Perpetual Contact: Mobile Communication, Private Talk, Public Performance (Katz & Aakhus, eds. Cambridge University Press 2002).

[13] For an interesting and thorough review of mobile communication systems, see Ling, The Mobile Connection: The Cell Phone's Impact on Society (Morgan Kaufmann 2004).

[14] Yacoub, Foundations of Mobile Radio Engineering (CRC Press LLC 1993).

[15] Stüber, Principles of Mobile Communication (Springer Science + Business Media 2011).

[16] Stüber, Principles of Mobile Communication (Springer Science + Business Media 2011).

[17] Adachi, Wireless Past and Future—Evolving Mobile Communications Systems, 84(1) IEICE Transactions on Fundamentals of Electronics, Communications and Computer Sciences 55–60 (2001).

[18] Malone, The Fourth Amendment and the Stored Communications Act: Why the Warrantless Gathering of Historical Cell Site Location Information Poses No Threat to Privacy, 39 Pepp. L. Rev. 701 (2011).

[19] Markgraf, How Far Can a Cell Tower Be for a Cellphone to Pick Up the Signal?, Chron.com (The Houston Chronicle), http://smallbusiness.chron.com/far-can-cell-tower-cellphone-pick-up-signal-32124.html (last visited Mar. 27, 2013).

[20] Hong & Rappaport, Traffic Model and Performance Analysis for Cellular Mobile Radio Telephone Systems With Prioritized and Nonprioritized Handoff Procedures, 35(3) IEEE Transactions on Vehicular Technology 77–92 (1986).

[21] Wikle, Cellular Tower Proliferation in the United States, 92(1) Geographical Review 45–62 (2002).

[22] Oliphant, The Mobile Phone Meets the Internet, 36(8) IEEE Spectrum 20–28 (1999).

that the battery in a mobile phone can be smaller, making sleek modern mobile phones possible.[23]

In the USA, a mobile provider receives about 800 frequencies to use across a city.[24] These frequencies can be reused so long as the cell towers using them are not adjacent to one another.[25] Since the switch from analog transmission to digital transmission, the number of calls that can be placed in a cell quadrant has tripled from approximately 56–168.[26]

In addition to cell towers, mobile carriers have base stations that consist of a cell tower and a small building housing the radio equipment.[27] A heavily populated area will require a large number of base stations, in addition to hundreds of cell towers, to handle all the traffic.[28] Each mobile carrier will also have a central office, called the Mobile Telephone Switching Office (MTSO), to manage the base stations and the connections between mobile phones and landlines.

To make a call, a number of steps occur between the time the user inputs a number and the time the recipient answers the call. First, when a phone is turned on, the mobile phone listens for a system identification code (SID).[29] This five-digit number is assigned by the FCC to each carrier.[30] The mobile phone listens for a SID on a control channel broadcast by the cell towers.[31] If a mobile phone is unable to find a control channel, it will display a "no service" message.

---

[23] Farina v. Nokia Inc., 625 F.3d 97 (3d Cir. 2010), cert. denied, 565 U.S. 928 (2011) (stating, "A cell phone functions by transmitting information between its low-powered radio transmitter and a base station, usually a tower containing a large antenna.") *See also* Pinney v. Nokia, Inc., 402 F.3d 430, 439–40, 38 A.L.R. Fed. 2d 701 (4th Cir. 2005).

[24] Noam, The Next Frontier for Openness: Wireless Communications, Competition for the Mobile Internet 21–38 (Springer US 2003). For more information on the radio spectrum allocation, see the FCC's discussion at http://www.fcc.gov/encyclopedia/radio-spectrum-allocation (last visited May 20, 2013).

[25] Noam, The Next Frontier for Openness: Wireless Communications, Competition for the Mobile Internet 21–38 (Springer US 2003).

[26] Bennett, Powering the Mobile Revolution: Principles of Spectrum Allocation (The Information Technology & Innovation Foundation, July 31, 2012), available at http://www.itif.org/publications/powering-mobile-revolution-principles-spectrum-allocation (last visited May 20, 2013).

[27] HTC Corp. v. IPCom GmbH & Co., KG, 667 F.3d 1270 (Fed. Cir. 2012) (describing base stations in relation to use by mobile phones and mobile carriers).

[28] Pinney v. Nokia, Inc., 402 F.3d 430, 440, 38 A.L.R. Fed. 2d 701 (4th Cir. 2005) (describing the relatively small range of each base station and the transfer of signal as the caller moves in and out of range of a base station).

[29] Kizza, Security in Wireless Networks, Guide to Computer Network Security 387–411 (Springer London 2013).

[30] Fox, Checking In: Historic Cell Site Location Information and the Stored Communications Act, 42 Seton Hall L. Rev. 769 (2012).

[31] Fox, Checking In: Historic Cell Site Location Information and the Stored Communications Act, 42 Seton Hall L. Rev. 769 (2012).

In addition to the SID, the mobile phone also transmits a registration request, which the MTSO uses to keep track of a phone's location on the cellular grid.[32] From the MTSO, the signal is transferred to the recipient's phone via landlines, other cell towers, or a combination of the two.[33] Every mobile phone has two unique strings of numbers associated with it that are used to facilitate this process.[34] The first number is the mobile identification number (MIN), which is the ten digit number dialed to connect with a particular mobile phone user.[35] The second is called an electronic serial number (ESN), which is immutable and assigned to the mobile phone by mobile carrier.[36]

At this point, the MTSO gets the call request and tries to connect the call with the intended recipient by looking at its location database to find the recipient.[37] The MTSO also picks which of the 168 frequencies the receiving phone will use and transmits this information over a control channel.[38] Once the recipient's phone and the closest tower switch to these frequencies, the call is connected.

If the recipient is moving while on the call, the base station will note when there is a change in signal strength.[39] When the signal begins to diminish, a nearby base station will note that the mobile phone is in range and will coordinate through the MTSO to switch cell towers, and the mobile phone is handed off from one cell tower to the other.[40]

---

[32] Donatelli, Locating Cellular Telephone Facilities: How Should Communities Answer When Cellular Telephone Companies Call, 27 Rutgers LJ 447 (1995).

[33] Tan, Wading Through the Rhetoric of the Telecommunications Act of 1996: Uncertainty of Local Zoning Authority over Wireless Telecommunications Tower Siting, 22 Vt. L. Rev. 461 (1997).

[34] Fawcett & Provost, "Combining Data Mining and Machine Learning for Effective User Profiling," in Proceedings of the Second International Conference on Knowledge Discovery and Data Mining (1996) (describing MIN and ESN).

[35] Fawcett & Provost, "Combining Data Mining and Machine Learning for Effective User Profiling," in Proceedings of the Second International Conference on Knowledge Discovery and Data Mining (1996).

[36] See U.S. v. Oliva, 686 F.3d 1106 (9th Cir. 2012), for additional opinion, *see* 493 Fed. Appx. 835 (9th Cir. 2012) and opinion amended and superseded on denial of reh'g en banc, 705 F.3d 390 (9th Cir. 2012) (describing the use of ESN for tracking phones); U.S. v. Fletcher, 635 F. Supp. 2d 1253 (W.D. Okla. 2009) (defining ESN); Patel, Weaknesses of North American Wireless Authentication Protocol, 4(3) IEEE Personal Communications 40–44 (1997).

[37] Kizza, Security in Wireless Networks, Guide to Computer Network Security 387–411 (Springer London 2013) (discussing the transmission of signals between towers and the MTSO).

[38] Cottrell, The Internet, Mobile Computing and Mobile Phones in Developing Countries, in m-Science: Sensing, Computing and Dissemination, at 7 (Canessa & Zennaro, eds., ICPT 2010) (stating, "The MTSO picks a frequency pair and tells the phone and relevant base station over the control channel. The base station and phone connect up on the frequency pair.")

[39] Stüber, Principles of Mobile Communication (Springer Science + Business Media 2011).

[40] For a description of the function of the MTSO, see Shubert v. Metrophone, Inc., 898 F.2d 401, 402 n.5 (3d Cir. 1990) (citing S. Rep. No. 99–541, 99th Cong., 2d Sess., at 9, reprinted at 1986 U.S. Code Cong. & Admin. News 3555, 3563). See also Fox, Checking In: Historic Cell Site Location Information and the Stored Communications Act, 42 Seton Hall L. Rev. 769 (2012).

As mentioned above, a mobile phone transmits a registration request when a user places or receives a call. This request creates a record that is stored by the mobile carrier.[41] The record "usually" includes the individual mobile phones involved (e.g., MINs and ESNs) and the cell towers used to transmit the call.[42] Mobile phones, even when not in use, are constantly communicating with the broader mobile network through the registration process.[43] Registration occurs approximately every 7 seconds when a mobile phone transmits its MIN and ESN to the nearest cell tower.[44]

Registration enables the mobile carrier to quickly and efficiently route calls.[45] The only way to stop a mobile phone from registering itself is by turning it off[46] and

---

[41] Malone, The Fourth Amendment and the Stored Communications Act: Why the Warrantless Gathering of Historical Cell Site Location Information Poses No Threat to Privacy, 39 Pepp. L. Rev. 701 (2011).

[42] Gruteser & Liu, Protecting Privacy, In Continuous Location-Tracking Applications, 2(2) IEEE Security & Privacy 28–34 (2004).

[43] McLaughlin, The Fourth Amendment and Cell Phone Location Tracking: Where Are We, 29 Hastings Comm. & Ent. L.J. 421 (2006).

[44] McLaughlin, The Fourth Amendment and Cell Phone Location Tracking: Where Are We, 29 Hastings Comm. & Ent. L.J. 421 (2006). For a discussion of cell site records generated by mobile carriers through the registration process, see In re U.S. for Historical Cell Site Data, 747 F. Supp. 2d 827 (S.D. Tex. 2010), subsequently vacated, 724 F.3d 600 (5th Cir. 2013).

[45] Pell & Soghoian, Can You See Me Now?: Toward Reasonable Standards for Law Enforcement Access to Location Data that Congress Could Enact, 27 Berkeley Tech. L.J. 117 126 n.28 (2012).

[46] In re Application of the U.S. for an Order Authorizing the Disclosure of Cell Site Location Information, 2009 WL 8231744 (E.D. Ky. 2009); In re Application for Pen Register and Trap/Trace Device with Cell Site Location Authority, 396 F. Supp. 2d 747, 756–57 (S.D. Tex. 2005) (concluding that *Smith* is inapplicable because cell site data is not voluntarily conveyed by the user but is instead "transmitted automatically during the registration process, entirely independent of the user's input, control, or knowledge"). In *U.S. v. Flores-Lopez*, the court stated:

And if the phone is either turned off or powered down to a level at which it appears to be turned off, the police can't obtain information from it, even its phone number, knowledge of which as we said is minimally invasive of privacy. The alternative to searching the cell phone forthwith or turning it off (really turning it off—not just powering it down) is to place it in a "Faraday bag" or "Faraday cage" (essentially an aluminum-foil wrap) or some equivalent, which isolates the cell phone from the phone network and from Bluetooth and wireless Internet signals." citing, Department of Justice, Computer Crime and Intellectual Property Section, "Awareness Brief: Find My iPhone" (June 18, 2009); Cindy Murphy, "Cellular Phone Evidence: Data Extraction and Documentation," http://mobileforensics.files.wordpress.com/2010/07/cell—phone—evidence—extraction—process—development–1–1–8.pdf. (Faraday bags or cages are found in consumer products such as microwave ovens to keep the microwaves in, and in coaxial cables to keep interfering radio signals out.) It is also possible to "mirror" (copy) the entire cell phone contents, to preserve them should the phone be remotely wiped, without looking at the copy unless the original disappears. See Keir Thomas, "Is Smartphone Security Good Enough?," PCWorld, Apr. 20, 2011, http://www.pcworld.com/businesscenter/article/225771/is_smartphone_security_good_enough.html; American Civil Liberties Union of Michigan, "ACLU Seeks Records about State Police Searches of Cellphones," Apr. 13, 2011, http://www.aclumich.org/issues/privacy–and–technology/2011–04/1542; Cellebrite, "UFED Ultimate," http://www.cellebrite.com/mobile-forensics-products/forensics-products/ufed-ultimate.html

U.S. v. Flores-Lopez, 670 F.3d 803, 809 (7th Cir. 2012).

in some cases removing the battery.[47] A mobile phone is constantly sharing some information about its location with a mobile carrier whenever the mobile phone is on.[48]

As either the caller or recipient moves around, the call is passed from one cell tower to another.[49] When the SID on the control channel is not from the caller's mobile carrier, the MTSO from the caller's mobile carrier is contacted by the MTSO of the cell tower being used to verify that the signal is valid.[50] This is commonly known as "roaming."[51]

As mentioned above, the advent of digital over analog tripled the amount of channels available for users to communicate. Digital also has a number of other benefits, including compression and manipulation of the signal that allows up to ten digital mobile phone calls to use the space of one analog mobile call.[52]

Digital mobile phones rely on frequency-shift keying (FSK) to send data.[53] FSK uses two frequencies, one for the binary 1s and one for the binary 0s.[54] Modulation and encoding schemes convert the analog information to digital and then back again all in seconds.[55] This rapid conversion requires that mobile phones house a lot of processing power.[56]

---

[47] U.S. v. Forest, 355 F.3d 942, 951–52 (6th Cir. 2004), cert. granted, judgment vacated, 543 U.S. 1100 (2005) (finding that, unlike dialed telephone numbers, cell site data is not "voluntarily conveyed" by the user to the mobile carrier but is transmitted automatically during the registration process entirely independent of the user's input, control, or knowledge).

[48] In addition, a cell tower can transmit a signal to a cell phone to determine the location of that cell phone.

[49] Fox, Checking In: Historic Cell Site Location Information and the Stored Communications Act, 42 Seton Hall L. Rev. 769 (2012).

[50] Cottrell, The Internet, Mobile Computing and Mobile Phones in Developing Countries, in m-Science: Sensing, Computing and Dissemination, at 7 (Canessa & Zennaro, eds., ICPT 2010).

[51] Cottrell, The Internet, Mobile Computing and Mobile Phones in Developing Countries, in m-Science: Sensing, Computing and Dissemination, at 13 (Canessa & Zennaro, eds., ICPT 2010) (stating, "If the SID on the control channel does not match the phone's SID then the phone knows it is roaming").

[52] Carne, Connections for the Digital Age: Multimedia Communications for Mobile, Nomadic and Fixed Devices (Wiley 2011). See also Wang & Guo, "The Development and Applications of Wireless Streaming Media Technology," in Proceedings of the International Conference on Computer Science and Electronics Engineering, Vol. 1 (Mar. 23–25, 2012).

[53] Yacoub, Foundations of Mobile Radio Engineering (CRC Press LLC 1993).

[54] Selvakumar, Nemalladinne, & Arumugam, Analysis of LTE Radio Frame by Eliminating Cyclic Prefix in OFDM and Comparison of QAM and Offset-QAM, Student Thesis, Linnaeus University, Sweden (2012).

[55] Sharma, Mishra & Saxena, Analog & Digital Modulation Techniques: An Overview, 3(1) International Journal of Computing Science and Communication Technologies 551–61 (July 2010), available at http://www.techniajournal.com/attachments/article/128/ANALOG%20%20DIGITAL%20MODULATION.pdf (last visited June 20, 2013).

[56] Ferreira, Dey, & Kostakos, "Understanding Human-Smartphone Concerns: A Study of Battery Life," in Proceedings of the 9th International Conference on Pervasive Computing 19–33 (Springer Berlin, Heidelberg 2011). See also Perrucci, Fitzek, & Widmer, "Survey on Energy Consumption Entities on Mobile Phone Platform," in Proceedings of the 73d IEEE Vehicular Technology Conference 1–6 (May 15–18, 2011).

## 5.3 What Is a Smartphone? How Does It Work?

A smartphone is "a mobile phone that offers more advanced computing ability and connectivity than a contemporary basic feature phone."[57] Smartphones allow users to make and receive calls just as mobile phones.[58] However, smartphones have additional features and capabilities that mobile phones do not. Smartphones allow users to install, configure, and run applications.[59] For example, an integrated digital assistant, such as "Siri"—the iPhone digital assistant—in the past would have only been available on a personal digital assistant (PDA) or a computer. Below are some of the actions smartphones are capable of performing today:

Smartphone capabilities are evolving at a blistering pace, and the features above will likely be antiquated by the time of a publication of a new edition of this book. For example, over the past 2 years, smartphones have started to integrate and utilize near field communication (NFC) technology, which allows the smartphone to send and receive information simply by placing the smartphone next to another device that has NFC capabilities.[60] The data transmitted using NFC by the smartphone can range from a file to a payment from a virtual wallet.[61] In fact, it is possible that by the time a new edition of this book publishes, the NFC will be a mainstream form of payment, meaning when you go to the supermarket instead of using a credit card you will simply use your smartphone.

Smartphones come with hardware similar to that of computers.[62] The physical outer body of the phone includes a screen and sometimes a keyboard.[63] The user

---

[57] Jeon, Kim, et al., "A Practical Analysis of Smartphone Security," in Human Interface and the Management of Information. Interacting with Information, Lecture Notes in Computer Science, Vol. 6771, 311–320 (Springer 2011); see also Barbu, The Ubiquitous Blackberry: The New Overtime Liability, 5 Liberty U. L. Rev. 47 (2010); Cheng, Iphone Jailbreaking Under the DMCA: Toward a Functionalist Approach in Anti-Circumvention, 25 Berkeley Tech. L.J. 215 (2010); Definition of Smartphone, PC Magazine Encyclopedia, http://www.pcmag.com/encyclopedia/term/51537/smartphone (last visited May 20, 2013).

[58] Charlesworth, The Ascent of Smartphone, 4(3) Engineering & Technology 32–33 (2009).

[59] Apple, Inc. v. Samsung Electronics Co., Ltd., 678 F.3d 1314 (Fed. Cir. 2012) (describing relationship between smartphones and applications).

[60] Agrawal & Bhuraria, Near Field Communication, IT Matters, 67; Curran, Millar, & Mc Garvey, Near Field Communication, 2(3) International Journal of Electrical and Computer Engineering 371–82 (2012).

[61] Want, Near Field Communication, 10(3) IEEE Pervasive Computing 4–7 (2011); Amin, Factors Affecting the Intentions of Customers in Malaysia to Use Mobile Phone Credit Cards, 31(7) Management Research News 493–503 (2008).

[62] Osawa, Is Smartphone Hardware Evolution Slowing?, Wall Street Journal (Mar. 15, 2013), http://blogs.wsj.com/digits/2013/03/15/is-smartphone-hardware-evolution-slowing/ (last visited Apr. 10, 2013).

[63] Kim & Lee, "Cultural Difference and Mobile Phone Interface Design: Icon Recognition According to Level of Abstraction," in Proceedings of the 7th International Conference on Human Computer Interaction with Mobile Devices & Services 307–10 (ACM 2005).

interface occurs through small buttons on the phone or touch screen capabilities.[64] Smartphones have internal memory capacities of 16, 32, 64, 128 GB, or greater.[65] Smartphones with an external micro-SD card slot can be further upgraded.[66] Most smartphones on the market have at least one camera, and oftentimes two—with the second being a lower resolution camera on the front-facing side to allow for video phone calls.[67]

Smartphones for the most part use a more advanced operating system than is found on mobile phones.[68] The smartphone operating system manages the hardware and software components of smartphones.[69] Smartphone operating system platforms range from systems that cover the entire mobile software stack and others that include the lower levels, relying on additional software to provide the user interface layer.[70] The vast majority of mobile operating systems includes the ability to run mobile applications.[71] The specific smartphone operating system varies based on the model. For example, the iPhone uses iOS, Microsoft uses Windows Mobile for its mobile market, and Google uses Android for its mobile phone market.[72] Today, the

---

[64] Eatoni Ergonomics, Inc. v. Research in Motion Corp., 486 Fed. Appx. 186 (2d Cir. 2012) (differentiating QWERTY keyboards and touchscreen models of mobile phones).

[65] Stuedi, Mohomed & Terry, "Wherestore: Location-Based Data Storage for Mobile Devices Interacting with the Cloud," in Proceedings of the 1st ACM Workshop on Mobile Cloud Computing & Services: Social Networks and Beyond (2010).

[66] A micro-SD card can be used as removable memory, which is one of the smallest flash memory cards on the market today. Here, SD stands for secure digital. Somorovsky, Meyer, et al., "Sec 2: Secure Mobile Solution for Distributed Public Cloud Storages," in Proceedings of the 2nd International Conference on Cloud Computing and Services Science 555–61 (SciTePress, Apr. 2012). Secure digital is a nonvolatile memory card format that can be used in portable devices, such as mobile phones, digital camera, GPS navigation system, etc. Chang, Chen & Zhou, Smart Phone for Mobile Commerce, 31(4) Computer Standards & Interfaces 740–47 (2009).

[67] Micheletti, iPhone Photography & Video for Dummies (For Dummies 2010).

[68] Lin & Ye, "Operating System Battle in the Ecosystem of Smartphone Industry," in Proceedings of the International IEEE Symposium on Information Engineering and Electronic Commerce 617–21 (May 2009).

[69] For a more in-depth discussion of the various issues around the mobile operating system landscape and providing further technical and operational details, refer to the article "Operating System Battle in the Ecosystem of Smartphone Industry." See Lin & Ye, "Operating System Battle in the Ecosystem of Smartphone Industry," in Proceedings of the International IEEE Symposium on Information Engineering and Electronic Commerce 617–21 (May 2009).

[70] A more detailed explanation can be found in Hall & Anderson, Operating Systems for Mobile Computing, 25(2) Journal of Computing Sciences in Colleges 64–71 (2009).

[71] For more information about mobile operating systems, see discussion later in the chapter. Another great resource for understanding mobile operating systems is the article published by Asokan that compares Android and iOS. See Asokan, Android vs. iOS–An Analysis, 4(1) Int'l J. of Computer Engineering & Tech 377–82 (Feb. 2013); Bellavista, Corradi, et al., A Survey of Context Data Distribution for Mobile Ubiquitous Systems, 45(1) ACM Computing Surveys 1–49 (2013).

[72] Colbert, Which Is the Superior Mobile OS: iOS, Android, or Windows 8?, Tech Republic, http://www.techrepublic.com/blog/tablets/which-is-the-superior-mobile-os-ios-android-or-windows-8/2684 (last visited Apr. 10, 2013). See also Mobile OS Comparison: Windows Phone 8 vs. iOS 6.0 vs. Android 4.1, available at http://www.phonearena.com/news/Mobile-OS-comparison-

dominant players would be the Google Android operating system, which is estimated to have approximately 40% of the US market, and Apple's hardware, which accounted for 37.8% of all smartphones in the USA as of January 31, 2013.[73]

## 5.4 What Is a Mobile Application?

A mobile application is software that is downloaded onto mobile phones and smartphones.[74] Mobile applications run the gamut in terms of functional capabilities ranging from email, to starting your car, to piloting a drone in Afghanistan.[75] Mobile applications can be purchased and downloaded through an online retailer, such as brand-specific channels or mobile carrier specific channels.[76] Prices of mobile applications vary.[77]

Constructing mobile applications for smartphones requires a rich set of skills ranging from programming to design.[78] The teams range from a two-man operation to the company electronic arts having an entire mobile application development division. Building mobile applications for a particular mobile operating system is no longer a simple or inexpensive process because of the diverse types of phones and operating systems.

---

Windows-Phone-8-vs-iOS-6.0-vs-Android-4.1_id31473 (last visited Apr. 10, 2013). Over the past 2 or 3 years, a smartphone patent war has been raging among major technology giants such as Microsoft, Google, Apple, Samsung, RIM, and HTC. See Goldstein, The Smartphone Patent War, in 1 Graph, NPR: Planet Money (Dec. 11, 2012), http://www.npr.org/blogs/money/2011/08/17/139723088/the-smart-phone-patent-war-in-1-graph (graphic that illustrates smartphone patent case trend); Ludlow, "Trends in Patent Litigation," Intellectual Asset Management, Sept.–Oct. 2011, at 15. For a more detailed discussion of the role of patents in software and hardware disputes, please refer to Chap. 8.

[73] Kellogg, In U.S. Market, New Smartphone Buyers Increasingly Embracing Android, Nielsen Wire Blog, http://www.nielsen.com/us/en/newswire/2011/in-u-s-market-new-smartphone-buyers-increasingly-embracing-android.html (last visited Apr. 26, 2013); Zeman, Apple iPhone Gains U.S. Market Share, InformationWeek Mobility blog, http://www.informationweek.com/mobility/smart-phones/apple-iphone-gains-us-market-share/240150233 (last visited Apr. 26, 2013).

[74] MDY Industries, LLC v. Blizzard Entertainment, Inc., 629 F.3d 928, 946 n.7 (9th Cir. 2010), as amended on denial of reh'g, (Feb. 17, 2011) and opinion amended and superseded on denial of reh'g, 2011 WL 538748 (9th Cir. 2011) (describing smartphones as devices that "allow users to install and run third-party software applications").

[75] iPhone App Pilots Drone Aircraft from 3000 Miles Away, LA Times Blogs (Sept 27, 2011), http://latimesblogs.latimes.com/technology/2011/09/iphone-drone-app-war.html (last visited Apr. 10, 2013).

[76] Holzer & Ondrus, Mobile Application Market: A Developer's Perspective, 28(1) Telematics and Informatics 22–31 (2011).

[77] Gans, Mobile Application Pricing, 24(1) Information Economics and Policy 52–59 (2012).

[78] Charland & Leroux, Mobile Application Development: Web vs. Native, 54(5) Communications of the ACM 49–53 (2011); Fling, Mobile Design and Development: Practical Concepts and Techniques for Creating Mobile Sites and Web Apps (O'Reilly Media 2009).

An alternative to creating native mobile applications is to develop mobile web applications that will work across all mobile phones and smartphones, much like a single website works on a computer regardless of its operating system.[79] Several solutions are available; some of the more widely used tools to build mobile web applications are Adobe Flash Builder and Flex, as well as HTML and JavaScript.[80] These tools allow developers to create mobile web applications for iOS (iPhone and iPad), Android, and BlackBerry Tablet OS.[81] The expertise to build and test mobile web applications using the above toolsets or others available in the marketplace is not nearly as cheap or as quick as building a webpage, but it is likely that over the coming years, it will become cheaper and easier to build mobile web applications.

It is arguably more cost-effective to build mobile web applications than to build native applications for each smartphone platform.[82] In addition to the economic benefits, when developers build mobile web applications, they can perform live updates direct to the smartphone, removing the need to go to the application store to update the application.[83] Developers of mobile web applications bypass the application store submission process, saving time in the product life cycle.[84] One downside is that since mobile web applications are not able to access the local capabilities on the smartphone, their functionality can be limited, unlike native mobile applications.[85]

Irrespective of whether a developer builds a native or mobile web application, it is essential that the tenets of the software engineering process, which we discuss in the software chapter, are applied to the mobile application development process to

---

[79] Charland & Leroux, Mobile Application Development: Web vs. Native, 54(5) Communications of the ACM 49–53 (2011).

[80] Wasserman, "Software Engineering Issues for Mobile Application Development," in Proceedings of the FSE/SDP Workshop on Future of Software Engineering Research 397–400 (ACM 2010).

[81] See Adobe Mobile app development http://www.adobe.com/devnet/devices/mobile-apps.html (last visited Apr. 26, 2013).

[82] Cavazza, Mobile Web App vs. Native App? It's Complicated, Forbes (Sept. 27, 2011), http://www.forbes.com/sites/fredcavazza/2011/09/27/mobile-web-app-vs-native-app-its-complicated/ (last visited Apr. 28, 2013).

[83] Ohrt & Turau, Cross-Platform Development Tools for Smartphone Applications, 45(1) Computer 72–79 (Sept. 2012); Gonçalves Walravens & Ballon, "How about an App Store?" Enablers and Constraints in Platform Strategies for Mobile Network Operators, in Proceedings of the 9th International IEEE Conference on Mobile Business and 2010 Ninth Global Mobility Roundtable 66–73 (2010).

[84] Charland & Leroux, Mobile Application Development: Web vs. Native, 54(5) Communications of the ACM 49–53 (2011). In addition, the end user gets forward compatibility, which allows their application and smartphone to keep running even when newer versions are released of either the software or the hardware. Charland & Leroux, Mobile Application Development: Web vs. Native, 54(5) Communications of the ACM 49–53 (2011).

[85] Charland & Leroux, Mobile Application Development: Web vs. Native, 54(5) Communications of the ACM 49–53 (2011).

ensure that the mobile application, whether native or web, is secure and high quality.[86]

## 5.5 What Is a Mobile Website?

A mobile website is a website enabled for mobile phones and smartphones.[87] While it may seem obvious, the ability to access the Internet on a mobile device with such a small screen requires more than just zooming in.[88] Developers must create a new version of a website for viewing on a mobile device. This requires rethinking how users interact with a particular website, what computer language is used to create the website, and the technology necessary to deliver the Internet content over cellular connections.[89]

With the spreading use of data consumption over 3G phones, users wanted a way to access more content from the Internet without being tied to a computer.[90] Developers responded to this by creating mobile browsers.[91] A mobile browser is a web browser designed for use on a small screen.[92] A mobile phone uses mobile browsers to access mobile websites.[93] Mobile browsers are optimized to show the viewer the most viewer-friendly version of the website. Essentially, the viewer sees a scaled down version of the regular site.[94]

[86] See Chap. 1 for discussion of software development methods and process. It is beyond the scope of this chapter to discuss these issues, but a great discussion can be found in the article "Mobile Application Software Engineering: Challenges and Research Directions." See Dehlinger & Dixon, Mobile Application Software Engineering: Challenges and Research Directions, available at http://www.mobileseworkshop.org/papers/7-Dehlinger_Dixon.pdf (last visited May 21, 2013).

[87] Raasch, How to Build a Mobile Website, Smashing Magazine (Nov 3, 2010), http://mobile.smashingmagazine.com/2010/11/03/how-to-build-a-mobile-website/ (last visited Apr. 10, 2013).

[88] Cui & Roto, "How People Use the Web on Mobile Devices," in Proceedings of the 17th International Conference on World Wide Web 905–14 (ACM 2008).

[89] Firtman, Programming the Mobile Web (O'Reilly Media 2010).

[90] Kaikkonen, "Full or Tailored Mobile Web-Where and How Do People Browse on Their Mobiles?, in Proceedings of the International Conference on Mobile Technology, Applications, and Systems Art. 28 (ACM 2008).

[91] For a discussion of the early origins of mobile web browsing, see Jaaksi, Developing Mobile Browsers in a Product Line, 19(4) IEEE Software 73–80 (2002).

[92] Shrestha, "Mobile Web Browsing: Usability Study," in Proceedings of the 4th International Conference on Mobile Technology, Applications, and Systems and the 1st International Symposium on Computer Human Interaction in Mobile Technology 187–94 (ACM 2007).

[93] Roto, Browsing On Mobile Phones, Nokia Research Center 10 (2005).

[94] Tian, Voight, et al., Performance Considerations for Mobile Web Services, 27(11) Computer Communications 1097–1105 (July 2004).

A mobile website uses Extensible Hypertext Markup Language, xHTML, to deliver wireless content.[95] Most websites on the Internet are written in HTML, but as the Internet and new mobile technologies continue to evolve, so too must the means of delivering content over these platforms.[96] Mobile browsers making use of XHTML will not look different to the viewer necessarily, but there are a host of benefits for developers, including ease of learning, ability to maintain, and preparation for the next phase of mobile web development.[97]

## 5.6 Mobile Phone Network Technologies

Mobile phones use mobile networks (a.k.a. cellular networks) to operate.[98] Mobile and wireless networks have grown at a ferocious pace in the past decade.[99] Today, mobile phones can come equipped with 2G, 3G, 4G, WLAN, Bluetooth, and other adapters.[100]

The G in 1G, 2G, 3G, and 4G stands for *generation* and refers to the generations of wireless telecommunication connectivity, with 1G being oldest and 4G being the newest.[101] First generation wireless technology (1G) is an analog voice-only mobile standard.[102] It was created in the 1980s and allows users to make calls in a single

---

[95] For a discussion on the origins of XHTML, see World Wide Web Consortium, XHTML 1.0: The Extensible HyperText Markup Language, 2000, http://www.w3.org/TR/xhtml1 (describing XHTML as "a family of current and future document types and modules that reproduce, subset, and extend HTML").

[96] For a discussion on the differences between HTML and XHTML, see World Wide Web Consortium, XHTML 1.0: The Extensible HyperText Markup Language, 2000, http://www.w3.org/TR/xhtml1

[97] For a discussion of the benefits to developers, see HTML vs. XHTML, http://www.webstandards.org/learn/articles/askw3c/oct2003/ (last visited July 19, 2013), and Zhang, Web Content Adaptation for Mobile Handheld Devices, 50(2) Communications of the ACM 75–79 (2007).

[98] Vaughan-Nichols, Wireless Middleware: Glue for the Mobile Infrastructure, 37(5) Computer 18–20 (2004).

[99] Comparing the findings of Varshney & Vetter, Emerging Mobile and Wireless Networks, 43(6) Communications of the ACM 73–81 (2000); with Wu, Talwar, et al., M2M: From Mobile to Embedded Internet, 49(4) IEEE Communications 36–43 (2011). Both show the explosive growth of the mobile market from the early 1990s to present.

[100] Dingwall, Municipal Broadband: Challenges and Perspectives, 59 Fed. Comm. L.J. 67 (2006) (comparing the differences between the various iterations of mobile technology).

[101] Broadcom Corp. v. Qualcomm Inc., 501 F.3d 297 (3d Cir. 2007) (discussing the different mobile technology developments). See generally Kumar, Liu, & Sengupta, Divya. Evolution of Mobile Wireless Communication Networks: 1G to 4G, 1 Int'l J. of Elect. & Comm. Tech. 68–72 (2010).

[102] Kumar, Liu, & Sengupta, Divya. Evolution of Mobile Wireless Communication Networks: 1G to 4G, 1 Int'l J. of Elect. & Comm. Tech. 68–72 (2010).

country and transmit data at speeds up to 2.4 kbps.[103] First generation connectivity is pretty much outdated and not in a great deal of use.[104]

## 5.7 Mobile Phone Network Technologies: 2G Mobile Communications

Second generation (2G) wireless telephone technology originally was launched on the GSM standard, which stands for Global System for Mobile Communications.[105] The advent of 2G took mobile communications from analog to digital.[106] This conversion allowed for services such as text messages, picture messages, and "multimedia messages," also known as "MMS."[107] Data is encrypted and transmitted on 2G mobile networks in a fashion that permits only the recipient to receive and read the data.[108]

Second generation mobile network technologies are either code division multiple access (CDMA) or time division multiple access (TDMA).[109] The TDMA technology divides the digital radio signals into time slots, while CDMA allocates a

[103] Kumar, Liu, & Sengupta, Divya. Evolution of Mobile Wireless Communication Networks: 1G to 4G, 1 Int'l J. of Elect. & Comm. Tech. 68–72 (2010).

[104] Ashiho, Mobile Technology: Evolution from 1G to 4G, Communication (June 2003), available at http://www.electronicsforu.com/EFYLinux/efyhome/cover/jun2003/Mobile-tech.pdf (last visited July 19, 2013).

[105] Kyocera Wireless Corp. v. International Trade Com'n, 545 F.3d 1340, 1350 (Fed. Cir. 2008) (stating, "The GSM standard is a comprehensive set of specifications for a second generation ('2G') mobile network").

[106] Kim, Can We Put New Wine in Old Bottles: The Highly Innovative Mobile Communications Market and Regulatory Rules, 2008 Int'l Bus. LJ 207–25.

[107] U.S. v. Hanjuan Jin, 833 F. Supp. 2d 977 (N.D. Ill. 2012), aff'd, 733 F.3d 718 (7th Cir. 2013) (detailing the change from 1G to 2G mobile standards).

[108] These phones have been hacked and devices have been built which are able to get through the security protocols. See Luckock, How Private Are Mobile Phone Calls?, Sky News (1 Nov 2010), http://news.sky.com/story/815332/how-private-are-mobile-phone-calls (last visited July 19, 2013); Kinch, GSM encryption can be cracked for $500, Mobile Industry Review (Aug. 25, 2009), http://www.mobileindustryreview.com/2009/08/gsm-encryption-can-be-cracked-for-500.html (last visited July 19, 2013).

[109] "The ubiquitous cell phone is a way of life in modern society." Wei, Ch. 22, "Wireless Telephony," in Communication Technology Update, 10/e (2012). See also Dahlman, et al., "Background of 3G Evolution," in Communications Engineering Desk Reference 259 (Academic Press 2009); Golden Bridge Technology, Inc. v. Nokia, Inc. 527 F.3d 1318, 1320 (Fed. Cir. 2008) (describing CDMA as a scheme "where multiple mobile phones communicate at the same time with the same base station over the same frequency range by using different numerical 'spreading codes' in their transmissions.")

special code to communicate over a multiplex physical channel for each user.[110] TDMA technologies include GSM, PDC, iDEN, and IS-136.[111]

GSM, long the standard for mobile voice-calling,[112] utilizes the cellular network construct to enable mobile devices to operate on different networks and in other countries.[113] Generally, base stations are positioned at regular geographic intervals, forming a net of transceivers.[114] Each transceiver operates within a small range, sufficient to overlap slightly with the surrounding transceivers' ranges, in a hexagonal pattern.[115] This slight overlap enables the handset to detect when a new transceiver arrives in range and allows for a handover, so when a handset moves, the call is not dropped.[116] The end result of this architecture is that it enables a user's calls to be seamlessly routed from one base station to the next.[117]

## 5.8 Mobile Phone Network Technologies: 2.5G Mobile Communications

Between 2G and 3G networks is the 2.5G standard, which enabled GSM mobile phones to transmit data and was achieved by the introduction of General Packet Radio Service (GPRS).[118] GPRS was standardized by the European Telecommunications Standards Institute (ETSI).[119]

---

[110] Bhalla & Bhalla, Generations of Mobile Wireless Technology: A Survey, 5(4) Int'l J. of Comp. Applications 26–32 (2010); Akhtar, "2G–4G Networks: Evolution of Technologies, Standards, and Deployment," in Encyclopedia of Multimedia Technology and Networking (Ideas Group Publisher 2010), available at http://www.techrepublic.com/whitepapers/2g-4g-networks-evolution-of--technologies-standards-and-deployment/2378579 (last visited May 22, 2013).

[111] Nilsson, Third-Generation Radio Access Standards, 76(3) Ericsson Review 110–21 (1999).

[112] Mouly & Pautet, Technical Report, Current Evolution of the GSM Systems, 2 IEEE Pers. Comm 9–19 (Oct. 1995).

[113] 2G is unlike 1G, where users were limited to voice calls in a single country, because 2G used digital and 1G used analog. Bhalla & Bhalla, Generations of Mobile Wireless Technology: A Survey, 5(4) Int'l J. of Comp. Applications 26–32 (2010).

[114] HTC Corp. v. IPCom GmbH & Co., KG, 667 F.3d 1270, 1273 (Fed. Cir. 2012) (describing mobile base stations).

[115] HTC Corp., 667 F.3d at 1273 (describing mobile base stations); Kyocera Wireless Corp. v. International Trade Com'n, 545 F.3d 1340 (Fed. Cir. 2008) (discussing roaming between base stations).

[116] See Brocade Communications Systems, Inc. v. A10 Networks, Inc., 843 F. Supp. 2d 1018 (N.D. Cal. 2012) (discussing wireless handoff from tower to tower).

[117] Base stations typically operate on one of two frequency bands: either 900 MHz or 1800 MHz. There are other bands in use in various countries but these two are the most widely used.

[118] See Silversman v. Motorola, Inc., 259 F.R.D. 163, 170 n.3 (N.D. Ill. 2009) (stating, "GSM refers to a family of mobile communications standards that currently operates in both second and third generations. GSM Edge is often seen as the bridge between 2G and 3G '2.5G,' so to speak), while GSM/UMTS is commonly referred to as '3G' and HSDPA as '3.5G' or '3G' plus." [citing Broadcom Corp. v. Qualcomm Inc., 501 F.3d 297, 304 (3d Cir. 2007)].

[119] Samjani, General Packet Radio Service [GPRS], 21(2) IEEE Potentials 12–15 (2002).

GPRS is based on Internet Protocols (IP) and enables users to utilize a wide range of applications—Internet access, intranet/corporate access, instant messaging, and multimedia messaging services (MMS), for instance, email.[120] With throughput rates of up to 40 Kbit/s, users have a similar access speed to a dial-up modem, but with the convenience of being able to connect from anywhere.[121] GPRS allows mobile wireless service providers to supply their mobile subscribers with packet-based data services operating GSM networks.[122]

GPRS is defined as a packet switched network where radio resources are used only when users are transmitting or receiving data. This means that rather than dedicating a radio channel to a mobile data user for a set period, the available radio resource can be shared between multiple users.[123] This optimized use of radio resources in turn allows for large numbers of GPRS users to share the same bandwidth and be served from a single cell.[124] The true number of users that can be supported varies based on the applications in use and how much data is being transmitted at the time. However, the mobile tower bases that support voice calls are used to support GPRS and as a consequence GPRS can be used wherever it is possible to make a voice call.[125]

Unlike GSM, where the cost of the data call correlates to the amount of time spent connected to the network, the cost of GPRS depends on the amount of data sent and received.[126] GPRS only transmits when data needs to be sent or received.[127] This means that when a user is not transmitting, the bandwidth is free for

---

[120] See Nanda, Balachandran & Kumar, Adaptation Techniques in Wireless Packet Data Services, 38(1) IEEE Comm. Mag. 54–64 (Jan. 2000).

[121] Ghribi & Logrippo, Understanding GPRS: The GSM Packet Radio Service, 34(5) Computer Networks 763–79 (2000).

[122] Buddhikot, Chandranmenon, et al., "Integration of 802.11 and Third-Generation Wireless Data Networks," in Proceedings of the Twenty-Second Annual Joint Conference of the IEEE Computer and Communications, 1 IEEE Societies 503–12 (2003).

[123] Ghribi & Logrippo, Understanding GPRS: The GSM Packet Radio Service, 34(5) Computer Networks 763–779 (2000).

[124] Ermel, Begain, et al., "Analytical Comparison of Different GPRS Introduction Strategies," in Proceedings of the 3rd ACM International Workshop on Modeling, Analysis And Simulation of Wireless and Mobile Systems 3–10 (Aug. 2000).

[125] Banerjee, Wu & Das, Mobility Support in Wireless Internet, 10(5) IEEE Wireless Communications 54–61 (2003).

[126] Kim, Humblet, et al., V. 92: The Last Dial-Up Modem?, 52(1) IEEE Transactions on Communications 54–61 (2004); Kridel, Rappoport, & Taylor, Chapter 3, The Demand For High-Speed Access To The Internet: The Case for Cable Modems, in Forecasting the Internet: Understanding the Explosive Growth of Data Communications (Loomis, et al. eds., Kluwer Acad. Pub. 2002).

[127] See Gyasi-Agyei & Sarker, "GPRS—Features and Packet Random Access Channel Performance Analysis," in Proceedings of the 8th IEEE International Conference on Networks, IEEE Computer Society 13–17 (2000).

transmissions by other users on the network.[128] Accordingly, users are charged for the amount of data they transmit, rather than connection time.[129] This design in turn enables mobile messaging devices using GPRS technology to have substantially higher data transmission speeds.[130]

## 5.9 Mobile Phone Network Technologies: 3G Mobile Communications

The next major evolution in mobile networks was the emergence of EDGE networks, which stands for Enhanced Data Rates for GSM Evolution.[131] EDGE is a high-speed pre-3G radio technology built on the GSM standard, but it is classified as 3G network technology. EDGE networks were built to deliver multimedia applications, such as streaming television to mobile phones at speeds up to 384 Kbps.[132] EDGE delivers up to 3× the data capacity of subscribers of GPRS.[133] EDGE uses the same TDMA (time division multiple access) frame structure, logic channels, and other components current GSM networks utilize, which allows existing GSM/GPRS networks to upgrade software and become an EDGE network.[134]

EDGE networks can carry greater bandwidth because they use eight phase shifting key (8PSK) encoding.[135] The 8PSK is a type of phase modulation scheme that is used by wireless communication devices to transmit data.[136] The 8PSK schema encodes three bits in a single symbol, which increases the data rate in the bandwidth when compared to other schemas, such as QPSK. 8PSK uses eight phase shifts,

---

[128] GPRS works with GSM transceivers by assigning uplink and downlink channels the same way as voice calls. The data is then uploaded or downloaded in chunks that correspond to the transmission rate of the GSM service.

[129] Yaiparoj, Harmantzis & Gunasekaran, On the Economics of GPRS Networks With Wi-Fi Integration, 187(3) European Journal of Operational Research 1459–1475 (2008).

[130] See Introduction to GSM / GPRS Wireless Modems, available at http://www.developershome.com/sms/GSMModemIntro.asp (last visited May 22, 2013).

[131] Furuskar, Mazur, et al., EDGE: Enhanced Data Rates for GSM and TDMA/136 Evolution, 6(3) IEEE Personal Communications 56–66 (1999).

[132] Stüber, Principles of Mobile Communication (Springer Science + Business Media 2011).

[133] Stüber, Principles of Mobile Communication (Springer Science + Business Media 2011).

[134] Furuskar, Mazur, et al., EDGE: Enhanced Data Rates for GSM and TDMA/136 Evolution, 6(3) IEEE Personal Communications 56–66 (1999).

[135] See generally Eriksson, Furuskar, et al., "Comparison of Link Quality Control Strategies for Packet Data Services in EDGE," in Proceedings of 49th IEEE Vehicular Technology Conference, Vol. 2, 938–42 (May 16–20, 1999); Kondur, et al., "Evolution of Wireless Mobile Communication Networks and Future of Cellular Market in India," available at http://airccj.org/CSCP/vol2/csit2444.pdf (last visited May 22, 2013).

[136] Priya, Rajesh & Muthaiah, Carrier Synchronization in Software Defined Radio for 8psk., 5 Int'l J. of Engineering & Tech. 81 (Feb.–Mar. 2013).

which allows for the transmission of more data in less time.[137] EDGE was deployed on GSM networks in the USA beginning in 2003.[138] While EDGE is considered pre-3G radio technology, EDGE meets the International Telecommunications Union's requirement for a 3G network and has been accepted by the ITU as part of the IMT-2000 family of 3G standards.

Code division multiple access networks evolved from 2G to 3G with the deployment of CDMA2000 networks.[139] CDMA2000 is the 3G mobile technology standard that uses CDMA channel access to transmit voice and data, as well as signal data, between mobile devices and cell towers. The deployment of 3G mobile phone networks (a.k.a. International Mobile Telecommunications-2000 (IMT—2000)) in the early 2000s allowed for the faster and more efficient transmission of packet switch data, providing mobile phone networks with the ability to offer users transmission speeds from 125 kbps to 2 Mbps.[140] The first 3G network was launched in 2001 by NTT DoCoMo in Japan.[141]

The security provided by 3G networks is stronger than 2G because the mobile device is able to authenticate the network to prevent network impersonation. Unfortunately, there exists several known security weaknesses within 3G technology.[142] A 3G network allows mobile phones to connect to the Internet or other IP networks to make voice and video calls, to download and upload data, and to surf the net.[143] For example, a 3G-enabled phone with the Skype application installed on it can make phone calls over a wireless network, preserving a user's costly voice minutes.[144]

---

[137] Wang & Yongacoglu, Performance of Trellis Coded-8PSK With Cochannel Interference, 42(1) IEEE Transactions on Communications 6–10 (1994).

[138] Dahlman, et al., "Background of 3G Evolution," in Communications Engineering Desk Reference 259 (Academic Press 2009).

[139] Akhtar, "2G–4G Networks: Evolution of Technologies, Standards, and Deployment," in Encyclopedia of Multimedia Technology and Networking (Ideas Group Publisher 2010), available at http://www.techrepublic.com/whitepapers/2g-4g-networks-evolution-of-technologies-standards-and-deployment/2378579 (last visited May 22, 2013).

[140] Dahlman, et al., "Background of 3G Evolution," in Communications Engineering Desk Reference 259 (Academic Press 2009).

[141] Banks & Fidoten, Chapter 19, Mobile Computing, in Grant & Meadows, Communication Technology Update and Fundamentals 280 (Focal Press 2008).

[142] Xenakis & Merakos, Security in Third Generation Mobile Networks, 27(7) Computer Communications 638–50 (2004).

[143] Akhtar, "2G–4G Networks: Evolution of Technologies, Standards, and Deployment," in Encyclopedia of Multimedia Technology and Networking (Ideas Group Publisher 2010), available at http://www.techrepublic.com/whitepapers/2g-4g-networks-evolution-of-technologies-standards-and-deployment/2378579 (last visited May 22, 2013).

[144] See Mossberg, Skype Does Better with Group Calls Than Mobile, The Wall Street Journal (Jan. 13, 2011), http://online.wsj.com/article/SB10001424052748704803604576077962539629004.html (last visited July 19, 2013).

Today, the most commonly utilized 3G technologies by mobile carriers are as follows:

- WCDMA stands for wideband code division multiple access, which is the radio access network used in Universal Mobile Telecommunications Systems modulation.[145] The UMTS modulation scheme used by WCDMA is quadrature phase shift keying (QPSK). In a QPSK signal, phase shifts on the I and Q signal represent bits of a symbol.[146]
- CDMA 1xEV-DO, also known as CDMA Evolution Data or EV-DO,[147] is a 3G technology add-on for CDMA networks that allows for downloads up to 2.4576 Mbps.[148]
- EDGE, which stands for Enhanced Data rates for GSM Evolution,[149] is a much faster version of GSM than was built upon the GSM standard.[150]
- CDMA 1xRTT is the equivalent of GPRS in the US market.[151] It is an advanced CDMA-based technology that allows transmission of data at speeds of up to 144 Kbps.[152]

---

[145] Valikhani v. Qualcomm Inc., 2009-1 Trade Cas. (CCH) ¶ 76518, 2009 WL 539915 (S.D. Cal. 2009); Park & Park, "A Survey of Security Threats on 4 g Networks," in Proceedings of the IEEE Globecom Workshops 1–6 (Nov. 26–30, 2007).

[146] CSR Technology Inc. v. Freescale Semiconductor, 2013 WL 503077 (N.D. Cal. 2013).

[147] See Broadcom Corp. v. Qualcomm Inc., 543 F.3d 683 (Fed. Cir. 2008); In re Sierra Wireless, Inc. Securities Litigation, 482 F. Supp. 2d 365 (S.D. N.Y. 2007).

[148] According to the *In re Apple & AT & TM Antitrust Litigation* court: "CDMA is one of two competing wireless network technologies in the United States, the other being GSM. Of the four major American carriers, ATTM and T-Mobile are GSM carriers and Verizon and Sprint are CDMA carriers." In re Apple & AT & TM Antitrust Litigation, 596 F. Supp. 2d 1288, 1295 n.2 (N.D. Cal. 2008). For a more technical discussion, refer to Performance of 1xEV-DO third-generation wireless high-speed data systems. See Bi, Brown, et al., Performance of 1xEV-DO Third-Generation Wireless High-Speed Data Systems, 7(3) Bell Labs Technical Journal 97–107 (2003), available at http://www.cdg.org/resources/files/white_papers/Perf_DO.pdf (last visited July 19, 2013).

[149] Broadcom Corp. v. Qualcomm Inc., 2009 WL 650576 (S.D. Cal. 2009).

[150] The court in *Edge Wireless, LLC v. US Cellular Corporation*, stated that "'EDGE' is an acronym for Enhanced Data rates for GSM Evolution (or Environment). EDGE is a type of technology that allows faster transmission of wireless data." Edge Wireless, LLC v. U.S. Cellular Corp., 2004 WL 1661992, *5 (D. Or. 2004).

[151] Rodriguez & Fridman, Performance of PEPs in Cellular Wireless Networks, Web Content Caching and Distribution 19–38 (Kluwer Acad. Pub. 2004); Zmijewska, "Evaluating Wireless Technologies in Mobile Payments-A Customer Centric Approach," in Proceedings of the International IEEE Conference on Mobile Business 354–62 (IEEE Computer Society 2005); Lawton, What Lies Ahead for Cellular Technology?, 38(6) Computer 14–17 (2005).

[152] Wingert & Naidu, CDMA 1XRTT Security Overview, Qualcomm White Paper (Aug. 2002); Kim, Lee, & Chu, "End-to-end Application Performance Impact on Scheduler in CDMA-1XRTT Wireless System," in Proceedings of the 61st IEEE Vehicular Technology Conference, Vol. 5, 2770–74 (Spring 2005).

Unlike Wi-Fi, which is often free in hotspots, you need to be subscribed to a mobile carrier to obtain 3G network connectivity.[153] This is commonly referred to as a data plan or network plan by mobile network carriers.[154] Today, most mobile phones connect to a 3G mobile network via SIM card or a 3G data card, which are generally provided by the mobile carrier.[155]

## 5.10 Mobile Phone Network Technologies: 4G Mobile Communications

4G and 5G mobile network technologies are now on the market and is projected to replace 3G technology sometime over the next decade.[156] An extension of 3G technology, 4G has greater bandwidth and service capabilities.[157] While there is a great deal of similarity in the technologies, the key features setting 4G apart include (1) integration of orthogonal frequency division multiplexing (OFDM),[158] a frequency immune to interference and designed to carry more data by splitting radio signals over different frequencies, and (2) Mobile Worldwide Interoperability for Microwave Access (WiMAX), a wireless broadband communications standard which uses OFDMA.[159] 4G mobile networks also use multiple-input multiple-output (MIMO), which uses two or more radio signals on a single radio channel.[160] These two tech-

---

[153] Balasubramanian, Mahajan & Venkataramani, "Augmenting Mobile 3G Using WiFi," in Proceedings of the 8th International Conference on Mobile Systems, Applications, and Services 209–22 (ACM 2010); Lee, Lee, et al., Mobile Data Offloading: How Much Can Wifi Deliver?, 40(4) ACM SIGCOMM Computer Communication Review 425–26 (Oct. 2010).

[154] Garber, Will 3G Really Be the Next Big Wireless Technology, 35(1) Computer 26–32 (2002).

[155] Putz & Schmitz, "Secure Interoperation Between 2G and 3G Mobile Radio Networks," in Proceedings of the First International Conference on 3G Mobile Communication Technologies Publ. No. 471 2000). *But* cf. Varoutas, Katsianis, et al., On the Economics of 3G Mobile Virtual Network Operators (MVNOS), 36(2) Wireless Personal Communications 129–42 (2006).

[156] Khan, Qadeer, et al., "4G as a Next Generation Wireless Network," in Proceedings of the International IEEE Conference on Future Computer and Communication 334–38 (Apr. 3–5, 2009).

[157] Hui & Yeung, Challenges in the Migration to 4G Mobile Systems, 41(12) IEEE Communications 54–59 (2003); Salkintzis, Interworking Techniques and Architectures for WLAN/3G Integration Toward 4G Mobile Data Networks, 11(3) IEEE Wireless Communications 50–61 (2004).

[158] Hara & Prasad, Multicarrier Techniques for 4G Mobile Communications (Artech House Publishers 2003); Yang, A Road to Future Broadband Wireless Access: MIMO-OFDM-based Air Interface, 43(1) IEEE Communications 53–60 (2005).

[159] Weinschenk, "Speeding Up WiMax," IT Business Edge, http://www.itbusinessedge.com/cm/community/features/interviews/blog/speeding-up-wimax (article no longer available). "Today the initial WiMax system is designed to provide 30 to 40 megabit-per-second data rates." Hu & Lu, "Open Wireless Architecture-The Core to 4G Mobile Communications," in Proceedings of the International Conference on Communication Technology Vol. 2 1337–42 (Apr. 9–11, 2003).

[160] Nema, Goel, & Singh, Integrated DWDM and MIMO-OFDM System for 4G High Capacity Mobile Communication, 3(5) Signal Process. Int. J. 132–43 (2010).

nological advances allow mobile phones operating on a 4G mobile network to stream higher quality audio/video streaming over end-to-end Internet Protocol.[161] The obvious benefit of providing speeds upward of 100 megabits per second (Mbps) is that users can consume more data, be it from a car, train, or automobile.[162] In summary, the real technical leap that occurred between 3G and 4G is the integration of already existing and new networks, services, and terminals, in order to satisfy ever-increasing user demands.[163]

While 2G mobile telecommunication focused on providing mobile phone users comprehensive mobile phone coverage (vis-a-vis one technology), and 3G mobile telecommunication networks focused on providing targeted coverage and integrated WLAN systems, 4G represents the full integration of WLAN and the use of a spectrum that is above the 3G 2 GHz band.[164] The above demonstrates the point that terminology for wireless evolution confuses even people experienced in wireless. For example, the ITU-R calls WiMAX "IMT-2000," meaning "3G," but one operator plans to deploy it calling it WiMAX 4G.[165] Irrespective of the particular name used to brand the technology, it is likely that both mobile phones and technology will continue to evolve in the coming years.[166]

## 5.11 What Is Mobile Messaging?

Mobile messaging refers to the ability to send and receive short text-based messages via mobile phones using the short message service (SMS) function offered by mobile network providers.[167] Messages can consist of words or numbers in any

---

[161] Khan, Qadeer, et al., "4G as a Next Generation Wireless Network," in Proceedings of the International IEEE Conference on Future Computer and Communication 334–38 (Apr. 3–5, 2009).

[162] Cvijetic, Tanaka, et al. "4+ G Mobile Backhaul Over OFDMA/TDMA-PON to 200 Cell Sites Per Fiber with 10 Gb/s Upstream Burst-Mode Operation Enabling <1 ms Transmission Latency," in Proceedings of the Optical Fiber Communication Conference and Exposition and National Fiber Optic Engineers Conference 1–3 (Mar. 3, 2012).

[163] Woh, Mahlke, et al., Mobile Supercomputers for the Next-Generation Cell Phone, 43(1) Computer 81–85 (2010). See Sullivan, 3G and 4G Wireless Speed Showdown: Which Networks Are Fastest?, PC World (Apr 16, 2012), http://www.pcworld.com/article/253808/3g_and_4g_wireless_speed_showdown_which_networks_are_fastest_.html (last visited July 19, 2013).

[164] Dahlman, Parkvall & Skold, 4G: LTE/LTE-Advanced for Mobile Broadband: LTE/LTE-Advanced for Mobile Broadband (Academic Press 2011).

[165] Bashah, Jorstad & Thanh, "Service Naming in Future Mobile Environments," in Proceedings of the International IEEE Conference on Parallel Processing Workshops 256–61 (IEEE Computer Society 2009).

[166] Huang, Qian, et al., "A Close Examination of Performance and Power Characteristics of 4G LTE Networks," in Proceedings of the 10th International Conference on Mobile Systems, Applications, and Services 225–38 (ACM 2012).

[167] See TruePosition Inc. v. Andrew Corp., 507 F. Supp. 2d 447, 456 n.6 (D. Del. 2007); Naughton, "Now 4 Billion People Know the Joy of Txt," The Guardian (May 5, 2012), http://www.guardian.co.uk/technology/2012/may/06/sms-text-messages-20th-birthday

alphanumeric combination.[168] At the most basic level, a mobile phone transmits and receives binary data.[169] To most mobile networks, the messages are simply a sequence of binary digits.[170] For example, the word "cool" would transmit as "01100011011011110110111101101100" when a text message is received or transmitted to a mobile phone. Mobile devices translate these sequences of digits into readable form for the end receiver.[171]

The message from the sending mobile phone is stored in a central SMS center, which then forwards it to the destination mobile.[172] This means that, where a recipient is offline, the SMS is stored and can be sent later.[173] It is also possible to specify the period after which the SMS message will be deleted from the SMS center, so that the SMS message will not be forwarded to the recipient mobile phone when it goes online.[174] This period is called the "validity period."[175] Another useful feature provided by the SMS center is the ability to be notified if an SMS has arrived successfully.[176]

SMS is essentially a universal mobile data service.[177] Originally standardized and implemented in GSM networks,[178] SMS interworking with fixed networks[179] has also been introduced. And, with personal communication system ("PCS")

---

[168] The first short message was sent in December 1992 from a personal computer (PC) to a mobile phone on the Vodafone GSM network in the UK. Originally, the amount of information you could transmit by SMS varied by network. GSM networks allowed messages of 160 characters, CDMA allowed 256 characters, and iDEN allowed 140 characters. See Seybold, Short Messaging Service (SMS), Mothering Magazine, June 25, 1999. Today, all networks have standardized on a 140-character message, and all networks have two-way SMS capability. See In re Mobilactive Media, LLC, 2013 WL 297950 (Del. Ch. 2013).

[169] Stüber, Principles of Mobile Communication (Springer 2011).

[170] Stüber, Principles of Mobile Communication (Springer 2011).

[171] Woods, Mobile Technologies from a Telecom Perspective, 52(1–2) The Reference Librarian 159–65 (2010).

[172] Lombera, Moser, et al., Mobile Decentralized Search and Retrieval Using SMS and HTTP, 18(1) Mobile Networks and Applications 22–41 (Feb. 2013).

[173] Brown, Shipman & Vetter, SMS: The Short Message Service, 40(12) Computer 106–10 (2007).

[174] Brown, Shipman & Vetter, SMS: The Short Message Service, 40(12) Computer 106–10 (2007).

[175] Basic Concepts of SMS Technology, available at http://www.developershome.com/sms_tutorial.asp?page=basicConcepts (last visited May 20, 2013).

[176] Peersman, Cvetkovic, et al., The Global System for Mobile Communications Short Message Service, 7(3) IEEE Personal Communications 15–23 (2000).

[177] Peersman, Griffiths, et al., A Tutorial Overview of the Short Message Service Within GSM, 11(2) Computing & Control Engineering Journal 78–89 (2000).

[178] "GSM" stands for "Global System for Mobile Communications." The most widely used of the three digital wireless telephony technologies (GSM, CDMA, and TDMA) is GSM that digitizes and compresses data and then sends it through a channel with two other user data streams, each in its own time slot. See Rahnema, Overview of the GSM System and Protocol Architecture, IEEE Communications Magazine 92–100 (Apr. 1993).

[179] See Collesei, Di Tria & Morena, "Short Message Service Based Application in the GSM Network," in Proceedings of the 5th IEEE International Symposium on Personal, Indoor and Mobile Radio Communications 939 (1994).

networks based on all three technologies, GSM,[180] CDMA,[181] and TDMA,[182] supporting SMS, these digital messages can readily be sent or received concurrently with data and voice communications. The SMS service description for fixed networks can be found in ES 201 986 "Short Message Service (SMS) for PSTN/ISDN; Service description."[183] The service functions in two ways, either as a user-based solution[184] or as a network-based solution.[185]

Of course, as mobile network systems and mobile phones advance, it will be possible to send more complex data types. There are four basic types of mobile messaging scenarios possible between the system and a mobile phone:[186]

- *PUSH SMS services:* PUSH services push relevant information from the application or service, through the network, to the mobile phone.[187] These services are usually deployed for system or service alerts, real-time notifications, and direct marketing offerings. For example, Blackberries use PUSH services to update email inboxes in a wireless context, and iPhones use PUSH services via Apple Push Notification Service to forward notifications to iPhone users. A bank can push a message to a customer that it has opened a new branch, or an application can push an update alert to a customer.[188]
- *PULL SMS services:* Mobile users "pull" or request information by sending an SMS from their mobile phones to a service number, often via a short code, linked

---

[180] See Telecommunication Industry Association/Electronic Industries Association (TIA/EIA) Standard, Short messaging service for spread spectrum systems, ANSI/TIA/EIA-637-A-1999 (approved Sept. 9, 1999).

[181] "CDMA" stands for "code division multiple access." It is a form of multiplexing which allows numerous signals to occupy a single transmission channel, optimizing the use of available bandwidth. See Wilson, Ganesh, et al., Packet CDMA Versus Dynamic TDMA for Multiple-Access in an Integrated Voice/Data PCN, 11 IEEE Journ. Select. Areas in Comm., 870 (Aug. 1993).

[182] "TDMA" stands for "time division multiple access." It is a technology that divides each cellular channel into three time slots in order to increase the amount of data that can be carried. Wilson, Ganesh, et al., Packet CDMA Versus Dynamic TDMA for Multiple-Access in an Integrated Voice/Data PCN, 11 IEEE Journ. Select. Areas in Comm., 870 (Aug. 1993).

[183] Final draft, ETSI ES 201 986 V1. 1.1 (2001–11).

[184] See Barwise & Strong, Permission-Based Mobile Advertising, 16 J. Interactive Marketing 14, 14–24 (2002).

[185] See Ranganathan & Campbell, "Advertising in a Pervasive Computing Environment," in Proceedings of the 2nd International ACM Workshop on Mobile Commerce 10–14 (2002).

[186] We limit this discussion to SMS-based services, but other rapidly emerging protocols are being adopted to provide these messaging services and will likely replace SMS at some point in the future.

[187] See Podnar, Hauswirth & Jazayeri, "Mobile Push: Delivering Content to Mobile Users," in Proceedings of the International Workshop on Distributed Event-Based Systems 563–70 (IEEE Computer Society 2002).

[188] See generally Pousttchi & Schurig, "Assessment of Today's Mobile Banking Applications From the View of Customer Requirements," in Proceedings of the 37th Annual Hawaii International Conference on System Sciences Track 7, Vol. 7, 70184.1 (IEEE Computer Society 2004).

to the application or service of the content provider.[189] Using the above example of mobile banking, PULL services embedded in a mobile banking application can enable customers to request a balance transfer or obtain a balance statement via SMS messages from the mobile phone.[190]

- *PUSH-PULL SMS services:* This service is initiated by a PUSH SMS from the application to the mobile user, prompting the user to reply via SMS.[191] As the above example demonstrates, mobile banking uses PUSH-PULL services to provide customers mobile banking or when an application requests the use of the mobile user's location to give directions.[192]
- *PULL-PUSH SMS services*: This service is initiated by the mobile user via SMS to the application provider, prompting the application to reply via SMS.[193] Mobile coupons are trending toward using PULL-PUSH services. For example, for mobile ads on mobile application where users are actually looking for services and products, the user will initiate via SMS a request for a particular product or service, and the mobile application will PUSH back a response to the user.[194]

The convenience and simplicity of SMS, combined with the evolution of pricing models (especially unlimited SMS bundles), have contributed to a significant growth of the SMS market in the USA and Europe over the past few years.[195] To date, the main application of SMS has been the exchange of text messages between mobile

---

[189] *See* Ogata & Yano, "Knowledge Awareness Map for Computer-Supported Ubiquitous Language-Learning," in Proceedings of the 2d IEEE Workshop on Mobile Technologies in Education 19–26 (2004).

[190] Peevers, Douglas & Jack, A Usability Comparison of Three Alternative Message Formats for an SMS Banking Service, 66(2) Int'l J. of Human-Computer Studies 113–23 (2008); Dickinger, Haghirian, et al., "An Investigation and Conceptual Model of SMS Marketing," in Proceedings of the 37th Annual Hawaii International Conference on System Sciences (Jan. 5–8, 2004).

[191] Dickinger, Haghirian, et al., "An Investigation and Conceptual Model of SMS Marketing," in Proceedings of the 37th Annual Hawaii International Conference on System Sciences (Jan. 5–8, 2004).

[192] Dickinger, Haghirian, et al., "An Investigation and Conceptual Model of SMS Marketing," in Proceedings of the 37th Annual Hawaii International Conference on System Sciences (Jan. 5–8, 2004).

[193] See Podnar, Hauswirth & Jazayeri, "Mobile Push: Delivering Content to Mobile Users," in Proceedings of the International Workshop on Distributed Event-Based Systems 563–70 (IEEE Computer Society 2002).

[194] See generally Unni & Harmon, Perceived Effectiveness of Push vs. Pull Mobile Location-Based Advertising, 7(2) J. of Interactive Advertising 28–40 (2007); Xu, Teo, et al., "The Role of Push-Pull Technology In Privacy Calculus: The Case of Location-Based Services," 26(3) J. of Management Information Systems 135–74 (Winter 2009–2010).

[195] Mobile services in developing countries will be addressed in the next edition of the book as well as several of the unique technologies used in these countries.

users,[196] but many content providers have entered this market offering a variety of services, including the following:

- Directory services (e.g., telephone directory, public transport timetables). SMS driven directory services are used around the world, for example, Telecom Namibia offers an SMS text message service that delivers a range of key classified business information using short messaging service (SMS) platforms across a multiple of mobile networks in Namibia.[197]
- Alerts regarding news, sports (e.g., notification of goals scored in football matches), finance (e.g., stock market reports, currency rates, bank services), and weather (e.g., GovDelivery provides alert and warning information provided by the National Weather Service).[198]
- Entertainment (games, competitions, quiz, interactive TV programs), SMS games, and quizzes.[199] For example, Snackable Media, a company that offers SMS-based games such as Predicto, boasts more than a million monthly active users, all paying a $9.95 per month subscription.[200]
- Chat rooms, SMS driven chat room services. For instance, a company, Mobilink, provides anonymous and group chat using the traditional SMS infrastructure. Mobilink subscribers can chat and make friends with other Mobilink subscribers in public chat rooms, just like in a web-based chat room.[201]
- Dating services. SMS driven dating services, for example, SMS Christian dating service, which is a text message mobile phone Christian dating services, utilize the latest technology for dating services online, SMS text messages, and mobile phone text message services.[202]

---

[196] See generally Short Message Service (SMS) in Fixed and Mobile Networks, at 4, CEPT (2004) 52 final (July 2004).

[197] See Telecom Namibia announces the launch of an SMS directory service, http://www.telecom.na/index.php/component/content/article/584 (last visited Apr. 28, 2013).

[198] See GovDelivery, https://public.govdelivery.com/accounts/USNWS/subscriber/new (last visited Apr. 28, 2013).

[199] Leppäniemi & Karjaluoto, Mobile Marketing: From Marketing Strategy To Mobile Marketing Campaign Implementation, 3(1) Int'l J. of Mobile Marketing 50–61 (2008).

[200] See Schonfeld, Don't Laugh At SMS Games: Snackable Media Sold $170 Million Worth Of Them Last Year (Jan. 18, 2010), http://techcrunch.com/2010/01/18/snackable-media-170-million/ (last visited Apr. 28, 2013). The article states that Predicto sends player's text messages with multiple-choice questions asking them to make predictions about celebrity news and pop culture. "Who will host the Tonight Show by 3/1?" "Will Best Actress nominee Julia Roberts wear an Armani gown to the Golden Globes?" Players text back their answers, and get a chance to win prizes up to $50,000. On average, people sign up for 3–4 months.

[201] See Mobilink World SMS Chat, http://www.mobilinkworld.com/index.php?option=com_content&task=view&id=254&Itemid=679 (last visited Apr. 28, 2013).

[202] See Fusion Free Christian Singles, http://www.fusion101.com/services/sms-text-christian-dating.htm (last visited Apr. 28, 2013); Eagle & Pentland, Social Serendipity: Mobilizing Social Software, 4(2) IEEE Pervasive Computing 28–34 (2005); Romm-Livermore & Setzekorn, Social Networking Communities and E-Dating Services: Concepts and Implication (Information Science Reference 2008).

- Social network messaging. SMS is used in social networking by Facebook or MySpace.[203] SMS social network messaging is even used in villages in India through a Twitter-like short message service (SMS) social marketing networking alternative called GupShup,[204] which facilitates "pocket social networking" for people without smartphones and was estimated to process four billion SMS messages per month as of August 2011.[205]
- Mobile advertising and commerce (e.g., mobile ads and offers). SMS is used in mobile marketing with several 100 million advertising SMS sent out every month in Europe alone.[206]

SMS was the foundation of instant messaging from companies like AOL and Yahoo, even before Facebook or MySpace.[207] SMS has spurred a great deal of content and service innovation, with new services being introduced continuously.[208] For example, some network operators have developed specific platforms for SMS content provision, including the authority to bill the end user on behalf of the content provider.[209] All this innovation has increased (and will continue to increase) the scope and complexity of mobile messaging and, by extension, the discoverability of mobile messages.[210] Of course, the medium for the mobile messaging is likely to evolve as mobile phones develop and the mobile application marketplace matures.[211]

---

[203] Han, Hui, et al., "Cellular Traffic Offloading Through Opportunistic Communications: A Case Study," in Proceedings of the 5th ACM Workshop on Challenged Networks 31–38 (Sept. 2010).

[204] See GupShup, http://gupshup.me/ (last visited Apr. 28, 2013).

[205] See India's SMS GupShup Raises $10 Million available at http://allthingsd.com/20110830/indias-sms-gupshup-raises-10m/ (last visited Apr. 28, 2013).

[206] See generally Tsang, Ho & Liang, Consumer Attitudes Toward Mobile Advertising: An Empirical Study, 8(3) Int'l J. of Elec. Comm. 65–78 (2004); Xu, Teo, et al., "The Role of Push-Pull Technology In Privacy Calculus: The Case of Location-Based Services," 26(3) J. of Management Information Systems 135–74 (Winter 2009–2010).

[207] See generally Ellison, Social Network Sites: Definition, History, and Scholarship, 13(1) J. of Computer-Mediated Comm. 210–30 (2007).

[208] Dickinger, Haghirian, et al., "An Investigation and Conceptual Model of SMS Marketing," in Proceedings of the 37th Annual Hawaii International Conference on System Sciences (Jan. 5–8, 2004).

[209] Streicher, Premium SMS Services Need Self-Regulation (Apr. 21, 2005), http://www.itweb.co.za/index.php?option=com_content&view=article&id=19602 (last visited July 19, 2013).

[210] See Maitland, van de Kar, et al., Mobile Information and Entertainment Services: Business Models and Service Networks, 6 Int'l J. Mgmt. Decision Making 47–64 (2005).

[211] This chapter does not cover all mobile SMS network technologies. Other available technologies include CDMA and a number of next-generation infrastructure, EVDO, HSPA, LTE, etc., currently being deployed to enable 3G/4G mobile services.

## 5.12 Future Mobile Devices

The future of mobile devices is uncharted and we are at the front end of the mobile revolution. Today, handheld holograms are not yet a commercial reality, but researchers at HP Labs have made prototypes of screens that can render 3D images and videos in smartphones, smart watches, tables, and other emerging mobile devices.[212] As we can see, smartphones are starting to assist people in taking control of their health and are enabling people to start running common medical tests.[213]

[212] Fattal, Peng, et al., A Multi-Directional Backlight for a Wide-Angle, Glasses-Free Three-Dimensional Display, Nature 495, 348–51 (Mar 21, 2013).

[213] See Peter Wayner, Monitoring Your Health With Mobile Devices (Feb. 23, 2012), http://www.nytimes.com/2012/02/23/technology/personaltech/monitoring-your-health-with-mobile-devices.html (last visited Apr. 28, 2013).

# Chapter 6
# Digital Forensic Investigations and eDiscovery

## 6.1 Forensic Technology 101

### *Forensic Software*

> It is a capital mistake to theorize before one has data. Insensibly one begins to twist facts to suit theories, instead of theories to suit facts.
>
> —Sherlock Holmes[1]

Forensic software is used to acquire and analyze digital evidence.[2] It is employed by a forensic examiner during a digital forensic investigation to discover and document relevant facts related to a case or issue.[3] These software tools are designed to assist forensic examiners in the analysis of digital evidence.[4] The number and variety of such software packages has increased dramatically over the last 30 years[5]—in

[1] Arthur Conan Doyle, "A Scandal in Bohemia," in The Adventures of Sherlock Holmes (1891).

[2] See Carrier, 3 File System Forensic Analysis (Addison-Wesley 2005).

[3] See Casey, Handbook of Computer Crime Investigation: Forensic Tools and Technology (Academic Press 2002); Carrier, 3 File System Forensic Analysis (Addison-Wesley 2005); Ayers, A Second Generation Computer Forensic Analysis System, 6 Digital Investigation S34-S42 (Sept. 2009).

[4] The digital crime scene is not unlike a physical crime scene. Each has their own evidence, witnesses, and timeline. See generally Carrier, Getting Physical with the Digital Investigation Process, in 2 International Journal of Digital Evidence (Fall 2003).

[5] See Baker, Brothers, et al., Chap. 10: Digital Evolution: History, Challenges and Future Directions for the Digital and Multimedia Sciences Section, in Forensic Science: Current Issues, Future Directions 252–91 (Ubelaker, ed., John Wiley & Sons 2012).



D. B. Garrie et al., *Uncovering Digital Evidence*,
https://doi.org/10.1007/978-3-031-68118-9_6

1989, there was only one such tool[6]; today, there are hundreds, perhaps thousands, all dedicated to finding a smoking gun amid billions of ones and zeros.[7]

At the outset, we should stress that forensic software is not like the eDiscovery[8] software used in resolving a dispute over electronic evidence. The latter type of software operates on the assumption that all parties are playing by the rules and that all relevant evidence that exists has been produced for review.[9] Digital investigations assume just the opposite,[10] that the opposing party most certainly is not playing by the rules and that relevant evidence has been renamed,[11] reformatted,[12] deleted,[13] encrypted,[14] overwritten,[15] or otherwise obfuscated in an attempt to hide its existence.[16]

A digital investigation seeks to preserve and analyze electronic data, to ensure that it is not lost.[17] Such electronic evidence runs the gamut and encompasses the

---

[6] Whitcombe, An Historical Perspective of Digital Evidence: A Forensic Scientist's View, 1(1) International Journal of Digital Evidence (Spring 2002).

[7] A simple search on the Internet reveals all the possibilities. In addition to the commercial products, there are a growing number of open-source applications that allow users free use of the software and the ability to further develop the tools for themselves.

[8] eDiscovery, also known as electronic discovery, is the name given to the most recent wave of discovery that involves digitally stored information. This can include emails, word processing documents, text messages, as well as any connected electronically stored information (ESI) such as metadata, GPS coordinates, credit card transactions, etc. More information on eDiscovery can be found in Chap. 10. See generally Comment 8.c., The Sedona Principles (2d ed. 2007) ("While [forensic data acquisition] is clearly appropriate in some circumstances, it should not be required unless exceptional circumstances warrant the extraordinary cost and burden"; also noting the need for careful protocols to address such collections). See also In re A & M Florida Properties II, LLC, 53 Bankr. Ct. Dec. (CRR) 17, 2010 WL 1418861 (Bankr. S.D. N.Y. 2010) (ordering sanctions against both the client and counsel where counsel's failure to gain an understanding of plaintiff's computer systems resulted in a delayed production of documents).

[9] Hartley, Current and Future Threats to Digital Forensics, ISSA Journal (Aug. 2007), digital archive available to members at http://www.issa.org/?page=ISSAJournal

[10] Hartley, Current and Future Threats to Digital Forensics, ISSA Journal (Aug. 2007).

[11] Dashora, Tomar, & Rana, A Practical Approach for Evidence Gathering in Windows Environment, 5(10) International Journal of Computer Applications 16–20 (2010).

[12] Garfinkel, Lessons Learned Writing Digital Forensics Tools and Managing a 30tb Digital Evidence Corpus, 9 Digital Investigation S80-S89 (2012).

[13] Adelstein, Live Forensics: Diagnosing Your System Without Killing It First, 49(2) Communications of the ACM 63–66 (2006).

[14] Yasinsac & Manzano, "Policies to Enhance Computer and Network Forensics," in Proceedings of the IEEE Workshop on Information Assurance and Security (June 5–6, 2001).

[15] Garfinkel, "Anti-Forensics: Techniques, Detection and Countermeasures," in Proceedings of the Second International Conference on i-Warfare and Security (2007).

[16] See generally In re Hecker, 430 B.R. 189, 196 (Bankr. D. Minn. 2010); Forte, & Power, A Tour Through the Realm of Anti-Forensics, 2007(6) Computer Fraud & Security 18–20 (June 2007).

[17] Brown, Computer Evidence Collection and Preservation (Charles River Media 2006) (Describing computer forensics as "the art and science of applying computer science to aid the legal process. Although plenty of science is attributable to computer forensics, most successful investigators possess a nose for investigations and a skill for solving puzzles, which is where the art comes in.").

underlying substantive data and associated data, such as data trails and time/date stamps,[18] which are often used to establish a timeline of important events when performing a digital investigation.[19] This chapter provides the reader with an overview of a digital forensic investigation.[20]

---

Although they are quite different specialties, this chapter recognizes that eDiscovery and computer forensics are not mutually exclusive. Whereas eDiscovery is typically sufficient, forensics offers more detail and should be viewed as complementing eDiscovery in many cases. Roth, "Introduction to Computer Forensics," Nev. Lawyer, June 2009, at 12, 15; Shannon, Electronic Discovery and Digital Forensics: An Overview, 10(1) J. of Nursing Law 67–69 (2005).

[18] Bradford, Brown, et al., "Towards proactive computer-system forensics," in Proceedings of the International Conference on Information Technology: Coding and Computing vol. 2, 648–52 (Apr. 5–7, 2004); Harris, Arriving at An Anti-Forensics Consensus: Examining How to Define and Control the Anti-Forensics Problem, 3 Digital Investigation 44–49 (2006).

[19] Schatz, Mohay & Clark, A Correlation Method for Establishing Provenance of Timestamps in Digital Evidence, 3 Digital Investigation 98–107 (2006); Carney & Rogers, The Trojan Made Me Do It: A First Step in Statistical Based Computer Forensics Event Reconstruction, 2(4) International Journal of Digital Evidence 1–11 (2004).

[20] Where sloppy, uninformed, or deceptive practices are used to respond to discovery requests, a court may determine that a forensic investigation of the producing party's computer systems is warranted to counter the loss of efficiency and the lack of good faith effort by the producing party. See generally Fennell v. First Step Designs, Ltd., 83 F.3d 526, 534 (1st Cir. 1996) (court denied request for discovery of defendant's entire hard drive because of costs, burdens, delays, and likelihood of discovering the evidence outweighed importance of requested evidence); Convolve, Inc. v. Compaq Computer Corp., 223 F.R.D. 162, 169 (S.D. N.Y. 2004), order clarified, 2005 WL 1514284 (S.D. N.Y. 2005) (plaintiffs not entitled to direct access to manufacturer's hard drives, servers, and databases absent demonstration of widespread destruction or withholding of relevant information by defendant); GTFM, Inc. v. Wal-Mart Stores, Inc., 49 Fed. R. Serv. 3d 219, 2000 WL 335558 (S.D. N.Y. 2000) (defendant ordered to allow plaintiffs' expert to conduct an on-site inspection of defendant's computer facilities to determine whether and how to extract relevant information where defendant had previously misrepresented its computer capabilities); Eugene J. Strasser, M.D., P.A. v. Bose Yalamanchi, M.D., P.A., 669 So. 2d 1142, 1145 (Fla. 4th DCA 1996) (if requesting party can demonstrate that deleted information could probably be retrieved from computer and there are no less intrusive means by which to do so, then a computer search is appropriate). The exact threshold that a requesting party will have to clear depends on the court. See generally McCurdy Group v. American Biomedical Group, Inc., 9 Fed. Appx. 822, 831 (10th Cir. 2001) (the mere suspicion that not all relevant information have been produced from a computer system will not support a motion to compel direct access to a producing party's computer system); Genworth Financial Wealth Management, Inc. v. McMullan, 267 F.R.D. 443, 448 (D. Conn. 2010) (computer imaging ordered in light of evidence of discovery misconduct including "admitted spoliation"); Stallings-Daniel v. Northern Trust Co., 52 Fed. R. Serv. 3d 1406 (N.D. Ill. 2002) (fishing expeditions are not permitted); Williams v. Massachusetts Mut. Life Ins. Co., 226 F.R.D. 144, 146 (D. Mass. 2005) (requesting party must present reliable information that the opposing party's representations are misleading or substantively inaccurate); Peskoff v. Faber, 244 F.R.D. 54, 59 (D.D.C. 2007) (forensic examination ordered; missing documents may have been caused by party's misconduct).

## *Where and How Information Is Stored*

Digital evidence is data "held on, or retrieved from, computer storage media in such a way that the information can be used as evidence in a court of law."[21] As the world of eDiscovery continues to expand, so too does the world of digital forensic investigations.[22]

Forensic software gives a forensic examiner access to electronically stored information (ESI) that is otherwise unavailable to a typical computer user.[23] An example of this is deleted data.[24] Even though deleted data disappears from visible view, it is not destroyed until it is overwritten by new data.[25] Even when overwritten, deleted data can sometimes be recovered, albeit at a very high cost, in the form of *shadow data*:

---

[21] Grenig & Gleisner, eDiscovery & Digital Evidence 13:1. See generally Casey, Digital Evidence and Computer Crime (Academic Press 2d ed. 2004); Casey, Handbook of Computer Crime Investigation: Forensic Tools and Technology (Academic Press 2002); Britz, Computer Forensics and Cyber Crime (2004); Vacca, Computer Forensics: Computer Crime Scene Investigation (Pearson Education 2002); Kruse & Heiser, Computer Forensics: Incident Response Essentials (Lucent Technologies 2002).

[22] Kahn, America's Cyber Future, Report for the Center for New American Security (May 31, 2011), available at https://www.cnas.org/publications/reports/americas-cyber-future-security-and--prosperity-in-the-information-age (last visited June 9, 2021); Baker, Brothers, et al., Chap. 10: Digital Evolution: History, Challenges and Future Directions for the Digital and Multimedia Sciences Section, Forensic Science: Current Issues, Future Directions 252–91 (Ubelaker, ed., John Wiley & Sons 2012). See generally R.S. Creative, Inc. v. Creative Cotton, Ltd., 75 Cal. App. 4th 486, 89 Cal. Rptr. 2d 353 (2d Dist. 1999). *But* cf. Wright v. AmSouth Bancorporation, 320 F.3d 1198, 56 Fed. R. Serv. 3d 1288 (11th Cir. 2003); Eugene J. Strasser, M.D., P.A. v. Bose Yalamanchi, M.D., P.A., 669 So. 2d 1142, 1144–1145 (Fla. 4th DCA 1996).

[23] See Casey, Digital Evidence and Computer Crime: Forensic Science, Computers, and the Internet (Academic Press 3d ed. 2011 [?]).

[24] See United States v. McAbee, 685 Fed. Appx. 682, 683 n.2 (10th Cir. 2017); U.S. v. Haymond, 672 F.3d 948, 952–53 (10th Cir. 2012) (deleted data formed the basis of defendant's conviction); U.S. v. Otero, 563 F.3d 1127, 1131 (10th Cir. 2009) (deleted data was found in the "'unallocated space' of the hard drive, where deleted data is stored before it is then overwritten with new data"); Dana Ltd. v. American Axle and Mfg. Holdings, Inc., 2012 WL 2524008 (W.D. Mich. 2012); Dana Ltd. v. American Axle and Mfg. Holdings, Inc., 2011 WL 4954061 (W.D. Mich. 2011); Howell v. Buckeye Ranch, Inc., 116 Fair Empl. Prac. Cas. (BNA) 455, 34 I.E.R. Cas. (BNA) 717, 2012 WL 5265170, *2 (S.D. Ohio 2012) (instructing plaintiff's counsel to advise defendants' counsel of any deleted data so as to allow for recovery attempt); Grant Mfg. & Alloying, Inc. v. McIlvain, 32 I.E.R. Cas. (BNA) 1592, 2011 WL 4467767 (E.D. Pa. 2011), judgment aff'd, 499 Fed. Appx. 157 (3d Cir. 2012); Peskoff v. Faber, 244 F.R.D. 54, 58 n.4 (D.D.C. 2007) ("The so-called 'slack space' of a computer is the 'unused space at the logical end of an active file's data and the physical end of the cluster or clusters that are assigned to an active file.' … Deleted data, or remnants of deleted data, is often found in a computer's slack space."); Marron, Discoverability of Deleted E-Mail: Time for a Closer Examination, 25 Seattle U. L. Rev. 895 (2001) (detailing how forensic examiners identify deleted emails).

[25] See Casey, Digital Evidence and Computer Crime 240 (2d. 2004). A more detailed explanation of deleted data can be found in the section titled Locating Digital Evidence—Allocated and Unallocated Space.

> [A] shadow of the data might remain [as] a result of the minor imprecision that naturally occur[s?] when data [is] being written on a disk. The arm that writes data onto a disk has to swing to the correct place, and it is never perfectly accurate. [Thus,] some parts of the data are overwritten leaving other parts untouched. A disk can be examined for shadow data in a lab with advanced equipment [...] and the recovered fragments can be pieced together to reconstruct parts of the original digital data.[26]

This data can be discoverable under Federal Rule of Civil Procedure 34, depending on the facts.

So where does this data lie? The answer focuses on the space not being used by a computer to store files—the "unallocated space." Unallocated space is best defined by understanding what it is not—allocated space.[27] Allocated space is the reserved area on a digital storage device (such as a computer's hard drive) where files are stored using magnetic or optical technology—in other words, allocated space is where files live.[28] Each file is made of 1 s and 0 s that are interpreted by the computer and its operating system as documents and programs.[29]

The ability to store a file on a digital device is a function of the *file system*, which is generally a component of the computer's *operating system*.[30] The file system tracks where a file is physically located on the storage medium (hard drive, thumb drive, CD, DVD, etc.); these physical locations are called *sectors* and *clusters*.[31] Sectors are the lowest common denominator ("LCD") for digital storage; they are where the hard drive reads and writes files to digital storage devices.[32] A cluster is a group of contiguous sectors that vary by multiples of 2, the storage size of which is determined by the file system; it is the LCD for the operating system to store files.[33] A hard drive or any digital storage device requires at least one cluster of storage to store an active file.[34] The unused space in this single cluster is referred to as the *slack*

---

[26] See Simon Property Group L.P. v. mySimon, Inc., 194 F.R.D. 639, 640, 47 Fed. R. Serv. 3d 247 (S.D. Ind. 2000).

[27] Wolfe, Evidence Analysis, 22(4) Computers & Security 289–91 (2003); Saltzer & Kaashoek, Principles of Computer System Design: An Introduction, Part I (Morgan Kaufmann 2009).

[28] Carrier, File System Forensic Analysis (Addison-Wesley 2007).

[29] Barr, Firmware Forensics: Best Practices in Embedded Software Source Code Discovery, 8 Digital Evidence & Elec. Signature L. Rev. 148 (2011).

[30] A file system is often organized in one of two formats, FAT and NTFS, discussed in §6:6. For an in-depth discussion of operating systems, see §2:5. See generally Saltzer & Kaashoek, Principles of Computer System Design: An Introduction, Part I (Morgan Kaufmann 2009); Silberschatz, Galvin & Gagne, 4 Operating System Concepts (Addison-Wesley 1998).

[31] See Buyya, 1 High Performance Cluster Computing: Architectures and Systems (Prentice Hall 1999).

[32] Clements, Principles of Computer Hardware (Oxford University Press, Inc. 2000).

[33] Kerr, Searches And Seizures in a Digital World, 119 Harv. L. Rev. 531 (2005).

[34] See Veenman, "Statistical Disk Cluster Classification for File Carving," in Proceedings of the Third International Symposium on Information Assurance and Security 393–98 (Aug. 29–31, 2007). See also White, Crime Scene to Court: The Essentials of Forensic Science §7.4.7 (The Royal Soc'y of Chemistry 2004).

*space* of the cluster.[35] The specific clusters storing active files are tracked by the file system.[36]

The operating system is responsible for tracking which clusters are in use and which are not.[37] Most Windows-based computers use file management structures that track the relative positions of a cluster in a binary list.[38] If the location is set to 0, the cluster is available for file storage; if the location is set to 1, it is occupied by an existing active file and is unavailable for use in saving another active file.[39]

For example, the line below identifies a text file (MyFile.txt) that is active (Status Bit = 1) and requires five clusters (with a "cluster size" of 4096 bytes) to store the file. The five cluster IDs are the four-digit numbers in the line below.

```
MyFile.txt (Status Bit = 1) = 2345+2346+2347+2353+2360.
&caret; = This is an Active File
```

To clarify, the first 4096 bytes of the text in the MyFile.txt document can be found inside of cluster identification number 2345, while the next 4096 bytes can be found inside of cluster ID 2346, and so on. Note that these five clusters are not all contiguous. This active file structure is known as a *fragmented* file.[40] The Status Bit is critical to allowing the file system to delete a file. When a user deletes the MyFile.txt and empties the Trash, Windows flips the Status Bit from 1 to 0:

```
MyFile.txt (Status Bit = 0) = 2345+2346+2347+2353+2360
(&caret; = This is a deleted file)
```

After the file system sets the Status Bit to 0, it immediately releases all associated clusters with the active file by changing the binary values from 1 s to 0 s:

```
ACTIVE FILE: 01001110110110000101...
(&caret; = Cluster ID 2345)

DELETED FILE: 01000000110100000100...
(&caret; = Cluster ID 2360)
```

[35] Gladyshev, & Patel, Finite State Machine Analysis of a Blackmail Investigation, 4(1) International Journal of Digital Evidence 1–13 (2005).

[36] See also Garcia-Molina & Salem, Main memory database systems: An overview, 4(6) IEEE Transactions on Knowledge and Data Engineering 509–16 (1992).

[37] See Morin, Gallard, et al., Towards an Efficient Single System Image Cluster Operating System, 20(4) Future Generation Computer Systems 505–21 (2004).

[38] See generally Nutt, Operating Systems (Addison-Wesley 3d ed. 2004).

[39] Veenman, "Statistical Disk Cluster Classification for File Carving," in Third International IEEE Symposium on Information Assurance and Security (Aug. 29–31, 2007).

[40] Van Baar, Alink & Van Ballegooij, Forensic Memory Analysis: Files Mapped in Memory, 5 Digital Investigation S52-S57 (2008).

Now that these five clusters have a binary status of 0, the Windows file system knows that they are part of the unallocated storage space and available to be claimed for use by another active file and overwritten.[41] Nearly all operating systems use a process similar to the one described above.[42]

So long as none of the five unallocated clusters are claimed for use by another file, the MyFile.txt is recoverable in its original form. All that it required is that the file system reset the Status Bit back to 1 (Status Bit = 1) and change the binary 0 s back to 1 s. However, when some or all of the clusters from the previous active file are reallocated by the file system, the original data in those clusters becomes, at best, partially recoverable, but, more likely, not recoverable at all.[43] Although isolated cluster fragments of the deleted MyFile.txt file may not yet be overwritten, there is no easy way to identify where those cluster fragments may be located among the hundreds of millions of possible clusters on a hard drive.[44]

This overwriting of clusters in the unallocated space occurs frequently (thousands of clusters a second) on a computer as new active files are created either by the user or automatically by the computer software.[45] This overwriting occurs because whenever there is activity on the computer (i.e., turning on the computer, writing or deleting file, installing a system update,[46] running disk defragmentation,[47]

[41] See generally Nutt, Operating Systems (Addison-Wesley 3d ed. 2004).

[42] See generally Nutt, Operating Systems (Addison-Wesley 3d ed. 2004).

[43] Garfinkel & Shelat, Remembrance of Data Passed: A Study of Disk Sanitization Practices, 1(1) IEEE Security & Privacy 17–27 (2003); Starek, Friedman, et al., Method and Apparatus for Real-Time Secure File Deletion, U.S. Patent No. 6,314,437 (issued Nov. 6, 2001).

[44] Karresand & Shahmehri, "Oscar—File Type Identification of Binary Data in Disk Clusters and RAM Pages," in International Federation for Information Processing, Volume 201, Security and Privacy in Dynamic Environments (Fischer-Hubner, Rannenberg, et al., eds. Springer 2006).

[45] See Fuji Photo Film Co., Ltd. and Fuji Photo Film U.S.A., Inc. v. Lexar Media, Inc., Defendant., 2007 WL 6372605 (N.D. Cal. 2007); In re Correra, 589 B.R. 76, 101–02 (Bankr. N.D. Tex. 2018); Kerr, Searches and Seizures in a Digital World, 119 Harv. L. Rev. 531 (2005).

[46] See Leach, Vanacour & Bishop, What Every Lawyer Needs to Know About Computer Forensic Evidence (Snell & Wilmer LLP 2010), available at https://www.swlaw.com/assets/pdf/publications/2010/02/19/PAPER_WhatEveryAttorneyNeedsToKnowAboutForensicEvidence.pdf (last visited June 9, 2021).

[47] See RKI, Inc. v. Grimes, 177 F. Supp. 2d 859, 877 (N.D. Ill. 2001) (at bench trial, "defendants' spoliation of evidence on their computer support[ed] a negative inference that defendants destroyed evidence of misappropriation" of trade secrets; "highly suspicious" deletions and defragmentation constituted "circumstantial evidence" of misappropriation); Gentex Corp. v. Sutter, 827 F. Supp. 2d 384, 389 (M.D. Pa. 2011); Leach, Vanacour & Bishop, What Every Lawyer Needs to Know About Computer Forensic Evidence (Snell & Wilmer LLP 2010), available at https://d33scoy2rrx0xd.cloudfront.net/assets/pdf/publications/2010/02/19/What%20every%20lawyer%20needs%20to%20know%20about%20computer%20forensic%20evidence%20by%20Sid%20Leach.pdf; Arent, Brownstone & Fenwick, Ediscovery: Preserving, Requesting & Producing Electronic Information, 19 Santa Clara Computer & High Tech. L.J. 131, 180 (2002) (citing *RKI, Inc. v. Grimes*).

or running antivirus software[48]), the file system uses an array of algorithms optimized for performance to reclaim space previously allocated.[49]

Developers of operating and file systems never intended the unallocated space to serve as file storage for active files.[50] The operating and file systems use unallocated space for the purpose of providing computers with additional space.[51] When a computer runs out of available storage clusters in the unallocated space, it stops operating.[52] During a computer's life span, a single storage cluster can be assigned to thousands of different files, as the cluster is released from one active file and assigned to another by the file system.[53]

Even without user intervention, computer systems regularly install software, run performance optimization applications, create automatic backups, and install Windows service packs, all resulting in the need to create and delete files.[54] For example, both Windows 7 and Windows Vista automatically schedule disk defragmentation actions to occur at least once a week, generally at night, in order to improve performance.[55] This automatic defragmentation, like nearly every other

---

[48] Rossein, Employment Discrimination Law and Litigation §14:48 (explaining that, in Mintel Intern. Group, Ltd. v. Neergheen, 30 I.E.R. Cas. (BNA) 396, 2010 WL 145786, *8 (N.D. Ill. 2010), the court relied on expert testimony in finding that any programs on defendant's laptop that would have destroyed metadata, such as antivirus software, were not user initiated).

[49] Zhe, Jun & Xiling, "Design and Realization of Efficient Memory Management for Embedded Real-Time Application," in Proceedings of the Sixth International Conference on ITS Telecommunications Proceedings (June 2006).

[50] See U.S. v. Pruitt, 638 F.3d 763, 765 n.2 (11th Cir. 2011) (noting that unallocated space "contains deleted data, usually emptied from the operating system's trash or recycle bin folder, that cannot be seen or accessed by the user without the use of forensic software"); Genger v. TR Investors, LLC, 26 A.3d 180 (Del. 2011) (discussing unallocated space).

[51] State v. Ritchie, 349 Or. 572, 577, 248 P.3d 405, 407 (2011) (explaining that "when a file is deleted, the data in the file remains in the physical location that originally was allocated, but the master file table is altered to indicate that that location now is 'unallocated,' i.e., available to be overwritten by new files").

[52] See Free up drive space in Windows 10, Microsoft, https://support.microsoft.com/en-us/windows/free-up-drive-space-in-windows-10-85529ccb-c365-490d-b548-831022bc9b32 (last visited June 9, 2021).

[53] See U.S. v. Triumph Capital Group, Inc., 211 F.R.D. 31, 46 n.6 (D. Conn. 2002) (explaining that "'[u]nallocated' or 'free space' is comprised of clusters that are available for storage of active files" and that "[f]ree space may contain remnants of, or entire files that were previously deleted").

[54] Arthur & Venter, An Investigation Into Computer Forensic Tools (Information and Computer Security Architectures (ICSA) Research Group, Department of Computer Science, Univ. of Pretoria 2004), available at http://icsa.cs.up.ac.za/issa/2004/Proceedings/Full/060.pdf (last visited May 10, 2021); Beckett & Slay, "Digital Forensics: Validation and Verification in a Dynamic Work Environment," in Proceedings of 40th Annual IEEE Hawaii International Conference on System Sciences 266a (IEEE Computer Society 2007); Hayes & Qureshi, "Microsoft Vista: Serious Challenges for Digital Investigations," in Proceedings of Student-Faculty Research Day, CSIS, Pace University A3 (2008).

[55] Ways to improve your computer's performance, Microsoft, https://support.microsoft.com/en-us/windows/ways-to-improve-your-computer-s-performance-c6018c78-0edd-a71a-7040-02267d68ea90 (last visited June 9, 2021).

activity that takes place when the computer is operating, overwrites unallocated space and makes data previously in those clusters effectively "unrecoverable."[56] In addition to these automatic functions, user actions also continuously overwrite unallocated space.[57] When users turn on their computer or open, create, and edit their documents during the course of the day, they typically overwrite thousands or hundreds of thousands of clusters in unallocated space.[58]

The likelihood of recovering deleted files from unallocated space is a function of time and use.[59] The longer a file is deleted, the more likely all its clusters have been reassigned to other active files, making the recovery of the deleted file impossible.[60] For example, if a key document had been deleted from the allocated space (reserved for active files) weeks or months earlier,[61] it could have been routinely overwritten by the many files created during the encryption process or by the general operation and daily use of the computers.[62] Consequently, the mere absence of a document is insufficient evidence that the "wiping" of the unallocated space removed it.[63]

Further, the wiping of unallocated space can happen in multiple circumstances, including the encryption of a hard drive. Encryption is defined as obscuring information with a key, called a cipher, such that it is only readable by someone who knows the cipher.[64] In the digital world, encryption operates by adding coding to

---

[56] Hayes & Qureshi, "A Framework for Computer Forensics Investigations Involving Microsoft Vista," in IEEE Long Island Systems, Applications and Technology Conference (May 2, 2008).

[57] Therefore, files in the smaller, unallocated space on the computer's hard drive reserved for emails, such as deleted email messages, get overwritten much faster as a result of normal usage. See TR Investors, LLC v. Genger, 2009 WL 4696062, *6 (Del. Ch. 2009), aff'd, 26 A.3d 180 (Del. 2011).

[58] See, e.g., United States v. Glenn, 935 F.3d 313, 318 (5th Cir. 2019) (program updates may destroy unallocated space data); Antioch Co. v. Scrapbook Borders, Inc., 210 F.R.D. 645, 651–52, 54 Fed. R. Serv. 3d 427 (D. Minn. 2002) (discussing that normal use of a computer may destroy data). Thus, while a computer is on, fragments are automatically deleted and overwritten each second.

[59] See Garrie & Spernow, Legally Correct But Technologically Off the Mark, 9 Nw. J. Tech. & Intell. Prop. 1, 20 (2010); *see generally,* e.g., U.S. v. Dobbs, 629 F.3d 1199, 1212 n.2 (10th Cir. 2011) (citing ROA Vol. 3 at 369) (expert was able to identify the existence of "a number of files that were overwritten that were picture files" but was unable to completely recover those files); State v. Cooley, 165 So. 3d 1237, 1248 (La. Ct. App. 3d Cir. 2015) (files in unallocated space can be recovered with "carving software"); Com. v. Rollins, 470 Mass. 66, 68–69, 18 N.E.3d 670 (2014).

[60] See People v. Kent, 79 A.D.3d 52, 910 N.Y.S.2d 78 (2d Dep't 2010), aff'd as modified, 19 N.Y.3d 290, 947 N.Y.S.2d 798, 970 N.E.2d 833 (2012).

[61] See Tener v. Cremer, 89 A.D.3d 75, 77, 931 N.Y.S.2d 552, 553–54 (1st Dep't 2011).

[62] See U.S. v. Otero, 563 F.3d 1127, 1131 (10th Cir. 2009); Philips Electronics North America Corp. v. BC Technical, 773 F. Supp. 2d 1149, 1169 (D. Utah 2011) (loading of large video files onto computer made previously deleted files unrecoverable from unallocated space).

[63] See Garrie & Spernow, Legally Correct But Technologically Off the Mark, 9 Nw. J. Tech. & Intell. Prop. 1, 7 (2010).

[64] See Spitalnick, Understanding Encryption and its Role in Security, 5 CPA Prac. Mgmt. F. 5 (2009) (stating that "[e]ncryption is the act of adding a cipher or string of characters to raw data.").

files in allocated space and deleting the remaining clusters of files from unallocated space.[65] This occurs in the same step as the additional coding to encrypted files, which use clusters from unallocated space, thus overwriting clusters in unallocated space.[66]

For an unencrypted storage device, the clusters in unallocated space are exponentially more costly and complex to preserve, review, and segregate.[67] While active files can be easily preserved, reviewed, and segregated by the custodian,[68] this is not the case for files residing in unallocated space.[69] Data in unallocated space is analogous to random, unbundled, and unorganized piles of confetti or shredded paper, while allocated space is analogous to pristine documents filed in labeled filing cabinets.[70] Reassembling raw clusters, if even possible, requires intensive use of forensic software followed by manual review and assembly, all at an extremely high cost.[71]

## 6.2 The Investigative Process of Forensic Examiners

### *Seven Phases of Forensic Examination*

A digital forensic investigation usually consists of seven phases: (1) evidence identification, (2) evidence acquisition, (3) evidence preprocessing, (4) evidence analysis, (5) report generation, (6) evidence preservation, and (7) testimony. These seven phases are discussed further below.[72]

---

[65] See generally Garrie & Spernow, "Legally Sound but Technologically Wrong" (Part 2 of 2), Daily Journal, April 30, 2010, at 6; Casey & Stellatos, The Impact of Full Disk Encryption on Digital Forensics, 42(3) ACM SIGOPS Operating Systems Review 93 (2008).

[66] See Garrie & Spernow, "Legally Sound but Technologically Wrong" (Part 2 of 2), Daily Journal, April 30, 2010, at 6.

[67] See Garrie & Spernow, "Legally Sound but Technologically Wrong" (Part 2 of 2), Daily Journal, April 30, 2010, at 6. Analysis is not limited to commercial or open-source tools as examiners frequently write their own software programs or scripts to conduct investigations. Individual investigators will often create their own checklists and protocols over time to ensure each investigation is equally thorough and properly documented.

[68] See Satpathy, Pradhan, & Ray, A Digital Investigation Tool based on Data Fusion in Management of Cyber Security Systems, 2(2) Int'l J. of Information Tech. 561–65 (2010); Bagley, Ferguson, & Leimich, "On the Digital Forensic Analysis of the Firefox Browser via Recovery of SQLite Artifacts from Unallocated Space," in Proceedings of the 6th International Conference on Cybercrime Forensics Education & Training (Canterbury Christ Church University, 2012).

[69] See Billard & Hauri, "Making Sense of Unstructured Flash-Memory Dumps," in Proceedings of the ACM Symposium on Applied Computing 1579–83 (2010).

[70] See Tecklenburg v. Appellate Division, 169 Cal. App. 4th 1402, 1407, 87 Cal. Rptr. 3d 460, 464 (3d Dist. 2009).

[71] Garrie & Spernow, Legally Correct But Technologically Off the Mark, 9 Nw. J. Tech. & Intell. Prop. 1, 8 (2010).

[72] Other models exist, for example, the Department of Justice has published a process model in the Electronic Crime Scene Investigation Guide that is based on a physical crime scene methodology;

For most phases of the investigation process, there is an analogous forensic software or hardware. Some forensic hardware and software are capable of servicing the entire investigation process, while others are focused on a narrow task within the process.[73] There are many forensic tools on the market that image computer devices and mobile devices and perform a variety of forensic analysis functions.[74] Where appropriate, the following sections will also include a discussion of the relevant tools available.

## *Seven Phases of Forensic Examination: Phase 1: Evidence Identification*

The first step in any digital investigation is identifying the type of evidence that may be available for analysis and its physical location.[75] In criminal cases, this may be limited to the evidence to which the person of interest had physical or logical access.[76] While this task may appear simplistic on its face, it increases in complexity when the person of interest uses an unexpected storage media, for example, if he uses a neighbor's unsecured wireless access router to access child pornography sites and then uses the neighbor's hard drive as a storage device for the images obtained.[77]

---

this includes preparation, collection, examination, analysis, and reporting. For a detailed discussion of methodologies, see generally Carrier and Spafford, Getting Physical with the Digital Investigation Process, 2(2) International Journal of Digital Evidence (Fall 2003).

[73] One of the early tools in the forensic investigation arsenal was EnCase, software produced by Guidance Software. One of the key functions of EnCase is the ability to run a command called "recover folders" that allows the recovery of lost files and subfolders within a folder. An integrated search function allows the examiner to run text searches on a drive. Since the original introduction of EnCase software, five additional versions of the software were released to capture more nuanced areas of the forensic market, such as enterprise level software, portable software, and data mapping. For specific information on EnCase software, see https://www.opentext.com/products/security-cloud

[74] The more common software providers include AccessData, Guidance Software, Paraben Forensic Tools, X-Ways Forensics, ADF Solutions, Cellebrite, Cyber Security Technologies, NIKSUN, RSA, Technology Pathways, OSForensics, FTK, and WetStone Technologies. Each of these companies produces a number of products for the various phases of the investigative process. This is only a partial list of mainstream software programs. Any software referenced in this chapter or in this book is not to be considered as an endorsement of the software or recommendation that said software is better or worse than any other software in the marketplace. Anti-forensic software tools which *act* to prevent data recovery are also widely available. See generally Southern New England Telephone Co. v. Global NAPs Inc., 624 F.3d 123, 143 (2d Cir. 2010).

[75] See, e.g., American Family Mut. Ins. Co. v. Gustafson, 2009 WL 641297, *2 (D. Colo. 2009) (requiring parties to establish terms of search along with forensic experts); Siemens Industry, Inc. v. Nagel, 2017 WL 4099788, *2 (W.D. Pa. 2017) (parties agreed to a stipulated protocol for a forensic examination).

[76] See Moenssens, Inbau, & Starrs, Scientific Evidence in Criminal Cases (Foundation Press 1973); O'Hara, & O'Hara, Fundamentals of Criminal Investigation (Charles C. Thomas Pub. Ltd. 1956).

[77] Schiesel, "Growth of Wireless Internet Opens New Path for Thieves," N.Y. Times, Mar. 19, 2005; The Associated Press, "NY men accused of downloading child porn after others use their Wi-Fi"

In complex civil cases, identifying what evidence might be relevant can be even more problematic as technological infrastructures encompassing hundreds of servers, desktops, laptops, cell phones, and tablet computers may be involved.[78] Each device may store only portions of the data deemed relevant and may be intermingled with privileged data.[79]

## *Seven Phases of Forensic Examination: Phase 2: Evidence Acquisition*

Criminal investigators have long recognized the importance of evidence hidden just below the surface, and digital evidence is no exception.[80] In the same way a crime scene investigator looks for fingerprints and tire tracks, digital crime scene investigators seek to collect pertinent evidence in the form of metadata and access logs, among others.[81] Since it is often unknown what is important at the time of collection, an image must be taken of all the evidence for later review.[82]

The method for acquiring digital evidence generally follows one of two methods.[83] The first method is to create a duplicate image of the device. The process of obtaining this image is called *imaging*.[84] Typically, it is the image that is used for further investigation, not the original device, as the image is an exact duplicate of the original storage device.

---

(posted Apr. 24, 2011, updated Mar. 22, 2019), https://www.syracuse.com/news/2011/04/ny_men_accused_of_downloading.html (last visited June 9, 2021). Just as pirated wireless incriminates the wrong individual, obtaining the evidence from the right individual is key to a proper conviction. Murphy, New Forensics: Criminal Justice, False Certainty, and the Second Generation of Scientific Evidence, 95 Cal. L. Rev. 721 (2007).

[78] See U.S. Bank Nat. Ass'n v. Parker, 2010 WL 559135, *1 (E.D. Mo. 2010).

[79] See Stengart v. Loving Care Agency, Inc., 201 N.J. 300, 308, 990 A.2d 650, 655 (2010); Supreme Court Rules of Evidence Committee, Final Report to the Supreme Court of Rhode Island (March 4, 2019), available at https://www.courts.ri.gov/Courts/SupremeCourt/SupremeMiscOrders/Order_Proposed_Amendments_to_RI_Rules4-15-19.pdf (report to Rhode Island Supreme Court Evidence Committee, in considering proposed amendments to rules of evidence, references the burdensome "massive document reviews" which take place in complex litigation in order to identify privileged material in digital discovery).

[80] There are two primary ways of collecting the evidence, but remote computing can effectuate either of those ends. Adelstein, Stillerman, & Joyce, Remote Collection of Computer Forensic Evidence, U.S. Patent No. 7,496,959 (issued Feb. 24, 2009).

[81] Carrier, Open Source Digital Forensics Tools: The Legal Argument, At Stake Research Report (Oct 2002), available at: http://dl.packetstormsecurity.net/papers/IDS/atstake_opensource_forensics.pdf (last visited May 1, 2021).

[82] See §6:6 on a review of imaging and how forensic tools take an image of a computer.

[83] Sedona Principles: Best Practices Recommendations and Principles for Addressing Electronic Document Production; *see generally* 5 Sedona Conf. J. 151, 162 (2004). See also Appendix A.

[84] See Oce North America, Inc. v. MCS Services, Inc., 2011 WL 197976, *1 (D. Md. 2011); United States v. Kim, 103 F. Supp. 3d 32, 40 (D.D.C. 2015) (imaging creates a "duplicate copy").

The image is created to preserve the present state of the device without changing the state of the device.[85] Forensic software creates a "static" bit-by-bit, sector-by-sector image of all the data on a storage device.[86] This method allows for a detailed analysis of the evidence acquired without changing the data located on the original device.[87] It is important to maintain the integrity of the information on the device, as any change in the information can have implications on the final evidence presented at trial (or for settlement negotiations).[88] For example, word processing software has the ability to update the metadata "[DATE]" fields in a document each time the document is opened. This function is useful when working on a report where continually updating the date field is necessary, but its existence means that if this document is opened during an investigation, the date on the face of the document will update automatically to the present time.

The imaging process can also create a hash digest that can later be used to validate the integrity of the forensic image.[89] This hash digest essentially creates a DNA type of identifier for files that is then compared to the original device to show that nothing was changed during the forensic investigation.

The second method for acquiring digital images is to create a file level copy using forensic software or hardware. This method is generally used when evidence needs to be acquired from a "live" system.[90] A "file level" copy can include most,

---

[85] See Covad Communications Co. v. Revonet, Inc., 258 F.R.D. 5, 9 (D.D.C. 2009) (ordering defendant to allow plaintiff's expert to make forensic images of defendant's drives and computers "to preserve information as it currently exists").

[86] The process of imaging a hard drive typically involves physically removing the hard drive from the device in question and attaching the hard drive to an imaging machine. This ensures that data and metadata on the hard drive are not altered, which would otherwise occur if the machine were turned on to access the data on the device. Where the parties have agreed not to produce metadata, or in a court where local rules prohibit metadata without a showing of good cause, parties may be hard-pressed to convince a judge that sloppy investigation technique is good cause for further investigation. See generally Aliki Foods, LLC v. Otter Valley Foods, Inc., 726 F. Supp. 2d 159, 178–80 (D. Conn. 2010); Covad Communications Co. v. Revonet, Inc., 258 F.R.D. 5, 9 (D.D.C. 2009).

[87] See Blitzer, Stein-Ferguson, & Huang, Understanding Forensic Digital Imaging (Academic Press 2008); Berg, Legal Ramifications of Digital Imaging in Law Enforcement, 2(4) Forensic Science Communications 1–19 (2000).

[88] Carrier & Grand, A Hardware-Based Memory Acquisition Procedure for Digital Investigations, 1(1) Digital Investigation 50–60 (2004); Conway, Preservation in the Digital World (Commission on Preservation and Access 1996); Kenneally & Brown, Risk Sensitive Digital Evidence Collection, 2(2) Digital Investigation 101–19 (2005).

[89] A hash digest, or hash value, is a mathematical formula applied to a file to create an individual alpha-numerical identifier. There are many types of algorithms available, with most people [?] generally recognizing MD5 hash values to be the most common. The MD5 hash algorithm is commonly used to validate the integrity of data. The algorithm is applied against source data to generate a unique 128-bit hash value. The algorithm is then used when data is shipped or taken out of storage after a period of time to generate a new 128-bit value. The two values are compared and if they match, then the match indicates that the data is intact and was not altered.

[90] For example, a file level copy would be created if the computer systems of interest cannot be powered off due to its "mission critical" status. Carrier, Risks of Live Digital Forensic Analysis, 49(2) Communications of the ACM 56–61 (2006); Carrier, Open Source Digital Forensics Tools: The Legal Argument (@Stake Research Report, Oct. 2002).

but not all, of the available data.[91] One should be advised that operating systems and databases are fluid by their nature, making it very difficult to create a file level copy.[92]

## *Seven Phases of Forensic Examination: Phase 3: Evidence Preprocessing*

Evidence preprocessing allows the forensic investigator to organize and categorize data prior to running an analysis of the evidence.[93] This decreases the overall time necessary to process evidence and provides a structured framework for the analysis phase.

A duplicate forensic image often contains two types of evidence: evidence in active files and evidence in deleted/free space, the allocated and unallocated space, respectively.[94] Forensic software catalogs these two types of potential evidence and makes them accessible for analysis.[95] Cataloging, usually called *indexing*, creates a searchable index of the files, so that the end user can quickly sort and search files across the storage device. The actual methods underlying indexing differ based on the software and the software options available to the forensic analyst. Unlike a duplicate forensic image, a "file level" forensic image is taken while a computer is actively running and, as such, only looks at the active files.[96]

---

[91] Casey & Stanely, Tool Review—Remote Forensic Preservation and Examination Tools, 1 Digital Investigation 284 (2004).

[92] The National Criminal Justice Reference Service (https://www.ncjrs.gov) releases regular reports on various hardware and software applications for digital evidence acquisition.

[93] Carrier & Spafford, Automated Digital Evidence Target Definition Using Outlier Analysis and Existing Evidence, in Proceedings of the Digital Forensic Research Workshop (2005).

[94] Kent, Chevalier, et al., Guide to Integrating Forensic Techniques into Incident Response, NIST Special Publication 800–86 (U.S. Department of Commerce, Aug. 2006); Beebe & Clark, Dealing with Terabyte Data Sets in Digital Investigations, in Advances in Digital Forensics 3–16 (IFIP International Conference on Digital Forensics, National Center for Forensic Science, Orlando, Fla., Feb.13–16, 2005).

[95] Carrier, Open Source Digital Forensics Tools: The Legal Argument (@Stake Research Report, Oct. 2002); Carrier, 3 File System Forensic Analysis (Addison-Wesley 2005). See also Hosmer & Gordon, Forensic Information Warfare Requirement Study (Wetstone Technologies, Cortland NY, 2002), stating:

The DOS and Windows 'delete' function does not completely erase file names or file content. Many computer users are unaware the storage space associated with such files merely becomes unallocated and available to be overwritten with new files. Pointers to the data are all that is changed, the data is not actually erased from the drive. Unallocated space is a source of significant 'security leakage' and it potentially contains erased files and file slack associated with the erased files. Often the DOS Undelete program can be used to restore the previously erased files. Like the Windows swap file and file slack, this source of ambient data can help provide relevant key words and leads that may have previously been unknown to the computer investigator.

[96] Carrier, Defining Digital Forensic Examination and Analysis Tools Using Abstraction Layers, International Journal of Digital Evidence (Winter 2003).

Preprocessing valid files includes identifying archives of data and decompressing and/or extracting the individual items so they can be analyzed.[97] Determining if a file is encrypted is also included at this level. Preprocessing deleted files is somewhat more complex.[98] Forensic software preprocessing on deleted files must be capable of recognizing that a hard drive may have been reformatted or that files on the hard drive may have been deleted and partially overwritten.[99] In either of these scenarios, the automated functions of the forensic software attempts to recover these files, where possible, and make the recovered content available for review by a forensic examiner.

Forensic software that is processing evidence should also be able to identify the metadata associated with each file where available.[100] Two types of metadata exist for each file: (i) time stamps maintained by the operating system[101] and (ii) time stamps and administrative details maintained by the software application that produced the file's content.[102]

---

[97] Typical archives are ZIP files and Outlook PST/OST files that contain email messages and attachments. Cohen, Advanced Carving Techniques, 4(3) Digital Investigation 119–28 (2007); Kessler, "Anti-Forensics and the Digital Investigator," in Proceedings of the 5th Australian Digital Forensics Conference, Edith Cowan University, Perth Western Australia (Dec. 3, 2007); Ayers, A Second Generation Computer Forensic Analysis System, 6 Digital Investigation S34-S42 (2009).

[98] Decherchi, Tacconi, et al., Text Clustering for Digital Forensics Analysis, 63 Computational Intelligence in Security for Information Systems 29–36 (2009); Lee, "Proposal for Efficient Searching and Presentation in Digital Forensics," in proceedings of Third International IEEE Conference on Availability, Reliability and Security 1377–81 (Mar. 4–7, 2008).

[99] Mohay, Computer and Intrusion Forensics (Artech House Publishers 2003); Pal & Memon, The Evolution of File Carving, 26(2) IEEE Signal Processing Magazine 59–71 (2009).

[100] Eoghan, Chap. 7, Handling a Digital Crime Scene, in Digital Evidence and Computer Crime: Forensic Science, Computers, and the Internet 526 (2011). See also Buchholz & Spafford, On the Role of File System Metadata in Digital Forensics, 1 J. of Digital Investigation 4 (Dec. 2004), stating:

In respect to metadata, some of the work [in digital forensics] also discusses the forensic value and/or quality of the information that is found. By forensic value we mean the possibility to draw conclusions about events on the system from the data. For example, time stamps have a high value from an event reconstruction perspective because they allow an ordering of file operations into a timeline. This is provided that the time stamps have not been tampered with and that the system's clock is correct. Access control information on its own, however, holds less value from an event reconstruction point of view, because it generally only reflects static system policies, but does not provide information about individual events. The information that can be derived from access control information is a (group of) user(s) that may have had access to an object on the system. At this point further evidence (e.g. in the form of time stamps or login data) is needed to draw any conclusions. Under quality we understand how believable the information is. Is it easy to tamper with the information on the system? For example, on some operating systems a file's access and modification time stamps can be arbitrarily set by its owner.

[101] These include the following fields of information: Created, Modified, Accessed, Record Update and Date of Deletion. See generally Buchholz & Spafford, On the Role of File System Metadata in Digital Forensics, 1(4) Digital Investigation 298–309 (2004).

[102] These include the following fields of information: Internal Create Date, Last Modified, Last Accessed, Author, Last Printed, Last Saved, Total Editing Time, etc. See generally Buchholz &

Operating system metadata differs based on the underlying file system. A FAT system records the type, size, location, and time stamps of files.[103] FAT is limited in what information is recorded, but with the introduction of NTFS,[104] more data components could be recorded such as individual user information and permissions.[105]

## *Seven Phases of Forensic Examination: Phase 4: Evidence Analysis*

In the evidence analysis phase, forensic examiners develop and test hypotheses about the acquired digital evidence.[106] The forensic examiner analyzes the images and attempts to identify the key elements under investigation that will satisfy the court in a civil or criminal case.[107] This includes examining the contents of files and, if necessary, recovering deleted data.[108] The evidence can then be divided into two groups: evidence that supports an analyst's theory and evidence that contradicts that theory. This is also the phase of the investigation where a determination is made as to whether there is any evidence of tampering or mass deletion of the evidence images.

---

Spafford, On the Role of File System Metadata in Digital Forensics, 1(4) Digital Investigation 298–309 (2004).

[103] FAT was formerly used by many operating systems on personal computers but now is relegated largely to removable media such as security keys, USB flash drives, and portable devices such as phones and cameras. Buchholz & Spafford, On the Role of File System Metadata in Digital Forensics, 1(4) Digital Investigation 298–309 (2004). See also Glisson, "Use of Computer Forensics in the Digital Curation of Removable Media," in Proceedings of Digital Curation: Practice, Promise and Prospects, School of Information and Library Science, Univ. of N. Carolina at Chapel Hill, NC 110–11 (Apr. 1–3, 2009).

[104] New Technology File System (NTFS) is the primary file system for the Windows operating system. It was introduced in 1993 as the successor to the FAT file system. See Pal & Memon, The Evolution of File Carving, 26(2) IEEE Signal Processing Magazine 59–71 (2009).

[105] See Glisson, "Use of Computer Forensics in the Digital Curation of Removable Media," in Proceedings of Digital Curation: Practice, Promise and Prospects, School of Information and Library Science, Univ. of N. Carolina at Chapel Hill, NC 110–11 (Apr. 1–3, 2009).

[106] See The Sedona Conference, Cooperation Guidance for Litigators & In-House Counsel (Sedona Conference Working Group Series, Mar. 2011), available at https://thesedonaconference.org/publication/Cooperation_Guidance_for_Litigators_and_In-House_Counsel (last visited June 9, 2021).

[107] Baryamureeba & Tushabe "The Enhanced Digital Investigation Process Model," in Proceedings of the 4th Annual Digital Forensic Research Workshop, Baltimore, MD (Apr. 2004); Reith, Carr, & Gunsch, An Examination of Digital Forensic Models, 1(3) International Journal of Digital Evidence 1–12 (2002).

[108] Carrier, Open Source Digital Forensics Tools: The Legal Argument (@Stake Research Report, Oct. 2002).

Forensic software used for analysis of evidence provides a forensic examiner with a framework whereby a forensic examiner can analyze the evidence.[109] This forensic software allows a forensic examiner to analyze evidence through the execution of keyword searches, timeline analysis, patterns of web usage, and content review,[110] to mention the most common criteria.[111] Additionally, this software allows a forensic examiner to access and review operational data not normally accessible to the user.

## *Seven Phases of Forensic Examination: Phase 5: Report Generation*

Following the review of evidence, a report is generated by the forensic examiner, detailing the protocols and processes that were followed, as well as the outcomes of the tests run against the hypothesis of the examiner.

Forensic software can generate reports detailing the forensic examiner's findings and observations. These forensic reports must provide enough data to allow a forensic examiner to recreate the exact environment upon which the original forensic examiner relied to draft their report.[112] The ability to replicate exactly the findings

[109] Garfinkel, Farrell, et al., Bringing Science to Digital Forensics with Standardized Forensic Corpora, 6 Digital Investigation S2-S11 (Sept. 2009); Noblett, Pollitt & Presley, Recovering And Examining Computer Forensic Evidence, 2(4) Forensic Science Communications 102–109 (2000).

[110] U.S. v. Flyer, 633 F.3d 911, 918 (9th Cir. 2011); U.S. v. Comprehensive Drug Testing, Inc., 621 F.3d 1162, 1176 (9th Cir. 2010); Wheeler v. State, 135 A.3d 282, 290 (Del. 2016); New Hampshire Ball Bearings, Inc. v. Jackson, 158 N.H. 421, 424–25, 969 A.2d 351, 356 (2009).

[111] Spafford & Weeber, Software Forensics: Can We Track Code To Its Authors?, 12(6) Computers & Security 585–95 (Oct.1993). Pearson, "Forensic Software Traces Tweaks to Images," 439(7076) Nature 520–21 (Feb. 2, 2006); Richard III, & Roussev, Next-Generation Digital Forensics, 49(2) Communications of the ACM 76–80 (2006).

[112] See United States v. Ganias, 824 F.3d 199, 215 n.35 (2d Cir. 2016); McCullock v. H.B. Fuller Co., 61 F.3d 1038, 1043–44, 42 Fed. R. Evid. Serv. 1047 (2d Cir. 1995); Jahn v. Equine Services, PSC, 233 F.3d 382, 393, 55 Fed. R. Evid. Serv. 1490, 2000 FED App. 0398P (6th Cir. 2000) (expert methodology can be reliable even where matter might be in debate because of other testimony); Smith v. Ford Motor Co., 215 F.3d 713, 720–21, 54 Fed. R. Evid. Serv. 79 (7th Cir. 2000) (district court abused discretion in relying on single, potentially irrelevant criterion in finding expert conclusions were based on unreliable methodologies, did not consider other factors, and failed to explain connection between factor selected by court and reliability under the circumstances); U.S. v. Martinez, 3 F.3d 1191, 1197–98, 37 Fed. R. Evid. Serv. 863 (8th Cir. 1993) (rejected by, Taylor v. State, 1995 OK CR 10, 889 P.2d 319 (Okla. Crim. App. 1995)); Spearman Industries, Inc. v. St. Paul Fire and Marine Ins. Co., 128 F. Supp. 2d 1148, 1150 (N.D. Ill. 2001) (court's function focuses on methodology, leaving the correctness of expert's conclusion or soundness of facts on which conclusion is based to fact finder). In addition, the report should include the forensic tools a forensic examiner used to illustrate and illuminate the environment in which the conclusions were drawn.

of a forensic examiner is essential to establishing the validity of the conclusions drawn in the initial investigation.[113]

## *Seven Phases of Forensic Examination: Phase 6: Evidence Preservation*

The goal of evidence preservation is to maintain defensible chain-of-custody documentation for all duplicate forensic images, case files, and reports. Flaws in the underlying digital evidence can prove fatal when presented as exhibits in court.[114]

Most forensic software applications and hardware devices are designed to facilitate maintaining the chain of custody. This is often accomplished by allowing examiners to track their analysis of the original or best evidence.[115]

## *Seven Phases of Forensic Examination: Phase 7: Testimony and Presentation*

In a litigation setting, counsel must review the report of the forensic examiner and evaluate the evidence before it is submitted. The *Daubert* test must be satisfied in order for scientific evidence to be admissible in court.[116] Due to the *Daubert* standards and the nature of digital evidence, forensic examiners seldom testify about their findings.[117] Digital evidence is either there or not there. Gray areas rarely exist.

---

[113] See generally Daubert v. Merrell Dow Pharmaceuticals, Inc., 509 U.S. 579, 113 S. Ct. 2786, 125 L. Ed. 2d 469, 37 Fed. R. Evid. Serv. 1 (1993).

[114] Casey, Digital Evidence and Computer Crime 211 (2d. 2004).

[115] American LegalNet, Inc. v. Davis, 673 F. Supp. 2d 1063, 1072 (C.D. Cal. 2009).

[116] Daubert v. Merrell Dow Pharmaceuticals, Inc., 509 U.S. 579, 113 S. Ct. 2786, 125 L. Ed. 2d 469, 37 Fed. R. Evid. Serv. 1 (1993).

[117] The courts have not dismissed using a *Daubert*-like framework for assessing the merits of a forensic report and the underlying forensic examiner expert testimony. In a case involving a spoliation of evidence claim supported by testimony based on the examination of a hard drive with large blocks of zeros surrounded by data, a court denied a motion to exclude the testimony on evidence that wiping programs exist that cannot be traced. The court found that the method used by the expert sufficiently filled the analytical gap between the data and the opinion. With a nod to the *Daubert* factors, the court noted that the expert had tested a hypothesis as to how the blocks of zeroes had appeared on the drive and had replicated the pattern of zeros. The court also approved evidence resulting from a load progression test that was found capable of repetition since the expert thoroughly documented each step in the test to establish that data had been written to the hard drive in the predicted manner. However, other courts have declined to use *Daubert* standard in determining whether to admit expert forensic testimony and the underlying forensic report. The state and federal courts with respect to admitting expert digital forensic testimony remain unsettled—no magic bullet exists. See generally Nucor Corp. v. Bell, 2008 WL 4442571, *4 (D.S.C. 2008).

If a case is made by the evidence, it is usually so overwhelming on its face that testimony is not required.

In non-litigation settings, such as an internal investigation, the presentation of evidence is determined by the individual case and the privacy laws and internal corporate rules that govern the situation.

### *Managing Digital Forensic Investigations*

For many reasons, including the ever-evolving nature of digital forensic investigations, counsel is ill-equipped to single-handedly implement a digital forensic investigation.[118] Forensic examiners use different forensic software, and it is important to understand that the genesis of these tools can have an impact on the conclusions drawn from the investigation. The information provided herein is designed to bridge the gap between the forensic expert and the attorney so that the forensic report can be utilized fully during the course of pretrial strategy and litigation.

## 6.3 How to Evaluate a Forensic Report

### *Introduction*

A forensic report, especially those involving digital evidence, must be reproducible by independent third parties. Facts discovered and opinions formed need to be documented and referenced to the source. Why? 1 s and 0 s do not lie. Therefore, the forensic reports that contain opinions that rest upon well-documented digital sources are much more likely to be able to withstand judicial scrutiny.[119]

---

[118] And, certainly, counsel does not want to be their own expert. See generally Harkabi v. SanDisk Corp., 275 F.R.D. 414, 419 (S.D. N.Y. 2010). See also Barrere, Betarte, & Rodriguez, "Towards Machine-Assisted Formal Procedures for the Collection of Digital Evidence," in Ninth Annual IEEE International Conference on Privacy, Security and Trust 32–35 (July 19–21, 2011); Biggs & Vidalis, "Cloud Computing: The Impact On Digital Forensic Investigations," in International Conference for Internet Technology and Secured Transactions 1–6 (Nov. 9–12, 2009); Mouhtaropoulos, Grobler & Li, "Digital Forensic Readiness: An Insight Into Governmental and Academic Initiatives," in 2011 IEEE European Conference on Intelligence and Security Informatics Conference 191–96 (Sept.12–14, 2011).

[119] Daubert v. Merrell Dow Pharmaceuticals, Inc., 509 U.S. 579, 595, 113 S. Ct. 2786, 2797, 125 L. Ed. 2d 469, 37 Fed. R. Evid. Serv. 1 (1993). *See* NutraSweet Co. v. X-L Engineering Co., 227 F.3d 776, 788–89, 55 Fed. R. Evid. Serv. 772, 47 Fed. R. Serv. 3d 584 (7th Cir. 2000) ("The district court did not abuse its discretion in concluding that the common and official acceptance of photographic analysis made it sufficiently reliable."); Clark v. Takata Corp., 192 F.3d 750, 758–59, 52 Fed. R. Evid. Serv. 1522 (7th Cir. 1999) (expert opinion properly excluded where based only on experience or training with no scientific data or supporting research material or other rigorous methodology).

The *Daubert v. Merrell Dow Pharmaceuticals, Inc.* decision describes a four-pronged test to determine whether scientifically derived evidence is admissible in federal court:

1. *Testing*: Has the scientific procedure been independently tested?
2. *Publication*: Has the scientific procedure been published and subject to peer review?
3. *Error rate*: Is there a known error rate, or potential to know the error rate, associated with the use of this scientific procedure?
4. *Acceptance*: Is the scientific procedure generally accepted by the relevant scientific community?

The *Daubert* inquiry test provides judges with an objective set of guidelines for accepting scientific evidence. The 1999 decision in *Kumho Tire v. Carmichael* extends the *Daubert* inquiry guidelines to any form of technical evidence.[120] Buttressing the case law is Rule 702 of the Federal Rules of Evidence, which provides guidelines for qualifying expert witnesses and minimizing adversarial bias in expert testimony. The purpose of these next sections is to provide the bench and the bar with a forensic analytical framework to apply when evaluating the weight and value of a forensic report.[121]

### *Examine the Mechanism Used to Collect the Digital Evidence Used in the Forensic Report*

The first factor focuses on the manner in which the evidence was acquired. The report should establish if the original evidence acquired was a duplicate bit-by-bit image of a hard drive or by live acquisition. As discussed earlier in the chapter, a bit-by-bit image of a hard drive is preferable to a live acquisition.

[120] Kumho Tire Co., Ltd. v. Carmichael, 526 U.S. 137, 158, 119 S. Ct. 1167, 1179, 143 L. Ed. 2d 238, 50 Fed. R. Evid. Serv. 1373 (1999).

[121] Many states have not codified or expressly adopted the *Daubert* standard for the admissibility of expert testimony. This includes California, Florida, Illinois, New York, New Jersey, and Pennsylvania. For example, in New Jersey, parties must satisfy three basic requirements for the admission of expert testimony: The testimony is beyond the ken of the average juror, the field testified to must be at a state of the art such that an expert's testimony could be sufficiently reliable, and the witness has sufficient expertise to offer the intended testimony. Practitioners are advised to be certain that the expert's reasoning satisfies the applicable standard, in order to avoid wasting money and effort compiling inadmissible evidence. State v. Kelly, 97 N.J. 178, 208, 478 A.2d 364, 379 (1984). For an individual review of state regulations, see Bernstein, The Unfinished Daubert Revolution (March 6, 2009). 10(1) Engage 35–38 (February 2009); George Mason Law & Economics Research Paper No. 09–18, available at http://ssrn.com/abstract=1354733

### *Ensure the Forensic Report Provides Sufficient Details of Sources so Process and Results May Be Replicated by a Third Party*

A digital forensic report should document with sufficient detail the steps undertaken by the examiner such that an independent third party could replicate the digital forensic conclusion. The forensic images should be available so that a third party could make a copy of the forensic image(s) and replicate the forensic examiner findings contained in the digital forensic report.

A report without the accompanying forensic images is a red flag. Where the conclusions are not reproducible by an independent third party with access to copies of the forensic images analyzed using similar analysis software, the court and counsel should grant little credence to forensic findings, absent exceptional circumstances.

### *Structure of Digital Forensic Report*

The report should not be tailored to support a particular outcome, as a material omission may constitute fraud. Examiners must resist overtures by attorneys, however well-intended or abstract, to submit any testimony or work product that is disrespectful of the truth, including overstating, understating, or omitting findings.

The findings should be concise and carefully circumscribed. The report should not volunteer an overabundance of information, which may be vulnerable to scrutiny under cross-examination. Further, all findings should be accurately qualified as to the limitations of the particular tool(s) used, the applicability of the current technology and industry standard best practices, the methodology or techniques (such as search criteria or formulae), and the scope of the investigation.

The scope of the investigation is not only limited by relevancy, but also by budget (i.e., time), which almost always places legitimate and significant constraints on what data is found or not found and the inferences to be drawn therefrom. Moreover, the digital forensic report only investigates those areas where responsive evidence can be found.

When evaluating a digital forensic report, counsel and the court should evaluate the substance of the report to ascertain if there is *information overload*. In this context, information overload rests on whether the digital forensic report contains hundreds of pictures, documents, or other such digital items in the body of the report that detract from the underlying conclusions contained in the report. The digital forensic report should provide a cohesive and logical framework on its face and should not delve into the underlying technical minutia.

### *Verify That the Forensic Report Establishes the Tools Used and Assumptions Made by the Forensic Examiner*

Many forensic examiners use a variety of forensic tools, and it is important that reviewers understand the genesis of these tools. The forensic tools a forensic examiner uses should be explicitly stated in the report to assist the reviewer in understanding the potential issues around the conclusions the forensic tool is being used to support.

## 6.4 Overview of Electronic Discovery

### *Introduction*

The basic principles that resolve legal disputes have changed little since Roman times. Parties in a dispute still come before a judge or panel to present evidence in support of their claims and defenses, and an adjudicator weighs the facts and makes a decision. All that has changed is the form of the evidence.

While evidence in Roman times was entirely tangible, including livestock and hard currency, evidence today is dominated by electronic data. These sources include electronic documents and multimedia such as email, text documents, spreadsheets, PDFs, audio recordings, Facebook postings, Twitter "tweets," and even YouTube videos. Whether or not one was born in the digital age, the facts critical to a case now require some level of comfort with digital data.

The process of information management, identification, preservation, collection, processing, review, analysis, production, and presentation of electronically stored information is called electronic discovery (hereinafter "eDiscovery").[122] Fueled by the interplay of law and technology and attracting some of the brightest minds of the

[122] See Sedona Best Practices Commentary on the Use of Search and Information Retrieval Methods in E-Discovery, noting that:

[A]s the ability to create and store massive volumes of electronic information mushrooms, the cost to store that information inversely plummets. In 1990, a typical gigabyte of storage cost about $20,000; today it costs less than $1 dollar. As a result, more individuals and companies are generating, receiving and storing more data, which means more information must be gathered, considered, reviewed and produced in litigation. But, with billable rates for junior associates at many law firms now starting at over $200 per hour, the cost to review just one gigabyte of data can easily exceed $30,000. These economic realities (i.e., the huge cost differential between the $1 to store a gigabyte of data and the $30,000 to review it) act as a driver in changing the traditional attitudes and approaches of lawyers, clients, courts and litigation support providers about how to search for relevant evidence during discovery and investigations. Escalating data volumes into the billions of ESI objects, review costs, and shrinking discovery timetables, all add up to equaling the need for profound change.

Available at https://www.wlrk.com/docs/TheSedonaConferenceBestPracticesCommentaryontheUseofSearchandInformationRetrievalMethodsinE-Discovery(2013).pdf

bench, bar, and business communities, eDiscovery is one of the most dynamic areas of law.[123] In practice, lawyers and executives must assess the merits and risks of a legal dispute or regulatory investigation using facts that are increasingly based in the digital domain.[124]

## *eDiscovery Process*

The eDiscovery process is complex, and the software solutions on the marketplace range from addressing a single stage of the eDiscovery process to supporting the entire process of eDiscovery. The diagram below encapsulates what is known as the Electronic Discovery Reference Model for eDiscovery.[125]

As the chart illustrates, the eDiscovery process breaks into the following stages[126]:

- *Information management*: Entities manage ESI according to an organization's information management policies.[127]
- *Identification*: Entities determine the scope of eDiscovery by identifying individuals and systems that will need to be collected.[128]
- *Preservation*: Entities ensure relevant systems preserve data tagged in the identification phase above.[129]
- *Collection*: Relevant parties perform the act of acquiring the ESI from systems.[130]

---

123 One indication of the amount of ongoing effort and investment generally to improve search and retrieval capabilities is evidenced by the research and development spending of Internet giants Google, Yahoo!, and eBay. According to published reports, Google spent $1.23 billion, Yahoo! spent $883 million, and eBay spent $495 million on core research and development activities in 2006. See Hertzberg, "I.T.'s Top 84 R&D Spenders" Baseline (Apr. 17, 2007), http://www.baselinemag.com/article2/0,1540,2114821,00.asp (last visited May 10, 2021).

124 Hickman v. Taylor, 329 U.S. 495, 507, 67 S. Ct. 385, 392, 91 L. Ed. 451 (1947) ("Mutual knowledge of all the relevant facts gathered by both parties is essential to proper litigation").

125 This model, additional resources, and a further discussion of each phase of eDiscovery are available at the EDRM website, http://www.edrm.net

126 Alexander, E-Discovery Practice, Theory, and Precedent: Finding the Right Pond, Lure, and Lines without going on a Fishing Expedition, 56 S.D. L. Rev. 25 (2011). See generally Race Tires America, Inc. v. Hoosier Racing Tire Corp., 674 F.3d 158, 161 (3d Cir. 2012).

127 Gelb & Gelb, What is "ESI" and Where Does It Reside?, Massachusetts E-Discovery & Evidence Preservation through Trial (Mass. CLE, Inc. 2011).

128 See generally Swofford v. Eslinger, 671 F. Supp. 2d 1274, 1281 (M.D. Fla. 2009); Kleen Products LLC v. Packaging Corp. of America, 2012 WL 4498465, *6 (N.D. Ill. 2012); Miller, From Conley to Twombly to Iqbal: A Double Play on the Federal Rules of Civil Procedure, 60 Duke L.J. 1 (2010); Gelb & Gelb, What is "ESI" and Where Does It Reside?, Massachusetts E-Discovery & Evidence Preservation through Trial (Mass. CLE, Inc. 2011).

129 See The Sedona Conference Database Principles Addressing the Preservation and Production of Databases & Database Information in Civil Litigation (Jacoby, ed., June 20, 2012).

130 See Rimkus Consulting Group, Inc. v. Cammarata, 688 F. Supp. 2d 598 (S.D. Tex. 2010); Garrie & Griver, Digital Issues in Mergers & Acquisitions, E-Discovery, & Information Technology Systems, 19 Widener L.J. 25 (2009); Kelleher, "Gathering and Producing Electronically Stored Information," in 1 Matthew Bender Practice Guide: California E-Discovery and Evidence, Ch. 9 (2012).

- *Processing*: Relevant parties cull the data to remove redundant and/or nonrelevant ESI and convert the ESI to fit the format for an effective review and, if necessary, for import into other eDiscovery software.[131]
- *Review*: Counsel reviews documents for privilege responsiveness, etc., usually with eDiscovery review software tools.[132]
- *Analysis*: Counsel analyze data further using keywords, custodians, legal issues, etc.[133]
- *Production*: Parties provide responsive data to opposing side.[134]
- *Presentation*: Counsel presents evidence to court, jury, etc. in furtherance of the dispute.[135]

The ERDM diagram also captures the economics of eDiscovery, with the largest costs resting with the review, analysis, production, and presentation stages of the eDiscovery process.[136] Increasingly, clients and the lawyers are attempting to

---

[131] See Moore v. Publicis Groupe, 287 F.R.D. 182, 190–91 (S.D. N.Y. 2012), adopted, 2012 WL 1446534 (S.D. N.Y. 2012); Panse, "Method and Apparatus for Processing Electronically Stored Information for Electronic Discovery," U.S. Patent No. 8,090,705 (Jan. 3, 2012).

[132] Moore v. Publicis Groupe, 287 F.R.D. 182, 193 (S.D. N.Y. 2012), adopted, 2012 WL 1446534 (S.D. N.Y. 2012) ("As with keywords or any other technological solution to ediscovery, counsel must design an appropriate process, including use of available technology, with appropriate quality control testing, to review and produce relevant ESI while adhering to Rule 1 and Rule 26(b)(2)(C) proportionality. Computer-assisted review now can be considered judicially-approved for use in appropriate cases."); Grossman & Cormack, Technology-Assisted Review In E-Discovery Can Be More Effective and More Efficient Than Exhaustive Manual Review, 17 Rich. J. L. & Tech. 11 (2011).

[133] Fanning & Drogt, E-Discovery and Its Global Implications, 22(3) Journal of Corporate Accounting & Finance 17–23 (2011); Legg & Dopson, Discovery in the Information Age–The Interaction of ESI, Cloud Computing and Social Media with Discovery, Depositions and Privilege, UNSW Law Research Paper No. 2012–11 (Univ. of New South Wales, Mar. 30, 2012).

[134] See Goodman v. Praxair Services, Inc., 632 F. Supp. 2d 494, 504–05 (D. Md. 2009); Moore v. Publicis Groupe, 287 F.R.D. 182, 193 (S.D. N.Y. 2012), adopted, 2012 WL 1446534 (S.D. N.Y. 2012); Pension Committee of University of Montreal Pension Plan v. Banc of America Securities, 685 F. Supp. 2d 456, 474 (S.D. N.Y. 2010) (abrogated on other grounds by Chin v. Port Authority of New York & New Jersey, 685 F.3d 135 (2d Cir. 2012)); Doppes v. Bentley Motors, Inc., 174 Cal. App. 4th 967, 994, 94 Cal. Rptr. 3d 802, 824–25 (4th Dist. 2009). See also Kelleher, "Gathering and Producing Electronically Stored Information," in 1 Matthew Bender Practice Guide: California E-Discovery and Evidence, Ch. 9 (2012); Manlowe, Samardzich & Shelton, Paradigm Shifts in e-Discovery Litigation: Cooperate or Continue to Pay Dearly, 78 Def. Counsel J. 170 (2011).

[135] See Garrie, Electronic Discovery and Keyword Mediation Mandates a Mastery of Technology and Law, 35 Am. J. Trial Advoc. 243 (2011); Marcus, Chap. 2, The Impact of Digital Information on American Evidence-Gathering and Trial—The Straw That Breaks the Camel's Back?, in Electronic Technology and Civil Procedure 29–48 (2012); Kamran, Chap. 32, Discovery of Electronically Stored Information, in 5 Information Security Management Handbook 473 (6th ed. 2011).

[136] See U.S. v. Briggs, 2011 WL 4017886, *2–3 (W.D. N.Y. 2011), for additional opinion, see, 2011 WL 4024766 (W.D. N.Y. 2011), on reconsideration in part, 831 F. Supp. 2d 623 (W.D. N.Y. 2011); Pace & Zakaras, Where the Money Goes (RAND Corp. 2012).

perform a case assessment early in the eDiscovery process to determine the appropriate strategy for settlement or trial.[137]

## 6.5 Predictive Coding (a.k.a. Computer-Assisted Review) Software and eDiscovery

### *Introduction*

Since the emergence of eDiscovery and the exponential growth of data creation,[138] the primary method of document retrieval has been some form of keyword searching.[139] There are many forms of keyword searching, and as the mountains of data

---

[137] See Garrie, Effective Keyword Selection Requires a Mastery of Storage Technology and the Law, 32 Pace L. Rev. 400 (2012); Withers, Computer-Based Discovery in Federal Court Litigation, 2000 Federal Courts L. Rev. 2, available at https://www.fjc.gov/content/computer-based-discovery-federal-civil-litigation-0 (last visited May 10, 2021) (suggesting parties adopt collaborative strategies on search protocols); see also Brownstone, Collaborative Navigation of the Stormy e-Discovery Seas, 10 Richmond J. Law & Tech. 53 (2004), available at http://law.richmond.edu/jolt/v10i5/article53.pdf (last visited May 10, 2021) (arguing that parties must agree to search terms and other selection criteria to narrow the scope to manageable data sets); The Sedona Principles, Second Edition, 2007, Comment 11.a ("For example, use of search terms could reveal that a very low percentage of files (such as emails and attachments) on a data tape contain terms that are responsive to 'key' terms. This may weigh heavily against a need to further search that source, or it may be a factor in a cost-shifting analysis. Such techniques may also reveal substantial redundancy between sources (i.e., duplicate data is found in both locations) such that it is reasonable for the organization to preserve and produce data from only one of the sources."). For some cases, the cost of review far outweighs any expected returns from winning a case, especially if the parties cannot agree on the parameters of the search.

[138] See Paul & Baron, Information Inflation: Can the Legal System Adapt?, 13(3) Richmond J. Law & Tech. 1, 2 n.2 (2007) ("Organizations have thousands if not tens of thousands of times as much information within their boundaries as they did 20 years ago."), available at http://law.richmond.edu/jolt/v13i3/article10.pdf (last visited May 10, 2021); Lyman & Varian, "How Much Information, 2003," http://www2.sims.berkeley.edu/research/projects/how-much-info-2003/ (last visited May 10, 2021) (research project); Kessler, "Days of Officially Drowning In Data Almost Upon Us," USA Today, Mar. 5, 2007, available at http://usatoday30.usatoday.com/tech/news/2007-03-05-data_N.htm (last visited May 10, 2021).

[139] In re Lorazepam & Clorazepate Antitrust Litigation, 300 F. Supp. 2d 43, 47, 57 Fed. R. Serv. 3d 1141 (D.D.C. 2004) (stating "[t]he glory of electronic information is not merely that it saves space but that it permits the computer to search for words or 'strings' of text in seconds."). See also In re CV Therapeutics, Inc. Securities Litigation, 2006 WL 2458720, *2 (N.D. Cal. 2006) (court endorses employment of search terms as reasonable means of narrowing production); F.T.C. v. Ameridebt, Inc., 2006 WL 618563, *1 (N.D. Cal. 2006) ("email could likely be screened efficiently through the use of electronic search terms that the parties agree upon"); Windy City Innovations, LLC v. America Online, Inc., 2006 WL 2224057, *3 (N.D. Ill. 2006) ("[k]eyword searching permits a party to search a document for a specific word more efficiently"); U.S. v. Amerigroup Illinois, Inc., 2005 WL 3111972, *2 (N.D. Ill. 2005) (referencing agreement by parties to search terms); Reino de Espana v. American Bureau of Shipping, 2006 WL 3208579, *3

keep increasing, so too does the complexity of keyword-searching software and methodologies.[140]

Selecting keywords for searching large volumes of ESI is an almost unavoidable step in the eDiscovery process.[141] This selection can be performed by the parties, the court, or a combination of both.[142] An efficient alternative involves a mediator, neutral, or special master with a clear understanding of the law and the underlying technology.[143] This can benefit both parties by expediting an agreement allowing the parties to maintain oversight of the keyword-selection process.[144] This serves both parties' interests because, as the *Zubulake* court noted, "it might be advisable to solicit a list of search terms from the opposing party for [the purpose of preservation], so that [opposing counsel] could not later complain about which terms were used."[145] A poorly designed search guarantees that the parties will have to perform a

---

(S.D. N.Y. 2006) (court approves of keyword search for names and email addresses as a "targeted and focused discovery search"); Medtronic Sofamor Danek, Inc. v. Michelson, 229 F.R.D. 550, 559, 56 Fed. R. Serv. 3d 1159 (W.D. Tenn. 2003) (court orders defendant to conduct searches using the keyword search terms provided by plaintiff); J.C. Associates v. Fidelity & Guar. Ins. Co., 2006 WL 1445173, *1 (D.D.C. 2006) (requiring search of files using four specified keywords); Alexander v. F.B.I., 194 F.R.D. 316, 47 Fed. R. Serv. 3d 904 (D.D.C. 2000) (court places limitations on the scope of plaintiffs' proposed keywords to be used to search White House email).

[140] More advanced keyword searches using "Boolean" operators and techniques borrowed from "fuzzy logic" may increase the number of relevant documents and decrease the number of irrelevant documents retrieved. These searches attempt to emulate the way humans use language to describe concepts. In essence, however, they simply translate ordinary words and phrases into a Boolean search argument. Thus, a natural language search for "all birds that live in Africa" is translated to something like "bird* + liv* + Africa".

[141] See, e.g., L-3 Communications Corporation v. Sparton Corporation, 313 F.R.D. 661, 666 (M.D. Fla. 2015) (use of keyword searching is "widely accepted," although far from perfect); Treppel v. Biovail Corp., 233 F.R.D. 363, 374–75 (S.D. N.Y. 2006).

[142] See, e.g., Victor Stanley, Inc. v. Creative Pipe, Inc., 250 F.R.D. 251, 255–56, 70 Fed. R. Serv. 3d 1052 (D. Md. 2008); McNulty v. Reddy Ice Holdings, Inc., 271 F.R.D. 569, 571 (E.D. Mich. 2011); William A. Gross Const. Associates, Inc. v. American Mfrs. Mut. Ins. Co., 256 F.R.D. 134, 136 (S.D. N.Y. 2009); Rhoads Industries, Inc. v. Building Materials Corp. of America, 254 F.R.D. 216, 222, 77 Fed. R. Evid. Serv. 1513 (E.D. Pa. 2008), order clarified, 254 F.R.D. 238 (E.D. Pa. 2008); Smith v. Life Investors Ins. Co. of America, 2009 WL 2045197, *7 (W.D. Pa. 2009); Mt. Hawley Ins. Co. v. Felman Production, Inc., 271 F.R.D. 125, 135 (S.D. W. Va. 2010).

[143] Mancia v. Mayflower Textile Servs. Co., 253 F.R.D. 354, 357 (D. Md. 2008) (citing Fed. R. Civ. P. 26–37 advisory committee's notes to the 1983 amendments); Skinner, The Role of Mediation for ESI Disputes, 70 The Alabama Lawyer 425, 426 (2009). See, e.g., Grant Street Group, Inc. v. Realauction.com, LLC, 2010 WL 4808510, *1–2 (W.D. Pa. 2010), report and recommendation adopted, 2010 WL 4689520 (W.D. Pa. 2010); Medtronic Sofamor Danek, Inc. v. Michelson, 229 F.R.D. 550, 559, 56 Fed. R. Serv. 3d 1159 (W.D. Tenn. 2003).

[144] See Zubulake v. UBS Warburg LLC, 229 F.R.D. 422, 432 (S.D. N.Y. 2004) (advising that discovery requests can be more effective if both parties "negotiate a list of search terms to be used in identifying the responsive documents"); see also Scheindlin, We Need Help: The Increasing Use of Special Masters in Federal Court, 58 DePaul L. Rev. 479 (2009).

[145] Zubulake, 229 F.R.D. at 432; see also, e.g., In re Pioneer Corporation, 2019 WL 5401015, *7 (C.D. Cal. 2019) ("The Parties shall meet and confer within 10 days of the date of this Order to determine a mutually agreeable set of 'keyword' search terms.").

series of subsidiary searches as gaps and problems in the original search become apparent.[146]

As always, the goal of discovery has been to satisfy the goal of Rule Number 1 of the Federal Rules of Civil Procedure to "secure the just, speedy and inexpensive determination of every action and proceeding." It is neither economically viable nor possible to have a perfect review of the entire document set.[147] The goal, therefore, is to balance the demands of justice, efficiency, and expense. This allows for a certain amount of error in making disclosures or responding to discovery requests.[148]

In recent history, computer-assisted review has distinguished itself as an alternative to keyword search for finding relevant documents within the ever-increasing document sets produced during discovery.[149] Computer-assisted review aims to reduce the number of documents reviewed by ranking the documents according to a

---

[146] See Grammel, Protecting Search Terms as Opinion Work Product: Applying the Work Product Doctrine to Electronic Discovery, 161 U. Pa. L. Rev. 2063, 2072–73 (2013) (discussing how sampling—i.e., the application of search terms to a randomly selected representative group of documents—can help attorneys determine whether the terms accurately capture the documents sought).

[147] Wood v. Capital One Services, LLC, 2011 WL 2154279, *8–9 (N.D. N.Y. 2011) (applying proportionality to deny use of search terms yielding over one million documents); Moore v. Publicis Groupe, 287 F.R.D. 182, 193 (S.D. N.Y. 2012), adopted, 2012 WL 1446534 (S.D. N.Y. 2012) (Rule 1 concerns must be taken into account in creating eDiscovery protocol).

[148] Lawson v. Spirit AeroSystems, Inc., 2020 WL 1813395, *3 (D. Kan. 2020). See The Sedona Conference Best Practices Commentary on Search & Retrieval Methods (August 2007), which states:

The Sedona conference has helped establish the benchmarks governing the evolution and refinement of reasonable, good faith practices for searching intimidating amounts of data. Principle 6 of The Sedona Principles, Second Edition (2007) notes that "[r]esponding parties are best situated to evaluate the procedures, methodologies and technologies appropriate for preserving and producing their own electronically stored information," and Principle 11 amplifies the point by stating that "[a] responding party may satisfy its good faith obligation to preserve and produce relevant electronically stored information by using electronic tools and processes, such as data sampling, searching, or the use of selection criteria, to identify data reasonably likely to contain relevant information."

[149] Baron, Law in the Age of Exabytes: Some Further Thoughts on "Information Inflation" and Current in E-Discovery Search, 17 Rich. J.L. & Tech. 9 (Spring 2011) (quoting Issues E-Discovery Institute Survey on Predictive Coding, E-Discovery Inst. 2 (Oct. 1, 2010), explaining that predictive coding is "a combination of technologies and processes in which decisions pertaining to the responsiveness of records gathered or preserved for potential production purposes … are made by having reviewers examine a subset of the collection and having the decisions on those documents propagated to the rest of the collection without reviewers examining each record."). See generally Lawson v. Spirit AeroSystems, Inc., 2020 WL 1813395, *6 (D. Kan. 2020) (collecting cases endorsing computer-assisted review as an alternative to manual review of keyword searches); Youngevity International, Corp. v. Smith, 2019 WL 1542300, *11 (S.D. Cal. 2019), report and recommendation adopted, 2019 WL 11274846 (S.D. Cal. 2019) (opining that computer-assisted review is "far more accurate" than manual review). See also In re Mercedes-Benz Emissions Litigation, 2020 WL 747195, *6 (D.N.J. 2020) (rejecting argument that further discovery would be too expensive where parties "chose to utilize search terms as opposed to technology-assisted review, despite wide recognition that technology-assisted review is cheaper, more efficient and superior to keyword searching"). For a hybrid approach, see Livingston v. City of Chicago, 2020 WL 5253848, *3 (N.D. Ill. 2020) (approving of defendant first using plaintiff-crafted search terms

calculated level of responsiveness.[150] Instead of looking at every email written by a custodian over a 3-year time period, computer-assisted review uses a number of factors including keywords, writing style, subject matter of the writing, and even punctuation style to determine the chain of documents that are most relevant to the matter.[151]

Computer-assisted review is a computerized process that uses "sophisticated algorithms to enable the computer to determine relevance, based on interaction with (i.e., training by) a human reviewer."[152] In other words, the software is trained by a senior attorney or partner to look for documents similar to documents that the training attorney tells the software are responsive. This is done by the attorney reviewing a relatively small "seed set" of documents and coding the documents as either responsive or not responsive.[153] "The computer identifies properties of those documents that it [then] uses to code other documents" until the "system's predictions and the reviewer's coding sufficiently coincide," at which point "the system has learned enough to make confident predictions for the remaining documents."[154]

Typically, this allows a set of hundreds of thousands of documents (or more) to be coded for responsiveness by the software, even though only a few thousand have actually been examined by attorneys.[155] In a common implementation of the technique, documents coded "nonresponsive" by the software—typically the bulk of

---

to cull down a collected data set to a review set and then using computer-assisted review to locate responsive documents within the review set).

[150] See generally Moore v. Publicis Groupe, 287 F.R.D. 182, *183–84 (S.D. N.Y. 2012), adopted, 2012 WL 1446534 (S.D. N.Y. 2012) (describing the function and use of predictive coding software); Grossman & Cormack, Technology-Assisted Review In E-Discovery Can Be More Effective and More Efficient Than Exhaustive Manual Review, 17 Rich. JL & Tech. 11–16 (2011).

[151] See generally Moore v. Publicis Groupe, 287 F.R.D. 182 (S.D. N.Y. 2012), adopted, 2012 WL 1446534, *183–84 (S.D. N.Y. 2012) (describing the function and use of predictive coding software); Baron, Using Visual Analytics in E-Discovery and E-Disclosure Cases, Presentation to Second UKVAC International Visual Analytics Summer School, Middlesex Univ., London (Sept. 3, 2012).

[152] See generally Moore v. Publicis Groupe, 287 F.R.D. 182 (S.D. N.Y. 2012), adopted, 2012 WL 1446534, *183–84 (S.D. N.Y. 2012) (describing the function and use of predictive coding software); Dynamo Holdings Ltd. Partnership v. C.I.R., 143 T.C. 183, 190–94, 2014 WL 4636526 (2014). For an example patent, see Privault, System and Method for Assisted Document Review, U.S. Patent No. 8,165,974 (issued Apr. 24, 2012).

[153] See generally Moore v. Publicis Groupe, 287 F.R.D. 182, *183–84 (S.D. N.Y. 2012), adopted, 2012 WL 1446534 (S.D. N.Y. 2012) (describing the function and use of predictive coding software); Garrie, Change is Coming: The Evolution of E-Discovery Economics, Dec. 2012, The Metropolitan Corporate Counsel, at 20 (discussing how predictive coding software works and a discussion of the basic math behind such software).

[154] See generally Garrie, Change is Coming: The Evolution of E-Discovery Economics, Dec. 2012, The Metropolitan Corporate Counsel, at 20 (discussing how predictive coding software works and a discussion of the basic math behind such software).

[155] See Moore v. Publicis Groupe, 287 F.R.D. 182, *183–84 (S.D. N.Y. 2012), adopted, 2012 WL 1446534 (S.D. N.Y. 2012); Global Aerospace Inc. v. Landow Aviation, 2012 WL 1431215 (Va. Cir. Ct. 2012). See also Kleen Products LLC v. Packaging Corp. of America, 2012 WL 4498465, *5 (N.D. Ill. 2012); Garrie, Change is Coming: The Evolution of E-Discovery Economics, Dec. 2012,

any document collection—may never be examined again, except for quality control sampling to ensure the software's interpretation of responsiveness matches that of the attorney running the software.[156] Those documents coded by the software as "responsive" may then be reviewed by attorneys for a final responsiveness determination as well as for privilege.

## *The Nuts and Bolts of Predictive Coding Software*

When using computer-assisted review, counsel should understand how the software addresses recall, precision, and accuracy, as early uses of computer-assisted review likely will require more education to the court.[157] Counsel should understand the following concepts when assessing computer-assisted review technology:

- *Recall* = number of documents predicted to be responsive / total number of actually responsive documents
- *Precision* = number of actually responsive documents / number of documents predicted to be responsive
- *Accuracy* = (true relevant documents retrieved + true nonrelevant documents not retrieved) / total documents[[158]]

There is a give and take between recall and precision. If recall is high (applying very broad search criteria), precision will be low (results will be overly inclusive). Conversely, if precision is high (applying stringent search criteria), recall will be low (results will be underinclusive).[159]

---

The Metropolitan Corporate Counsel, at 20 (discussing how predictive coding software works and a discussion of the basic math behind such software).

[156] See Moore v. Publicis Groupe, 287 F.R.D. 182, *183–84 (S.D. N.Y. 2012), adopted, 2012 WL 1446534 (S.D. N.Y. 2012); Global Aerospace Inc. v. Landow Aviation, 2012 WL 1431215 (Va. Cir. Ct. 2012). See also Kleen Products LLC v. Packaging Corp. of America, 2012 WL 4498465, *5 (N.D. Ill. 2012).

[157] See Moore v. Publicis Groupe, 287 F.R.D. 182, *189–90 (S.D. N.Y. 2012), adopted, 2012 WL 1446534 (S.D. N.Y. 2012); Global Aerospace Inc. v. Landow Aviation, 2012 WL 1431215 (Va. Cir. Ct. 2012). See also Kleen Products LLC v. Packaging Corp. of America, 2012 WL 4498465, *5 (N.D. Ill. 2012).

[158] Garrie, Predictive Coding Endorsed by the Southern District of New York—People Plus Technology Equals Smart Search, Daily Journal (May 1, 2012).

[159] Garrie, Predictive Coding Endorsed by the Southern District of New York—People Plus Technology Equals Smart Search, Daily Journal (May 1, 2012). The F-score is intended to account for this trade-off. It is a statistical measure used in text retrieval applications specifically to measure the compromise between precision and recall: $F = 2(P * R)(P + R)$. For example, if our recall is 80%, but our precision is only 10%, the F-score is 17%. This is sometimes known as the balanced F-score or F1 measure because it gives equal weight to both recall and precision. The F-score can be weighted if more emphasis needs to be placed on recall (the F2 measure) or on precision (the F0.5 measure), according to user requirements.

Richness is another important concept when looking at computer-assisted review statistics.[160] Richness is simply the percentage of relevant documents in the total population. Richness is a measure related to the population, not to the performance of the computer-assisted review application. Thus, in a collection with a small number of relevant documents across a much larger population of documents, such as finding evidence of well-hidden corporate criminal activity, the richness will be low because only a few relevant documents were returned. Conversely, in a medical malpractice suit, almost all of the documents produced by the medical facility regarding a particular patient will be responsive, which will result in a higher richness score.

## *Conclusion*

When deployed and used properly by counsel, these new technologies can reduce clients' bills, increase efficiency, and avoid wasting valuable resources, energy, and efforts.[161] In the end, the goal for counsel should be to develop an effective strategy that assures the eDiscovery issues do not subsume the case or cost their clients millions of unnecessary dollars as it did in *Moore*.[162]

While many agree that computer-assisted review offers distinct advantages to Boolean keyword searches, having the court mandate that a party use a particular method of technology is arguably overstepping its bounds.[163] Best practices dictate that the methods for eDiscovery should be cost-effective, efficient, and reliable. The courts have not been inclined to require the most advanced technology for every case at the expense of efficiency and costs.

In federal district courts across the country, judges and panels have introduced standing orders for the implementation of evolving methods of eDiscovery

[160] Garrie, Predictive Coding Endorsed by the Southern District of New York—People Plus Technology Equals Smart Search, Daily Journal (May 1, 2012).

[161] See generally Moore v. Publicis Groupe, 287 F.R.D. 182 (S.D. N.Y. 2012), adopted, 2012 WL 1446534 (S.D. N.Y. 2012) (for Judge Peck's order approving of the use of computer-assisted review).

[162] Transcript of proceedings before Hon. Nan R. Nolan on February 21, 2012, in Kleen Products LLC v. Packaging Corporation of America, et al., No. 10-cv-05711 (N.D. Ill.) (Plaintiffs asking the court to require the producing parties to use a particular form of eDiscovery, specifically computer-assisted review. Plaintiffs believe that defendants' use of Boolean keyword searches is not reliable enough to meet the standard for reasonableness. Defendants are arguing their method of keyword and phrases meets the requirements of best practices.), available at http://www.umiacs.umd.edu/~oard/teaching/708x/spring12/slides/6/transcript.pdf (last visited May 10, 2021).

[163] See In re Mercedes-Benz Emissions Litigation, 2020 WL 103975, *1 (D.N.J. 2020) (declining to order technology-assisted review where defendants objected after noting that "no court has ordered a party to engage in TAR over the objection of that party" and "[t]he few courts that have considered this issue have all declined to compel predictive coding").

technology into the discovery process.[164] While these orders are a step forward in integrating technology into the discovery phase of litigation, they leave little room for expansion. This leaves concern for new technologies such as computer-assisted review and its ability to make headway in the rapidly changing world of eDiscovery.

Discovery is no small task, and the costs associated with collecting and culling electronic documents can be monumental.[165] However, the aim should still be making the litigation about the issues and not about discovery. The goal of adding technology to the discovery process should be to provide a solution that will allow lawyers to focus more on issues and less on discovery. This will require legal practitioners to remain up to date on the most viable method for data retrieval for the sake of their clients and their caseload.

## 6.6 Issues to Consider When Evaluating eDiscovery Solutions and Providers

### *Introduction*

The transformation of discovery into eDiscovery has wreaked havoc on the practice and business of law, creating more money for vendors at large and for some lawyers irrespective of the economy. It is virtually impossible to have litigation without some amount of eDiscovery. From the emails sent between employees around the LIBOR rate, to digital footprints left by high-tech criminals in the *New York Times* email breach, to employees involved in contentious divorce proceedings, the digital world is involved. This has led to a third party in the relationship between lawyers and litigants—the eDiscovery vendor. Today, eDiscovery can be fully outsourced, or done entirely internally, or some place in between.

Irrespective of where one falls in the spectrum, at some point a corporation will undoubtedly involve one or more eDiscovery software and/or vendors. The remainder of this article provides ten tips for counsel to consider when evaluating eDiscovery software or services. Of course, these are broad and general tips and require tweaking to be effective within a company.

---

164 See ArrivalStar S.A. v. U.S., 106 Fed. Cl. 760, 760 n.1 (2012).

165 See, e.g., Rajala v. McGuire Woods, LLP, 2010 WL 2949582, *6 (D. Kan. 2010); Pinstripe, Inc. v. Manpower, Inc., 2009 WL 2252131, *4 (N.D. Okla. 2009); Proctor & Gamble Co. v. S.C. Johnson & Son, Inc., 2009 WL 440543, *1 (E.D. Tex. 2009).

### *Weigh the Legal Risks and the Company Culture*

It is necessary that one weighs the legal risks and the company culture to see if bringing an eDiscovery solution, or a component of the solution, in-house is a good idea. One of the most common reasons a company fails to deploy an eDiscovery solution is the company culture. Some legal departments are structured such that the idea of being responsible for managing discovery is simply not part of the job description. Other companies struggle to get outside counsel onboard and acquiesce to using the solution their outside firm uses. While this is happening less and less, it still does happen. At other times, the system is purchased but the champion of the tool leaves the legal department, and the eight-figure system simply dies on the vine. It is critical before looking at eDiscovery solutions that counsel be aware of the corporate culture within which they are operating. For example, I have advised several global companies to utilize a managed service approach to eDiscovery because the company culture lent itself better to utilizing vendors and they had outsourced a large portion of their IT functions, making delivery of any eDiscovery solution a great deal more complex.

### *Try Before You Buy*

Companies should follow the "try before you buy" principle, meaning they should test the eDiscovery solution using an old case of their own, not a case provided by a vendor. The vendor is never going to provide a case that is not going to work, because, if it fails, you will not buy their solution. In line with this concept, counsel should encourage as many people in the legal department as possible to step up and try the vendor's product. Ideally, counsel should bring in the end users of the software or the team members who will work directly with outside vendors to make sure they have input in the review and selection process. Often these end users have a better idea of how the solution will be utilized and will most likely have a wish list of improvements for future software purchases.

### *Is the Solution Being Used by the Seller?*

Verify that the eDiscovery solution you are buying is being used by the person selling it. One should never purchase an eDiscovery solution from a vendor whose own legal team does not use the product. In addition, do not hesitate to ask around and see what other companies are using for their in-house software and outside vendor services. It is rare that an eDiscovery solution provider will provide a bad reference. Thus, it is strongly suggested that you reach out through your own network and ask to speak with people who have bought and used the system, as they often will be able to deliver an unvarnished view. When one reaches out to them, it is useful to consider asking questions that include the following: How easy or hard was the eDiscovery solution to install? How much work is required to manage the eDiscovery solution? What would they do differently if they were starting from scratch? In addition, ask about the skill level of the vendor, customer service, and overall abilities of an eDiscovery solution or outside eDiscovery service provider. It is recommended that one have the conversation face-to-face. It is certainly a conversation that can save counsel a great deal of money, time, and headache.

### *Cost-Benefit Analysis*

Perform a cost-benefit analysis of your existing eDiscovery vendor services. Before buying an eDiscovery solution or using an eDiscovery vendor anything, it is important to understand the cost-benefit dynamic:

- High cost + low benefit = do not purchase
- Low cost + high benefit = purchase solution
- High cost + high benefit = depends
- Low cost + low benefit = depends

Today, counsel often assumes that bringing a solution in-house will deliver value and lower costs, but it is critical that counsel validate this assumption before acting. Counsel should know the answers to these questions:

- How much money does the company currently spend with outside vendors on each case in identifying, collecting, and/or preserving data?
- How much does the company spend on eDiscovery vendors for the other components of the eDiscovery process?
- What is the cost to purchase, implement, and adopt an eDiscovery solution for some or part of the eDiscovery?
- What impact does having an in-house eDiscovery cost have on the company's legal spend?

Answers to these questions can be acquired promptly as one need only go to the accounting department and run a few reports to get an accurate estimate. If this is not available, then alternative paths exist, such as meeting with the CFO of the company to determine the current spend to eDiscovery vendors. Experience suggests that if the company spends more than $5000 per case with an eDiscovery vendor to identify, collect, or preserve, and the company has more than 20 active matters a year, it might pay to evaluate bringing some of the eDiscovery activities in-house. While bringing eDiscovery in-house sounds daunting, the reality is that although front-end work for counsel and technologists exists, the time savings, peace of mind, and the monetary cost savings can be substantial and often outweigh the initial costs incurred in setting up and getting an eDiscovery solution operating.

Counsel should be mindful when calculating the monetary cost that the total cost of ownership of an eDiscovery solution is more than just the software itself. Counsel must be mindful that there will be technology costs (storage, server, and head count) and legal costs (an in-house person to manage and oversee the process). A company can incur the following costs depending on the eDiscovery solution or service being sourced:

- New technology assets to administer the solution (e.g., purchase a machine and several additional software applications to ensure litigation hold software operates properly)
- Additional technology head count to support the machine
- Personnel to administer the legal holds and ensure the litigation hold solution software is being utilized by counsel

While the total cost of using an eDiscovery vendor or eDiscovery system is higher than just the prices of the software, additional benefits are realized that go beyond being able to administer compliant legal holds, including the following:

- Avoiding the need to retain counsel to administer the litigation hold beyond validating that the company is preserving as required.
- Knowing that the company has mitigated the real-world risk that comes with an ad hoc litigation hold system.
- Saving money by avoiding the costly exercise of working with outside counsel chasing down IT or employees to ensure the litigation hold letter was delivered—arguably this is "priceless."

The above highlights some of the additional costs and benefits that should be included when calculating the cost-benefit of bringing eDiscovery in-house.

## *Testing, Testing, Testing: Scalability, Security, Usability, Accuracy, Etc.*

While everything should work in the demo, it should also be tested with larger data sets and preferably with the company's own data. If the eDiscovery provider or software vendor says it is going to cost a couple of bucks to run a proof of concept, pay it. Why? It is better to pay a little up front than to go all in with a single software solution or vendor, only to lose the company's shirt (and its data!) in the process. This tip applies whether the company is testing eDiscovery software or an outside vendor service. The problem with using vendor data to run a test is that their data is meant to highlight how smooth and efficient their software is. But the real world is anything but smooth sailing, especially when it comes to eDiscovery. Using data from a prior case will give the company an idea of how the software compares to prior software, as well as if the testing software is challenged with the same hurdles as the previous software.

### *Does the Company Have Appropriate Internal Protocols and Processes?*

Before a company buys eDiscovery software, make sure it has the internal protocols and processes to address the use of eDiscovery software or services. Preparation is the best preventative measure one can take. Make sure internal case-handling protocols map to the software or services the company is using. Maintaining a clear schedule of tasks and checklists will keep all parties on the same page and timeline, as well as clearly defining expectations for each team member. These internal protocols should also include detailed plans on managing pre-litigation tasks, such as issuing a litigation hold notice. If one does not have protocols and process addressing vendor software or services, every time the software is used by a different member of the legal team, a different ad hoc process will emerge. This translates to more time and money spent re-documenting the eDiscovery process and members of the legal team being given multiple sets of instructions on how to run a case.

### *Who Is the Internal Owner?*

Before acquiring an eDiscovery solution or using an eDiscovery vendor, it is critical that the company has identified an internal owner to resolve issues, ensure people use it, and manage the nuts and bolts on a daily basis.

It is critical that there is an internal owner who will be responsible for working with their fellow in-house counsel, outside counsel, and other vendors. While it may seem counterintuitive to bring in yet another person to the process, having a single person responsible for the coordination of identification, preservation, collection, search, and production of ESI will help the company realize substantial savings and lower eDiscovery risks overall. Often, this individual can also prove to be an invaluable resource in assisting their in-house colleagues and outside counsel in the often complex search and production process.

### *Investigate the Long-Term Viability of an eDiscovery Solution or Vendor*

Software and technology changes rapidly, unlike the long-term nature of litigation. Consequently, when evaluating an eDiscovery solution or vendor, it is critical that counsel perform a risk analysis to ensure that the vendor is financially stable, meaning they are unlikely to file for bankruptcy. Take caution not to invest in software only for it to disappear from the market. While it is possible to put software code in escrow, this is a high-risk solution. A company should also be mindful of the fact that it is very possible the software provider or solution provider will be acquired, as there is a great deal of activity in the eDiscovery vertical, so counsel should make sure that the contract terms cover the life cycle of the caseload or provide a process by which the company can migrate to another vendor or solution.

## *Involve the CIO and Technology Assets in the Selection*

Involve the Chief Information Officer and other technology assets when selecting eDiscovery software, hardware, or services to ensure that the solution purchased does not overwhelm IT internal resources.

Today, the gap between IT and legal is certainly shrinking, which is great for many reasons. However, if counsel engages IT after a solution is selected, they risk the solution not actually working. Almost all eDiscovery solutions require some IT support, which usually translates into headcount to ensure the systems are available to run an eDiscovery solution. Of course, any eDiscovery system is handling sensitive documents, so ensuring the security of the environment within which the eDiscovery solution runs is also tantamount and usually requires input from IT at some level. For example, when a company buys an eDiscovery identification and collection platform, it will most likely require internal IT assets to assist legal in identifying and collecting data. Another benefit of dialoguing with IT prepurchase is that counsel will get a better grasp of the support costs. For example, we know of several great eDiscovery predictive coding solutions that operate great in Windows environment, but when they are run in a non-Windows environment, installing software patches and updates can be a bit trickier and require additional costs.

## *Does the Company's Demand Justify Investment?*

Verify that the company's demand is sufficient to justify the investment by looking across the entire legal department, compliance, and any other department that might work with outside counsel on a regular basis. Often overlooked when selecting an eDiscovery software solution is whether the company's case load justifies bringing such a system in-house, even if the budget is available. It is prudent for counsel to verify that the company's case load is sufficient to justify the investment and share this information with the technology stakeholder as well, to avoid IT purchasing a solution that is not necessary. At larger companies, the case load assessment requires counsel to reach across different legal groups to determine the current case load, and while this process may seem tedious, it is essential. For example, a midsize company might think that they do not have an active enough case docket to justify buying an eDiscovery solution. However, if the legal team reaches out to the compliance department, such a solution might be a huge cost saver, because that department is managing dozens of internal investigations and would benefit by having an in-house eDiscovery platform to manage such investigations. With this tip, unlike evaluating the cost-benefit for the legal department, the focus is on ascertaining the internal demand for an eDiscovery solution across the entire organization.

# Chapter 7
# Encryption

## 7.1 Encryption

### *What Is Encryption?*

Data encryption translates data into another form, or code, so that only people with access to a secret key (formally called a decryption key) or password can read it. Encrypted data is commonly referred to as ciphertext, while unencrypted data is called plain text. Currently, encryption is one of the most popular and effective data security methods used by governments and organizations. Two main types of data encryption exist—asymmetric encryption, also known as public-key encryption, and symmetric encryption.

The purpose of data encryption is to protect digital data confidentiality as it is stored on computer systems or transmitted using the Internet or other computer network protocols. This provides confidentiality and drive key security initiatives including authentication, integrity, and non-repudiation. Authentication allows for the verification of a message's origin, and integrity provides proof that a message's contents have not changed since it was sent. Additionally, non-repudiation ensures that a message sender cannot deny sending the message. The use of encryption has been used for thousands of years. In Khufu, Egypt, we find the first use of hieroglyphic encrypted symbols in the tomb of Amenemhet. Kings used secret codes. Cardinal Richelieu in 1642 had the great cryptologist, Rossignol, to the decipher his messages. More recently, George Washington relied on encrypted messages; World War II had the Enigma machine saving countless lives. Since the dawn of the nuclear age governments have relied on encryption codes for national security purposes. Now, in the digital age organizations have had to incorporate encryption in their security equation.

 
D. B. Garrie et al., *Uncovering Digital Evidence*,
https://doi.org/10.1007/978-3-031-68118-9_7

## *Why Is Encryption Necessary?*

More than ever before, personal and confidential information is transmitted over the Internet in clear text and potentially exposed.[1] Many people today increasingly rely on technology, but do not fully understand the importance of data, software, and systems security.[2] Moreover, security professionals have trouble using programs and tools intended for security purposes.[3] As a result, several companies have recently suffered major data breaches resulting in high profile litigation.[4] Damages can be massive, and additional losses can include credit monitoring for all customers (direct and indirect), years of systemic and obtrusive audits,[5] long-term impact to profitability/revenue projections, systemic and companywide obtrusive audits to identify and correct not just the source of the leak but other broken business processes that were discovered during these audits, data theft, and destruction of files, servers, and storage systems.[6] A basic knowledge of encryption and cybersecurity is necessary to help a user understand how he or she is an important part of the network that keeps their own data, and the data of their employer, safe. We have recently seen as an example a major shipping company not only lost control of their

[1] "A major catalyst for email encryption were revelations about widespread online surveillance in documents leaked by Edward Snowden, the former National Security Agency contractor." Agence France-Presse, NSA Spying Inspires ProtonMail End-to-End Encrypted Email Service (May 19, 2014),http://gadgets.ndtv.com/internet/news/nsa-spying-inspires-protonmail-end-to-end-encrypted-email-service-526769 (last visited Sept. 18, 2017); *see also* Miners, NSA Sniffing Prompts Yahoo to Encrypt Traffic Between Its Data Centers (Apr. 3, 2013), http://www.computerworld.com/s/article/9247410/NSA_sniffing_prompts_Yahoo_to_encrypt_traffic_between_its_data_centers (last visited Sept. 18, 2017).

[2] *See* Garrie, The BYOD Dilemma: How to Keep Your Assets from Turning Into Liabilities (2014), http://blog.legalsolutions.thomsonreuters.com/wp-content/uploads//2014/02/BYOD-white-paper.pdf (last visited Sept. 18, 2017).

[3] Sasse & Flechais, Usable Security: Why Do We Need It? How Do We Get It?, *in* Security and Usability: Designing Secure Systems That People Can Use 13, 14 (O'Reilly Media 2005).

[4] Equifax, Sony, Target, and eBay are among the most recent victims. *See*, e.g., Kevin McCoy, Equifax Hit with at Least 23 Class-Action Lawsuits Over Massive Cyberbreach (Sept, 11, 2017), https://www.usatoday.com/story/money/2017/09/11/equifax-hit-least-23-class-action-lawsuits-over-massive-cyberbreach/653909001/ (last visited Sept. 18, 2017); *see also* Ellis, Lawsuits say Sony Pictures should have expected security breach (Dec. 20, 2014), http://www.cnn.com/2014/12/20/us/sony-pictures-lawsuits/ (last visited Jan. 6, 2015).

[5] *See* FTC Red Flags Rule, http://www.ftc.gov/sites/default/files/documents/federal_register_notices/identity-theft-red-flags-and-address-discrepancies-under-fair-and-accurate-credit-transactions-act/071109redflags.pdf (last visited Sept. 18, 2017).

[6] The event coordination site Meetup was shut down in 2014 for 7 days by a hack known as a distributed denial-of-service attack (DDoS), causing losses in the hundreds of thousands of dollars, in addition to the disruption of communities whose organizers rely on the website. *See* Newman, Aggressive Hackers Brought Meetup Down. Here's How It Came Back (Mar. 10, 2014), http://www.slate.com/blogs/future_tense/2014/03/10/ddos_attacks_brought_meetup_down_but_now_it_has_better_network_security.html (last visited Sept. 18, 2017).

network but had no secure backup to remount their data. They lost months of business and reputation.

### Overview of Chapter

The purpose of this chapter is to provide the reader with a foundational knowledge of encryption and relate it to the realities of electronic information security that are becoming more and more a part of our daily lives. The chapter has three parts: It will start with an overview of encryption, then go into some of its applications, and will end by covering some of the ways in which employers can educate their employees on encryption and cybersecurity.

The first part will go over the basics of encryption and look into some various types. It will begin with a definition and explanation of encryption keys—the tools used to unlock encrypted data—before going into an overview of three major types of encryption: symmetric encryption, asymmetric encryption, and hashing. While the theory of encryption shares the same principles, the use of encryption for data in transmission or at rest in a stored state will be implemented differently and require different security protocols.

The second part will address some of the applications and tools of encryption. This will include a look at some important tools used to authenticate data—digital certificates and digital signatures. It will also survey some ways in which the various types of encryption are put to use, including a widely used encryption program known as "Pretty Good Privacy," cryptographic protocols used to secure Internet data transfer (SSL/TLS), and the mechanics of username/password logins.

## 7.2 Basics of Encryption

### Introduction

Encryption is the conversion of data from one format to another format that is indecipherable by normal means, thus protecting the content of the data from prying eyes. It is the process of transforming data using a mathematical or logical function and delivering it to the recipient who then "unpacks" it using the appropriate methods or processes.[7] The input is referred to as plaintext. Plaintext can be any form of information such as text, binary code, or even an image that needs to be transformed into a format that is unreadable by anyone except those who possess the secret to

[7] Oriyano, Cryptography: InfoSec Pro Guide (McGraw Hill 2013).

unlocking it.[8] Encryption transforms plaintext into ciphertext, which contains the original message in a scrambled form.[9]

## *Algorithms: Executing Encryption*

One of the more challenging aspects of the encryption process, and arguably the most puzzling for the bench and bar, is the algorithm/cipher process.[10] The algorithm or cipher consists of discrete steps that mandate how the encryption/decryption process is to be performed. To take a simple example, an algorithm could be to convert the letters in a message into numbers corresponding to their place in the alphabet, thus yielding an encrypted message or ciphertext. To decrypt the ciphertext, the algorithm would dictate that this process is reversed by converting the numbers back to their corresponding letters. The algorithm is thus the set of directives by which the encryption/decryption is executed.[11]

## *Keys: Unlocking the Secrets of Encrypted Data*

Before getting into the specifics of various types of encryption, let us first go over what a key is. In technical terms, a key "is a discrete piece of information that enacts a specific result or output for a given cryptographic operation."[12] An encryption key can be thought of in the same way as a physical key or, perhaps more appropriately, a combination for a locker; they are special tools used to unlock something.[13] In encryption, keys are the pieces of information that unlock the original plaintext input of the encrypted data. The algorithm employed in a given encryption process defines the encryption key.[14] It can be thought of as the design of the lock, which

[8] "The '789 Patent describes a method of translating (or 'encrypting') ordinary data (called 'plaintext') into encoded data (called 'ciphertext'), so that the plaintext may not be viewed by an unintended reader." Paone v. Microsoft Corp., 771 F. Supp. 224, 225 (E.D.N.Y. 2011).

[9] Paone, 771 F. Supp. at 225.

[10] "In addition to a dearth of briefing on the topic of whether the specification discloses an algorithm for the functions claimed, lacking before the Court is the expert testimony upon which it ordinarily relies when construing means-plus-function terms." Widevine Technologies, Inc. v. Verimatrix, Inc., 2009 Markman 3734106, 2009 WL 3734106, *15 (E.D. Tex. 2009).

[11] "The algorithm is a type of mathematical formula for transforming the contents of the movie file into gibberish." DVD Copy Control Assn., Inc. v. Bunner, 31 Cal. 4th 864, 871, 4 Cal. Rptr. 3d 69, 75 P.3d 1 (2003), as modified, (Oct. 15, 2003).

[12] Oriyano, Cryptography: InfoSec Pro Guide 17 (McGraw Hill 2013).

[13] Cryptography at 17.

[14] "A CSS-protected DVD can be decrypted by an appropriate decryption algorithm that employs a series of keys stored on the DVD and the DVD player. In consequence, only players and drives containing the appropriate keys are able to decrypt DVD files and thereby play movies stored on

determines the specific cuts and grooves in the key that make it work; the more cuts, the more complicated to pick the lock.[15]

### *Symmetric-Key Encryption: The Oldest and Most Widely Used Type of Encryption*

Symmetric encryption works by using the same key to encrypt as to decrypt.[16] It is what is used in applications such as True Crypt, VeraCrypt, and Microsoft's BitLocker. The nature of the method, however, requires that both the transmitter and the receiver of an encoded message be in possession of the key, which means that they must find a way to transmit the key itself securely.[17] For that reason, as telecommunications became increasingly common in the early 1970s, researchers focused on a solution that would provide security without requiring the transmitter and receiver to previously have securely exchanged a key.[18] This research would lead to the development of public-key encryption, which will be addressed shortly.[19]

The symmetry of the keys is just one factor that should be noted as essential in defining an encryption method. It is important to keep in mind that symmetric key encryption is only the tip of the iceberg and that legal definitions of encryption must be precisely worded so as to account for the range of forms that it can take. In *Tristrata, Inc. v. Microsoft Corp.*,[20] Microsoft's proposed construction of "encrypt"[21] "limits encryption to symmetric encryption,"[22] by failing to account for other forms of encryption, which do not use the same key to encrypt as to decrypt.

---

DVDs." Universal City Studios, Inc. v. Reimerdes, 111 F. Supp. 2d 294, 310 (S.D. N.Y. 2000), judgment entered, 111 F. Supp. 2d 346 (S.D. N.Y. 2000), aff'd, 273 F.3d 429 (2d Cir. 2001).

[15] Cryptography at 17.

[16] Oriyano, Cryptography: InfoSec Pro Guide 17 (McGraw Hill 2013).

[17] Beal, Symmetric-key Cryptography, http://www.webopedia.com/TERM/S/symmetric_key_cryptography.html (last visited Sept. 18, 2017).

[18] Differ & Hellman, New Directions in Cryptography, IEEE Transactions Info. Theory, IT-22, 6, 644 Nov. 1976.

[19] New Directions in Cryptography at 647.

[20] Tristrata, Inc. v. Microsoft Corporation, 2013 Markman 5645984, 2013 WL 5645984, *10 (N.D. Cal. 2013), aff'd, 594 Fed. Appx. 653 (Fed. Cir. 2014).

[21] "Use a key to disguise a message in such a way as to hide its substance from those who do not know the key." Tristrata, 2013 WL 5645984 at *10.

[22] 2013 WL 5645984 at 35.

## *Asymmetric-Key Encryption (or Public-Key Encryption)*

The goal of asymmetric-key encryption is to develop a system in which two entities, which have not previously exchanged a secure key, are able to use publicly available or known techniques to establish a secure connection for data transmission.[23] The basic process by which such a "public-key" system operates is as follows:

> Each user generates a pair of inverse transformations, E and D, at his terminal. The deciphering transformation D must be kept secret, but need never be communicated on any channel. The enciphering key E can be made public by placing it in a public directory along with the user's name and address. Anyone can then encrypt messages and send them to the user, but no one else can decipher messages intended for him. Public key cryptosystems can thus be regarded as multiple access ciphers.[24]

In other words, in that system, the user generates two keys and makes only one of them—the encoding key—public.[25] When other users send data to the first user, they can access that public encoding key to encrypt the data. Once it is encrypted, the message can only be decrypted with the private decoding key—barring the possibility of a hacker with the time, computing resources and motivation to devote to cracking the encryption. While in the early days of computing, that may have been a rarity, due to the computer power that exists in modern technology, it is less a matter of whether or a not a system will be cracked, but how soon.[26]

While the distinction between symmetric and asymmetric encryption may seem mostly clean-cut in theory, as with anything, in practice there can be gray areas. An early example, *Rackman v. Nintendo of America, Inc.*, illustrates how the line between different types of encryption can be blurred in the legal context, even when relatively clear from a purely technical perspective.[27]

The Nintendo Entertainment System video game console utilized a security system in which game cartridges inserted into the console contained a microprocessor ("the key chip") that exchanged data with an identical chip ("the lock chip")

---

[23] Tristrata, Inc. v. Microsoft Corporation, 2013 Markman 5645984, 2013 WL 5645984, *35 (N.D. Cal. 2013), aff'd, 594 Fed. Appx. 653 (Fed. Cir. 2014).

[24] Differ & Hellman, New Directions in Cryptography, IEEE Transactions Info. Theory, IT-22, 648 Nov. 1976.

[25] "This system is called a 'public key' system because one key can be made public without compromising the secrecy of the remaining key." Advanced Software Design Corp. v. Fiserv, Inc., 625 F. Supp. 2d 815, 820 (E.D. Mo. 2008). For illustration, "say Company A and Compnay B want to use public key encryption to exchange data. Each company would provide the other company with its public key. That would allow each company to encrypt data being sent to the other company. However, if the public key was stolen, the encrypted data would be safe, because it takes the private key (which ideally neither company would share, as neither needs to share it) to decrypt the data." Spernow, Garrie, and Kelley, What it takes to Frustrate the Hacker Knocking at Your Door, Law Firm Cybersecurity 52 (ABA Book Publishing 2017).

[26] Lenstra & Verheul, Selecting Cryptographic Key Sizes, Lecture Notes in Computer Sci. 1751 446 (2000), at 449.

[27] Rackman v. Nintendo of America Inc., 34 U.S.P.Q.2d 1068, 1994 WL 665794 (S.D. N.Y. 1994).

contained in the console.[28] If the data matched, the cartridge was authentic.[29] The system was effective due to the difficulty in reverse engineering the "secret" that the key chip and the lock chip both kept (cf. symmetric encryption).[30]

Arguing "for a looser definition of public-key cryptography which requires only that the private key cannot practically be determined from the public key," Rackman contended that this violated his patent for the use of public-key encryption in game cartridges.[31] Basing its decision largely on the prosecution history of the patent (as opposed to its plain text), the court wound up distinguishing public-key encryption partially by the degree of difficulty in deriving one key from the other:

> [I]n order to be a public-key cryptographic security system … Nintendo's system must do more than just make it practically difficult for a competitor to derive the key chip, given public access to the lock chip … . [T]he use of public-key cryptography envisioned in the '857 patent presumes a special mathematical relationship between private and public key resulting in the computational infeasibility of deriving the former from the latter.[32]

Even though the technologies may feel distinct conceptually, the legal language defining them might seem a bit fine, or least vulnerable to a bit of legal gaming. These gray areas are fertile grounds for litigation. To navigate them effectively, it is important to understand precisely where a legal definition fails to square up with the technological nature of a given form of encryption.

American jurists often find themselves overwhelmed intellectually with these scientific/technical descriptions—as a result, they try to redefine these terms into something that satisfies them but is often quite different than an engineer's definition. Most issues in fact turn not on the definition but the failure to implement encryption properly. Therefore, especially in litigation, you need to first establish and educate the court on the scientific description untainted by the facts of your case. This will save you and the court a lot of time. In addition, when drafting agreements that involve scientific/technical terms, insert in a defining footnote the term or protocol along with the technical source of the term or protocol.

### *Hashing: One-Way Encryption*

Hashing is a distinct and different area of encryption. Hashing takes plaintext and transforms it into ciphertext in a way that is not intended to be decrypted. It does not keep the information secret but rather focuses authenticating by preserving the integrity of the data and ensuring that the data received is what the sender intended

---

[28] Rackman, 1994 WL 665794 at *4.

[29] 1994 WL 665794 at *4.

[30] 1994 WL 665794 at *5.

[31] 1994 WL 665794 at *5.

[32] 1994 WL 665794 at *7.

the receiver to have. It is one-way encryption.[33] The hashing function executed on the plaintext data is responsible for generating a fixed-length value that is relatively easy to compute in one direction, but almost impossible to reverse.[34]

The hashing process outputs what is referred to as a hash, hash value, or message digest.[35] The value should be unique for every different input that enters the process.[36] This property of hashes allows one to detect even the slightest changes to data of any type. Basically, anything that is hashed and then changed, even minutely, will result in an entirely different hash value from the original value. The most popular hashing algorithm is called MD5, which can be manipulated, unlike HD7.

Still, defining *hashing* can be a point of dispute in litigation. *Pacid Group, LLC v. Apple, Inc.* was a patent case concerning, among other things, how to construe the term "secure hash operation" and its relevant permutations in the patents at issue.[37] Plaintiffs argued for a broader, two-factor interpretation focusing on the relationship between the input and the output,[38] while defendants insisted on a considerably narrower four-factor definition focusing on the specific characteristics of the output.[39] The court landed somewhere between the two.[40] Following the tendency of the Federal Circuit's claim construction teachings, it avoided construing the technical terms based on citations to prior art and focused more on the intrinsic language of the patents in dispute.[41] Thus, while it is important to have a solid understanding of

---

[33] Oriyano, Cryptography: InfoSec Pro Guide 115 (McGraw Hill 2013).

[34] Cryptography, at 115.

[35] "[T]ypically a relatively unique representation (also called a 'fingerprint' or the 'message digest') of the data is first generated using a process in which the data is 'condensed' or 'hashed,' for example by means of a one-way hash function into a relative small value, thereby fixing its contents … ." RMail Ltd. v. Amazon.com, Inc., 2013 Markman 968246, 2013 WL 968246, *34 (E.D. Tex. 2013).

[36] "A hash has the following properties: (i) it should be computationally infeasible to find another input string that will generate the same hash value; and (ii) the hash does not reveal anything about the input that was used to generate it." Serverside Group Ltd. v. Tactical 8 Technologies, L.L.C., 985 F. Supp. 2d 900, 938 (N.D. Iowa 2013), adhered to on reconsideration, 985 F. Supp. 2d 944 (N.D. Iowa 2014).

[37] The PACid Group, LLC v. Apple, Inc., 2010 Markman 2813654, 2010 WL 2813654 (E.D. Tex. 2010).

[38] "(1) that the output is deterministic (i.e., repeatable in that the same inputs always produce the same outputs), and (2) that the output has no known relationship with the input that may be used to recover the input from the output." The PACid Group, LLC, 2010 WL 2813654 at 11.

[39] "(1) that the output is always the same binary length regardless of the size of the input, (2) that it is computationally infeasible to determine the input from the output, (3) that it is computationally infeasible to determine two inputs that produce the same output, and (4) that on average, approximately 50 percent of the secure has output bits are changed when only one single bit is changed." 2010 WL 2813654 at 11.

[40] The court accepted the first part of defendants' definition, rejected (2) and (3), and partially accepted (4). 2010 WL 2813654 at 11–13.

[41] "While it has previously been noted that cited prior art can guide the construction of a claim term because it may indicate the meaning of the term to a person of skill in the art at the time of the invention, Defendants' incorporation of 'computationally infeasible' imports an unclaimed limitation into the proposed construction." 2010 WL 2813654 at 12.

the technical background of hashing (or any other form of encryption), the specific circumstances of each case will often dictate how these technical areas are approached.

Hashing is used in a great number of contexts, some of which we will address in the remainder of the chapter. As a preview to the following section, here are a few of the places where hashes play an important role today:

- Digital certificates[42]
- Verifying downloaded software[43]
- Password storage[44]
- Digital signatures[45]

## 7.3 Tools and Applications of Encryption

### *Challenges to Contemporary Encryption*

In transport mode, only the packet payloads are encrypted. The headers are sent intact in the open. This makes deployment a little easier and requires less infrastructure. You can still have AH (Authentication Header) in the transport mode and verify the source address of the packets. While the message is safe, an adversary can see the start and endpoint of a message.

Layer Two Tunneling Protocol (L2TP) is another industry-developed protocol and is endorsed by Microsoft and Cisco. Although used frequently in hardware-based encryption devices, its use in software is relatively limited. In tunnel mode, the entire packet—header and all—is encapsulated and encrypted, placed in another packet, and forwarded to a central VPN processor. The endpoints decrypt the packets and then forward them to the correct IP. A benefit of this method is that outsiders can't even tell what the final destination for the encrypted packet is. Another advantage is that the VPN can be controlled and administered from a few central points. The downside is that this requires dedicated hardware at both ends to do the tunneling.

The most basic method of attack on encryption today is brute force, or trying random keys until the right one is found. Of course, the length of the key determines the possible number of keys and affects the plausibility of this type of attack. It is

---

[42] "The first step of validating a certificate is to first verify the certificate's integrity. This is done by first creating a one-way hash of the certificate contents (using the hash algorithm indicated in the certificate)." Goulet, Summarizing PKI Certificate Validation (Jan. 19, 2009), http://blog.securism.com/2009/01/summarizing-pki-certificate-validation/ (last visited Jan. 6, 2015).

[43] Hashing ensures that downloaded software is in the state in which the author intended.

[44] Many operating systems rely on hashing to verify stored passwords instead of storing passwords themselves.

[45] See § 7:12.

important to keep in mind that encryption strength is directly proportional to key size, but as the key size increases, so do the number of resources required to perform the computation.

Alternative methods of breaking a cipher include side-channel attacks and cryptanalysis. Side-channel attacks go after the implementation of the cipher, rather than the actual cipher itself. These attacks tend to succeed if there is an error in system design or execution. Likewise, cryptanalysis means finding a weakness in the cipher and exploiting it. Cryptanalysis is more likely to occur when there is a flaw in the cipher itself.

Data protection solutions for data encryption can provide encryption of devices, email, and data itself. In many cases, these encryption functionalities are also met with control capabilities for devices, email, and data. Companies and organizations face the challenge of protecting data and preventing data loss as employees use external devices, removable media, and web applications more often as a part of their daily business procedures. Sensitive data may no longer be under the company's control and protection as employees copy data to removable devices or upload it to the cloud. As a result, the best data loss prevention solutions prevent data theft and the introduction of malware from removable and external devices as well as web and cloud applications. In order to do so, they must also ensure that devices and applications are used properly and that data is secured by auto-encryption even after it leaves the organization.

As we mentioned, email control and encryption is another critical component of a data loss prevention solution. Secure, encrypted email is the only answer for regulatory compliance, a remote workforce, BYOD, and project outsourcing. Premier data loss prevention solutions allow your employees to continue to work and collaborate through email, while the software and tools proactively tag, classify, and encrypt sensitive data in emails and attachments. The best data loss prevention solutions automatically warn, block, and encrypt sensitive information based on message content and context, such as user, data class, and recipient. While data encryption may seem like a daunting, complicated process, data loss prevention software handles it reliably every day. Data encryption does not have to be something your organization tries to solve on its own. Consider a top data loss prevention software that offers data encryption with device, email, and application control, and rest assured that your data is safe.

Endpoint users are the greatest security risk along with the failure to manage data and its inherent security level as it returned to storage.

## *Introduction to the Tools and Applications of Encryption*

So far we have covered the basic incarnations of encryption and generally how each option works. This part will point out a few of the practical applications of encryption and some of the specific tools involved in these applications. Among them are systems for secure communication, identification, authentication, e-commerce, key management, and secure computer access.[46] This is not meant to be an exhaustive examination, but rather a brief overview of encryption's practical manifestations and the factors that come into play. Encryption methods vary in the amount of data they can process in a given time frame and the type of key needed for decryption. The type of encryption used may be dictated by regulatory or industry standards or by individual preference or by software compatibility.

### *Digital Certificates: Passports of the Digital World*

One of the key issues in asymmetric and symmetric encryption is key distribution. A digital certificate identifies the holder of a particular key.[47] It is like a digital passport. At a high level, a digital certificate is generated by an authentication system, and it provides identity verification.[48] Depending on the type of certificate, the user may have to answer queries or enter information to verify their identity, thus protecting against undesirable results such as fraud.

A vast majority of the devices we use on a daily basis to communicate in a safe and secure manner would not work properly without digital certificates. Digital certificates are necessary for identity and authority verification in public-key infrastructure (PKI).[49] Digital certificates bind public keys to their holding parties and indicate the actions that the holder of the key is allowed to exercise.[50]

Digital certificates are the "signature" of the Internet commerce world. These use a combination of encryption types to provide authentication. They prove that who you are connecting to is really who they say they are. Simply put, a certificate is a "certification" of where the information is coming from. A certificate contains the public key of the organization encrypted with either its private key or the private key of a signing authority. Using a signing or certificate authority is considered the more secure method of the two. If you can decrypt the certificate with their public key, then you can reasonably assume the website belongs to that organization. Certificates are usually tied to a particular domain. They can be issued by a central entity, called a certificate authority (CA), or created and signed locally as described above. There are several of these organizations, the biggest of which is VeriSign, the company that also runs the domain names system. They have sanctioned many other companies to offer certificates under their authority. Getting a certificate from VeriSign or

---

[46] Oriyano, Cryptography: InfoSec Pro Guide 230–31 (McGraw Hill 2013).

[47] "The digital certificate contains information identifying the website (i.e., the website's name, web address), the website's public key, and a digital signature." Stambler v. RSA Sec., Inc., 2003 WL 22749855, *2 (D. Del. 2003), aff'd, 123 Fed. Appx. 982 (Fed. Cir. 2005).

[48] U.S. Patent No. 6,321,339 B1 (issued Nov. 20, 2001).

[49] Public-key infrastructure refers to the system for the creation, storage, and distribution of digital certificates. Vacca, Public Key Infrastructure: Building Trusted Applications and Web Services 8 (Auerbach 2004).

[50] Oriyano, Cryptography: InfoSec Pro Guide 180 (McGraw Hill 2013).

one of the companies it authorizes is like having someone vouch for you. Generally, they will not issue you a certificate until they verify the information you are putting in the certificate, either by phone or via some kind of paper documentation, such as a corporate charter. Once they "certify" you, they will take this information, including the URLs you are going to use the certificate for, and digitally "sign" it by encrypting it with their private key. Then a web server or other program can use this certificate. When outside users receive some data, such as a web page from the server, and it has a certificate attached, they can use public-key cryptography to decrypt the certificate and verify your identity. Certificates are used most often at e-commerce websites, but they can also be used for any form of communications. SSH and Nessus both can use certificates for authentication. VPNs also can use certificates for authentication instead of passwords.

## *Username/Password Logins: Hashing in Action*

Hashing is vital to password management. Consider a scenario where a user is trying to log into his computer. A user types his username and password into a workstation or system, which verifies that the password entered matches the username. In order for the computer to do this, however, it needs to have first executed a hashing function on the password when the user initially created the account on the workstation. At that point, it stores the resulting hash value—not the password itself—in a directory. This is to help secure the password from unauthorized intruders. When the user reenters the password on another login attempt, the computer hashes it and compares the result of that function with the value stored in its directory. In this way, hashing allows for the computer to verify that a password matches a given username without storing the password in a database, where it could be vulnerable to any number of extraction methods or potential targeted attacks.

It is important to keep in mind, however, that while this process is useful, it is not a complete solution. There are many risks to security that exist in tandem with password use, including (though not limited to) keystroke loggers, phishing software, or, the lowest-tech of all, lost or stolen passwords that were written down on paper or stored in some other nonsecure way.[51]

The use of "salt" is a way to provide additional protection for hashed passwords. It basically increases the amount of effort needed to break hashed passwords by adding data to the password and hashing the combination.[52] In 2013, Adobe was hacked, and while they used hashing to obfuscate passwords on their servers, once someone was able to extract all the hashed passwords, it was conceivably possible

[51] Al-Sinani & Mitchell, Implementing PassCard: A CardSpace-based Password Manager, Tech. Rep.: Royal Holloway U. London 1 (Dec. 2010).

[52] *See* MarkCC, Passwords, Hashing and Salt (Mar. 2, 2013), http://www.goodmath.org/blog/2013/03/02/passwords-hashing-and-salt/ (last visited Sept. 18, 2017).

to break the hashing algorithm within a few months.[53] Salting would have made this unfeasible in any reasonable amount of time. The US Navy did this technique during World War II, but they called it padding.

The reasonable standard for password security became a point of focus in *In re LinkedIn User Privacy Litigation*, a class action brought on behalf of 6.5 million users of LinkedIn.com whose passwords were stolen and posted online after the website was hacked.[54] The plaintiffs claimed that LinkedIn was engaging in fraudulent business practices by making representations in their Privacy Policy that deceived the public into thinking that their password security was better than it was.[55] LinkedIn moved to dismiss based on the idea that the plaintiffs would not have known that their unsalted hashing algorithm was below industry standard.[56] The plaintiffs then argued that "even if the average consumer would not have understood that unsalted, SHA-1 encryption was below the industry standard, the popular media would have found that disclosure newsworthy and would have disseminated the information to consumers."[57] The motion to dismiss was denied.

## *Digital Signatures: Authenticating Electronic Information*

Digital signatures are checks set in place to determine the authenticity of electronic information.[58] They are useful for ensuring that documents, transactions, driver files, and other pieces of software originate from the party claimed and have not been altered.[59] Digital signatures serve much the same function as handwritten signatures; they verify that the signer agrees to the contents of the document.[60] While this makes the document more secure in terms of authenticity, it does not do anything to make the contents of the document confidential. The following example shows how public-key encryption, hashing, and digital certificates come into play in creating digital signatures:

- Let's say Harry wants to send a message to Sally with a digital signature. Harry creates his message and hashes it. He then encrypts the hash value using his

---

[53] Mandalia, Adobe Hack Password Dump Shows Users Still Pathetic at Choosing Passwords (Nov. 5, 2013), http://www.techienews.co.uk/972757/adobehack- password-dump-analysis-shows-users-still-pathetic-choosing-passwords/ (last visited Sept. 18, 2017).

[54] In re LinkedIn User Privacy Litigation, 2014 WL 1323713 (N.D. Cal. 2014).

[55] LinkedIn, 2014 WL 1323713 at *7.

[56] 2014 WL 1323713 at *7.

[57] 2014 WL 1323713 at *7.

[58] "The use of digital signatures in communications with the state is defined in Government Code section 16.5 and allows electronic signatures that conform to the Secretary of State's regulations." Ni v. Slocum, 196 Cal. App. 4th 1636, 1655–56 (Cal. App. 1st Dist. 2011).

[59] Tyson, How Encryption Works, http://computer.howstuffworks.com/encryption6.htm (last visited Jan. 6, 2015).

[60] Oriyano, Cryptography: InfoSec Pro Guide 196 (McGraw Hill 2013).

private key, combines this encrypted bundle to the plaintext message, and sends the combination to Sally.
- Sally receives the message and sees that it came from Harry. She then pulls out his public key from the certificate authority (CA)[61] that they both trust and decrypts the hash. If it is decrypted successfully, the identity of the sender is validated. Once the hash is decrypted, Sally reruns the original hashing algorithm Harry used on the plaintext message and compares that hash value to the one she just decrypted. If the two match, then Sally knows that the message has not been altered.

## *Pretty Good Privacy: Bringing Encryption to the People*

"Pretty Good Privacy," or PGP, is a data encryption program developed in 1991 by Phil Zimmerman that provides cryptographic security and authentication for data communication.[62] Zimmerman created it in an effort to make strong encryption systems publicly available, and he distributed it for free.[63] PGP provides users with a reasonably simple way to encrypt files, produce private and public keys, use digital signatures, and more.[64] Nowadays, most people use the open source version of PGP, known as GPG, by going to the GPG website where the source code and binaries are available.[65] Once installed, the user has to generate his or her own key. The user can then upload a public key to the key server where others can search for and download it in order to send the user encrypted messages.

PGP is not as common today as it once was, and a push for an automatic "end-to-end" encrypted email service has been gaining momentum recently.[66] Automatic email encryption puts the burden of the encryption process on the service provider

[61] "The entity responsible for enrollment, creation, management, validation, and revocation of digital certificates." Cryptography, at 176.

[62] Garfinkel, PGP: Pretty Good Privacy 10 (O'Reilly 1995).

[63] PGP: Pretty Good Privacy, at 10.

[64] "'PGP' stands for 'pretty good privacy,' and that encryption device was generally effective at protecting e-mail conversations from outside monitoring … . PGP is also used to erase data from hard drives." United States v. Fullmer, 584 F.3d 132, 141 (3d Cir. 2009).

[65] Lambert, Email Encryption: Using PGP and S/MIME (Jul. 11, 2013), http://www.techrepublic.com/blog/it-security/email-encryption-using-pgp-and-s-mime/ (last visited Sept. 18, 2017).

[66] Agence France-Presse, NSA Spying Inspires ProtonMail End-to-End Encrypted Email Service (May 19, 2014), http://gadgets.ndtv.com/internet/news/nsa-spying-inspires-protonmail-end-to-end-encrypted-email-service-526769 (last visited Sept. 18, 2017).

rather than the user.[67] While major services such as Google and Yahoo have enhanced their security measures, widespread encrypted email service is still not yet a reality.[68]

## *Secure Sockets Layer (SSL): Securing Internet Data Transfer*

Secure Sockets Layer (SSL) and its later iteration, Transport Layer Security (TLS), are cryptographic protocols that help to ensure the security of servers, primarily public servers, by providing "authentication, privacy, and integrity."[69] SSL and TLS are in widespread common use, particularly for confidential user information in e-commerce and email, and their most recent iterations are held to be reasonably secure, when employed correctly.[70] (An exception is the Open SSL vulnerability known as Heartbleed.[71]) SSL and TLS allow clients and web servers to communicate securely using a two-layered security process that involves both symmetric and asymmetric keys.[72]

Let us take an example in which a client is using an e-commerce site and needs to supply sensitive information. The interaction between the client and the web server goes as follows: The client generates a randomly selected symmetric key and then uses the server's public key to encrypt his key.[73] Next, the client sends this encrypted key to the server, which in turn decrypts the key with its private key.[74] Once this is done, the two systems can communicate using good old symmetric

---

[67] Jason Stockman, codeveloper of a new end-to-end encrypted email service called ProtonMail, explains "'There's no installation. Everything happens behind the scenes automatically.'" Agence France-Presse, NSA Spying Inspires ProtonMail End-to-End Encrypted Email Service (May 19, 2014), http://gadgets.ndtv.com/internet/news/nsa-spying-inspires-protonmail-end-to-end-encrypted-email-service-526769 (last visited Sept. 18, 2017).

[68] Agence France-Presse.

[69] Lee, Malkin, et al., Cryptographic Strength of SSL/TLS Servers: Current and Recent Practices, Proceedings of 7th ACM SIGCOMM, 83 (2007).

[70] Cryptographic Strength of SSL/TLS Servers: Current and Recent Practices, at 85.

[71] Hunt, Everything You Need to Know About the Heartbleed SSL Bug (Apr. 9, 2014), http://www.troyhunt.com/2014/04/everything-you-need-to-know-about.html (last visited Sept. 18, 2017).

[72] "In reality, a client and a server engage in an SSL 'handshake' involving several different communication steps between the client and the server: initial 'hellos,' server authentication using an SSL certificate, potential client authentication, sending (by the client) and decryption (by the server) of a pre-master secret, generation of a master secret, generation of session keys, and formal completion of the handshake. Later communications within the same session then use the generated session keys to both encrypt and decrypt all the information transmitted during the session." In re Under Seal, 749 F.3d 276, 280 n.3 (4th Cir. 2014).

[73] Oriyano, Cryptography: InfoSec Pro Guide 196 233-34 (McGraw Hill 2013).

[74] Cryptography, at 233–34.

encryption.[75] When the client is finished, the session is ended and the symmetric key is discarded.[76]

## *Three Major Encryption Types: DES, AES, and RSA*

Accepted as a standard of encryption in the 1970s, DES encryption is no longer considered to be safe. It encrypts just 56 bits of data at a time and it is easily hacked. 3DES is a version of block cipher used today. Triple Data Encryption Standard (3DES) works as its name implies. Instead of using a single 56-bit key, it uses three separate 56-bit keys for three times the protection, but it takes longer to encrypt data. Block lengths are critical to the final resultant key strength. Financial institutions and businesses still use it, but newer forms of encryption will replace it.

Advanced Encryption Standard (AES), a more secure type of encryption, is used by governments and security organizations as well as businesses for confidential communication transmissions. AES uses "symmetric" key encryption that introduces end user security issue.

AES differs from other encryption types in that it encrypts data in a single block, instead of as individual bits of data. The block sizes determine the name for each kind of AES encrypted data:

- AES-128 encrypts blocks of a 128-bit size.
- AES-192 encrypts blocks of a 192-bit size.
- AES-256 encrypts blocks of a 256-bit size.

In addition to having different block sizes, each encryption method has a different number of rounds. These rounds are the processes of changing a plaintext piece of data into encrypted data or ciphered text. AES-128, for example, uses 10 rounds, and AES-256 uses 14 rounds.[77]

Today, AES encryption is used widely in many applications, and it is widely accepted as a secure encryption method.

"Rivest-Shamir-Adleman" (RSA) is another encryption tool to send data online using a public key; it is a secure means to send information between people unknown each other.

The fishes—Twofish, Blowfish, and Threefish—are other publicly available encryption tools that are utilized to password protect software products on the market.

[75] Cryptography, at 233–34.

[76] Cryptography, at 233–34.

[77] HP Tech Types: Linsey Knerl 8.20.

## Key Management

A chain is as strong as its weakest link. You may have the most sophisticated encryption for stored data and transmission of data, but the before and after something is encrypted are the most vulnerable links. This could take the form of leaving the information out in the open unencrypted, e.g., on a desk or in an unsecured laptop, or a careless or compromised employee. "Loose lips sink ships."

If you use symmetric-key encryption, the issue is how can you share the key in a "secure manner." Geography is probably the biggest determiner of why and how you would exchange keys and need to access the encryption key.

A critical factor in key security is the regular updating of keys and their management. This again implicates the need for a secure means in the exchange keys. One on one management of encryption keys might not seem a difficult task, but consider the inordinate magnitude of thousands of keys in any large corporation.

The life cycle of keys

- Creation
- Distribution
- Storage
- Backup (separate system)
- Tracking use of key
- Auto expiration date encoded
- Ability to terminate a user's key

Consider the number of keys times the number of expirations times the terminations or revocations.

In multilateral nation-state scenarios, the storage of data or the communication of data may raise issues of the need to use some higher encryption levels. Recently, US Department of State's Directorate of Defense Trade Controls (DDTC) announced interim final rule that amended the "Encryption Rule" under the International Traffic in Arms Regulations (ITAR) (22 C.F.R. §120.54).[78] This brought clarity to sensitive material transiting the Internet beyond the USA.

Another area of concern is where certain nation-states require companies to provide a "backdoor" to their systems or products. This requires a careful examination on your part of how authentication or encryption protocols may be compromised for your organization as a whole. The use of encryption must be examined along with other security concepts such as dual authentication, air gaping, and insider threats. In these situations, you may need to consider entirely separate and independent air gapped systems in your business model.[79]

---

[78] 84 Fed. Reg. 70887 to 70893 ("Interim Final Rule").

[79] Walsh, NJIT Cyber Investigations and the Law (2018).

## *Encryption Checklist*

[ ] How can encryption help—risk analysis
[ ] Value of data vs. cost of encryption—risk analysis
[ ] What are your family jewels, who may want your IP
[ ] Know your enemies' crypto skill level
[ ] Level and type of encryption
[ ] Transmission or storage or both divide into levels of and different security means
[ ] Access and management of keys
[ ] Air gap between encrypted and non-encrypted data
[ ] Encryption is one step in your security process, e.g., hash stored data
[ ] Layer your data on your servers to make security water tight compartments
[ ] Human interaction must be limited and compartmented
[ ] Vendor, supply chain, and third party access issues
[ ] Dual authentication
[ ] Legal, finance, PR, human resources, IT CISCO, B of D all need IN
[ ] Legal needs to give a current legal risk assessment and exposure
[ ] Human element: security background and reinvestigation checks

Your security protocol must be comprehensive across your organization and professionally built and involve all elements of the management team—ask for help!

## *Glossary of Cryptographic Keys*

- **A 40-bit key**—key with a length of 40 bits, once the upper limit of what could be exported from the USA and other countries without a license. Considered very insecure. *See* key size for a discussion of this and other lengths.
- **authentication key**—key used in a keyed-hash message authentication code, or HMAC.
- **benign key**—(NSA) a key that has been protected by encryption or other means so that it can be distributed without fear of it being stolen. Also called **BLACK key**.
- **content-encryption key (CEK)**—a key that may be further encrypted using a KEK, where the content may be a message, audio, image, video, executable code, etc.
- **crypto ignition key**—an NSA key storage device (KSD-64) shaped to look like an ordinary physical key.
- **cryptovariable**—NSA calls the output of a stream cipher a key or key stream. It often uses the term **cryptovariable** for the bits that control the stream cipher, what the public cryptographic community calls a key.
- **data encryption key (DEK)**—used to encrypt the underlying data.
- **derived key**—keys computed by applying a predetermined hash algorithm or key derivation function to a password or, better, a passphrase.
- **DRM key**—a key used in digital rights management to protect media.

- **electronic key**—(NSA) key that is distributed in electronic (as opposed to paper) form. *See* EKMS.
- **ephemeral key**—a key that only exists within the lifetime of a communication session.
- **expired key**—key that was issued for a use in a limited time frame (cryptoperiod in NSA parlance) which has passed and, hence, the key is no longer valid.
- **FIREFLY key**—(NSA) keys used in an NSA system based on public-key cryptography.
- **key derivation function (KDF)**—function used to derive a key from a secret value, e.g., to derive KEK from Diffie-Hellman key exchange.
- **key encryption key (KEK)**—key used to protect MEK keys (or DEK/TEK if MEK is not used).
- **key production key (KPK)**—key used to initialize a keystream generator for the production of other electronically generated keys.
- **key fill**—(NSA) loading keys into a cryptographic device. *See* fill device.
- **master key**—key from which all other keys (or a large group of keys) can be derived. Analogous to a physical key that can open all the doors in a building.
- **master encryption key (MEK)**—used to encrypt the DEK/TEK key. **master key encryption key (MKEK)**—used to encrypt multiple KEK keys. For example, an HSM can generate several KEK and wrap them with an MKEK before export to an external DB—such as OpenStack Barbican. [1] one-time pad **(OTP or OTPad)**—keying material that should be as long as the plaintext and should only be used once. If truly random and not reused, it's the most secure encryption method. *See* one-time pad article.
- **one-time password (OTP)**—one-time password based on a prebuilt single use code list or based on a mathematical formula with a secret seed known to both parties, uses event or time to modify output (see TOTP/HOTP).
- **paper key**—(NSA) keys that are distributed in paper form, such as printed lists of settings for rotor machines, or keys in punched card or paper tape formats. Paper keys are easily copied. *See* Walker spy ring, *RED key*.
- **poem key**—keys used by OSS agents in World War II in the form of a poem that was easy to remember. *See* Leo Marks.
- **public/private key**—in public-key cryptography, separate keys are used to encrypt and decrypt a message. The encryption key (**public key**) need not be kept secret and can be published. The decryption or **private key** must be kept secret to maintain confidentiality. Public keys are often distributed in a signed public-key certificate.
- **pre-placed key**—(NSA) large numbers of keys (perhaps a year's supply) that are loaded into an encryption device allowing frequent key change without refill.
- **RED key**—(NSA) symmetric key in a format that can be easily copied, e.g., *paper key* or unencrypted *electronic key*. Opposite of *BLACK* or *benign key*.
- **revoked key**—a public key that should no longer be used, typically because its owner is no longer in the role for which it was issued or because it may have been compromised. Such keys are placed on a certificate revocation list or **CRL**.

- **session key**—key used for one message or an entire communication session. *See traffic encryption key.*
- **symmetric key**—a key that is used both to encrypt and decrypt a message. Symmetric keys are typically used with a cipher and must be kept secret to maintain confidentiality.
- **traffic encryption key (TEK)/data encryption key (DEK)**—a symmetric key that is used to encrypt messages. TEKs are typically changed frequently, in some systems daily and in others for every message. See *session key*. DEK is used to specify any data form type (in communication payloads or anywhere else).
- **transmission security key (TSK)**—(NSA) seed for a pseudorandom number generator that is used to control a radio in frequency hopping or direct-sequence spread spectrum modes. *See* HAVE QUICK, SINCGARS, and electronic warfare.
- **seed key**—(NSA) a key used to initialize a cryptographic device so it can accept operational keys using benign transfer techniques. Also, a key used to initialize a pseudorandom number generator to generate other keys.
- **signature key**—public-key cryptography can also be used to electronically sign messages. The private key is used to create the electronic signature; the public key is used to verify the signature. Separate public/private key pairs **must** be used for signing and encryption. The former is called **signature keys**.
- **stream key**—the output of a stream cipher as opposed to the key (or *cryptovariable* in NSA parlance) that controls the cipher.
- **training key**—(NSA) unclassified key used for instruction and practice exercises.
- **type 1 key**—(NSA) keys used to protect classified information. *See* Type 1 product.
- **type 2 key**—(NSA) keys used to protect sensitive but unclassified (SBU) information. *See* Type 2 product.
- **Vernam key**—type of key invented by Gilbert Vernam in 1918. *See stream key.*
- **zeroized key**—key that has been erased (see zeroisation).

**Glossary References** Schneier, Applied Cryptography (Wiley & Sons 2d ed.); National Information Assurance (IA) Glossary, Committee on National Security Systems, CNSS Instruction No. 4009, 2010; Walsh, Cyber Investigations and the Law (NJIT 2018); Practices, Proceedings of 7th ACM SIGCOMM, 83 (2007); Wikipedia

## *Conclusion*

Encryption along the concepts and applications surrounding it are part of a larger picture: cybersecurity. Cyber threats are on the rise worldwide, with business and government leaders declaring them a major priority.[80] The field of cryptography is vast and this chapter can only touch on the surface concepts, but that does not lessen the importance of security for all users of the Internet and mobile devices. Best practice in cybersecurity is constantly evolving as the give and take continues between hackers and network defense systems, so it is important to stay updated and informed. Many excellent guides to Internet security and encryption exist with more detail and examples than we are able to provide; but gaining some knowledge, however slight, of the systems that come into play every time you hit "send" on an email or download a file can only be beneficial, and we hope that it may encourage you to do further research in the field.

[80] *See*, e.g., Garrie, Cybersecurity Becoming Real Issue for Boards of Directors, Daily J., Jun. 2, 2014; Barlyn, Wall Street watchdog to bolster reviews of brokerage security, Reuters, Oct. 29, 2014, http://www.reuters.com/article/2014/10/29/us-finra-cybersecurity-examinations-idUSKBN0II2DA20141029 (last visited Sept. 18, 2017).

# Chapter 8
# Law Firm Cybersecurity

## 8.1 Introduction

It is often said that water takes the path of least resistance. This is equally true of hackers seeking to break into law firm computer systems. This chapter discusses methods and practices to frustrate these hackers. As part of the discussion, we outline the rationale for why the digital communications and client files of law firms constitute high-value targets to a wide range of diversely motivated actors, many of whom are armed with increasingly sophisticated technologies (as well as proven low-tech methods) for penetrating a firm's systems. This chapter does not cover the specific forms of exposures (Trojans, denial-of-service attackers, etc.); instead, we focus on the best practices in preventing the hack. In doing so, we seek to provide context for the reality that law firms' security chains are only as strong as their weakest internal and external links.

At the outset, it is critical that law firms recognize the long-term incentives for targeting law firms[1] and the range of consequences to a firm of a successful attack. Principally, threat actors will have two central objectives: (1) to gain administrator or specific user access to a firm's computer systems or (2) to cause physical or virtual damage to a firm's computer or data storage systems.

[1] American Bar Association, Cybersecurity Legal Task Force Section of Science & Technology Law, Report to the House of Delegates: Resolution 109 (August 2014) at 4, http://www.americanbar.org/content/dam/aba/administrative/house_of_delegates/resolutions/2014_hod_annual_meeting_109.authcheckdam.pdf (last visited Oct. 1, 2017) ("The threat of cyber attacks against law firms is growing. Lawyers and law offices are facing unprecedented challenges from the widespread use of electronic records and mobile devices. There are many reasons for hackers to target the information being held by law firms. They collect and store large amounts of critical, highly valuable corporate records, including intellectual property, strategic business data, and litigation-related theories and records collected through e-discovery.")



D. B. Garrie et al., *Uncovering Digital Evidence*,
https://doi.org/10.1007/978-3-031-68118-9_8

The first goal, achieving access, allows cybercriminals to possess a client's data and communications and would generally enable a sufficiently sophisticated actor to transfer, alter, or delete this information, often without detection.[2] The second goal, causing physical or virtual damage to a firm's systems, constitutes a malicious and destructive act upon the enterprise[3] that generally requires no special access, because the attacks are either external or "insider" driven (e.g., a denial-of-service attack) or exploitative (e.g., attacking an unpatched operating system). Significantly, both forms of attacks can be deployed to steal confidential and market-sensitive information, as well as to hold data and systems hostage as part of an extortion scheme that requires a ransom to be paid (ransomware).[4]

Cyberattacks can be launched directly against a firm's systems or by exploiting employees, clients, vendors, and suppliers; for example, providers of software, data storage, human resource (HR) materials, and eDiscovery are all vectors through which threat actors may breach a law firm's systems.[5] In sum, law firms must understand that they are just as susceptible to cyberattacks as any other company, if not more so, and there are many potential points of entry for hackers.

In fact, law firms are often particularly attractive targets for cybercriminals. They are frequently high-value targets due to their possession of privileged and confidential attorney-client information. This includes confidential and sensitive communications, trade secrets, financial data, and intellectual property (IP), as well as market-sensitive information about litigation, government investigations, mergers, and acquisitions.

Irrespective of the nature and purpose of the attack, firms must anticipate the wide-ranging potential harms and consequences of being hacked. On top of the monetary costs of remediation, the long-term harms can be crippling and may

---

[2] Panko, Business Data Networks and Telecommunications (Prentice Hall 2003) ("The hacker is now in a position to wreak havoc in the system by means such as reading or altering sensitive information, changing or deleting key files, wiping out the hard drive, and using the compromised target to launch attacks against other targets.") While this access can be actively used to cause harm to a firm, it is also possible to use that access to passively ingest a firm's, or client's, sensitive data. Imagine a law firm that has a robust patent prosecution practice. If a cybercriminal wanted to engage in corporate espionage, it is unlikely it would be able to access a company's research, but once that information is sent to the law firm to prepare the patent application, it might be in significant jeopardy if the law firm does not have proper cybersecurity processes in place.

[3] Bento and Regina, "Empirical Test of a Hacking Model: An Exploratory Study," Communications of the Association for Information Systems: Vol. 14, Article 32 (2004) at 681, available at http://aisel.aisnet.org/cais/vol14/iss1/32 (last visited Oct. 1, 2017) ("When hackers are unable to achieve control of the target, they often express their frustration by launching Denial-of-Service (DoS) attacks (such as *Smurf*, *Fraggle* and *Syn*) that disrupt services or make them inaccessible to legitimate users, networks, and systems.")

[4] Proctor, Ransomware Hackers Pose Threat to B.C. Law Firms—British Columbia, CBC News, http://www.cbc.ca/beta/news/canada/british-columbia/ransomware-hackers-pose-threat-to-b-c-law-firms-1.2898490 (last visited Oct. 1, 2017).

[5] *See* Huggins, Supplier Security, Managing Partner 17 (Mar. 20, 2015).

include damage to client relationships, disruption of day-to-day operations, reputational harm, and loss of internal and public confidence in the firm's continuity.[6]

Inevitably, a breach will also implicate difficult cost-benefit (and hindsight) analyses about the need for enhanced security, client and regulatory disclosure, government cooperation, media response, remediation, and enterprise resiliency. A successful attack on a law firm draws quick and repeated inquiries from clients, regulators, and the media. Attacks on law firms are of great interest to these constituencies (as well as to a firm's competitors and the public at large), not only because of the highly sensitive nature of attorney-client matters—and the often embarrassing secrets revealed—but also because many firms have developed extensive best practices in advising their clients on issues of cybersecurity, data privacy, information protection, crisis management, and contingency planning. This is an irony that has not been lost on the diverse community of hackers that seek to target law firms.

The nature, timing, coordination, and messaging of a firm's response to a breach are therefore critical and require substantial preparation before the breach takes place.

## 8.2 The Threat Landscape for Law Firms

In the wake of the mounting number of high-profile cyberattacks,[7] law firms can no longer metaphorically put their head in the sand. The impression that "only large law firms" or "only a few law firms" are subject to cyberattacks is a mistaken feeling of comfort. There is consensus among those in the field that there are only three types of operating enterprises left in the world (including law firms): those that have been hacked; those that are going to be hacked; and those that have been hacked, but don't know it.

Thus, it is critical for law firms to realize—and realize quickly—that they are attractive targets and vulnerable to a wide range of threat actors seeking access to their information. Indeed, because law firms act as warehouses of sensitive and personally identifiable client data, they are in many ways the perfect victims: high-impact, high-vulnerability, silent sufferers.[8]

As a result, the Federal Bureau of Investigation and other authorities have issued a series of alerts to warn law firms and their clients about the increasing risk of

[6] Compounding the problem, most insurance carriers do not recognize all of these long-term harms resulting from a data breach as an insurable risk.

[7] *See* Storm, Ransomware Attack on DLA Piper Puts Law Firms, Clients on Red Alert, The American Lawyer, (Jun. 27, 2017), http://www.americanlawyer.com/id=1202791614770/Ransomware-Attack-on-DLA-Piper-Puts-Law-Firms-Clients-on-Red-Alert

[8] Simshaw, Legal Ethics and Data Security: Our Individual and Collective Obligation to Protect Client Data, 32 Am. J. Trial Advoc. 549, 550 (2015).

cyberattacks.[9] Indeed, recent events prove what law enforcement officials have been warning companies about for years. As hacking tools and hackers for hire proliferate in certain corners of the Internet, it has become easier for criminals to breach computer networks as a way to further a range of crimes, from insider trading to IP and identity theft to extortion.

In 2016, LawFirm CyberSecurity Scorecard reported "… 40% of surveyed law firms had experienced a data breach in 2016 and did not know about it."[10] In June of 2017, DLA Piper—a large multinational firm with estimated revenues of $2.5 billion—was reportedly attacked by "wiper-ware," leaving the firm completely without access to its own data.[11]

Perhaps most notorious among law firm breaches was the leak of millions of documents and records from Panama City-based law firm Mossack Fonseca in April 2016, which exposed the business, financial, and tax dealings of thousands of world leaders, public figures, and popular celebrities, as well as their global networks of friends, family members, and advisors.

The implications of the Mossack Fonseca breach and the ensuing disclosures (the "Panama Papers") are still playing out legally, politically, and in the court of public opinion—and will for years to come. Depending upon regional geopolitics, authorities around the world are either now gathering evidence for potential criminal cases against the firm and its clients or attempting to spin the discussion about the significance of this information.

Putting aside questions about who was responsible for the Panama Papers breach and the motivations therefor, experts quickly reached important conclusions about the nature of the attack:[12]

- The breach was long-standing (occurring over more than a year) and was not discovered by the firm until public disclosures of the records.
- The outflow of client-sensitive information was voluminous (dating back to the 1970s and estimated at 4.2 million emails, 3 million database files, 2.1 million PDFs, 1.1 million images, 320,166 text files, and 2242 files in other formats).
- The dissemination was continuous and widespread. There was a global appetite and capacity to analyze and further publicize the data as "news worthy" (an effort that is still ongoing).
- The consequences to the firm and its clients will be long term; investigations have been opened in numerous jurisdictions and public disclosures are continuing.

---

[9] Goldstein, Law Firms Are Pressed on Security for Data, DealBook (Mar. 26, 2014), http://dealbook.nytimes.com/2014/03/26/law-firms-scrutinized-as-hacking-increases/

[10] Report, Law Firm Cyber Security Scorecard The State of the Legal Industry Right Now, LogicForce (2017), available for download at https://www.logicforce.com/reports/detail/cyber-security-q1 (last visited Oct. 1, 2017).

[11] Roberts, Law Firm DLA Piper Reels Under Cyber Attack, Fate of Files Unclear, Fortune (Jun. 29, 2017), http://fortune.com/2017/06/29/dla-piper-cyber-attack/

[12] *See* Temperton and Burgess, "Panama Papers: The Security Flaws at the Heart of Mossack Fonseca," Wired UK, Apr. 6, 2016, http://www.wired.co.uk/news/archive/2016-04/06/panama-papers-mossack-fonseca-website-security-problems

- Mossack Fonseca, as many firms do, relied upon antiquated and vulnerable information technology (IT) platforms, lax data and encryption protections, and outdated security access protocols.

According to authorities, the growing attacks on law firms also reflect the enhanced ability of threat actors to scour the digital landscape for sophisticated types of information and tools. In February 2016, a posting appeared on an underground Russian website called DarkMoney.cc, in which the person offered to sell his hacking services to other would-be cyber thieves and identified specific law firms as potential targets.[13] Of note, YouTube also hosts videos that offer hacking tutorials.[14]

Law firm hackers, like commercial fishermen casting wide nets, often seek to gather large amounts of information indiscriminately and then analyze it later to see how it could be of value. This, in turn, can make it even more difficult to determine the actors responsible and the ultimate objectives of their attacks.

Understandably, the risks to law firms have raised concerns among clients, many of whom have now taken matters into their own hands. Many clients are now asking for certifications about security, whereas others are conducting their own assessments of the firms they hire. Even major corporate clients that might not independently question their law firm's cybersecurity practices are increasingly being compelled to do so by government agencies like the Securities and Exchange Commission's Office of Compliance Inspections and Examinations (OCIE).[15] The State of New York has recognized the need for enhanced cybersecurity by being the first state to implement mandatory cybersecurity requirements on financial institutions. The regulation will require third-party vendors, such as law firms, to be compliant with cybersecurity best practices.[16]

In response to this new phenomenon, some law firms now affirmatively disclose that they are compliant with cybersecurity standards such as ISO 27001.[17] Other law firms even view their investments in cybersecurity as offering a potential competitive advantage to attract clients.[18]

---

[13] *See generally* Hong and Sidel, "Hackers Breach Law Firms, Including Cravath and Weil Gotshal," Wall St. J., Mar. 29, 2016, http://www.wsj.com/articles/hackers-breach-cravath-swaine-other-big-law-firms-1459293504

[14] Segall, YouTube's "RAT" Problem, CNN (Jul. 29, 2015), http://money.cnn.com/2015/07/29/technology/youtube-ratting-problem/index.html

[15] Rashbaum et al., Cybersecurity: Business Imperative for Law Firms, N.Y.L.J. (Dec. 10, 2014).

[16] Tribe, As Cybersecurity hurdles loom, smaller firms face big challenges, The American Lawyer (Sept. 27, 2016), http://www.americanlawyer.com/id=1202768670107/As-Cybersecurity-Hurdles-Loom-Smaller-Firms-Face-Big-Challenges?slreturn=20160929162108

[17] Pratt, Law Firm Makes a Case for Security Certification, CIO (Aug. 28, 2015), http://www.cio.com/article/2969323/security/law-firm-makes-a-case-for-security-certification.html

[18] *See* Cybersecurity Ignorance Is Big Risk for Law Firms & Corporate Counsel, ALM Legal Intelligence Analysts Find, ALM, Dec. 16, 2015, http://www.alm.com/press-room/cybersecurity-ignorance-is-big-risk-for-law-firms-corporate-counsel-alm-legal-intelligence-analysts-find/

Notwithstanding the material risks to attorney-client relationships—and the protection of communications, IP, business strategies, public market transactions, and sensitive governmental affairs—the legal industry has generally operated within a set of cybersecurity guidelines that are vague on basic standards and best practices. (Note, though, that the ABA Model Rules of Professional Responsibility were updated, especially in Model Rules 1.1 and 1.6, to address cybersecurity.)[19] Also, the Florida Supreme Court has recognized the need for increased awareness of technology and cybersecurity by requiring technology-related CLE courses.[20]

Inevitably, cybersecurity standards for the legal profession will change, either voluntarily (e.g., through the American Bar Association), by regulation (e.g., the Federal Trade Commission, Department of Justice, SEC), or because of the concerns and liability claims of clients. Until appropriate guidelines are set, however, it is essential for every firm to understand and assess the cyber exposures it faces.

## 8.3 Don't Be the Low-Hanging Fruit

As mentioned previously, many firms do not realize that everyone is a potential target. You may be a target because of who you do business with, information you have, or the simple fact that you are on the Internet. So, how do you go about protecting yourself? One of the easiest ways is to take simple measures that prevent you from being an easy target. While skilled or determined hackers will be able to bypass most basic security measures, simply having them in place will deter many threat actors. The following sections discuss simple ways to avoid being the low-hanging fruit.

## 8.4 Don't Be the Low-Hanging Fruit—The First Step: Proper Password Management

One of the first and best ways to avoid being low-hanging fruit is proper password management. To understand password management, you need to understand how passwords are stored in a Windows environment. In Windows, passwords are not stored in plain text; instead, the hash of a password is stored. Some of you reading

[19] Model Rules of Prof'l Conduct R. 1.1, cmt. 2 (Am. Bar Ass'n 2012) ("To maintain the requisite knowledge and skill, a lawyer should keep abreast of changes in the law and its practice, including the benefits and risks associated with relevant technology"); *see also* Model Rules of Prof'l Conduct R. 1.6(c) ("A lawyer shall make reasonable efforts to prevent the inadvertent or unauthorized disclosure of, or unauthorized access to, information relating to the representation of a client.")

[20] Li, Florida Supreme Court approves mandatory tech CLE classes for lawyers, ABA Journal (September 30, 2016), http://www.abajournal.com/news/article'florida_supreme_court_approves_mandatory_tech_cles_for_lawyers

this might have heard the word *hash* in the context of computer forensics; the term is used similarly here.[21] A hash is a numeric value of a fixed length that uniquely identifies a piece of data. Windows creates a hash that corresponds to each password by executing a mathematical formula on the password; the result is a series of letters and numbers that represent the password. Windows then stores the hash and does not store the password. So, when you enter a password into your Windows computer, the computer executes the hash formula on the password and compares the result to the stored hash of the password. If the hashes match, the computer knows you entered the right password and lets you log onto your computer. This process protects the security of your password by storing only the hash and not the password itself. The key is that the hash formula only works one way, meaning that you can't take a hash and turn it back into a password.

Windows allows both uppercase and lowercase letters, numbers, and punctuation symbols to be included in a password. With that set of characters, there are 6,634,204,312,890,625 possible different passwords if one restricts the length of the password to 8 characters. Hackers are often left to "brute-force" crack a password, which means that they have to try all of those combinations until they are successful. Attackers may alternatively attempt *birthday Attacks*, which target collisions in hash functions, where two distinct inputs result in the same hash. If hackers could enter a password every second, it would still take them 210 million years to guess. That sounds pretty safe, right? Not really. In 2012, Jeremi Gosney of Stricture Consulting Group created a computer that was able to guess 350 billion passwords per second.[22] As a result, he could crack any eight-character Windows password in less than 6 hours. Not so safe now, are we? Well, consider this: If you used ten characters for our passwords—a mere two more characters—Gosney's machine would take five and a half years to crack them.

Of course, Mr. Gosney's research was done in 2012. Machines and password-cracking methods have evolved since then. Still, realize that to be successful, password-cracking routines need to try different passwords over and over. Windows has a built-in prevention mechanism to prevent anyone from repeatedly trying passwords. You can set Windows to lock an account after any number of consecutively entered bad passwords.[23] A good rule of thumb is five bad passwords in a row. That means after five guesses, the account is locked. When the account is locked, it no longer allows someone to log into the account. That action has two results. First, the hacker cannot make any more password guesses until the account is unlocked. Second, the person who (legitimately) uses the account immediately finds out that

---

[21] Konheim, Hashing for Storage: Data Management, in Hashing in Computer Science: Fifty Years of Slicing and Dicing (Wiley 2010).

[22] Goodin, 25-GPU Cluster Cracks Every Standard Windows Password In <6 Hours, Ars Technica (Dec. 9, 2012), http://arstechnica.com/security/2012/12/25-gpu-cluster-cracks-every-standard-windows-password-in-6-hours/

[23] Account lockout threshold, Microsoft: Technet, July 17, 2014, https://technet.microsoft.com/en-us/library/hh994574.aspx

they cannot use it anymore. This person reports the lock to the IT department, which then is alerted to the possibility that someone is trying to hack the account.

Another great weapon against brute-force attacks is to *change your password frequently*.[24] If a hacker is trying to brute-force attack your password and you change the password, in essence that causes the hacker to have to start all over again from the beginning in guessing passwords. Changing passwords monthly is a good idea but can sometimes be a bit much for most users. A change every 90 days should strike a good balance between being a nuisance and practicing good password management.

Proper password management also means training your users to use good passwords. So far we have been talking about brute-force attack: guessing all combinations of letters and numbers. Another, sometimes easier method is what is called a *dictionary attack*.[25] Hackers are known to start guessing passwords by trying words in the dictionary. Sometimes that will include foreign-language dictionaries as well. Think you are smart by changing the letter "I" to a "1" or an "S" to a "$" in your password? That is called password "munging." Hackers compensate for munging nowadays as well. Best advice here? Forget words in the dictionary.

Unfortunately, with complex passwords, users often find themselves at a loss to remember the passwords. As a result, many resort to writing down passwords on a sticky note and putting that note on their monitors. If an organization allows that activity to occur, it might as well return to the use of "1234" as a password. The solution for remembering passwords is a password management application.[26] Many password management applications are available, and many of them are free. Some are web based so that users can access their passwords from multiple locations. The use of a password-protected Word document or Excel spreadsheet is also acceptable.

Some organizations still tolerate the most egregious violation of sound security hygiene: password sharing.[27] The biggest problem with this practice is that it removes all accountability for actions in an environment. If multiple people know passwords to one's account, it is exceedingly difficult to properly ascribe blame if that account is then used in an unauthorized fashion. All too often, computer forensic investigations grind to a screeching halt because it is determined that multiple

---

[24] Cocks, The Importance of Changing Passwords, NSK (Oct. 2, 2009), http://blog.nskinc.com/topic/data-security/IT-Services-Boston/The-Importance-of-Changing-Passwords (last visited 10/1/2017).

[25] Goodin, 25-GPU Cluster Cracks Every Standard Windows Password In <6 Hours, Ars Technica (Dec. 9, 2012), http://arstechnica.com/security/2012/12/25-gpu-cluster-cracks-every-standard-windows-password-in-6-hours/

[26] Glaser, You Need a Password Manager. Here Are Some Good Free Ones, Wired (Jan. 24, 2016), http://www.wired.com/2016/01/you-need-a-password-manager/; Silver et al., Password Managers: Attacks and Defenses, Usenix (Aug. 2014), https://www.usenix.org/system/files/conference/usenixsecurity14/sec14-paper-silver.pdf

[27] Whitty et al., Individual Differences in Cyber Security Behaviors: An Examination of Who Is Sharing Passwords, 18 Cyberpsychol. Behav. Soc. Networks 3 (Jan. 2015), available at http://www.ncbi.nlm.nih.gov/pmc/articles/PMC4291202/ (last visited Oct. 1, 2017).

people had access to the account in question and therefore it was impossible to determine who was responsible for the offending action. Some organizations feel the need to share passwords with their IT department. That practice is unnecessary. Proper planning would allow IT to get into any device through the ability to reset a password.

Proper password management extends to mobile devices as well. While "bring your own device" (BYOD) is prevalent today, that doesn't stop a company from extending its password policies to those mobile devices.[28] In fact, since version 2003, Microsoft Exchange has had a feature built in that allows a company to force mobile devices to be encrypted and require a password of a certain length that would be changed periodically.[29]

One other thing to keep in mind is that brute-force password cracking works best when the database containing the hashes is stolen. Once stolen, the hashes can be brute-force cracked offline without any detection. Therefore, proper protection of your computers to prevent the stealing of hashes is important (this is discussed later).

To summarize, implement and practice the following password policies:

- Ignore words from the dictionary.
- Use passwords at least ten characters in length; the bigger the better.
- Implement a lockout policy in your environment to catch brute-force attempts.
- Change your passwords every 90 days.
- Do not ignore or exclude mobile devices.
- Do not ignore or exclude administrative accounts running on servers.

## 8.5 Don't Be the Low-Hanging Fruit—Don't Forget to Apply Patches

We have discussed password policies as a basic step to ensure that your system will not be low-hanging fruit that is particularly appealing to hackers. Another important and easy step a company can take to help shore up its defenses is to apply updates and patches in a timely fashion. While it would be unreasonable to insist that a company apply patches as soon as they are released, especially to production servers, statistics on exploited companies show that administrators generally take way too long to apply patches. The 2015 Verizon data breach investigations report showed that 99.9% of companies that were compromised through the exploitation of a known vulnerability were actually compromised more than a year after the

[28] Lord, BYOD Security: Expert Tips on Policy, Mitigating Risks, & Preventing a Breach, Digital Guardian (Jan. 12, 2016), https://digitalguardian.com/blog/byod-security-expert-tips-policy-mitigating-risks-preventing-breach

[29] Lord, BYOD Security: Expert Tips on Policy, Mitigating Risks, & Preventing a Breach.

vulnerability was published and publicized.[30] That statistic means that administrators were waiting for more than a year to patch known vulnerabilities. That delay is clearly not a best practice. While actual best practices will depend on the nature, risk profile, and systems of a given business, the regular and reasonably timely application of patches is essential to maintaining good security hygiene for any organization.[31]

The following areas should be considered, first and foremost, when applying patches:

1. Patches to operating systems (Windows, Linux, Mac)
2. Patches to firewalls, wireless routers, and other network devices
3. Patches to user applications such as Microsoft Office, Adobe Acrobat, Adobe Flash
4. Recommended configuration changes

Item number 4 is as important as the first three but is often overlooked. It does not require installing updated files; rather, it usually involves adjusting the system settings to improve security. Those changes may be to the Windows Registry or an option in an application. An example is the disabling of older versions of Secure Sockets Layer, or SSL, on a web server.[32] SSL deals with encrypted communication between a client and a server, and older versions are vulnerable to some attacks.

## 8.6 Don't Be the Low-Hanging Fruit—Secure Your Perimeter

Owners of homes and businesses protect them with locks, guards, alarm systems, and other forms of security. The type of protection may be as simple as a lock on a door, but quite often it involves multiple layers of security with notifications for various events. Access to gain entry into a facility is controlled by keys, codes, and identification. The more guarded the facility, the more layers in place. Your network can and should also be controlled in the same way.[33] Protecting your perimeter is an important deterrent to those who wish to gain access to your environment.

---

[30] Report, 2015 Data Breach Investigations, Verizon Enterprise Solutions, available at https://msisac.cisecurity.org/whitepaper/documents/1.pdf (last visited 10/1/2017).

[31] For more information, see A Practical Methodology for Implementing a Patch Management Process, SANS (2003), https://www.sans.org/reading-room/whitepapers/bestprac/practical-methodology-implementing-patch-management-process-1206 (last visited Oct. 1, 2017); Rosato, Best Practices for Applying Service Packs, Hotfixes and Security Patches, Microsoft: Developer Network, https://msdn.microsoft.com/en-us/library/cc750077.aspx (last visited Oct. 1, 2017).

[32] What Is SSL (Secure Sockets Layer) and What Are SSL Certificates?, Digicert, https://www.digicert.com/ssl.htm (last visited Oct. 1, 2017).

[33] Edwards, Security At the Edge: Locking Down the Network Perimeter, IT Security (Feb. 4, 2008).

One of the most basic protections for your perimeter, and another way to avoid being the low-hanging fruit, is a firewall. What is a firewall? Basically, a *firewall* is a device that sits between your network and the Internet. A firewall acts as a gateway or a traffic cop, monitoring communication going between your environment and the rest of the world.[34] A firewall can deny traffic, allow traffic, or just monitor and log traffic. Some are simple: Plug them in, make some configuration changes, and let them go. Others are more complex, requiring hours to properly configure.

The above diagram illustrates the placement of a firewall within a network. The diagram also shows two purposes of a firewall. The first is connectivity between laptops and desktops in your environment and the Internet.[35] The second is connectivity for servers that communicate with the outside world.[36] Those types of servers may be email servers, web servers, or FTP servers but are collectively known as *forward-facing servers*, in that they are directly accessible by others using the Internet.[37] Note that the email and FTP servers are in a separate area from the rest of the network. This placement is commonly known as a demilitarized zone (DMZ).[38] The reason for placing forward-facing servers in the DMZ is because those servers need more open communication to the outside world and are more likely to be compromised due to their accessibility from the outside world.[39] Should those servers become compromised, the rest of your network can be protected by limiting the type of network traffic that occurs between the servers in the DMZ and the rest of the computers in your environment.[40]

Placing a firewall around your forward-facing systems allows the firewall to act as a traffic cop for communications between your network and the Internet.[41] What can that traffic cop do? First, it can limit the communications.[42] For example, your email server may have a built-in web server so that employees can retrieve email via a web browser. A proper way to implement that feature is not to allow traffic over unencrypted HTTP (e.g., http://myemail.com) but only over encrypted HTTPS (e.g. https://myemail.com). The firewall can limit that traffic by allowing only HTTPS

[34] Ingham and Forrest, A History and Survey of Network Firewalls (Technical Report TR-CS-2002-37), University of New Mexico (2002), available at http://www.cs.unm.edu/~treport/tr/02-12/firewall.pdf (last visited Oct. 1, 2017).

[35] Ingham and Forrest, A History and Survey of Network Firewalls.

[36] Ingham and Forrest, A History and Survey of Network Firewalls.

[37] *See generally* Security Best Practices to Protect Internet Facing Web Servers, Microsoft, http://social.technet.microsoft.com/wiki/contents/articles/13974.security-best-practices-to-protect--internet-facing-web-servers.aspx

[38] Rouse, DMZ (demilitarized zone) [definition], TechTarget, http://searchsecurity.techtarget.com/definition/DMZ

[39] Rouse, DMZ (demilitarized zone) [definition].

[40] Rouse, DMZ (demilitarized zone) [definition].

[41] Lewis and Knopf, CPAs, PC, Computer Protection: Call a Traffic Cop, 3 Financial Rx 3 (Mar. 2010), http://www.lewis-knopf.com/newsletters/financial-rx-article/computer-protection-call-a-traffic-cop/

[42] Lewis and Knopf, CPAs, PC, Computer Protection: Call a Traffic Cop.

traffic to get to the web server. A properly configured firewall should be set up to enable only that traffic which is necessary and deny all other traffic. The other thing that a traffic cop can do is look for traffic that should not occur. What if your email server all of a sudden started accepting FTP requests or starting sending traffic to another FTP server? Your firewall can be configured to look for that traffic and block it. Another example would be finding unencrypted, readable data being sent over HTTPS, which is an avenue for encrypted communications. Your firewall can also act as a traffic cop by looking for traffic going to certain IP addresses or coming from certain IP addresses that may be suspicious.[43]

One common misstep that many people make is neglecting to implement password controls on their firewall. The most egregious of violations is when people do not change the out-of-the-box password for the administrative account. In November of 2014, an article in *Network World* discussed a website that broadcasted more than 73,000 Internet-accessible cameras.[44] How were the hackers able to do that? They just used the default passwords for each camera, connected, and started broadcasting. A properly functioning firewall would block the hacker from broadcasting anything. However, if the default password on a firewall is not changed, the hackers will instead use that account to give themselves an open door to come into your network and steal whatever they want.

Another device that can help with protecting a firm's perimeter is an intrusion detection system (IDS).[45] An IDS sits inside your network and monitors traffic for suspicious activity.[46] Think of an IDS as an antivirus (AV) application, but for network traffic. Your AV is programmed to look for applications with specific signatures or behaviors indicating that they are viruses.[47] An IDS looks for patterns or behaviors that would indicate someone may have hacked into your computer network and is stealing data.[48] An IDS system is not a replacement for a firewall, nor is a firewall a replacement for an IDS. The two devices work in tandem to block traffic and identify malicious traffic.[49]

---

[43] For an example of creating these types of rules, see Add or Edit Firewall Rule, Microsoft: Technet, https://technet.microsoft.com/en-us/library/cc753558.aspx (last visited Oct. 1, 2017).

[44] Smith, Peeping into 73,000 Unsecured Security Cameras Thanks to Default Passwords, Network World (Nov. 6, 2014), http://www.networkworld.com/article/2844283/microsoft-subnet/peeping-into-73-000-unsecured-security-cameras-thanks-to-default-passwords.html

[45] Berge, What Is Intrusion Detection?, SANS, https://www.sans.org/security-resources/idfaq/what-is-intrusion-detection/1/1 (last visited Oct. 1, 2017); Rouse, Intrusion Detection (ID) [definition], TechTarget, http://searchmidmarketsecurity.techtarget.com/definition/intrusion-detection

[46] Berge, Understanding Intrusion Detection Systems, SANS, https://www.sans.org/reading-room/whitepapers/detection/understanding-intrusion-detection-systems-337 (last visited Oct. 10, 2017).

[47] Rouse, Antivirus Software [definition], TechTarget, http://searchsecurity.techtarget.com/definition/antivirus-software

[48] Berge, Understanding Intrusion Detection Systems, SANS, https://www.sans.org/reading-room/whitepapers/detection/understanding-intrusion-detection-systems-337 (last visited Oct. 10, 2017).

[49] Snyder, Do You Need an IDS or IPS, or Both?, TechTarget, http://searchsecurity.techtarget.com/Do-you-need-an-IDS-or-IPS-or-both

## 8.7 Don't Be the Low-Hanging Fruit—Have Someone Monitor Your Borders

Just like your alarm system needs someone to respond to it, or your guards need someone to whom they report, your firewall needs somewhere to report. Better yet, your company needs to have someone monitor the firewall and respond to potential security incidents. Monitoring firewalls, and other security systems, is one of the most neglected security activities. An organization may have all the protection in the world, but it is useless if no one is there to monitor what is going on. Take the example mentioned previously regarding the blocking of certain IP addresses. How does a firm know what IP addresses to block? Monitoring of firewall or IDS systems could indicate consistent, malicious activity coming from a specific IP address. With that information, the firewall could be configured to block all traffic to and from that address.

Monitoring helps with setting a baseline of expected network traffic.[50] Creation of a baseline is key to finding malicious activity.[51] The reason that organizations will forgo monitoring, or not monitor correctly, is that the amount of data generated by a firewall or IDS system can be daunting. For large organizations, it can be downright impossible.[52] The solution is to generate a baseline of what is expected traffic.[53] A Security Information and Event Management (SIEM) tool can both aggregate large quantities of data and use this information to establish baselines. A baseline will show what types of traffic one can expect in one's environment. A baseline will also provide information as to how much data will typically traverse the firewall to the outside Internet. With that information, rules can be created to identify unusual types of network traffic or large increases in traffic.[54] To illustrate this concept, consider the following scenario. An organization reports a data breach. The investigation reveals that stolen information was compressed into ZIP files and the ZIP files were renamed as JPG files. The fake JPG files were then put on the company's website and downloaded through that public-facing website. No alarms were triggered because JPG files being downloaded from a website is quite normal. However,

---

[50] White Paper, Baseline Process Best Practices, Cisco (Oct. 3, 2005), available at http://www.cisco.com/c/en/us/support/docs/availability/high-availability/15112-HAS-baseline.html (last visited Oct. 1, 2017).

[51] Beal, Intrusion Detection (IDS) and Prevention (IPS) Systems, Webopedia (July 15, 2005), http://www.webopedia.com/DidYouKnow/Computer_Science/intrusion_detection_prevention.asp

[52] Bejtlich, Top Seven Network Traffic Monitoring Challenges, TechTarget, http://searchnetworking.techtarget.com/tip/Top-seven-network-traffic-monitoring-challenges

[53] *See*, e.g., Brandenburg, How to Set a Network Performance Baseline for Network Monitoring, TechTarget, http://searchnetworking.techtarget.com/How-to-set-a-network-performance-baseline-for-network-monitoring

[54] Avoiding Network Traffic Confusion with Consistent Firewall Rules, TechTarget, http://searchsecurity.techtarget.com/magazineContent/Avoiding-Network-Traffic-Confusion-with-Consistent-Firewall-Rules

if the client had included a trigger for very large JPG files, such as these were, then it is possible the activity could have been detected and stopped.

One trap that organizations commonly fall into is the "set it and forget it" mindset.[55] Security is an ever-evolving discipline. What was once considered a good practice can become a bad practice as the relevant technology evolves. For example, years ago it was considered a secure practice to dispose of hard drives by using a magnet to wipe them clean.[56] With today's new hard drives, not only is that practice not considered a best practice, but magnets, except for extremely powerful ones, are ineffective in wiping hard drives.[57] The other issue with "set it and forget it" is that hackers are constantly evolving their methods and attacks.[58] With each new vulnerability that is published by Microsoft, Apple, US-CERT (through the CVE list), or others, hackers attempt to exploit those vulnerabilities on unpatched systems. Especially in the case of a vulnerability that doesn't have a fix, or has an automated fix, the only way for a company to protect itself is to adjust its protections.

Perimeter controls should not stop at just a firewall or IDS system. A firewall may protect one entry point into your network, but there are usually many entry points into a given system. Consider the following list:[59]

1. *Mobile devices.* Cell phones and tablets are quite often used outside of your network. Therefore, these devices constitute another entry point into your perimeter. Any plan dealing with perimeter protections should include defenses for these devices. Encryption (discussed later and in Chap. 7) and proper password management (previously discussed) should be considered. However, one also needs to consider limiting the type of data accessible by mobile devices, as well as mobile device management (MDM) tools that allow remote deactivation or wiping of stolen devices.
2. *Wireless networks.* Whether used for internal staff or guests, wireless networks are another entry point into your environment. Some companies do away with wireless networks altogether. Best practices will segment or separate guest networks from the rest of a firm's network environment, often with physically separate network cables, switches, and routers to prevent any access to the firm's environment by a wireless network. Routine scanning is also important to identify new wireless networks that may pop up in your environment. A cell phone

[55] Donovan, The Days of a "Set It and Forget It" Approach to Endpoint Security Are Over, Says ESG, FierceITSecurity (Jan. 13, 2015), http://www.fierceitsecurity.com/story/days-set-it-and-forget-it-approach-endpoint-security-are-over-says-esg/2015-01-13

[56] Wright, Overwriting Hard Drive Data, SANS (Jan. 15, 2009), https://digital-forensics.sans.org/blog/2009/01/15/overwriting-hard-drive-data/

[57] Wright, Overwriting Hard Drive Data.

[58] Hackers Are Evolving, Comms. Bus., Dec. 14, 2015, http://commsbusiness.co.uk/features/hackers-are-evolving/

[59] For a deeper analysis of new points of entry that affect perimeter security, see Buecker et al., Understanding IT Perimeter Security (IBM, 2008), available at http://www.redbooks.ibm.com/redpapers/pdfs/redp4397.pdf (last visited Oct. 1, 2017).

or tablet acting as a wireless hot spot, when not monitored, can be a recipe for disaster.

3. *Portable storage devices.* Tapes, CD/DVD, and USB drives must all be considered perimeter devices, as they can contain client data and be accessed outside of your environment. Encryption of these devices is discussed later, but some firms choose to restrict their use altogether by employing technological restrictions on their use.

## 8.8 Encryption

As discussed in Chap. 7, encryption can be a very effective tool in protecting a law firm's sensitive data in the event its perimeter security measures are breached.

## 8.9 Summary

Many organizations are hacked simply because they are easy to hack. The first step to keep your firm from being hacked is to avoid being an easy target: the low-hanging fruit. Timely updating of computers, having a proper password policy, and implementing even a basic firewall all go a long way toward making sure your organization is not hacked just because it was the easiest target. These controls will not only make it difficult for a hacker to enter your network, but they will allow for monitoring of traffic taking place between your network and the Internet.

Until political and law enforcement solutions evolve, law firms will remain primarily responsible for their own defense. As a result, it is now incumbent upon all law firms to understand why they represent a potentially attractive target, as well as the varied and multifarious ways to avoid becoming an easy target for hackers. To this end, although the discussion in this chapter is not an exhaustive list or a description of the methods and practices that exist, it is meant to serve as an introduction to common practices available to frustrate the hacker knocking at your door.

# Chapter 9
# Artificial Intelligence

## 9.1 Introduction

The history of AI is most fairly captured by first acknowledging the philosophical ideas that inspired the eventual creation of AI. As early as the twelfth and thirteenth centuries, inventors created "automatons" which are referred to as the early ancestors of robots.[1] The word "automaton" comes from Greek and means "acting on one's own will."[2] These self-operated mechanical creations included automatic wine dispensers to water operated orchestra automatons whereby falling water would rotate drum pegs that then moved levers which created different sounds.[3]

Fast forward to the 1940s, American writer Isaac Asimov wrote a short story called "Runaround."[4] This work of fiction featured robots developed by engineers using tree laws of robotics. The laws of robotics were that (1) the robots should not injure humans through action or inaction; (2) the robot should follow commands of humans unless it would cause a violation of the first law; and (3) the robot must prevent its own destruction as long as it does not conflict with the first and second

---

[1] M. B. (2018, July 18). *Automatons: The ancestors of the current robots*. OpenMind. https://www.bbvaopenmind.com/en/technology/robotics/automatons-the-ancestors-of-the-current-robots/#:~:text=The%20Al%2DJazari%20automatons,the%2012th%20and%2013th%20centuries

[2] Tableau Software LLC. (n.d.). *What is the history of Artificial Intelligence (AI)?* Tableau. https://www.tableau.com/data-insights/ai/history#definition

[3] M. B. (2018, July 18). *Automatons: The ancestors of the current robots*. OpenMind. https://www.bbvaopenmind.com/en/technology/robotics/automatons-the-ancestors-of-the-current-robots/#:~:text=The%20Al%2DJazari%20automatons,the%2012th%20and%2013th%20centuries

[4] Haenlein, M., & Kaplan, A. (n.d.). A brief history of artificial intelligence: – researchgate. https://www.researchgate.net/profile/Michael-Haenlein/publication/334539401_A_Brief_History_of_Artificial_Intelligence_On_the_Past_Present_and_Future_of_Artificial_Intelligence/links/60cd82e5a6fdcc01d482dc23/A-Brief-History-of-Artificial-Intelligence-On-the-Past-Present-and-Future-of-Artificial-Intelligence.pdf

 
D. B. Garrie et al., *Uncovering Digital Evidence*,
https://doi.org/10.1007/978-3-031-68118-9_9

law. This work, though fiction, influenced robotics, AI, and computer science for decades to come.[5]

Alan Turing is known widely for his code breaking machine called The Bombe which was used by Britain to decode the German army code during the World War II.[6] He then published a seminal paper, *Computing Machinery and Intelligence*, that clearly outlined the potential computerization of humanlike thinking, reasoning, and problem-solving.[7] Turing suggested that machines ought to be able to use data and information the same way humans use it to make decisions and solve problems.[8] This was a major turning point for AI because not only did he theorize the ability of computers to behave this way but also how these intelligent machines should be built and tested.[9]

Through the 1950s, there were a handful of notable foundational developments in the world of AI. First, Arthur Samuel created the first checker game program where the computer played the game independently.[10] Later in 1959, Samuel would coin the term "machine learning" while describing his checker-master computer program.[11] Up until 1955 when John McCarthy used the term "artificial intelligence," the idea of intelligent machine capabilities had gone without a popular term or common name.[12] From this time through the 1980s, we saw artificial intelligence become a mainstream idea through the plethora of books and films that touched on or explored the idea of robots.[13]

The 1980s saw a more widespread acceptance of the pursuit of meaningful artificial intelligence. After the American Association of Artificial Intelligence known

[5] Haenlein, M., & Kaplan, A. (n.d.). A brief history of artificial intelligence: – researchgate. https://www.researchgate.net/profile/Michael-Haenlein/publication/334539401_A_Brief_History_of_Artificial_Intelligence_On_the_Past_Present_and_Future_of_Artificial_Intelligence/links/60cd82e5a6fdcc01d482dc23/A-Brief-History-of-Artificial-Intelligence-On-the-Past-Present-and-Future-of-Artificial-Intelligence.pdf

[6] Haenlein, M., & Kaplan, A. (n.d.). A brief history of artificial intelligence: – researchgate. https://www.researchgate.net/profile/Michael-Haenlein/publication/334539401_A_Brief_History_of_Artificial_Intelligence_On_the_Past_Present_and_Future_of_Artificial_Intelligence/links/60cd82e5a6fdcc01d482dc23/A-Brief-History-of-Artificial-Intelligence-On-the-Past-Present-and-Future-of-Artificial-Intelligence.pdf

[7] Turing, A. M. (1970, January 1). *Alan M. Turing, Computing Machinery and intelligence*. PhilPapers. https://philpapers.org/rec/TURCMA

[8] Anyoha, R. (2017, August 27). *The history of Artificial Intelligence*. Science in the News. https://sitn.hms.harvard.edu/flash/2017/history-artificial-intelligence/

[9] Anyoha, R. (2017, August 27). *The history of Artificial Intelligence*. Science in the News. https://sitn.hms.harvard.edu/flash/2017/history-artificial-intelligence/

[10] Tableau Software LLC. (n.d.). *What is the history of Artificial Intelligence (AI)?* Tableau. https://www.tableau.com/data-insights/ai/history#definition

[11] Tableau Software LLC. (n.d.). *What is the history of Artificial Intelligence (AI)?* Tableau. https://www.tableau.com/data-insights/ai/history#definition

[12] Tableau Software LLC. (n.d.). *What is the history of Artificial Intelligence (AI)?* Tableau. https://www.tableau.com/data-insights/ai/history#definition

[13] Tableau Software LLC. (n.d.). *What is the history of Artificial Intelligence (AI)?* Tableau. https://www.tableau.com/data-insights/ai/history#definition

as the Association for the Advancement of Artificial Intelligence (the "AAAI") was founded in 1979, they held their first conference the following year. While there were several notable developments mentioned earlier, by the mid 1980s, the AAAI warned of a drought of funding for AI projects which would stunt the growth and development of this area.

It wasn't until 1997 that the next cornerstone development in the world of artificial intelligence occurred—the creation of Deep Blue by IBM.[14] Deep Blue was a chess playing computer program that was able to beat the then-world chess champion, Gary Kasparov. The match between Gary and the Deep Blue program came with high expectations. Deep Blue was able to process 200 million potential moves *per second.* It was also able to calculate 20 moves ahead.[15] Through these two key processes and displays of AI, the world champion chess player was beaten by a computer.

In the next 20 years or so, we saw piecemeal mainstream implementations that utilized AI and/or robotics that are probably still top of mind for most people. In 2002 the first Roomba was released. A year later, NASA landed the Spirit Rover and Opportunity Rover on Mars and were able to control the rovers to navigate Mars unassisted by humans. The Internet saw the popularization of social media networks such as Facebook and Twitter, who were utilizing AI to improve user experience and target marketing and advertising. In 2010, Microsoft launched the XBox 360 Kinect which was the first gaming hardware that linked the human user movements and the gaming system by translating the movement into game commands.[16] A year later, we saw Apple release Siri—the first mainstream virtual assistant.[17] And that same year of 2011, nearly 15 years after Deep Blue's seminal chess victory, the world experienced another computer program, Watson, that utilizes natural language processing to beat two former Jeopardy champions in a televised game.[18]

When we think about AI today, we often think of Alexa or ChatGPT. But it was actually nearly 60 years ago when the first natural language processing chatbot was created by Joseph Weizenbaum.[19] We may also think of self-driving cars that seem to have recently become mainstream, when in fact The Stanford Cart was one of the

---

[14] Tableau Software LLC. (n.d.). *What is the history of Artificial Intelligence (AI)?* Tableau. https://www.tableau.com/data-insights/ai/history#definition

[15] Haenlein, M., & Kaplan, A. (n.d.). A brief history of artificial intelligence: – researchgate. https://www.researchgate.net/profile/Michael-Haenlein/publication/334539401_A_Brief_History_of_Artificial_Intelligence_On_the_Past_Present_and_Future_of_Artificial_Intelligence/links/60cd82e5a6fdcc01d482dc23/A-Brief-History-of-Artificial-Intelligence-On-the-Past-Present-and-Future-of-Artificial-Intelligence.pdf

[16] Tableau Software LLC. (n.d.). *What is the history of Artificial Intelligence (AI)?* Tableau. https://www.tableau.com/data-insights/ai/history#definition

[17] Tableau Software LLC. (n.d.). *What is the history of Artificial Intelligence (AI)?* Tableau. https://www.tableau.com/data-insights/ai/history#definition

[18] Tableau Software LLC. (n.d.). *What is the history of Artificial Intelligence (AI)?* Tableau. https://www.tableau.com/data-insights/ai/history#definition

[19] Tableau Software LLC. (n.d.). *What is the history of Artificial Intelligence (AI)?* Tableau. https://www.tableau.com/data-insights/ai/history#definition

first autonomous vehicles created in 1961, more than 60 years ago. By 1979, the Stanford Cart was able to navigate without human intervention. Later the first driverless car was created by Ernst Dickmann in Munich. The car was able to drive nearly 60 miles per hour effectively if there weren't other human drivers or obstacles.

## 9.2 Types of Artificial Intelligence

**Narrow** Artificial narrow intelligence is also referred to as "Weak AI." This type of AI can be trained to perform only a single or narrow task. Typically, the interface's ability to complete the narrow task is significantly faster than a human.[20] However, the limitation of course is that it must perform within the defined task. All of the natural language processing artificial intelligence that we are currently used to such as Siri, Alexa, and Cortana may seem limitless but are in fact merely advanced examples of Narrow AI.[21] Even AI that appears more sophisticated such as ChatGPT is still Narrow AI since it is limited by the text based interaction.[22]

Functions[23] within Narrow AI fall into two main categories. Reactive Machine AI describes instances of AI where there is nothing functionally stored, so the interface is incapable of referring back to its previous outputs. Instead, the AI does a specific task, and that is the end of the loop. Deep Blue mentioned earlier is an example of Reactive Machine AI. The AI within Deep Blue wasn't referring back to its previous moves and rationales. Instead, it was analyzing all of the potential next moves and then calculating the potential outcome for those moves. Limited memory AI, as the name suggests, has some *limited* memory recall, unlike Reactive Machine learning. Not only can it recall past functions or actions, but it also can monitor specific interactions over time. Therefore, limited memory AI can use past information to make its next decision. Over time, this AI can also work to improve its overall performance by comparing its chosen action to the outcome of that action. While these algorithms often have the look and feel of general AI (see below), their functionality does not meet that definition. What follows are some of the most widely used examples of limited memory AI.

- *Generative AI.* Presently, one of the most hot button versions of limited memory AI is Generative AI. Generative AI can use its limited memory to create new content. This is the type of AI that is responsible for ChatGPT. ChatGPT is

[20] IBM Team, (2023, October 16). *Understanding the different types of artificial intelligence*. IBM Blog. https://www.ibm.com/blog/understanding-the-different-types-of-artificial-intelligence/

[21] IBM Team, (2023, October 16). *Understanding the different types of artificial intelligence*. IBM Blog. https://www.ibm.com/blog/understanding-the-different-types-of-artificial-intelligence/

[22] IBM Team, (2023, October 16). *Understanding the different types of artificial intelligence*. IBM Blog. https://www.ibm.com/blog/understanding-the-different-types-of-artificial-intelligence/

[23] IBM Team, (2023, October 16). *Understanding the different types of artificial intelligence*. IBM Blog. https://www.ibm.com/blog/understanding-the-different-types-of-artificial-intelligence/

powered by a Large Language Model. A Large Language Model is a deep learning mechanism that can perform various natural language processing tasks.[24] The algorithm uses the large datasets to interpret an input to then predict or generate some type of content.[25]

- *Large Language Models*. The uses of Large Language Models ("LLMs") are far and wide and go well beyond the mainstream understandings of the application.[26] This varies from creating software code to comprehending protein structures. LLMs can have major positive implications for the healthcare field (more on this later), but generally, this technology can be used to help develop vaccines or even find cures for illnesses.[27] Notably, these LLMs require pretraining and continual fixes.[28] The most easily understood example of LLMs is information retrieval on the Internet.[29] Each time you type in a search in Google, an LLM produces a response to your search prompt. The search engine can retrieve information relevant to your search and then communicate a response.[30]
- *Virtual Assistants*. Another widely popularized version of limited memory AI is virtual assistant. Virtual assistants such as Alexa and Siri can understand your questions and provide relevant answers. This type of limited memory AI leverages both Large Language Model technology and Natural Language Processing. The cornerstone identifiable technology utilized for virtual assistants is their ability to not just process your language prompt but to create its own human language verbal interaction. These types of virtual assistants are typically able to interface with natural language and operate across multiple platforms. For example, you may speak to your virtual assistant, and she may be able to add an event to your calendar, add a grocery item to your reminder list, and then turn your smart home lights on.[31]
- *Chatbots*. Sometimes chatbots get lumped into this type of limited memory AI. But like most things, not all types of chatbots are created equally. However, there are various types of chatbot AI. You'll see similar technical similarities

[24] Elastic. (n.d.). *What is a large language model?: A comprehensive llms guide*. https://www.elastic.co/what-is/large-language-models

[25] Elastic. (n.d.). *What is a large language model?: A comprehensive llms guide*. https://www.elastic.co/what-is/large-language-models

[26] IBM Team, (2023, October 16). *Understanding the different types of artificial intelligence*. IBM Blog. https://www.ibm.com/blog/understanding-the-different-types-of-artificial-intelligence/

[27] Elastic. (n.d.). *What is a large language model?: A comprehensive llms guide*. https://www.elastic.co/what-is/large-language-models

[28] Elastic. (n.d.). *What is a large language model?: A comprehensive llms guide*. https://www.elastic.co/what-is/large-language-models

[29] Elastic. (n.d.). *What is a large language model?: A comprehensive llms guide*. https://www.elastic.co/what-is/large-language-models

[30] Elastic. (n.d.). *What is a large language model?: A comprehensive llms guide*. https://www.elastic.co/what-is/large-language-models

[31] Yasar, K., & Botelho, B. (2023, October 2). *What is a virtual assistant (AI assistant)?: Definition from TechTarget*. Customer Experience. https://www.techtarget.com/searchcustomerexperience/definition/virtual-assistant-AI-assistant

utilized in website chatbot customer service products as well. However, these are often written communications between the user and the output. It is important to note that some chatbots that provide the user only a small subset of options to choose from instead of typing in an entire prompt are not generating a response. Instead, it is retrieving information that it has been taught. The next, more sophisticated type of chatbot is a conversational agent. This interaction is more humanistic and can be based on either text or voice.[32]

- *Self-Driving Cars.* The final example, for purposes of understanding the basics of limited memory AI, is the self-driving car. The autonomous car operates on limited memory AI by using the information at its disposal to make real-time decisions. These decisions span everything from when to break, how to turn, when to apply the accelerator, and every single other action.

**Computer Vision** The next form of AI that we often come across in daily life but may not recognize the name of or its technological ability is computer vision AI. Computer vision, as the name suggests, involves the computer's ability to leverage its neural networks to enable photo tagging (think of when Facebook suggests a tag based on someone's face previously tagged in your album or your iPhone where you can search by face).On a more professional level, healthcare imaging also utilizes this type of AI.

**General** Artificial general intelligence is also referred to as "strong AI." The critical aspect of strong AI is that it is a theoretical form of artificial intelligence that can replicate human level reasoning. Strong AI can, in effect, use information or skill derived or gathered and apply it to further reasoning without any human intervention.[33] Ultimately, strong AI strives to accomplish the same reasoning, problem-solving, and logic processes as the human brain. To date, true general AI does not yet exist.

**Super AI** "Artificial superintelligence" is similar to strong AI—it is also theoretical. Building off the premises laid out with regard to the goals of strong AI, super AI would be able not just to make humanlike reasoning and other cognitive skills, but it would *surpass* a human's ability to do these things.[34] But like general AI, super AI does not yet exist.

**Theory of Mind** The final general umbrella of AI is another not yet realized form of artificial intelligence. Theory of mind AI would be able to interact with people in

---

[32] Yasar, K., & Botelho, B. (2023, October 2). *What is a virtual assistant (AI assistant)?: Definition from TechTarget.* Customer Experience. https://www.techtarget.com/searchcustomerexperience/definition/virtual-assistant-AI-assistant

[33] IBM Team, (2023, October 16). *Understanding the different types of artificial intelligence.* IBM Blog. https://www.ibm.com/blog/understanding-the-different-types-of-artificial-intelligence/

[34] IBM Team, (2023, October 16). *Understanding the different types of artificial intelligence.* IBM Blog. https://www.ibm.com/blog/understanding-the-different-types-of-artificial-intelligence/

a whole new way—by understanding thoughts and emotions. It would be able to make inferences related to human motivation, emotions, and intentions. Emotion AI is currently being developed. The intended uses span voice analyzation and emotional responses.

## 9.3 Some Common Examples of Current Applications of AI[35]

**Speech Recognition** Speech recognition technology is being further integrated into our everyday lives. Not only do we interact with this technology during back and forth with virtual assistants such as Amazon Echo or Siri, but we also interface with smart assistants in our cars or even transcriptions that convert human speech to written text on our cell phones or computers.[36] Automatic speech recognition (ASR) allows a computer to recognize and process human speech.[37]

**Customer Service** Virtual agents are commonly utilized for customer service. These customer service agents are able to provide quick and accurate service. Users are able to receive answers to frequently asked questions, receive updates on their shipping statuses, or even reorder items that have gotten lost in the mail.[38] The format of these interfaces can range from virtual agents on websites all the way to Facebook Messenger.[39]

**Digital Surveillance** AI algorithms are used to review video footage including security camera videos to scan for objects and subjects. Using facial recognition technology, the AI is able recognize people from an existing database. This technology can be used by investigators and law enforcement to track down suspects involved in crimes and assist in building evidence for a case.

**Online Recommendations** Search and recommendation algorithms track a user's online activity over time to learn what that user's interests and behaviors. Using machine learning and deep learning, this data is analyzed to provide specific recommendations catered to that user.

---

[35] IBM. (n.d.). *What is Artificial Intelligence (AI)?* https://www.ibm.com/topics/artificial-intelligence

[36] SHAIP. (2023, June 21). *Automatic speech recognition (ASR) – definition, use cases, example*. Shaip. https://www.shaip.com/blog/automatic-speech-recognitiona-complete-overview/

[37] IBM. (n.d.). *What is speech recognition?* https://www.ibm.com/topics/speech-recognition

[38] IBM. (n.d.). *What is Artificial Intelligence (AI)?* https://www.ibm.com/topics/artificial-intelligence

[39] IBM. (n.d.). *What is Artificial Intelligence (AI)?* https://www.ibm.com/topics/artificial-intelligence

## 9.4 The Future of AI[40]

**Education** AI has wide applications in education. From a student perspective, students will be able to more securely store the information—thanks to facial recognition and other biometric methods of security. AI can also help to digitize textbooks which may in effect increase the availability of textbooks and educational materials in general. Utilizing natural language processing and machine learning, students will be able to experience education in ways unlike any other generation.[41] AI can also help detect plagiarism. While we have seen universities unveil policies regarding the acceptable use of AI, many universities have confronted the inevitable reality of AI use by students and draw the line at copying ideas and generating assignments as one's own.

**Healthcare** In addition to the advanced imaging processes related to proteins and other conditions noted above, there are also myriad other potential uses within the mental healthcare field. One of the new and major movements in the mental healthcare space is the utilizing of prescription digital therapeutics (PDTs). These are prescriptions of a digital mode of therapy, not a prescription of physical medication that comes to mind when we think of a "prescription."[42] Not only are these prescriptions convenient and private, but these FDA approved prescriptions are already being used to help treat a variety of conditions such as ADHD and PTSD.[43] One example of this is EndeavorRx. EndeavorRx is "the only doctor prescribed video game treatment for kids with ADHD."[44] As of the date of this writing, there are already 14 FDA approved PDTs for the treatment of 11 diseases or disorders. We can anticipate that these offerings will continue to grow. There are also a growing number of chatbot based mobile mental health apps. As the AI used in these apps

[40] Thomas, M. (2023, March 3). *The future of AI: How Artificial Intelligence Will Change the world.* Built In. https://builtin.com/artificial-intelligence/artificial-intelligence-future

[41] Thomas, M. (2023, March 3). *The future of AI: How Artificial Intelligence Will Change the world.* Built In. https://builtin.com/artificial-intelligence/artificial-intelligence-future

[42] Otsuka. (2023, October 5). *Otsuka Brandvoice: Prescription digital therapeutics are expanding what it means to treat mental health.* Forbes. https://www.forbes.com/sites/otsuka/2023/06/26/prescription-digital-therapeutics-are-expanding-what-it-means-to-treat-mental-health/?sh=67cfdc0c4bcf&gclid=Cj0KCQiA7OqrBhD9ARIsAK3UXh1Ngt4JYubxRGH6L9s_ezEJTw8FzF_pouZ2TT6vus0mb4B6hQhpfhoaArqNEALw_wcB

[43] Otsuka. (2023, October 5). *Otsuka Brandvoice: Prescription digital therapeutics are expanding what it means to treat mental health.* Forbes. https://www.forbes.com/sites/otsuka/2023/06/26/prescription-digital-therapeutics-are-expanding-what-it-means-to-treat-mental-health/?sh=67cfdc0c4bcf&gclid=Cj0KCQiA7OqrBhD9ARIsAK3UXh1Ngt4JYubxRGH6L9s_ezEJTw8FzF_pouZ2TT6vus0mb4B6hQhpfhoaArqNEALw_wcB

[44] *EndeavorRx® – ADHD video game treatment for kids: FDA-authorized.* EndeavorRx. (2023, December 20). https://www.endeavorrx.com/

continues to evolve, we can anticipate the increased effective use of these technologies.[45]

**Manufacturing** As AI becomes more deeply embedded in the processes and systems of manufacturing, we can anticipate that there will be a new wave of attempts to increase efficiency and productivity.[46] We will see artificial intelligence utilize algorithms to optimize supply chain management and improve efficiency through decreased downtimes and proactive detection of machine issues. When these inadequacies are detected, the issue will be resolved (either through automation or human intervention), and the unplanned downtime will have been eliminated or at least drastically reduced. Not only will the system not have to wait for the issue to come to a screeching halt and then wait for diagnostics and then repair, but the repair will be the only actual intervention.[47] AI algorithms are particularly helpful in this setting because not only can they analyze large amounts of data quickly and efficiently, but they can find irregularities that are otherwise undetectable.[48]

**Customer Services** With the proliferation of generative AI, we can expect to see more integrations within electronic platforms of customer service to further tailor and ultimately improve the customer experience. As the CEO of Salesforce AI described the next wave of integration of AI in customer service, "The next wave of AI is primed to transform customer service, turning the industry on its head in the most exciting way possible."[49] One of the current strains on the customer service industry is trying to balance the high expectations of customers against managing resources. This new shift from AI that can retrieve programmed answers to common questions to AI that can predict a customer's needs and present them with personalized responses and solutions the way a human could will help manage these

[45] Haque and Rubya. An Overview of Chatbot-Based Mobile Health Apps: Insights from App Description and User Reviews (2023) available at https://www.ncbi.nlm.nih.gov/pmc/articles/PMC10242473/

[46] Cooper, G. (2023, August 16). *The future of AI in manufacturing*. MHA. https://www.mha.co.uk/insights/the-future-of-ai-in-manufacturing#:~:text=Enhanced%20Efficiency%20and%20Productivity&text=Intelligent%20automation%20systems%20powered%20by,potential%20failures%2C%20reducing%20unplanned%20downtime

[47] Cooper, G. (2023, August 16). *The future of AI in manufacturing*. MHA. https://www.mha.co.uk/insights/the-future-of-ai-in-manufacturing#:~:text=Enhanced%20Efficiency%20and%20Productivity&text=Intelligent%20automation%20systems%20powered%20by,potential%20failures%2C%20reducing%20unplanned%20downtime

[48] Cooper, G. (2023, August 16). *The future of AI in manufacturing*. MHA. https://www.mha.co.uk/insights/the-future-of-ai-in-manufacturing#:~:text=Enhanced%20Efficiency%20and%20Productivity&text=Intelligent%20automation%20systems%20powered%20by,potential%20failures%2C%20reducing%20unplanned%20downtime

[49] Dow Jones & Company. (2023, July 18). *Paid program: How ai is reshaping customer service*. The Wall Street Journal. https://partners.wsj.com/salesforce/how-generative-ai-will-revolutionize-customer-service/

competing service agency pains.[50] Downstream, this will cause a complete revolutionization of what consumers come to know and expect when it comes to customer service. Companies who are able to leverage the successful realization of the powers of these technologies into a platform or integration that can empower them to provide these important improvements will possess an important competitive advantage for years to come.

**Marketing** Over the last decade, we have seen the restandardization of how online marketing is done. No longer are marketing departments relying on cold calls or door to door sales pitches. Instead, companies are leveraging online information of their customers—thanks to many data privacy laws—with the affirmative consent of its customer. Companies are able to utilize the Internet to track items that customers look at and automatically email them reminders to purchase or perhaps even sweeten the deal with a small discount on the item they looked at but never purchased. AI could soon provide a new way for companies to gauge potential customers' feelings about their items. One great example of this is Affectiva, an emotion artificial intelligence company in Boston. Their technology can capture the subconscious reactions and instinctual movements and then correlate those emotions with consumer behavior. This is to say AI could effectively predict whether you will purchase a product or share an advertisement just based on the way the subtle muscles in your face react when a new advertisement pops up on your screen.[51]

This AI use case has not gone unnoticed by US regulators for fear of abuse of personal data. For example, in February, 2024, FTC Chairwoman Linda Khan called out how AI-based behavioral advertising has fueled companies' abuse of private data and cautioned that AI model training is "emerging as another feature that could further incentivize surveillance."[52] She announced that the FTC is specifically monitoring how companies notify consumers when they intend to use data collected in different contexts. Chairwoman Khan cautioned that companies must "actively notify users of this change rather than quietly and retroactively rewriting their terms of service." The FTC has recently announced several settlements with companies alleged to have improperly used consumers' health, geolocation, and browsing data in the AI context.[53]

There are many other recent statements and actions from US government regulators and enforcers expressing concern about AI usage in various contexts, some of which are explored below. One notable example is the SEC's recent settlement of

[50] Dow Jones & Company. (2023, July 18). *Paid program: How ai is reshaping customer service.* The Wall Street Journal. https://partners.wsj.com/salesforce/how-generative-ai-will-revolutionize-customer-service/

[51] Somers, M. (2019, March 8). *Emotion AI, explained.* MIT Sloan. https://mitsloan.mit.edu/ideas-made-to-matter/emotion-ai-explained

[52] "Smalley, S. (2024, February 27). FTC's Khan warns tech industry that agency will strictly enforce AI data privacy." The Record. https://therecord.media/ftc-warns-tech-industry-ai-data-privacy

[53] Id.

charges for "AI washing" against two investment advisers for making false and misleading statements about their purported use of artificial intelligence (AI).[54] The firms agreed to settle the SEC's charges and pay $400,000 in total civil penalties. And on April 3, 2024, the Congressional Research Service issued a report entitled "Artificial Intelligence and Machine Learning in Financial Service," that among other things, discussed policy and regulatory issues related to AI/ML in the financial sector.[55]

This is a rapidly evolving area for regulation and legislation that practitioners need to stay abreast of in real time.

## 9.5 Challenges with AI

There are a number of challenges facing AI. First there is generally mistrust from much of the general public. In a survey of over 2000 adults in the USA, only 39% of survey takers think AI is safe and secure.[56] Meanwhile, almost 80% of survey takers thought that AI could be used maliciously.[57] One way we have seen AI used to manipulate people is through deepfakes. Deepfakes are altered videos that intentionally make it appear as though an often famous person is saying or doing something that they in fact did not do. For example, there was a viral video of David

---

[54] https://www.sec.gov/news/press-release/2024-36 ("We find that Delphia and Global Predictions marketed to their clients and prospective clients that they were using AI in certain ways when, in fact, they were not," said SEC Chair Gary Gensler. "We've seen time and again that when new technologies come along, they can create buzz from investors as well as false claims by those purporting to use those new technologies. Investment advisers should not mislead the public by saying they are using an AI model when they are not. Such AI washing hurts investors").

[55] https://crsreports.congress.gov/product/pdf/R/R47997 ("Adoption of the technology also brings challenges and risks. While AI may eliminate some human bias in financial services, it may also introduce or exacerbate bias. Certain AI-market specific factors—such as using the same data to train models and concentration of technology and technological capacity—may encourage monocultures, or herd-like behavior, that introduce systemic risk. The ability of certain models to learn on their own, free from human oversight, may also allow them to engage in market manipulation, conflicts of interest, or other unlawful activity. Financial industry use of the technology has attracted policymaker interest. For example, Executive Order 14110 on the 'Safe, Secure, and Trustworthy Development and Use of Artificial Intelligence' briefly discusses the Biden Administration's view of AI/ML in finance, among a host of other issues. In addition, the House Committee on Financial Services created a bipartisan AI Working Group to address these issues in January 2024").

[56] Mearian, L. (2023, October 3). *With AI, there's a trust gap based on gender, age*. Computerworld. https://www.computerworld.com/article/3707795/ai-trust-gap-based-on-gender-age.html#:~:text=Only%2039%25%20of%20survey%20respondents,AI%20assurance%20and%20government%20regulation

[57] Mearian, L. (2023, October 3). *With AI, there's a trust gap based on gender, age*. Computerworld. https://www.computerworld.com/article/3707795/ai-trust-gap-based-on-gender-age.html#:~:text=Only%2039%25%20of%20survey%20respondents,AI%20assurance%20and%20government%20regulation

Beckham speaking nine languages, when he actually only speaks one.[58] This example is relatively lighthearted, but the risks that this same technology can be used to create videos of political figures delivering frightening messages could spread disinformation and fear and eventually be weaponized and threaten democracy as we know it.[59]

The survey also revealed that over 50% of adults thought AI would cause job loss.[60] It is estimated that by 2023, AI can account for up to 30% of the hours worked today.[61] Experts in the area have speculated that the key to integrating AI in our work is by learning to work alongside the technology and focusing on human strengths. For example, in a customer service setting, we could leverage AI to answer routine questions and provide quick access to information to customers. Meanwhile, this would allow human associates to build strong relationships with customers while solving more complex problems.[62] On the other hand, with the increasing focus on AI across multiple industries, there are several careers that will likely grow in demand. For instance, Forbes predicts that AI related careers such as AI data privacy experts, AI augmentation specialists, and AI supply chain management specialists will dramatically increase in years to come.[63] This increase in professional opportunities also leads to a demand in education for the required training and certifications and expectations on regulatory bodies.

One of the ways in which we can leverage the strengths of AI while controlling the potential negative effects is by implementing thoughtful legislation.[64] We already see this being done in the UK where the Artificial Intelligence Regulation Bill has been brought to the House of Lords. The proposed legislation also proposes a new "AI Authority."[65] The AI Authority would have general oversight into all AI related activities in the UK. In the EU, the AI Act has been enacted and is now in effect and

---

[58] Bonderud, D. (n.d.). *What are deepfakes? how they work + how to spot one – norton*. United States. https://us.norton.com/blog/emerging-threats/what-are-deepfakes

[59] Marr, B. (2023, October 5). *The 15 biggest risks of Artificial Intelligence*. Forbes. https://www.forbes.com/sites/bernardmarr/2023/06/02/the-15-biggest-risks-of-artificial-intelligence/?sh=413a2a752706

[60] Mearian, L. (2023, October 3). *With AI, there's a trust gap based on gender, age*. Computerworld. https://www.computerworld.com/article/3707795/ai-trust-gap-based-on-gender-age.html#:~:text=Only%2039%25%20of%20survey%20respondents,AI%20assurance%20and%20government%20regulation

[61] Thomas, M. (n.d.). *12 risks and dangers of Artificial Intelligence (AI)*. Built In. https://builtin.com/artificial-intelligence/risks-of-artificial-intelligence

[62] WSJ. (2023, July 18). *Paid program: How AI is reshaping customer service*. The Wall Street Journal. https://partners.wsj.com/salesforce/how-generative-ai-will-revolutionize-customer-service/

[63] Amdur, E. (2023, October 5). *14 AI jobs of the future – now*. Forbes. https://www.forbes.com/sites/eliamdur/2023/08/24/14-ai-jobs-of-the-future%2D%2Dnow/

[64] JD Supra. (n.d.). *UK AI regulation bill proposes new AI regulator*. JD Supra. https://www.jdsupra.com/legalnews/uk-ai-regulation-bill-proposes-new-ai-1727245/

[65] JD Supra. (n.d.). *UK AI regulation bill proposes new AI regulator*. JD Supra. https://www.jdsupra.com/legalnews/uk-ai-regulation-bill-proposes-new-ai-1727245/

comes with extensive compliance requirements for covered entities.[66] In the USA, the White House recently issued an Executive Order on Safe, Secure, and Trustworthy Use of AI in the federal government, which among other requirement imposed the obligation for government agencies to appoint a Chief AI Officer to oversee usage and implementation of AI.[67] This was quickly followed up by "AI Bill of Rights" which outlines the intentions of the federal government in combating bad actors utilizing AI with an interest in protecting the general public.[68] The Bill of Rights goes on to outline a number of things including the ways in which AI technology should be developed, how algorithms should be developed in a way that does not allow for discrimination in its application, as well as data privacy considerations.[69] These recent instances of the executive branch issuing rules governing certain AI usage are not exclusive. For example, in January of 2023, the National Institute of Standards and Technology issued the AI risk management framework, developed in concert with industry and intended to be a voluntary set of guiding principles for the responsible use of AI, and then in March of 2023 launched the Trustworthy and Responsible AI Resource Center.[70] The standards will continue to evolve, and the USA, the UK, and the EU will define the parameters for the use of AI in the West to protect the general welfare.

## 9.6 Managing AI: Governance and Oversight

A 2022 survey conducted by the international law firm Baker McKenzie of 500 US-based, C-level executives revealed gaps in corporate handling of AI risk.[71] While 75% of the surveyed companies use AI tools, 64% of companies lack a Chief Artificial Intelligence Officer ("CAIO") to oversee the company's AI strategy. Moreover, only 41% of respondents said they have AI expertise at the board level.

Although many of these companies have some form of AI policies to manage risk, a CAIO is essential to truly understand the risks of AI which span data privacy,

---

[66] Gilcrhist, K.and Jordache, R (2024, March 3): *World's first major act to regulate AI passed by European lawmakers*. CNBC. https://www.cnbc.com/2024/03/13/european-lawmakers-endorse-worlds-first-major-act-to-regulate-ai.html; *see also* https://www.europarl.europa.eu/news/en/press-room/20240308IPR19015/artificial-intelligence-act-meps-adopt-landmark-law

[67] https://www.whitehouse.gov/briefing-room/statements-releases/2023/10/30/fact-sheet-president-biden-issues-executive-order-on-safe-secure-and-trustworthy-artificial-intelligence/

[68] The United States Government. (2023, November 22). *Blueprint for an AI bill of rights*. The White House. https://www.whitehouse.gov/ostp/ai-bill-of-rights/

[69] Id.

[70] https://www.nist.gov/itl/ai-risk-management-framework

[71] Risky Business: Identifying Blind Spots in Corporate Oversight of Artificial Intelligence (March 30, 2022), available at: aisurveypptfinalmarch20222.pdf (bakermckenzie.com)

legal liability, compliance with state and local regulations, and algorithm bias in recruitment, to name a few.[72]

Some companies, such as Meta, have created oversight boards—independent bodies that people can appeal to regarding content decisions made with respect to social media and AI.[73] On April 5, 2024, Meta, utilizing feedback from the Oversight Board, announced its decision to label a wider range of video, audio, and image content as "Made with AI" when applicable.[74] While Meta's oversight board is more involved than what is likely necessary for most companies, appropriate oversight is crucial to internal governance. This importance of this issue was highlighted during recent congressional testimony provided by Bradford Newman, the coauthor of this book, to the US Senate on October 31, 2023, during a Health, Education, Labor, and Pension Subcommittee hearing on artificial intelligence and the future of work.[75]

---

[72] Goldman, S. (2022, June 7): This AI Attorney Says Companies Need a Chief AI Officer Pronto. Venture Beat https://venturebeat.com/ai/this-ai-attorney-says-companies-need-a-chief-ai-officer-pronto/ (quoting the coauthor of this book who serves as the cochair (and past chair) of the American Bar Association AI Subcommittee: "When Bradford Newman began advocating for more artificial intelligence expertise in the C-suite in 2015, 'people were laughing at me,' he said. Newman, who leads global law firm Baker McKenzie's machine learning and AI practice in its Palo Alto office, added that when he mentioned the need for companies to appoint a chief AI officer, people typically responded, 'What's that?'… From a corporate governance standpoint, AI is different as well, he continued: 'Unlike, for example, the financial function, which is the dollars and cents accounted for and reported properly within the corporate structure and disclosed to our shareholders, artificial intelligence and data science involves law, human resources and ethics,' he said. 'There are a multitude of examples of things that are legally permissible, but are not in tune with the corporate culture…. What will help, said Newman, is to appoint a chief AI officer (CAIO)—that is, a C-suite level executive that reports to the CEO, at the same level as a CIO, CISO or CFO. The CAIO would have ultimate responsibility for oversight of all things AI in the corporation.

'Many people want to know how one person can fit that role, but we're not saying the CFO knows every calculation of financial aspects going on deep in the corporation – but it reports up to her,' he said. So a CAIO would be charged with reporting to the shareholders and externally to regulators and governing bodies. 'Most importantly, they would have a role for corporate governance, oversight, monitoring and compliance of all things AI'. Newman added").

[73] Meta, Oversight Board, available at: https://about.fb.com/news/tag/oversight-board/#:~:text=The%20Oversight%20Board%20is%20an,Visit%20the%20Transparency%20Center

[74] Meta, Our Approach to Labeling AI-Generated Content and Manipulated Media (April 5, 2024), availableat:https://about.fb.com/news/2024/04/metas-approach-to-labeling-ai-generated-content-and-manipulated-media/

[75] https://www.c-span.org/person/?138494/BradfordNewman; https://www.c-span.org/video/?531500-1/senate-hearing-artificial-intelligence-future-work; see also: https://techcrunch.com/2018/05/15/society-needs-the-artificial-intelligence-data-protection-act-now/?guccounter=1&guce_referrer=aHR0cHM6Ly93d3cuZ29vZ2xlLmNvbS8&guce_referrer_sig=AQAAAKqk4ooFjZlBGByQiicHbSWOdgH0m3lkrvbZ1GnuoupCH3_nw8ZDp-3BlINEtc4XUqHZqgtn68_0qeOXzBO7Vvy6xA0BvJ8GK-lGslreh9GIKqky-m3lYgEHAiGynCQ9KCV3eXiVnAgbiUVeuCM-EoP32fhkaN4ifPC9AlGlK0LH, discussing potential federal AI legislation that requires covered entities to appoint a Chief AI Officer. Mr. Newman's legislative proposal for the Artificial Intelligence Data Protection Act was turned into a House of Representatives Discussion Draft Bill in the 115th Congress, 2nd Session, 2018.

## 9.7 AI Regulation in the USA

The USA currently does not have federal regulation of AI.[76] As noted above, in October 2023, President Biden issued an executive order to establish standards for safe, secure, and trustworthy AI development.[77] The executive order calls on Congress to pass new bipartisan data privacy legislation. The order also seeks to harness AI to advance equity and civil rights by preventing discriminatory algorithms and bias. States, on the other hand, have enacted a number of laws which regulate various aspects of AI, especially with regard to use cases involving employment and privacy.

For example, in 2023, New York's Local Law 144 of 2021 took effect, which regulates automated employment decision tools.[78] Namely, the law prohibits employers and employment agencies from using automated employment decision tools (referred to as "AEDT") unless required notice is provided and a bias audit is completed. AEDTs use machine learning, data analytics, and artificial intelligence to aid employers in making employment decisions. While AEDT is meant to replace discretionary decision-making, the law is meant to stop the perpetuation of implicit biases. New York City also released its Artificial Intelligence Action Plan in 2023 as a roadmap to guide productive, safe growth of AI.[79]

Illinois enacted the Artificial Intelligence Video Interview Act in 2020.[80] The Act provides that an employer who asks applicants to record video interviews and uses AI analysis of the applicant-submitted videos must (1) notify applicants prior to the interview that AI may be used to consider the applicant's suitability; (2) provide applicants with information regarding how AI works to evaluate applicants; and (3) obtain the applicant's consent.

California's Governor Gavin Newsom signed an executive order in 2023 to study the use and development of AI throughout the state in order to create a responsive

---

[76] On March 13, 2024, the EU adopted the Artificial Intelligence Act (AI Act) as a comprehensive framework for AI. The AI Act takes a risk-based approach, outlining four levels of risk for AI systems from minimal risk to unacceptable risk. The Act bans those systems deemed too risky that pose a safety threat. For example, high risk AI systems include critical infrastructure (such as transportation), educational or vocational training, or law enforcement. The text of the Act is available at https://www.europarl.europa.eu/doceo/document/TA-9-2024-03-13-TOC_EN.html. *See also* Shaping Europe's Digital Future, AI Act, available at: https://digital-strategy.ec.europa.eu/en/policies/regulatory-framework-ai

[77] President Joseph R. Biden Jr., Executive Order on the Safe, Secure, and Trustworthy Development and Use of Artificial Intelligence (Oct. 30, 2023), available at: https://www.whitehouse.gov/briefing-room/presidential-actions/2023/10/30/executive-order-on-the-safe-secure-and-trustworthy-development-and-use-of-artificial-intelligence/

[78] https://www.nyc.gov/assets/dca/downloads/pdf/about/DCWP-AEDT-FAQ.pdf

[79] https://www.nyc.gov/office-of-the-mayor/news/777-23/mayor-adams-releases-first-of-its-kind-plan-responsible-artificial-intelligence-use-nyc#/0

[80] Artificial Intelligence Video Interview Act, available at: https://www.ilga.gov/legislation/ilcs/ilcs3.asp?ActID=4015&ChapterID=68

and safe process for deployment within the state government.[81] A number of assemblymembers and state senators have introduced bills regulating AI and discrimination,[82] safety standards,[83] protection for actors and artists,[84] and automated decision-making.[85] Until such time as the federal government enacts preemptive AI legislation, the clear trend will be an increase in state and local AI legislation and regulation.

## 9.8 Bias in AI

AI tools have human progenitors which, consciously or not, embed their own personal biases. When a task for an AI task is initially defined, the AI designer's bias can creep in. However, defining what constitutes bias when it comes to AI is becoming increasingly complex. For example, it would not be desirable for generative AI tools tasked with "generate an image of a successful CEO" to generate only images of Caucasian, middle-aged males.

However, the topic of bias in generative AI was recently complicated by the release of Google's Gemini, which created controversy by intentionally "overcorrecting" for bias, which ironically resulted in increased bias in the tool. Gemini was criticized for creating historically inaccurate output, such as an image of America's Founding Fathers as black or the Pope as a woman.[86] Bias in AI used outside of the generative AI use case, where inputs and outputs are less transparent, presents equally if not more important issues when it comes to decisions used for loans, admission to college, and similarly important use cases. For example, in recognition of the increasing use of AI in hiring decisions, monitoring employee performance,

---

[81] Executive Department, State of California, Executive Order N-12-23 (Sept. 6, 2023), available at: https://www.gov.ca.gov/wp-content/uploads/2023/09/AI-EO-No.12-_-GGN-Signed.pdf

[82] Assemblymember Bauer-Kahan Introduces Bill to Eliminate Bias in AI Decision-making (Feb. 15, 2024), available at: https://a16.asmdc.org/press-releases/20240215-assemblymember-bauer-kahan-introduces-bill-eliminate-bias-ai-decision

[83] Senator Wiener Introduces Legislation to Ensure Safe Development of Large-Scale Artificial Intelligence Systems and Support AI Innovation in California (Feb. 8, 2024), available at: https://sd11.senate.ca.gov/news/20240208-senator-wiener-introduces-legislation-ensure-safe-development-large-scale-artificial

[84] Assemblymember Kalra, SAG-AFTRA, Introduce First of its Kind Legislation on Generative AI in Performer Contracts (Sept. 13, 2023), available at: https://a25.asmdc.org/press-releases/20230913-assemblymember-kalra-sag-aftra-introduce-first-its-kind-legislation

[85] A New Landmark for Consumer Control Over their Personal Information: CPPA Proposes Regulatory Framework for Automated Decision-making Technology (Nov. 27, 2023), available at: https://cppa.ca.gov/announcements/2023/20231127.html

[86] Google CEO Pichai says Gemini's AI image results "offended our users" (Feb. 28, 2024), available at https://www.npr.org/2024/02/28/1234532775/google-gemini-offended-users-images-race; see also "Google Gemini is 'the tip of the iceberg': AI bias can have 'devastating impact' on humanity, say experts" (March 6, 2024) available at https://www.foxbusiness.com/media/google-gemini-tip-iceberg-ai-bias-devastating-impact-humanity-experts

and determining of pay or promotions, the Equal Employment Opportunity Commission ("EEOC") released a technical assistance document to guide employers using AI to avoid bias.[87] The document is aimed at preventing discrimination against workers and those seeking employment and explains how Title VII of the Civil Rights Act impacts an employer's use of AI systems.

## 9.9 AI Use in the Legal World

### A. Ethical Concerns

In 2023, a personal injury lawyer representing a plaintiff in the Southern District of New York made headlines for using ChatGPT to locate case law for his opposition to defendant's motion to dismiss.[88] In Mata v. Avianca, plaintiff's counsel asked ChatGPT to find case law regarding a complex issue concerning the court's jurisdiction based on the potential application of a foreign treaty. In response, ChatGPT fabricated six cases, which purported to support plaintiff's position and which the plaintiff's counsel cited to the court without cite-checking. The issue came to a head after opposing counsel could not locate the cases plaintiff cited, and it turned out ChatGPT had "hallucinated" (i.e., made up the cases and even the names of judges). Not surprisingly, the court sanctioned the plaintiff's counsel.

In response to the increasing use of generative AI by lawyers nationally, 16% or more than 1600 US district and magistrate judges have banned filings created by AI or mandated the disclosure of AI usage.[89] The California State Bar recently released guidelines for lawyers regarding AI usage that, although not mandatory, provide a framework for the ethical use of AI with clients and the courts.[90] Other state bars are likely to follow California's lead.

### B. Cases Regarding AI

Generative AI is trained by data all across the Internet. This raises the following question: Should AI developers pay every owner of IP-protected material scraped from the Internet to train AI? As of 2024, this issue is still being litigated and is still largely unclear.

---

[87] Equal Employment Opportunity Commission, Select Issues: Assessing Adverse Impact in Software, Algorithms, and Artificial Intelligence Used in Employment Selection Procedures Under Title VII of the Civil Rights Act of 1964 (May 18, 2023), available at: https://www.eeoc.gov/laws/guidance/select-issues-assessing-adverse-impact-software-algorithms-and-artificial

[88] *Mata v. Avianca, Inc.*, No. 1:22-cv-01461 (PCK) (S.D.N.Y. Jun. 22, 2023).

[89] Judges and Law Scholars Divided Over AI Standing Orders (March 22, 2024), available at: https://www.law360.com/pulse/articles/1810715/judges-and-law-scholars-divided-over-ai-standing-orders

[90] The State Bar of California, Practical Guidance for the Use of Generative Artificial Intelligence in the Practice of Law (Nov. 16, 2023), available at: https://www.calbar.ca.gov/Portals/0/documents/ethics/Generative-AI-Practical-Guidance.pdf

A group of authors, including Sarah Silverman, sued OpenAI, the creator of ChatGPT, for copyright infringement for training its AI tool on copyrighted books.[91] In the court's most recent order in the Silverman case, all but the plaintiffs' direct infringement and unfair competition claims were dismissed, including claims for vicarious infringement, violation of the Digital Millennium Copyright Act, negligence, and unjust enrichment. District Court Judge Araceli Martinez-Olguin found that the main weakness of plaintiffs' claims is that they "have not alleged that the ChatGPT outputs contain direct copies of the copyrighted books." The Silverman case has been consolidated with another action against OpenAI by another author, Paul Tremblay.[92]

Getty Images filed a lawsuit against Stability AI for infringing more than 12 million photographs including their associated metadata in its products, Stable Diffusion and DreamStudio.[93] On January 26, 2024, the court dismissed Stability AI's motion to dismiss without prejudice.

[91] *Silverman* et al *v. OpenAI, Inc.*, et al, No. 4:23-cv-03416-TLT (N.D. Cal. 2023).

[92] *Tremblay* et al *v. OpenAI, Inc.*, et al, No. 4:23-cv-03223-AMO (N.D. Cal. 2023).

[93] *Getty Images (US), Inc. v. Stability AI, Inc.*, No. 1:23-cv-00135-GBW (D. Del. 2023).

# Chapter 10
# Web 3.0

## 10.1 Blockchain and Why It Matters

Blockchain has captured the imagination of developers, entrepreneurs, libertarians, and businesses large and small and is becoming a household name that can conjure up mystifying images of cryptography, Bitcoin, and geek-tech. But it is nothing more than a method of accounting, by a public ledger, which uses voluntary participants, often referred to as "nodes," to verify transactions. Because a blockchain relies on remote technology to verify and update the transactions registered on it, blockchain dispenses with the need for a single, centralized custodian with all of the information—like a bank, registrar, or other ledger keeper—to maintain records.

Blockchain technology employs cryptography to provide a secret key. This secret key allows the holder to unlock all data held in the anonymous public address or "wallet" and allows the holder of the key to transfer whatever electronic data is registered on a corresponding public address, to any other public address. While all the information on a blockchain may be public, because the public addresses are anonymous, blockchain technology allows for public access to the transaction database but provides privacy to the underlying addressees or users. The electronic data can be anything that exists digitally, including digital assets such as cryptocurrency like Bitcoin or Ether,[1] to equity interests in a company, making blockchain ideal technology for the finance and securities industries.

Blockchain technology—also known as distributed ledger technology (DLT)—was first implemented in 2009 as part of the Bitcoin protocol (or program) and is currently used by financial companies, insurance conglomerates, food distributors and supermarkets to track food provenance, and the shipping industry and in certain real estate transactions. In addition, entities like the Depository Trust and Clearing Corporation (the DTCC), which provides clearing and settlement services of the

[1] A digital asset and cryptocurrency issued and distributed on the Ethereum blockchain protocol.



D. B. Garrie et al., *Uncovering Digital Evidence*,
https://doi.org/10.1007/978-3-031-68118-9_10

vast majority of US securities transactions, and the Society for Worldwide Interbank Financial Telecommunication (SWIFT), a worldwide electronic payment network, as well as various participants in the Internet of Things (IoT), are actively looking to incorporate blockchain technology as the basis for their recordkeeping.

Blockchain is also helpful to law enforcement and forensics research as it allows a secure, immutable audit trail that is time-stamped and can be viewed but not changed by anyone with access to the ledger. As a result, blockchain has assisted law enforcement in identifying and prosecuting criminals that were paid in or with cryptocurrency. The most prominent criminal prosecution involving cryptocurrency to date was the identification, arrest, and conviction of Ross Ulbricht, who ran the multibillion dollar criminal enterprise known as Silk Road, an illegal marketplace on the dark web where users contracted murders for hire, laundered money, and bought and sold drugs.

Because blockchain technology exists exclusively as electronic data, it also allows for the creation of self-executing contracts, known as smart contracts. The parties to the smart contract reduce the basic terms of their agreement to a computer code and find an online source to act as a verification that a triggering event has occurred, such as entitlement to payment once a transaction has been consummated, and then the code's contract automatically transfers currency.

In short, blockchain has the potential to transform the underlying layer, or back-office functions, of nearly all recordkeeping in our society, and everyone from manufactures to financial institutions is seeking to incorporate this revolutionary technology into their operations, making blockchain an important tool for people to understand.

## 10.2 Blockchain and the Use of Smart Contracts

Smart contracts, a term coined by computer scientist and lawyer, Nick Szabo, in his seminal article *Smart Contracts: Building Blocks for Digital Markets*, are an automated contract that does not require human involvement to be executed or enforced. Szabo described a smart contract as "a set of promises, specified in digital form, including protocols within which the parties perform on these promises."[2]

A simpler way of looking at a smart contract is as an "if, then" equation; if X condition is met, then Y occurs. At the moment that an agreed-upon condition occurs, the smart contract self-executes and the transfer is recorded on the blockchain.

Once participants agree to terms, conditions, and outcomes, the smart contract is coded and recorded on the blockchain. The coding of most smart contracts contains references to an external data source which is required for the smart contract to

[2] Szabo, Smart Contracts: Building Blocks for Digital Market, Entropy #16, available at http://www.fon.hum.uva.nl/rob/Courses/InformationInSpeech/CDROM/Literature/LOTwinterschool2006/szabo.best.vwh.net/smart_contracts_2.html.

function, called an "oracle." After a smart contract is recorded on chain, it cannot be modified without the participating parties' permission. This last characteristic ensures that a smart contract will always produce the desired outcome when agreed-upon conditions are met; it also makes contracts nearly impossible to unilaterally modify if circumstances change, forbearance is warranted, or a programming error is found, as a court or individual recordkeeper has no control over the underlying data.

Smart contracts are ideal for real estate sales, bond payments and servicing, securities transfers, loan payments, loss payments under insurance contracts, and many other agreements relating to financial data.

Initially, smaller companies in the blockchain space and on the Ethereum network were the only ones utilizing smart contracts. Larger companies were hesitant to employ smart contracts, while the base layer or "rails" were still being developed. However, presently, companies have started not only adopting smart contracts but created their own initiatives, such as JPMorgan and Google.[3]

## 10.3 Bitcoin's Rise: The 2017 ICO Boom and the SAFT

In January of 2017, Bitcoin was trading at approximately $1000 a coin. By December of 2017, it had risen to $19,000 a coin. It is still unclear what fueled the drastic price increase, but many believe that the prominence of initial coin offerings (or "ICOs") contributed to this rise.[4] During the 2017 ICO boom, between July and November, approximately 430 companies raised more than $3 billion. From January 2014 to December 2017, $6.4 billion was raised by ICOs.[5] Most companies purported to raise funds from investors by issuing a digital asset often referred to as a "token" or "coin." In general, the US Securities and Exchange Commission has typically regarded ICOs as an offering of securities, in which case, ICOs made available to those living in the USA must be registered with the SEC or fall under an exemption.[6]

Many ICOs used a form of agreement called a SAFT as safe means of selling tokens, exempt from securities registration requirements to raise money. SAFT stands for Simple Agreement for Future Token. SAFTs were based off a Simple

[3] Bert-Jan Butijn, Jens K. Roehrich, Kostas Selviaridis, and Wendy van der Valk, Beyond the Blockchain Technology Hype: When Does it Make Sense to Use Smart Contracts? (Feb. 20, 2023), available at: https://cmr.berkeley.edu/2023/02/beyond-the-blockchain-technology-hype-when-does-it-make-sense-to-use-smart-contracts/.

[4] Others have claimed that a "whale" or an individual that held a large amount of Bitcoin caused the surge in pricing. Orcutt, "One Bitcoin 'whale' may have fueled the currency's price spike in 2017," MIT Technology Review (Nov. 2004), https://www.technologyreview.com/2019/11/04/132066/one-bitcoin-whale-may-have-fueled-the-currencys-price-spike-in-2017/.

[5] Galka, Four Years of Token Sales, Visualized in One Graphic (Dec. 11, 2017), https://elementus.io/blog/token-sales-visualization/.

[6] SEC, Cryptocurrency/ICOs, Five Things to Know about ICOs (March 8, 2024), available at: https://www.sec.gov/securities-topics/ICO.

Agreement for Future Equity. In a written investor alert dated May 9, 2017, titled "Investor Bulletin: Be Cautious of SAFEs in Crowdfunding,"[7] in bold and italics, the SEC stated "Despite its name, a SAFE may not be 'simple' or 'safe.'" Since issuing its warning about SAFEs, the SEC has aggressively asserted that SAFTs are securities and that digital assets offered in connection with SAFTs must abide by the US securities laws.

In 2020, the SEC launched a website to help companies and potential investors understand whether an ICO qualifies as security and whether a particular ICO is subject to SEC regulation.[8] As noted below, the SEC has since devoted considerable resources to enforcement efforts in this domain.

## 10.4 Regulation of Digital Assets in the USA

A number of institutions regulate digital assets issued by financial technology ("fintech") companies including (1) the Securities and Exchange Commission ("SEC"), (2) the Commodity Futures Trade Commission ("CFTC"), (3) the Federal Trade Commission ("FTC"), (4) the Consumer Financial Protection Bureau ("CFPB"), (5) the Office of the Comptroller of the Currency ("OCC"), and (6) the Financial Depository Insurance Commission ("FDIC").

## 10.5 Regulation of Digital Assets in the USA—SEC

For a number of years, the Securities and Exchange Commission has provided guidance to the cryptocurrency sector through enforcement actions concerning transactions utilizing digital assets. Early cases such as *Securities and Exchange Commission v. Trendon T. Shavers and Bitcoin Savings and Trust*[9] and *In the Matter of Erik T. Voorhees*[10] indicated that investment schemes involving digital assets can be deemed to constitute the unregistered sale of securities and be subject to the federal and state securities laws.

The SEC has issued limited guidance as to how new technologies fit into current statutory frameworks; and it has primarily regulated via enforcement action, and publishing summaries of these actions, and any settlements, to provide guidance to others.

---

[7] SEC, Investor Bulletin: Be Cautious of SAFEs in Crowdfunding (May 9, 2017), available at https://www.sec.gov/oiea/investor-alerts-and-bulletins/ib_safes.

[8] SEC, Spotlight on Initial Coin Offerings (ICOs), https://www.sec.gov/ICO.

[9] Securities and Exchange Commission v. Shavers, Fed. Sec. L. Rep. (CCH) P 97596, 2013 WL 4028182 (E.D. Tex. 2013), adhered to on reconsideration, 2014 WL 12622292 (E.D. Tex. 2014).

[10] See In the Matter of Erik T. Voorhees, Securities Act Release No. 33-9592, 109 S.E.C. Docket 3, 2014 WL 2465620 (June 3, 2014).

For example, in the SEC Division of Enforcement's 2019 Annual Report, released in November 2019, the Codirectors of the Division highlight that the Division's activities "in the digital asset space matured and expanded" in 2019.[11] This took shape in the form of first-ever cases brought related to the unlawful promotion of ICOs and a number of other cases brought related to fraud and registration violations connected to digital assets.

In addition, the Division has sought to provide guidance to practitioners in the digital asset space through some of the language they have used in their settlements. For example, in three cases brought in 2019 against issuers of digital assets, the settlements that resulted provided the issuers with a path to compliance with securities registration requirements when the initial sales of securities were illegally made or made without an exemption. Proper registration of securities and compliance with the required disclosures to investors are paramount concerns to the SEC, whose enforcement actions have typically sought to "send the clear message that, if a product is a security, regardless of the label attached to it, those who issue, promote, or provide a platform for buying and selling that security must comply with the investor protection requirements of the federal securities laws."[12]

The SEC, beginning under Chair Jay Clayton in 2018 and continuing under current Chair Gary Gensler through 2023, formerly disapproved of more than 20 exchange rule filings for spot Bitcoin exchange-traded products ("ETPs"). That changed in 2024.[13] The Commission marked the start of 2024 by approving the listing and trading of a number of spot Bitcoin exchange-traded product (ETP) shares while noting, however, that its action is limited to ETPs holding only Bitcoin. This historic shift by the SEC came in direct response to a ruling by the US Court of Appeals for the District of Columbia following the Commission's disapproval of the listing and trading of Grayscale's proposed ETP. The federal appellate court held that the SEC needed to provide a greater explanation as to its reason for disapproval.[14] The Commission also noted a number of protections to be included for investors, such as requirements that sponsors of Bitcoin ETPs must provide full and truthful disclosure of their products and that existing rules and standards of conduct apply to the purchase and sale of approved ETPs.[15]

[11] Securities and Exchange Commission, Division of Enforcement, 2019 Annual Report, at 6 (Nov. 2019), available at https://www.sec.gov/files/enforcement-annual-report-2019.pdf.

[12] 2019 Annual Report, at 6.

[13] Gary Gensler, Statement on the Approval of Spot Bitcoin Exchange-Traded Products (Jan.10, 2024), available at: https://www.sec.gov/news/statement/gensler-statement-spot-bitcoin-011023.

[14] See *Grayscale Investments, LLC v. SEC*, No. 22-1142, 82 F.4th 1239 (D.C. Cir. 2023).

[15] Gary Gensler, Statement on the Approval of Spot Bitcoin Exchange-Traded Products (Jan. 10, 2024), available at: https://www.sec.gov/news/statement/gensler-statement-spot-bitcoin-011023.

## 10.6 Regulation of Digital Assets in the USA—Consumer Protection Agencies

The consumer protection agencies, like the CFPB and FTC, exist largely to ensure that consumers are unharmed by business practices that fall within their jurisdiction while attempting to maintain competitive marketplaces. While fintech firms increase competition in the marketplace and assist consumers, sometimes those efficiencies present unforeseen risks to consumers. The CFPB has often taken a measured approach and attempted to engage private fintech firms in dialog before issuing enforcement actions. For example, the CFPB has a "no-action letter" policy, which withholds enforcement actions against some consumer-friendly innovations in an effort to promote innovation and provide safe harbor to qualifying firms. Other policies, like the CFPB's Office of Innovation and sandbox programs, seek to allow qualifying companies to experiment with fintech in a regulated setting while reducing potential risk to consumers in the process.

The FTC is more limited in its ability to impose enforcement actions related to fintech activities, as it has a robust investigative capacity but limited supervisory authority. Most of the FTC's involvement with fintech companies has been in the context of acting as an organizer of hearings, reports, workshops, and conferences to discuss new technology and the potential risks they pose. For example, from 2016 to 2024, the FTC has brought approximately 20 cases against technology, telecommunications, and money service firms related to adoption of financial technology.

While the FTC is limited in its enforcement capacity, it has not stopped short in warning consumers of crypto risks. From 2018 to 2024, the FTC issued roughly 13 consumer alerts warning the public of cryptocurrency scams and 7 reports concerning fintech and cryptocurrency. For example, the FTC released a report finding that consumers reported losing more than $1 billion in cryptocurrency in scams since 2021.[16] The FTC's message is clear: Consumers must be wary of cryptocurrencies.

## 10.7 Regulation of Digital Assets in the USA—Banking Regulators

The primary banking regulators, including the Federal Reserve, Federal Deposit Insurance Corporation ("FDIC"), Office of the Comptroller of the Currency ("OCC"), and National Credit Union Administration, have also been involved in the regulation of digital assets. In particular, these entities seek to reduce risk to participants in the banking industries by adjusting rules to fit the new challenges and

[16] Federal Trade Commission, New Analysis Finds Consumer Reported Losing More than $1 Billion in Crptocurrency to Scams since 2021(June 3, 2022), available at: https://www.ftc.gov/news-events/news/press-releases/2022/06/new-analysis-finds-consumers-reported-losing-more-1-billion-cryptocurrency-scams-2021.

opportunities offered by fintech, issuing guidance on fintech topics, and supervising the relationship between member banks and nonbank fintech companies.

Banking regulators have offered regulatory sandboxes to allow member banks and their technology service providers (TSPs) to experiment and test new fintech solutions in controlled environments. For example, in 2019, the OCC proposed an Innovation Pilot Program aimed at supporting the testing of products and services that benefit consumers, businesses, and communities.[17] One important feature of this program would be the open line of communication and feedback between regulators and participants which would allow for a more streamlined dialog in the absence of statutory and regulatory waivers. Similar programs have been enacted by the other banking entities, including the Federal Reserve (Federal Reserve Innovation Program), the FDIC (FDIC Tech Lab), and more broadly the OCC (OCC Office of Innovation).

However, the FDIC is still promoting exercising caution toward crypto. In July of 2022, the FDIC issued a "fact sheet" defining what the public needs to know about FDIC deposit insurance and crypto companies.[18] The fact sheet makes clear that the FDIC does not insure crypto companies, nor by extension crypto-assets or any nonbank entity, such as crypto custodians, exchanges, brokers, wallet providers, and neobanks.

On January 3, 2023, the FDIC, in tandem with the OCC and the Federal Reserve System, released additional guidance regarding crypto-asset risks to banking organizations sparked by concern regarding the "significant volatility and the exposure of vulnerability in the crypto-asset sector."[19] The joint statement notes that banking organizations must be aware of the key risks associated with crypto-assets and its participants to ensure such risks "do not migrate to the banking system." The agencies include a litany of concerns, including "legal uncertainties related to custody practices, redemptions, and ownership rights, some of which are currently the subject of legal processes and proceedings" in addition to "risk management and governance practices in the crypto-asset sector exhibiting a lack of maturity and robustness." [20]

[17] Office of the Comptroller of the Currency, OCC Innovation Pilot Program, available at https://www.occ.treas.gov/topics/supervision-and-examination/responsible-innovation/occ-innovation-pilot-program.pdf. See also Office of the Comptroller of the Currency, Responsible Innovation, https://www.occ.treas.gov/topics/supervision-and-examination/responsible-innovation/index-responsible-innovation.html.

[18] Federal Deposit Insurance Corporation, Fact Sheet: What the Public Needs to Know About FDIC Deposit Insurance and Crypto Companies (July 28, 2022), available at: https://www.fdic.gov/news/fact-sheets/crypto-fact-sheet-7-28-22.pdf.

[19] Joint Statement on Crypto-Asset Risks to Banking Organizations (Jan. 3, 2023), available at: https://www.fdic.gov/news/press-releases/2023/pr23002a.pdf.

[20] *Id.*

## 10.8 Issues Raised by SEC/CFTC Enforcement Actions and Litigation, 2018–2024

Enforcement actions conducted by the Securities and Exchange Commission and Commodity Futures Trading Commission are not precedential. Past decisions need not be followed or distinguished in future decisions. Nonetheless, enforcement actions reflect how the SEC and CFTC interpret federal securities and commodities laws with respect to cryptocurrency. Federal lawsuits brought by the SEC or CFTC, on the other hand, can be precedential.

## 10.9 Issues Raised by SEC/CFTC Enforcement Actions and Litigation, 2018–2020—DAO Report and the *Howey* Test

To its credit, prior to the initiation of any enforcement actions against issuers of initial coin offerings, on July 27, 2017, the Securities and Exchange Commission released an investigative report (the "DAO Report") finding that the digital assets issued by the Digital Autonomous Organization (the "DAO") constituted securities under the federal securities laws.[21] The SEC relied on the *Howey* test as the foundation of its analysis.

*Howey* is a decades-old, Supreme Court decision,[22] which analyzed whether an investment in an orange grove qualified as an "investment contract"[23] and therefore a security under the Securities Exchange Act of 1934 (the "Exchange Act"). Despite its age, the *Howey* test is still used today to define securities. *Howey* defined an investment contract as "a contract, transaction or scheme whereby a person invests his money in a common enterprise and is led to expect profits solely from the efforts of the promoter or a third party."[24] The definition establishes a four-part test to determine whether a particular scheme is an investment contract. For an investment contract to be a security under *Howey*, the following factors must be present: (1) an investment of money, (2) in a common enterprise, (3) with an expectation of profits, and (4) which are derived solely from the efforts of the promoter.

Significantly, the DAO Report noted that "form should be disregarded for substance" in analyzing digital asset offerings.[25] The DAO Report was clear that, technological advances notwithstanding, a digital asset that meets the characteristics of

[21] Report of Investigation Pursuant to Section 21(A) of the Securities Exchange Act of 1934: The DAO, Exchange Act Release No. 34-81207, 2017 WL 7184670 (July 25, 2017).

[22] *SEC v. W.J. Howey Co.*, 328 U.S. 293, 298–99 (1946).

[23] Exchange Act §3(a)(10), 15 U.S.C.A. §78c(a)(10).

[24] *Howey*, 328 U.S. at 298–99.

[25] The DAO Report, Exchange Act Release No. 34-81207, 2017 WL 7184670, *8.

an investment contract is a security. Among other things, the DAO Report asserted that investors who purchased digital assets issued by the DAO "were investing in a common enterprise and reasonably expected to earn profits through that enterprise," with such profits being derived from the "managerial efforts of others," including the founders and curators of the DAO, who also served the function of nodes on a blockchain.[26] The DAO Report gave particular attention to the tradability of the underlying digital asset in secondary markets as an indicator of whether or not the asset was a security.

After issuing the DAO Report, the SEC began prosecuting enforcement actions against issuers of digital assets for violation of US securities laws despite protestations that the digital assets issued were cryptocurrency or were SAFTs and somehow exempt from US securities laws.

## 10.10 Issues Raised by SEC/CFTC Enforcement Actions and Litigation, 2018–2020—SAFT Enforcement Actions

In the early case of *In the Matter of Simply Vital Health, Inc.*, the Securities and Exchange Commission took action against a blockchain-based health tech company SimplyVital Health, Inc. ("SimplyVital") for failing to verify investors were accredited.[27] The company conducted a presale of its "HLTH" token to raise funds for its blockchain platform. Tokens were to be sold in two phases: a private sale followed by a crowd sale. The private sale required a minimum investment of $10,000 from accredited investors through a Simple Agreement for Future Tokens (SAFTs). Under the terms of the SAFT, investors would receive HLTH tokens once they launched. But despite these efforts to comply with the registration exemptions, the company fell short in taking reasonable steps to verify that its investors were actually accredited. SimplyVital was aware some investors were pooling funds to meet the minimum investment requirement, but did not try to determine whether the participants in the pool were also accredited. As result, SimplyVital's token sale failed to qualify for exemption under Regulation D and violated Sections 5(a) and 5(c) of the Securities Exchange Act.

Since *In the Matter of Simply Vital Health*, the SEC has issued new rule amendments which impact the potential exemption applicable under Regulation D.[28] For

[26] 2017 WL 7184670, *9.

[27] *In the Matter of Simply Vital Health, Inc.*, Securities Act Release, No. 33-10671, 2019 WL 3780055 (Aug. 12, 2019).

[28] SEC Harmonizes and Improves "Patchwork" Exempt Offering Framework (Nov. 2, 2020), available at: https://www.sec.gov/news/press-release/2020-273.

Rule 504 of Regulation D, the 2020 amendment raised the maximum offering amount from $5 to $10 million, which is still the limit in 2024.[29]

## 10.11 Issues Raised by SEC/CFTC Enforcement Actions and Litigation, 2018–2020—Kik Interactive and Telegram

Even when investors are verified as accredited, selling tokens in two phases—a private sale to wealthy investors and a crowd sale to the general public—may violate US securities laws. After Canadian mobile messenger maker, Kik Interactive ("Kik"), raised $100 million from selling tokens, the Securities and Exchange Commission filed a lawsuit to enjoin Kik, disgorge all revenue generated from token sales, and seek civil penalties.[30]

Kik had offered and sold digital assets to professional investment funds and other select, wealthy investors using a Simple Agreement for Future Tokens (SAFTs). Kik's SAFT entitled purchasers to the future delivery of "Kin" a digital asset for Kik's "decentralized economy," which did not yet exist. Under the SAFT, investors bought Kin at a discount to the price that the general public would pay, and Kik promised to deliver Kin pursuant to a schedule: half at the time that it delivered tokens to the general public and half on the 1-year anniversary of the first delivery. Kik raised approximately $49 million in this offering.

Kik then offered Kin to the general public and had public investors sign up for this public sale while still offering and selling discounted Kin to investment funds and wealthy investors through its SAFT. Kik sold about $50 million of Kin to the general public in exchange for Ether. In addition to the fact that the decentralized economy Kik had marketed did not exist, no goods or services were offered on Kik's platform in return for Kin.

The SEC alleged Kik violated Section 5 of the Securities Act through its entire offer and sale of Kin, including sales to accredited investors by SAFT. Though Kik argued that its SAFT sales were private offerings, exempt from registration requirements under Rule 506(c), the SEC disagreed for three reasons:

- Kik's SAFT sales violated Section 5 because they were part of, and not separate from, the public sale of Kin. The SEC noted that sales made through SAFTs were contingent on the public also buying Kin in the offering and that Kik conducted a single marketing campaign that publicly referred to only one sale.
- Even if Kik's offering were to be treated as two separate offerings, Kik could not show "two" separate offerings under SEC rules. "A person may not separate

[29] Private Placements under Regulation D – Investor Bulletin (Aug. 17, 2022), https://www.sec.gov/oiea/investor-alerts-and-bulletins/private-placements-under-regulation-d-investor-bulletin.

[30] See *U.S. Securities and Exchange Comission, v. Kik Interactive Inc.*, 2019 WL 2365305 (S.D. N.Y. 2019) (Complaint).

parts of a series of related transactions, the sum total of which is really one offering, and claim that a particular part is a nonpublic transaction."[31] The SEC argued Kik's SAFT sales and Kin sales must be considered integrated because they were part of a single plan of financing, involved issuance of the same class of securities (i.e., identical and fungible Kin), were made at or about the same time, involved functionally similar consideration, and were for the same general purpose.
- Even if SAFT sales to accredited investors were a separate offering, such sales still failed exemption because Kik did not take steps to restrict the purchasers from immediately reselling to the public.

Another early case is illustrative. Telegram, a mobile messaging application, used a SAFT to raise approximately $1.7 billion between January and March 2018 from sales of, approximately, 2.9 billion digital assets called "Grams." The SEC alleged that "Telegram sold more than 1 billion Grams to 39 U.S. purchasers, raising $424.5 million from the U.S. market." Telegram intended to use the proceeds from its offering of Grams to finance creation of its own blockchain protocol, the "Telegram Open Network" or "TON Blockchain." In asserting that Grams were not a currency because no products or services could be purchased with Grams, the SEC also asserted that Grams were securities as they were purchased by investors with the expectation of profit. Telegram intended to sell Grams in the US capital markets by October 31, 2019, prompting the SEC to seek and obtain a preliminary injunction enjoining the offering of Grams.[32] After approximately 8 months of battling the SEC, Telegram agreed to return over $1.2 billion to investors and to pay a civil penalty of $18.5 million.

All told, the SEC reasoned that those who bought Kin (from Kik) or Grams (from Telegram) would be deprived of the important disclosures that SEC reporting and a registration statement would have provided, such as information regarding the digital assets, the issuer's business operations, financial condition, risk factors, and management. In October of 2020, the US District Court for the Southern District of New York issued a permanent injunction against Kik from violating the registration provisions of Sections 5(a) and 5(c) of the Securities Act of 1933. Moreover, Kik was ordered, until 2023, to provide notice to the SEC prior to engaging in enumerated future issuances, offers, sales, and transfers of digital assets and pay a $5 million penalty.

Both cases serve as an ample reminder that there is no easy way to circumvent US securities laws, SAFT, or otherwise.

---

[31] Nonpublic Offering Exemption, 1933 Act Release No. 33-4552, 27 Fed. Reg. 11316, 1962 WL 69540, *4 (Nov. 6, 1962); *S.E.C. v. Mattera*, Fed. Sec. L. Rep. (CCH) P 97759, 2013 WL 6485949, *12 (S.D. N.Y. 2013).

[32] *S.E.C. v. Telegram Group Inc.*, Fed. Sec. L. Rep. (CCH) P 100769, 2020 WL 1430035 (S.D. N.Y. 2020), appeal withdrawn, 2020 WL 3467671 (2d Cir. 2020).

## 10.12 Issues Raised by SEC/CFTC Enforcement Actions and Litigation, 2018–2020—Unregistered and Nonexempt Crypto-Exchanges

By cease-and-desist order dated November 8, 2018, EtherDelta, an online trading platform and its operator, agreed to pay fines for violating Section 3(a)(1) of the Exchange Act and Rule 3b-16, in operating an unlicensed exchange.[33] EtherDelta provided a user-friendly interface that resembled online securities trading platforms where users could enter orders to buy or sell specified quantities of digital assets at a specified price (in Ether) and with a specified time-in-force. Orders were fulfilled through smart contracts. EtherDelta neither registered with the Securities and Exchange Commission as a national securities exchange nor operated pursuant to any registration exemptions. As a result, EtherDelta violated Exchange Act Sections 5 and 21C(a).

Pursuant to Exchange Act Rule 3b-16(a), a system must be registered as a national exchange if it is "a market place or facilities for bringing together purchasers and sellers of securities or for otherwise performing with respect to securities the functions commonly performed by an exchange" (as those terms are used in Section 3(a)(1) of the Exchange Act) if such a system (1) brings together the orders for securities of multiple buyers and sellers and (2) uses established, nondiscretionary methods (whether by providing a trading facility or by setting rules) under which such orders interact with each other, and the buyers and sellers entering such orders agree to the terms of the trade. One exemption to the registration requirement is an alternative trading system ("ATS").[34] An ATS that complies with ATS regulations and operates pursuant to the Rule 3a1-1(a)(2) exemption is not required to register as a national securities exchange. EtherDelta, however, did not take steps to comply with ATS regulations either.

The SEC asserted that EtherDelta operated as a marketplace for bringing together the orders of multiple buyers and sellers in digital assets that included securities as defined by Section 3(a)(10) of the Exchange Act. The purchasers of such digital assets invested money with a reasonable expectation of profits, including through the increased value of their investments in secondary trading, based on the managerial efforts of others.[35] EtherDelta brought together orders by receiving and storing orders in tokens in the EtherDelta order book and displaying the top 500 orders

---

[33] *In the Matter of Zachary Coburn*, Exchange Act Release No. 34-84553, 2018 WL 5840155 (Nov. 18, 2018).

[34] Exchange Act Rule 3a1-1 exempts an organization, association, or group of persons that complies with Regulation ATS, which, among other things, requires registering as a broker-dealer, filing a Form ATS with the Commission, and establishing written safeguards and procedures to protect subscribers' confidential trading information. 17 C.F.R. §240.3a1-1(a)(2).

[35] See *SEC v. Edwards*, 540 U.S. 389, 393 (2004); *SEC v. W.J. Howey Co.*, 328 U.S. 293, 301 (1946); Report of Investigation Pursuant to Section 21(A) of the Securities Exchange Act of 1934: The DAO, Exchange Act Release No. 34-81207, 117 S.E.C. Docket 745, 2017 WL 7184670 (July 25, 2017).

(including token symbol, size, and price) as bids and offers on the EtherDelta website. EtherDelta further provided the means for these orders to interact and execute through the combined use of the EtherDelta website, order book, and preprogrammed trading protocols defined in the EtherDelta smart contract. In the Commission's assessment, these established, nondiscretionary methods allowed users to agree upon the terms of their trades in tokens on EtherDelta. EtherDelta's manager agreed to disgorge over $300,000 in profits and paid a $75,000 penalty.

## 10.13 Issues Raised by SEC/CFTC Enforcement Actions and Litigation, 2018–2020—Duality of Jurisdiction

More recent lawsuits by the Securities and Exchange Commission and the Commodity Futures Trading Commission show the expansive reach of enforcement of US federal securities and commodities laws. In a pair of enforcement actions brought by the SEC and CFTC, XBT Corp. SARL (doing business as First Global Credit) ("XBT") found itself in the crosshairs of both commissions for offering unregistered Bitcoin swaps.[36]

XBT settled with both the SEC and CFTC for alleged violations regarding solicitations and acceptances of futures orders from 24 US customers, including accepting Bitcoin for margin trades. At the time, XBT was not registered with the CFTC as a futures commission merchant ("FCM") or with the SEC on a registered national securities exchange. According to the SEC's order, from 2014 until 2019, XBT had at least 90 investors who conducted more than 18,000 security-based swaps representing more than $100 million in transactions "based on US-listed securities." Of those transactions, $43.8 million in trades were made by US residents. The SEC ordered XBT to pay over $130,000, including disgorgement and a civil penalty, while the CFTC ordered XBT to pay an additional $100,000. The civil penalty levied by the CFTC could have been much greater but "was substantially reduced in light of [XBT]'s cooperation and remediation."

US regulators keep a watchful eye on foreign companies soliciting investments from US customers. That included 1pool Ltd. ("1pool"), a company based in the Marshall Islands, and its CEO, a resident of Austria. In a consent order entered into between 1pool, its CEO, and the CFTC, the CFTC found that the CEO, through 1pool, illegally offered retail commodity transactions—a regulated transaction under federal commodities laws—that were margined in Bitcoin.[37] As set forth in the order, the offer and sales were improper because 1pool failed to register as an

[36] *In the Matter of: XBT Corp. SARL d/b/a First Global Credit, Respondent*, CFTC No. 20-04, Comm. Fut. L. Rep. P 34615, 2019 WL 5718287 (Oct. 31, 2029); *In the Matter of XBT Corp SARI d/b/a First Global Credit*, Securities Act Release Nos. 33-10723, 34-87428, 2019 WL 5624341 (Oct. 31, 2019).

[37] *CFTC v. 1pool Ltd.*, Comm. Fut. L. Rep. (CCH) P 34468, 2019 WL 1605201 (D.D.C. 2019); *SEC v. 1pool Ltd. a.k.a. 1Broker and Patrick Brunner*, No. 1:18-CV-02244-TNM (D.D.C.),

FCM and further failed to put anti-money laundering (AML) procedures in place. Similarly, the SEC found that 1pool and its CEO solicited investors from the USA to buy and sell security-based swaps. The SEC stated that 1pool improperly transacted in these swaps on a registered national securities exchange, failed to register as a dealer, and lacked anti-money laundering procedures.

The SEC and CFTC's jurisdiction over transactions facilitated outside of the USA is limited when there are no US persons involved in the relevant transactions. If, however, a foreign entity solicits US investors or executes a regulated transaction, such as a retail commodity transaction or security-based swap, with a US investor, the CFTC and SEC's jurisdiction are triggered. In recent years, especially with respect to digital assets, the CFTC and SEC have been quick to assert their jurisdiction both against foreign issuers and foreign initiated transactions. Often under financial pressure to settle, firms sometimes agree to jurisdiction when the CFTC and SEC's standing are tenuous.

## 10.14 Issues Raised by SEC/CFTC Enforcement Actions and Litigation, 2018–2020—Outsourcing Does Not Mitigate Liability and BCOT

Outsourcing initial coin offering sales does not abate liability for the sale of unregistered securities. Blockchain of Things Inc. ("BCOT"), maker of blockchain development tools, raised nearly $13 million through an initial coin offering. BCOT intended to use the funds to develop its blockchain-based technology and platform that, according to BCOT, would facilitate third-party secure messaging, digital asset generation, and digital asset transfer over blockchain. To sell its token, BCOT engaged resellers in South Korea, Vietnam, Japan, and the UAE. BCOT's reseller agreements provided that each foreign reseller would have exclusive sales rights within its respective geographic territory (i.e., South Korea, Vietnam, Japan, and the UAE). However, the agreements did not require resellers to ensure potential purchasers were in fact residents of the respective geographic territories. Because direct contact with purchases was through the foreign resellers, BCOT had no visibility into the resellers' token sales or into the identity of the potential purchasers. BCOT's resellers succeeded in selling more than $12 million in tokens to more than 1380 individuals. When the SEC began an investigation into whether BCOT had broken federal securities laws through the offer and sale of its token, BCOT accepted a settlement with the Securities and Exchange Commission.[38]

---

Litigation Release No. 24330, 2018 WL 5734344 (S.E.C. Release No. 2018); *SEC v. 1pool Ltd. a.k.a. 1Broker and Patrick Brunner*, 2018 WL 4658195 (D.D.C. 2018) (Complaint).

[38] *In the Matter of Blockchain of Things, Inc.*, Securities Act Release No. 33-10736, 2019 WL 7020130 (Dec. 18, 2019).

While the SEC order does not clarify whether any of 1380 purchasers were US individuals, it included sales to these individuals in its assessment of unregistered and nonexempt sales. Moreover, though BCOT itself sold tokens to 69 US investors (accounting for less than 5% of the total coin sales), the SEC did not limit remedial measure to just US customers. Rather, all customers of BCOT's coins could request a refund. In addition to returning funds to investors, BCOT agreed to register its tokens as securities, to cease and desist from violating federal securities laws in the future, and further agreed to pay a $250,000 penalty.

## 10.15 Issues Raised by SEC/CFTC Enforcement Actions and Litigation, 2018–2020—Penalties for Illegally Issuing Unregistered Digital Assets

Penalties for offering unregistered digital assets that are not exempt from registration can vary widely based on the asserted offense and response. For example, in the case of *In the Matter of Gladius Network LLC*, Gladius saved itself from civil penalties by self-reporting its unregistered initial coin offering to the Securities and Exchange Commission.[39] Gladius had raised money via an unregistered offering of digital assets called GLA. GLA could be acquired directly from Gladius or purchased in secondary markets. Gladius raised $12.7 million worth of Ether during its ICO.

Thereafter, Gladius notified the SEC of its unregistered offering. The SEC determined that GLA Tokens were securities and that Gladius had violated US securities laws, but did not impose a penalty against Gladius, demonstrating that issuers who proactively and voluntarily seek to remediate an unregistered securities offering can avoid fines. In fact, the SEC made a point of highlighting Gladius' cooperation in not issuing a fine. The Gladius Order states:

> The Commission is not imposing a penalty because of the significant steps Gladius took to remediate the violation. Gladius, which was evaluating the applicability of the federal securities laws to its ICO, self-reported to staff in the Commission's Division of Enforcement in the summer of 2018, and informed Commission staff that it wanted to do what was necessary to take prompt remedial steps. It cooperated with the staff's investigation, providing information quickly and in a form useful to the staff. It also voluntarily agreed to the remedial steps listed in the undertakings in this order, including the provision of compensation to investors.[40]

[39] *In the Matter of Gladius Network LLC*, Securities Act Release No. 33-10608, 2019 WL 697993 (Feb. 20, 2019).

[40] 2019 WL 697993, *2.

## *Block.one*

While self-reporting may stave off civil penalties, when an ICO is so large it raises funds in the billions from individuals around the world, the penalties for not complying with US securities laws may be outweighed by the sheer upside of crowdfunding through a coin offering.

Block.one's ICO for the EOS blockchain made headlines in 2018 as one of the largest crowdfunded projects of all time. Block.one offered and sold $900 million worth of digital assets to raise capital for development of the EOS blockchain and EOS.IO software. Block.one raised several billion dollars, including from residents in the USA. After Block.one failed to register its offering with the SEC or qualify for a registration exemption, the SEC investigated the company for offering and selling unregistered securities.[41]

Foreseeing the risk associated with running an unregistered, nonexempt coin offering in the USA, Block.one tried to discourage purchase of tokens by persons within the USA. Though Block.one sold ERC-20 Tokens directly through the EOS.IO website, it blocked US IP addresses from accessing the website's token sale page. In addition, Block.one required all customers to agree to the Token Purchase Agreement, which included provisions that US persons were prohibited from purchasing tokens. But despite these measures to prevent US purchases, Block.one did not verify that purchasers were not US-based persons. Nor did Block.one try to prevent resale of tokens to US purchasers in secondary markets.

The SEC determined that purchases had occurred in the USA through the EOS.IO website. The Commission further determined that the digital assets offered and sold by Block.one were nonexempt, unregistered securities. Block.one was fined $24 million—a penalty of pennies on the dollar compared to the billions raised by Block.one in its ICO. Perhaps more potent than the pecuniary penalty, however, Block.one was ordered not to commit future securities violations, which could have hamstrung future fundraising efforts. But Block.one sought and was granted a waiver from the SEC, allowing the company to rely on Regulation A and D exemptions for future projects. In the end, Block.one's censure was relatively insignificant considering the scale of the company's sale of unregistered securities.

---

[41] *In the Matter of Block.one*, Securities Act Release No. 33-10714, 2019 WL 4793292 (Sept. 30, 2019).

## 10.16 Issues Raised by SEC/CFTC Enforcement Actions and Litigation Through 2023—SEC Crackdown on Unregistered Tokens and Retail Exchanges

The SEC has ramped up its efforts to prevent the sale of unregistered securities. In 2023, it filed at several lawsuits against companies that sold unregistered securities, including the following:

1. In *SEC v. Genesis Global Capital, LLC and Gemini Trust Company, LLC*, the SEC alleged that, through the Gemini Earn Cryptocurrency Asset Lending Program, Genesis and Gemini engaged in the unregistered offer and sale of securities to US retail investors.[42]
2. In *SEC v. Justin Sun*, the SEC charged Sun and three of his companies, Tron Foundation Limited, BitTorrent Foundation Ltd., and Rainberry, Inc., with offering and selling Tronix (TRX) and BitTorrent (BTT) without registering and for manipulating the secondary market for TRX through wash trading.[43]
3. In *SEC v. Coinbase*, the SEC charged Coinbase as operating as an unregistered broker through offering Coinbase Prime and Coinbase Wallet and offering a staking program without first registering with the SEC. The SEC also alleged Coinbase operates a trading platform allowing US customers to buy, sell, and trade cryptocurrency without registering with the SEC as a broker, national securities exchange, or clearing agency.[44] This case has ignited an epic legal battle, with Coinbase aggressively defending itself. The dispute, which is guaranteed to generate appellate—and perhaps even Supreme Court—review, will result in clarification of, and likely new, law concerning the scope of the US securities law as applied to the blockchain industry.
4. In *SEC v. LBRY, Inc.*, the SEC alleged LBRY sold unregistered securities when it issued its own token, LBC, and received approximately $12.2 million in proceeds. Judge Barbadoro of the US District Court for the District of New Hampshire ordered LBRY to pay a civil penalty of $111,614 and permanently enjoined LBRY from further violations of the registration provisions of the federal securities laws and from participating in unregistered offerings of crypto-asset securities.[45]

State enforcers have also entered the arena. For example, in *James v. Mek Global Limited and Phoenixfin PTE Ltd d/b/a KuCoin*, New York Attorney General Letitia

[42] *SEC v. Genesis Global Capital, LLC and Gemini Trust Company, LLC*, No. 1:23-cv-00287 (S.D.N.Y. Jan. 12, 2023).

[43] *SEC v. Justin Sun, et al.*, No. 1:23-cv-02433 (S.D.N.Y. March 3, 2023).

[44] *SEC v. Coinbase, Inc. and Coinbase Global, Inc.*, No. 1-23-cv-04738 (S.D.N.Y. June 6, 2023).

[45] *SEC v. LBRY, Inc.*, No. 1:21-cv-00260- PB, (D. N.H. March 29, 2021), appeal filed on August 8, 2023.

James sued KuCoin for failing to register with the State of New York prior to allowing investors to buy and sell cryptocurrencies on its platform.[46]

These cases demonstrate the SEC's effort to regulate blockchain and highlight that "if a [centralized] platform offers trading of digital assets that are securities and operates as an 'exchange,' as defined by the federal securities laws, then the platform must register with the SEC as a national securities exchange or be exempt from registration."[47]

## 10.17 Issues Raised by SEC/CFTC Enforcement Actions and Litigation, 2018–2020—Limitations on Disgorgement

In *Liu v. Securities and Exchange Commission*,[48] the US Supreme Court limited the Commission's power to seek disgorgement and held that the amount of a disgorgement award in a SEC civil enforcement action could not exceed net profits from wrongdoing, in light of disgorgement's function as equitable relief under 15 U.S.C.A. §78u(d)(5).

## 10.18 Issues Raised by SEC/CFTC Enforcement Actions and Litigation, 2018–to the Present—Paid Promotions Must Be Disclosed

Particularly in light of the prevalence of social media as a means of promotion, parties must be extremely cautious not to improperly promote an initial coin offering.

---

[46] *James v. Mek Global Limited and Phoenixfin PTE Ltd d/b/a KuCoin*, No. 1:20-cv-02806-GBD-RWL, (S.D.N.Y. March 9, 2023).

[47] SEC, Cryptocurrency/ICOs, What Market Professionals Need to Know, available at: https://www.sec.gov/securitiestopics/ICO#:~:text=If%20a%20platform%20offers%20trading,or%20be%20exempt%20from%20registration.

[48] *Liu v. SEC*, 140 S. Ct. 1936 (2020).

## *ICO Rating*

Operating under the trade name "ICO Rating," a Russian website reviewed and rated ICOs and published its reports and ratings in social media posts.[49] The website promoted itself as "a rating agency that issued independent analytical research, evaluation of ICO projects and assigning them ratings." ICO Rating generated significant web traffic from the USA and contracted with a state-side provider to host its website in the USA. Research and ratings were published in English and included figures fashioned in US dollars.

But unbeknownst to the website's readers, ICO Rating received a fee to rate, produce, and publish research reports on ICO projects on its website and social media networks. For its failed disclosure, ICO Rating was found in violation of Section 17(b) of the Securities Act by the SEC. The Russian website agreed to disgorge $100,000 in profits and paid prejudgment interest and civil penalties of more than $165,000.[50]

## *Centra Tech, Inc.*

Paid promotions on social media are also subject to the same disclosure requirements. For example, Centra Tech, Inc. ("Centra"), a Miami-based company, conducted an ICO to raise funds for a crypto debit card.[51] To promote its ICO, Centra sought celebrity endorsement by Floyd Mayweather and DJ Khaled. Both celebrities were compensated for promoting Centra on their social media accounts, but neither disclosed in their posts that they were being compensated by Centra. The pair were found in violation of Section 17(b) of the Securities Act for touting an ICO that involved the offer and sale of securities on social media without disclosing their receipt of compensation from the issuer for doing so. Both celebrities were disgorged of their endorsement earnings and ordered to desist of future violations.

The SEC continues to charge celebrities and social media influencers for touting and making misleading statements about crypto-assets without disclosing payments being received. In 2022, the SEC charged reality TV star and businesswoman, Kim Kardashian, for touting EMAX tokens, offered and sold by EthereumMax.[52] The SEC found that Kardashian failed to disclose the $250,000 payment she received for

---

[49] Its URL is http://www.icorating.com/, but many company security protocols deem it a gaming site, so block it.

[50] *In the Matter of ICO Rating*, Securities Act Release No. 33-10673, 2019 WL 3947981 (Aug. 20, 2019).

[51] *In the Matter of Floyd Mayweather Jr.*, Securities Act Release No. 33-10578, 2018 WL 6266203 (Nov 29, 2018); *In the Matter of Khaled*, Securities Act Release No. 33-10579, 2018 WL 6266204 (Nov. 29, 2018).

[52] *In the Matter of Kimberly Kardashian*, Securities Act Release No. 3-21197 (Oct. 3, 2022).

her post on Instagram about the EMAX tokens, which contained a link to EthereumMax's website, where investors can purchase tokens. Kardashian, without admitting or denying the charges, agreed to pay $1.26 million, including $260,000 in disgorgement and a penalty of $1,000,000 in addition to agreeing to not promote any crypto-asset securities for 3 years. In 2023, the SEC charged former NBA player Paul Pierce for touting the same EMAX tokens.[53] Pierce settled the charges for a penalty of $1,115,000 and $240,000 for disgorgement and prejudgment interest and agreed not to promote any crypto-asset securities for 3 years. Gurbir S. Grewal, Director of the SEC's Division of Enforcement, stated that "the federal securities laws are clear that any celebrity or other individual who promotes a crypto asset security must disclose the nature, source, and amount of compensation they received in exchange for the promotion."[54]

## 10.19 Issues Raised by SEC/CFTC Enforcement Actions and Litigation, 2018–to the Present—Brokerage Fees to Unregistered Brokers-*ICOBOx*

In September, 2019, the Securities and Exchange Commission commenced an enforcement action against ICOBox and its founder Nikolay Evdokimov for acting as unregistered brokers of digital asset offerings and organizing an illegal $14 million securities offering of ICOBox's digital tokens. The SEC further alleged that ICOBox acted as an unregistered broker-dealer by "facilitating initial coin offerings that raised more than $650 million for dozens of clients."[55] In March of 2020, the US District Court for the Central District of California found that defendants had illegally sold and offered ICOS tokens, which were securities subject to the registration requirements of the federal securities laws. The court permanently enjoined ICOBox and Evdokimov from violating the securities registration provisions of Section 5(a) and 5(c) of the Securities Act of 1934. The court ordered defendants to pay disgorgement totaling $16,059,428.99 and Evdokimov to pay a civil fine of $192,768.

[53] *In the Matter of Paul Anthony Pierce*, Securities Act Release No. 3-21305, (Feb. 17, 2023).

[54] SEC Charges Kim Kardashian for Unlawfully Touting Crypto Security (Oct. 3, 2022), available at: https://www.sec.gov/news/press-release/2022-183.

[55] *SEC v. Icobox and Nikolay Evdokimov*, 2019 WL 4507480 (C.D. Cal. 2019), Litigation Release No. 24601, 2019 WL 4511566 (S.E.C. Release No. 2019); *SEC v. Icobox and Nikolay Evdokimov*, 2019 WL 4507480 (C.D. Cal. 2019) (Complaint).

## 10.20 Issues Raised by SEC/CFTC Enforcement Actions and Litigation 2023—Sam Bankman-Fried and the Fall of FTX

In 2022, the SEC charged Sam Bankman-Fried with violating Section 17(a) of the Securities Act and 10(b)(5) of the Exchange Act for organizing a scheme to defraud equity investors in FTX Trading Ltd., a crypto trading platform which Bankman-Friend was CEO and cofounder. While promoting FTX as a safe crypto-asset trading platform, Bankman-Fried improperly used FTX customers' funds for his privately held crypto hedge fund, Alameda Research LLC, and gave Alameda special treatment on the FTX platform. Bankman-Fried raised more than $1.8 billion from investors who bought stake in FTX. He used these funds, diverted through Alameda, to purchase lavish real estate in the Bahamas and make sizeable political donations.[56]

Bankman-Fried also failed to inform investors of the risk from FTX's exposure to Alameda's holdings of overvalued, illiquid assets, such as FTX-affiliated tokens. When the prices of crypto-assets fell in 2022, Bankman-Fried's actions were exposed when Alameda's lenders demanded repayment of billions of dollars of loans. Yet, despite the writing on the wall, Bankman-Fried used addition FTX customer funds to aid Alameda and give himself and other executives personal loans.

In November of 2023, Bankman-Fried was convicted, and on March 28, 2024, a federal district court judge for the Southern District of New York sentenced Bankman-Fried to 25 years in prison for stealing roughly $11 billion from customers, investors, and lenders of the FTX platform. Bankman-Fried is expected to appeal the decision.

The SEC brought another major case in 2023 against the largest crypto-asset trading platform in the world, Binance, for similarly misleading investors. The SEC brought 13 charges against Binance Holdings Limited and its CEO, Changpeng Zhao, for violating the federal securities laws.[57] The SEC alleged that Binance and Zhao conducted the unregistered offer and sale of crypto-assets and mislead investors. Binance and Zhao claimed US customers were restricted from Binance.com, but Zhao and Binance secretly allowed high-value US customers to continue trading on the platform. Also, Zhao and Binance improperly exercised control of customers' assets, which were then commingled and diverted, including to Zhao's own entity, Sigma Chain.

The SEC also secured emergency relief by a consent order to ensure the Binance defendants would return to the USA any assets held for customers of the crypto trading platform, Binance.US. The consent order ensured that customers could withdraw their assets from the platform or to ensure those who kept assets on the

---

[56] *SEC v. Samuel Bankman-Fried*, No. 1:22-cv-10501, (S.D.N.Y. Dec. 13, 2022); *CFTC et al. v. Bankman-Fried et al.*, No. 1:22-cv-10503 (S.D.N.Y. Dec. 13, 2022).

[57] *SEC v. Binance Holdings Limited, Bam Trading Services Inc., Bam Management US Holdings Inc., and Changpeng Zhao*, No 1:23-cv-01599 (D.D.C. June 5, 2023).

platform were protected while the case was pending. Gurbir S. Grewal, Director of the SEC's Division of Enforcement, stated that "[g]iven that Changpeng Zhao and Binance have control of the platforms' customers' assets and have been able to commingle customer assets or divert customer assets as they please, as we have alleged, these prohibitions are essential to protecting investor assets."[58]

In November of 2023, Binance pleaded guilty and agreed to pay over $4 billion for violations of the Bank Secrecy Act, failure to register as a money transmitting business, and violating the International Emergency Economic Powers Act. Zhao, a Canadian citizen, pleaded guilty for failing to maintain an effective anti-money laundering program in violation of the Bank Secrecy Act and stepped down as Binance's CEO.

## 10.21 Trading Platforms and Money Service Business Laws

Until 2008, currency transactions were among the least regulated transactions in US financial markets. Following Dodd-Frank and attendant changes to the Commodities Exchange Act, commodities markets now face increased regulation. Regulatory requirements differ based on the type of product traded, whether a transaction is physically or cash-settled, the type of person trading the product (i.e., retail or institutional investors), and whether the instrument is traded on an exchange or over-the-counter.

Foreign exchange ("FX") transactions are regulated with varying levels of scrutiny depending on the attributes of the particular trade and the potential risks such posed to consumers. Regulators separate FX transactions into two categories, spot transactions, which are settled within 2 days of the transaction date, and forward or futures transactions, which generally have quarterly delivery dates and extended lifespans based on the terms of an underlying agreement.

Money service businesses serve a large segment of the unbanked or self-banked population and provide services like currency exchange, check cashing, money transfer, prepaid stored value cards, money orders, and traveler's checks. A dealer in foreign exchange is a type of money service business which deals in and exchanges currency as a business. A money transmitter is a type of money service business which provides money transfer services or payment instruments. Both dealers in foreign exchange and money transmitters are regulated businesses.

[58] SEC Secures Emergency Relief to Protect Binance.US Customers' Assets (June 17, 2023), available at: https://www.sec.gov/news/press-release/2023-110.

## 10.22 Trading Platforms and Money Service Business Laws—Federal Law

A dealer in foreign exchange is defined to include a person who accepts currency in exchange for other currency as a business, other than a person who does not exchange currency in an amount greater than $1000 in currency or other monetary instruments for any person on any day in one or more transactions.[59]

A money transmitter is defined to include a person that "provides money transmission services, or any other person engaged in the transfer of funds."[60] The term "money transmission services" means "the acceptance of currency, funds, or other value that substitutes for currency from one person *and* the transmission of currency, funds, or other value that substitutes for currency to another location or person by an means."[61]

Nonbank financial institutions engaging as a dealer in foreign exchange or in money transmission are considered to be money service businesses that, unless exempted, must register with Financial Crimes Enforcement Network and must be licensed in the states where the nonbank financial institution operates (if required by the state).[62] Whether a nonbank financial institution is a dealer in foreign exchange or a money transmitter is a matter of facts and circumstances.

## 10.23 Trading Platforms and Money Service Business Laws—Virtual Currencies

The Financial Crimes Enforcement Network (FinCEN) has outlined the extent to which FinCEN regulations have jurisdiction over persons "creating, obtaining, distributing, exchanging, accepting, or transmitting virtual currencies."[63] The guidance defines "virtual currency" as a "medium of exchange that operates like a currency

[59] 31 C.F.R. §1010.100(ff)(1).

[60] See 31 C.F.R. §1010.100(ff)(5)(i)(A) and (B).

[61] See 31 C.F.R. §1010.100(ff)(5)(i)(A).

[62] 31 C.F.R. §1010.100(ff)(5)(i). FinCEN supervisory authority is pursuant to the Bank Secrecy Act ("BSA"), 31 U.S.C.A. §§5311 to 5332.

[63] See FinCEN Guidance No. FIN-2013-G001: Application of FinCEN's Regulations to Persons Administering, Exchanging, or Using Virtual Currencies, at 1 n.1 (Mar. 18, 2013), available at https://www.fincen.gov/sites/default/files/shared/FIN-2013-G001.pdf; see also FIN-2014-R011, Request for Administrative Ruling on the Application of FinCEN's Regulations to a Virtual Currency Trading Platform (October 27, 2014), available at https://www.fincen.gov/sites/default/files/administrative_ruling/FIN-2014-R011.pdf; FIN-2014-R012, Request for Administrative Ruling on the Application of FinCEN's Regulations to a Virtual Currency Payment System (October 27, 2014), available at https://www.fincen.gov/sites/default/files/administrative_ruling/FIN-2014-R012.pdf.

in some environments, but does not have all the attributes of real currency," specifically that "virtual currency does not have legal tender status in any jurisdiction."[64]

FinCEN's guidance divides the participants in "generic virtual currency arrangements" into three categories: "users," "exchangers," and "administrators."[65] A user is a person who "obtains virtual currency to purchase goods or services on the user's behalf."[66] An exchanger engages in the business of exchanging virtual currency for traditional currency or other virtual currency.[67] Finally, an administrator "is a person engaged as a business in issuing (putting into circulation) a virtual currency, and who has the authority to redeem (to withdraw from circulation) such virtual currency."[68] The guidance explains that "users" are not money transmitters under these regulations.[69] On the other hand, an exchanger of virtual currency that "(1) accepts and transmits a convertible virtual currency or (2) buys or sells convertible virtual currency for any reason is a money transmitter under Federal law, unless a limitation to or exemption from the definition applies to the person."[70] While an administrator is generally considered to be a money transmitter, it relates to centralized virtual currencies (such as E-gold or Liberty Reserve).

## 10.24 Trading Platforms and Money Service Business Laws—Implications of Being a Money Service Business

Dealers in foreign exchange and money transmitters are required to (a) register with the Financial Crimes Enforcement Network (FinCEN), (b) conduct a comprehensive risk assessment of its exposure to money laundering, (c) implement an anti-money laundering program based on such risk assessment, and (d) comply with the recordkeeping, reporting, and transaction monitoring obligations. Examples of such requirements include the filing of currency transaction reports[71] and suspicious activity reports,[72] whenever applicable, general recordkeeping maintenance,[73] and recordkeeping related to the sale of negotiable instruments.[74] Furthermore, to the extent that any of the dealer's or transmitter's transactions constitute a "transmittal

[64] FinCEN Guidance No. FIN-2013-G001, at 1.
[65] FinCEN Guidance No. FIN-2013-G001, at 2.
[66] FinCEN Guidance No. FIN-2013-G001, at 2.
[67] FinCEN Guidance No. FIN-2013-G001, at 2.
[68] FinCEN Guidance No. FIN-2013-G001, at 2.
[69] FinCEN Guidance No. FIN-2013-G001, at 2.
[70] FinCEN Guidance No. FIN-2013-G001, at 3.
[71] 31 C.F.R. §1022.310.
[72] 31 C.F.R. §1022.320.
[73] 31 C.F.R. §1010.410.
[74] 31 C.F.R. §1010.415.

of funds"[75] under FinCEN's regulations, then such entity must also comply with the "Funds Transfer Rule"[76] and the "Funds Travel Rule."[77] It is a violation of federal law for a business to operate as an unlicensed money transmitter.

## 10.25 Conclusion

The regulation of blockchain-related financial products can be as complicated as the computer science underlying a blockchain protocol. There are many different levels where regulation can occur, from state level money service business laws to federal (and state) securities laws. The federal courts are being confronted with novel legal issues, as well as the application of the age-old Howey test to brand new blockchain technology and use cases. Each year, for the foreseeable future, the law of blockchain and crypto will continue to evolve, side by side with the development of the underlying technology itself. Given the USA's decentralized patchwork of regulation, legal risk and uncertainty in the USA can be a significant impediment to fintech companies and the release of blockchain products to the public. As a result, all participants in the blockchain economy will be wise to keep their friends close and their lawyers closer.

[75] 31 C.F.R. §1010.100(ddd).

[76] 31 C.F.R. §1010.410(e).

[77] 31 C.F.R. §1010.410(f).

# Index




D. B. Garrie et al., *Uncovering Digital Evidence*,
https://doi.org/10.1007/978-3-031-68118-9

MIX
Papier aus verantwortungsvollen Quellen
Paper from responsible sources
FSC® C105338

If you have any concerns about our products,
you can contact us on
**ProductSafety@springernature.com**

In case Publisher is established outside the EU,
the EU authorized representative is:
**Springer Nature Customer Service Center GmbH**
**Europaplatz 3, 69115 Heidelberg, Germany**

Printed by Libri Plureos GmbH
in Hamburg, Germany